THE SOCIOLOGY
OF
MENTAL ILLNESS

THE SOCIOLOGY OF MENTAL ILLNESS

Bernard J. Gallagher III
VILLANOVA UNIVERSITY

PRENTICE-HALL, INC., Englewood Cliffs, New Jersey   07632

Library of Congress Cataloging in Publication Data

Gallagher, Bernard J., III
    The sociology of mental illness.
    Bibliography: p. 349
    Includes index.
    1. Social psychiatry. 2. Psychology, Pathological—
Etiology—Social aspects. 3. Mentally ill—Care and
treatment—Social aspects. I. Title. [DNLM:
1. Mental disorders. 2. Social environment. WM31
G162s]
RC455.G23   616.8'9   79-20858
ISBN 0-13-820928-6

Prentice-Hall Series in Sociology
Neil J. Smelser, Series Editor

Printed in the United States of America

10 9 8 7 6 5 4 3 2 1

Editorial/production supervision and interior design by Scott Amerman
Cover design by RL Communications
Cover sketch by permission of Vincent Bugliosi
Manufacturing buyer: Ray Keating

PRENTICE-HALL INTERNATIONAL, INC., *London*
PRENTICE-HALL OF AUSTRALIA PTY. LIMITED, *Sydney*
PRENTICE-HALL OF CANADA, LTD., *Toronto*
PRENTICE-HALL OF INDIA PRIVATE LIMITED, *New Delhi*
PRENTICE-HALL OF JAPAN, INC., *Tokyo*
PRENTICE-HALL OF SOUTHEAST ASIA PTE. LTD., *Singapore*
WHITEHALL BOOKS LIMITED, WELLINGTON, *New Zealand*

Contents

10
Patterns of Mental Illness:
Social Class, Race, and Social Mobility   241

IV
The Social Role
of the Mental Patient   275

11
Becoming a Mental Patient   277

12
The Patient in Treatment   297

13
Life As An Ex-Mental Patient   325

Preface

This book is about one of the most personally devastating and mysterious problems that afflicts mankind—mental illness. Countless publications have discussed physical illness but there have been relatively few writings on mental illness. This is mainly because mental illness has only been recently examined scientifically. In past years it was relegated to poetry or theology because it was mistakenly confused with eccentricity or possession. In the nineteenth century some attempts were made to analyze mental illness as a real pathology but researchers were blinded to the social aspects of mental illness because of the biological orientation of the time.

Today there is a growing body of evidence that mental illness is a sociological problem as well as a biological phenomenon. Most of this evidence appears in articles published in professional journals. Some of it appears in monographs on selected issues. This book is the first to organize the sociological literature on mental illness. I have not written it simply to meet the need for a textbook on the sociology of mental illness. I was alarmed by the stinging biases typically found in writings on mental illness. Medical researchers view mental illness only as a biological issue while psychoanalysts consider it as the product of childhood experiences and sociologists posit that it stems from social stress or life crises. Since there is evidence that mental illness can be the product of a number of factors, I wrote this book to review the sociological research on mental illness and to briefly summarize the position of other schools of thought as well. Anything short of a multidimensional approach to a multicausal phenomenon like mental illness is unfair to the readers and a serious professional risk.

I am not interested in making a false dedication to some relative, friend, or "guiding light" who had absolutely nothing to do with the research and writing of the book. Certainly I am heavily indebted to Mary Ann Griesser for her many hours of typing and to Carole Champlin for her useful editorial advice. But the only dedicative urge I feel is not to a person but to a cause—the elimination of ignorance about mental illness. I speak of ignorance not simply in terms of the symptoms and origins of mental illness but, more importantly, in terms of the stigmatizing and damaging ways in which so many people think of it. If this book helps further that cause, then it is a success for me.

Bernard J. Gallagher III

I

An Overview

1

Mental Illness
and Society

Mental illness is one of the most serious problems in the world today. Simply stated, it causes a living hell for both the afflicted person and those around him. This anguish was vividly illustrated by Charles Manson in a doodling he made while on trial for the famous Tate-LaBianca murders. It is uncertain whether Manson was purposely drawing his concept of a tortured person or actually uncovering a disorder of his own. Nevertheless, this author was so impressed with how Manson's simple sketch emotionally represented the inner world of mental illness that he used the drawing for the cover of this book. (Ironically, permission to use Manson's sketch was given by Vincent Bugliosi, the prosecuting attorney in the Tate-LaBianca trial and coauthor of *Helter Skelter*.) Aside from the agonizing *personal* pain of mental illness, it is also a major *social* problem as evidenced by a large number of studies reporting that an alarmingly high percentage of the world population is mentally ill.[1] In addition, the size of the mentally ill population appears to be growing as the same studies indicate that the rate of mental illness has increased seven-fold since the end of World War II.[2]

---

[1]Studies estimating the rate of mental illness in the United States report that approximately 20 percent of Americans are mentally ill. There is a wide array of estimates in these studies ranging from 1.7 percent to 69 percent. See: Bruce P. Dohrenwend and Barbara Snell Dohrenwend, "Social and cultural influences on psychopathology," *Annual Review of Psychology*, 25 (1974), p. 423.

[2]Part of this increase is due to a more liberal definition of mental illness in the post World War II studies. See: Bruce P. Dohrenwend, "Sociocultural and social-psychological factors in the genesis of mental disorders," *Journal of Health and Social Behavior*, 16 (1975), p. 368.

Social Forces and Mental Illness

In the last few decades there has been an increased recognition of the important relationship between sociocultural forces and mental illness. A growing body of research has consistently shown that both the causes (etiology) and distribution (epidemiology) of mental illness are frequently linked with the world of the interpersonal. It is ironic that one of the first persons to emphasize the relationship between social forces and psychopathology was an individual trained in physical medicine— Sigmund Freud. In fact, credit is largely due to Freud, the founder of psychoanalysis, for the discovery of the interpersonal origin of mental disorder. He viewed personality as the product of the interaction of innate, instinctual urges (chiefly sex and aggression) and social factors. He believed that the personality is shaped by the interpersonal experiences of each individual person throughout the socialization process. From this perspective, one's interactions with nuclear family members, as an infant and young child, and with peers, as an older child and adolescent, are together responsible for the make-up of the final personality. According to Freud, certain types of mental illness (*functional*)[3] result from unsatisfactory, even traumatic, experiences with the significant people in one's life during the process of personality formation.

Since Freud's death, his followers have extended his theories on the relationship between social forces and the abnormal personality. These "Neo-Freudians" place even more emphasis on the role of interpersonal relationships than Freud did. Alfred Adler, for instance, stressed that mental disorder originates from "inferiority feelings" caused by an overprotective or neglectful childhood.[4] Karen Horney held that a disturbance in the parent-child relationship can scar the developing personality and cause life-long mental anguish.[5] Otto Rank, another famous Neo-Freudian, traced the origin of psychopathology to separation from the womb of the mother.[6] This painful experience, which he called "birth trauma," can lead to mental illness in people who find the interpersonal world threatening and consequently unconsciously desire to return to the peaceful environment of the womb. Other theoreticians commonly designated as "Neo-Freudians" include Otto Fenichel, Heinz Hartmann, Erik Erikson, Erich Fromm and Harry Stack Sullivan.

Of all types of social influences, those within the nuclear family are most frequently responsible for mental illness. A number of pathological family patterns have been uncovered. One is what is called "family

---

[3]*Functional* disorders are those considered to originate from psychological causes and are therefore considered distinct from the *organic* illnesses which are biologically based. The functional illnesses consist of the functional psychoses, the neuroses and the personality disorders. They are described and explained separately in Chapters 3 through 7.

[4]Alfred Adler, *Problems of Neurosis* (New York: Harper and Row, 1964).

[5]Karen Horney, *The Neurotic Personality of Our Time* (New York: W. W. Norton, 1937).

[6]Otto Rank, *The Trauma of Birth* (New York: Robert Brunner, 1952).

schism." Here the family is divided into two warring camps headed by the parents. This forces the children to choose one side, often causing a concomitant splitting of their own identities into two antagonistic parts. Where the family is "skewed," one parent dominates the group usually through excessive dependency on the other parent. This type of relationship typically proceeds at the expense of parental satisfaction of the children's needs.

Other potentially damaging familial experiences include the lack of a mother figure. Here the child is denied the warmth and affection necessary for normal personality development. Observations of such maternally-deprived children make it clear that ". . . when deprived of maternal care, a child's development is almost always retarded—physically, intellectually, and socially—and symptoms of physical and mental illness may appear."[7] On the other hand, a mother-child relationship which is too cohesive can also jeopardize mental health by creating a personality which is pathologically dependent on others and not able to function adequately alone.[8]

The list of intrafamilial experiences that lead to mental illness is well-documented and growing constantly. It is no longer a body of knowledge shared exclusively by mental health experts but is rapidly disseminated to the public through a number of popular publications.[9] In fact, psychiatric knowledge has entered into legal conflict situations in which children have charged their parents with raising them improperly! In the chapters that follow, various intrafamilial theories of mental disorder are presented and evaluated.

The Role of Culture

There is also an important relationship between mental illness and the wider social forces commonly known as culture. Culture influences the very way mental illness is defined. Thus the same behavior can be considered healthy or normal in one culture and ill or abnormal in another. Indeed, some argue that mental illness is esssentially a semantic or cultural issue because, they contend, it is nothing more than deviation from certain norms of a particular culture. From this perspective, the proposition that some people be considered mentally ill is futile since no one can be considered mentally ill. This is an extreme position with a

---

[7]John Bowlby, *Child Care and the Growth of Love* (Baltimore: Penguin Books, 1968), p. 21.

[8]H. R. Schaffer, "The too-cohesive family: a form of group pathology," *International Journal of Social Psychiatry*, 10 (1964), pp. 266–275.

[9]A recent analysis of columns on mental health problems in popular magazines published over fifty years revealed a four-fold increase in the number of problems discussed between 1923 and 1973. See: Edmund G. Doherty and Rosalie Young, "The expanding universe of mental health problems" (Paper presented at the annual meeting of the Society for the Study of Social Problems, San Francisco, California, 1978).

small band of followers but it does raise important points. Cultural forces, for instance, can affect the *symptoms* of mental illness. In fact, there are some forms of mental illness that are only found among members of a particular culture. Psychiatrists raised in Western cultures find it difficult to understand these disorders and consequently label them bizarre, exotic, and unclassifiable. Actually, they are comprehensible from the perspective of the cultural system in which they are found. Sometimes they are regarded as divinely inspired signs to be worshipped and followed in some religious sense. A description of these phenomena is presented in chapter two.

Culture can also affect the *rate* of mental disorder in different societies. Freud expressed the view that culture directly interferes with mental health by frustrating human instincts.[10] He held that this occurs to a greater degree in civilized, sophisticated cultures such as our own. In these settings, culture exists and continues to exist only through the individual's renouncement of his instinctive desires. The whole structure of culture, with its elaborate set of norms and values, puts prohibitions on man's innate drives of aggression and egoistic self-satisfaction. Freud believed that man's own pursuit of culture is responsible for human misery because that pursuit requires the repression of innate needs and desires. He also held that civilized man would be much happier if he gave up the perpetuation of culture and returned to more primitive conditions! This thesis astonished many people in Freud's time and continues to raise some eyebrows today. There are, of course, those who do not believe that modern industrial society is generative of more mental disturbance than other kinds of society.[11] However, the most recent empirical evidence shows that fast-paced, industrial societies, particularly the capitalistic ones, are least conducive to mental health.[12]

Culture can also affect mental health by the restrictions it places on people in particular social roles. In American culture there are numerous examples, all of which are presented in part three of this book. One is the female sex role which is responsible for menopausal depression. Some women during their "change of life" experience a sudden breakdown and assert that their lives are not worth living. Why? A medical explanation holds biological changes are responsible for the change in mood. But it is more likely that these women react to menopause with depression because of the limited definition of the female sex role in American culture. If women have based their lives on a narrow range of fulfilling experiences, such as childbearing and childrearing, they have no alternative channels through which to gain satisfaction when

---

[10]Sigmund Freud, *Civilization and its Discontents* (New York: W. W. Norton, 1961).

[11]Alex Inkeles, "The modernization of man," in *Modernization: The Dynamics of Growth*, ed. Myron Weiner (New York: Basic Books, 1966).

[12]In one such study, mental illness, suicide, and alcoholism were combined to form an "anxiety index." The researcher found that Japan, West Germany, and France are the principal high anxiety countries of the world. See: R. Lynn, *Personality and National Character* (Oxford: Pergamon Press, 1971).

childbearing is no longer possible. They feel then at menopause that they have lost their only function in society, and depression is the result.[13]

Societal Views Toward Mental Illness Through History

It has only been in the last 100 years that mental illness has been researched in a scientific way. Primitive people viewed mental illness as magic. One of their doctrines was that an evil being, such as the devil, could control the mind of a person. This is called _demonology_. The course of treatment was to exorcise demons from the person by use of procedures which were often cruel and barbaric by modern standards. If less painful techniques failed, such as prayers, loud noises, and foul odors, the person would be whipped and starved. One particularly crude practice was _trephination_ in which the disturbed person's skull was chipped away to allow demons to escape.

Ancient Greeks and Romans made a number of speculations about mental illness. They assumed that the cause of mental illness was a disturbance within the natural body itself.[14] Around 700 B.C. the physician-priest Alcmaeon hypothesized that brain processes caused sensation and concluded that difficulties in reasoning resulted from an illness of the brain. Hippocrates (460–367 B.C.) stated that mental illness originated from an excess or imbalance among the four humors of the body. His classification of temperaments—choleric, melancholic, sanguine, and phlegmatic—corresponded to excesses in the four humors: yellow bile, black bile, blood, and phlegm respectively. In addition, he believed that hysteria, a disorder involving the loss of use of a body part, was a uniquely female disorder caused by a uterus which wandered throughout the body.

Plato (429–347 B.C.) departed from a purely physiological explanation and argued for the role of divine intervention. He described four kinds of madness, two of which implied possession by good spirits. These were prophetic madness, such as Apollo's oracle at Delphi, and poetic madness, which provided creative abilities. The other two types were erotic madness and ritual madness, which was induced by orgiastic religious ceremonies.

Aristotle (384–322 B.C.) revitalized Hippocrates' emphasis on bodily functions. His theory, however, was far from progressive since he claimed that the heart is the causal agent in mental illness.

Asclepiades (ca. 100 B.C.) rejected the biological theory of Hippocrates and stressed the importance of environmental factors. He dif-

---

[13]This argument is expressed in greater detail elsewhere. See Ernest Becker, "Social science and psychiatry: the coming challenge," _The Antioch Review_, 23 (1963), pp. 353–366.

[14]These people were so certain that mental illness was biologically caused that in A.D. 47, a Roman physician tried to cure the Emperor's symptoms with an electric eel. This may have been the first use of "shock therapy."

ferentiated between delusions, hallucinations, and illusions as well as acute and chronic onsets.[15] Aretaeus (A.D. 30–90) is credited with the observation that mental illness is an exaggeration of the normal personality. He grouped illnesses according to patterns of symptoms, something which no one had previously considered.

In ancient Palestine insanity was connected with the supernatural. Little thought was given to medical or other aspects of mental illness. In fact, there is some evidence that magical practices were designed to cast out the demons of madness as primitive man had done centuries before.

During the Middle Ages treatment of mental illness was in the hands of priests who believed that demonic forces were at work in the mind of the afflicted. Consistently, they would sprinkle the disordered person with holy water and shout obscene epithets at Satan to hurt his pride. Actually, two kinds of possession were recognized. In one form the person was unwillingly seized by the devil as God's punishment for sins. These people were considered to be mentally ill. In the second form, the person deliberately entered into a pact with the devil. These were witches with supernatural powers. By the end of the fifteenth century the distinction between these two forms of possession was blurred, and many unfortunates were labeled as witches and accused of causing pestilence and floods. The actions by officials of the Catholic and Protestant churches[16] furthered the belief in witches and prompted a multitude of arrests, hangings, and other grotesque executions of suspected witches, many of whom were actually suffering from mental illness.[17]

The Dutchman Johann Weyer (1515–1588) attacked demonology. He insisted that witches were ill and should be treated humanely. Although he formulated no theories of his own, he was skillful in describing disorders well known today. He was particularly important in helping to counteract the barbaric treatment of mentally ill people who were constantly threatened with execution or expulsion from the community.

During the eighteenth century in Europe the mentally ill were no longer killed or tortured as common practice. Instead they were chained and confined in jail with criminals. Although many feel that medical scientists were responsible for ending this practice, Foucalt reports that the change was initiated by prisoners who were indignant at being forced to live with madmen.[18] They viewed their enforced association with the mentally ill as the ultimate punishment and humiliation.

The situation of the mentally ill was similar in the United States. By

[15]A delusion is a belief that is not consistent with reality. A hallucination is a sensory perception not associated with real external stimuli. An illusion is a false sensory perception of real external sensory stimuli.

[16]In 1484 Pope Innocent VIII issued a papal bull urging the clergy to search exhaustively for witches. This decree ushered in a violent and tragic period in Western history.

[17]Pressing victims to death was another method of execution that is reported to have been used in Salem, Massachusetts in the late 1600s.

[18]Michael Foucault, *Madness and Civilization* (New York: Vintage Books, 1973).

1860, twenty-eight of thirty-three states had public asylums for the insane to keep them isolated from society. This was a reflection of the belief that the causes of mental illness were diseases of the brain that should be treated by physicians. In both the European prisons and the American asylums, the mentally ill were condemned to lives of misery and, in most cases, permanent separation from society.

Humane treatment was begun in France through the efforts of Philippe Pinel, a founder of modern psychiatry (1745–1826). Pinel invoked the concept of individual freedom, made so salient in the French Revolution, in calling for reforms in treating the mentally ill. At the Bicêtre Hospital, he removed patients' chains, allowed them access to hospital grounds, and instructed the staff to employ human kindness. The results of his efforts were dramatic as many recovered who were considered incurable. Pinel's reform movements were formalized at the Salpetrière Hospital where personnel were trained to be more than custodians and were instructed in keeping systematic records on each patient. Record keeping itself reflected the new belief that the mentally ill patient could be cured. But the policy of nonrestraint, promulgated by Pinel and other reformers of the time, such as Tuke, was slowly adopted throughout the Western world. Pinel's ideas were tested in the United States largely through the efforts of Benjamin Rush (1745–1813) who is considered the father of American psychiatry. Rush, concerned with social reforms, introduced methods based on moral treatment at the Pennsylvania Hospital. His views were not entirely consistent, however, since, in his widely-used textbook on psychiatry published in 1812, he reaffirmed his beliefs in bloodletting, purgatives, and in the "tranquilizer," a special chair in which patients were tied down and suspended in mid-air.

In 1841, Dorothea Lynde Dix (1802–1887), a Massachusetts school teacher, initiated the investigation of deplorable and brutal conditions prevalent in asylums. For forty years she worked diligently for the building of state-supported hospitals. She initiated the principle of public responsibility for the mentally ill. A measure of her effectiveness is the striking increase in the number of people treated in mental hospitals; from 2,561, or 14 percent, of the estimated ill in 1840, the figures rose to 74,028, or 69 percent, of the estimated ill in 1890.

From an etiological perspective, Hippocrates' original belief that all mental disorders were biological in origin was revived in the early nineteenth century when psychiatry was first scientifically organized. This period was characterized by the unquestioned belief that pathological bodily conditions and brain tissue dysfunctions were solely responsible for mental disorder. This perspective became known as the *somatogenic* view since it looked for the origin of mental illness in the body or soma. Western Europe was the center of psychiatric investigation during this period. Unfortunately, specialists in mental disorder did not concern themselves with each other's work due to their preoccupation with their own limited research. This was responsible for a rather chaotic approach to mental illness at that time. Many did not recognize any difference between neurological and psychological phenomena partly because the study of mental illness was undertaken exclusively by physicians. The French psychiatrist Morel (1809–1873), for example, worked on the premise that mental disease was the unfortunate result of hereditary neural weakness. Others, such as the German psychiatrist Griesinger (1817–1868) and the Frenchman, Magnon (1835–1916), were oriented to biological explanations of mental disorder simply because they studied only diseases involving overt somatic symptoms such as paralysis and alcoholism.

Research in the late 1800s brought some empirical evidence to support the somatogenic hypothesis. *Dementia paralytica,* commonly known as *paresis,* had been discovered in 1798 among patients at the Bethelem Hospital in Pennsylvania. It was noted that paralysis, delusions of grandeur, and dementia (loss of mental powers) were associated with the disorder but the cause of the illness eluded researchers. In 1894, Fournier discovered that 65 percent of paretic patients had had syphilis. It was postulated that the syphilitic infection had impaired brain tissues, but researchers could not determine why syphilis was not found in all paretic cases. An ethically questionable experiment in 1897 by Kraft-Ebing laid that question to rest. He injected paretic patients who had denied having had syphilis with the syphilitic virus. Surprisingly, none of them developed syphilis which demonstrated that syphilitic infection leads to paresis. Apparently Fournier had naively relied on patients' self-reports of having had syphilis, not a very useful way to detect a fact which many people would prefer to hide.

During the somatogenic period, the first organized attempt at classifying mental illness was undertaken by Emil Kraepelin (1855–1926). He observed that there were two major types of disorder. One was a disorder of *mood* expressed by excited behavior (mania) or melancholic behavior (depression) which he called the *manic-depressive psychosis.* The other disease involved a disorder of *thought,* often progressive, which he called *dementia praecox* since it resembled premature senility. It is now known as *schizophrenia.* Kraepelin's classifications proved to be less controversial than his etiological beliefs since he viewed the manic-depressive psychosis as an irregularity in metabolic function and dementia praecox as an imbalanced chemical state caused by abnormal secretions of the sex glands.

In the late nineteenth century, John P. Gray, superintendent of Utica State Hospital and editor of the American Journal of Insanity, became the chief advocate of the somatogenic position. Around this time a "great struggle" was beginning between somatogenic theorists such as Gray and a new school of thought which suggested that mental disorders could be caused solely by a disturbance in the patient's psychological state. This approach to mental illness, known as the *psychogenic* view, first became established within modern psychiatry through the study of hysteria. Hysteria is associated with somatic symptoms such as loss of sight, hearing, or partial anaesthesia. It had been believed that hysteria was a purely physiological disorder until the application of hypnosis provided new insight. Although the Austrian physician, Messmer,[19] discovered hypnosis, it was first applied to hysterical patients in France by Charcot and his student, Janet, who demonstrated that individuals under a hypnotic state could artificially produce symptoms identical to hysteria. This discovery, combined with the recognition that many hysterical patients had physical symptoms that were anatomically impossible,[20] forced investigators to conclude that abnormalities of psychological processes alone can produce mental disorder. The insight was limited, however, in that it failed to specify the causal direction of the relationship; that is, does the abnormal psychological process produce mental disorder or vice versa?

The causal link between psychological processes and mental illness was first established clearly by Sigmund Freud (1856–1939) who, with the assistance of Josef Breuer in the late 1800s, studied the unconscious segment of the human mind. Freud's discovery of the unconscious origin of psychological difficulties, along with his theory that the personality consists of three interdependent parts: the instincts (Id), the seat of moral regulations (Superego), and the agent which functions to reach compromises between the parts of the personality and the constraints of reality (Ego), must be viewed as the cornerstone of modern psychiatry. This school of thought, commonly known as psychoanalysis, served as both a theory of personality development and as a means to treat particular types of mental disorders. From clinical observations, Freud postulated the sequential development of the personality through the satisfaction of specific needs at various stages of "psychosexual" development. He believed that mental illness results from an interruption of this process so that the aim of psychoanalytic treatment should be to trace the origin of the experiences in earlier life that gave rise to the abnormality. Since Freud's theories were based on the importance of sexual and aggressive strivings of the unconscious id, he devoted a great deal of energy to developing techniques that would allow access to that part of the personality. His efforts led to the production of more sophisticated techniques than hypnosis such as dream interpretation, free association, and a simple "talking out" technique known as abreaction. All of these allowed access to the unconscious, a previously unknown part of the human personality.

Around the beginning of the twentieth century, many ideas were espoused which stressed the role of the sociocultural environment in the

[19]This is the origin of the term "mesmerized" which essentially means to be hypnotized.

[20]An example is "glove anaesthesia" where the patient loses feeling in the hand from the wrist to the fingertips. Anatomically, this is impossible since the nerves are not distributed in such a way that the entire hand can be anaesthetized without losing feeling in parts of the arm as well. These patients lost the feeling of their *concept* of the hand as a unit.

development of mental illness. During the 1880s, as industrialization and urbanization were rapidly expanding, articles appeared in popular magazines pleading for Americans to wake up and avoid the loss of their moral fiber which was being threatened by the competitive jungle of modern industrial society. As early as 1844, C. D. Hayden concluded that "[It is our] free institutions which promote insanity . . . life in our republic has all the excitement of an Olympic contest. A wide arena is thrown open and all fearlessly join in the maddening rush for the laurel wreath. . . ."[21] Many more articles appeared articulating the theme that the competition engendered by modern industrial society had debilitating effects on individuals. Before the turn of the century, G. A. Blumer, the distinguished editor of the American Journal of Insanity, warned that "Either the average brain of today has become a more unstable structure than the average brain of our ancestors; or else the average stress of environmental forces brought to bear on the brains of our generation has become more severe than formerly."[22] He believed that the alarming increase in the rate of mental illness in the United States was caused by the preoccupation of Americans with social mobility. W. A. White suggested in 1903 that a return to a simpler life style was desirable. He felt that " . . . the frontiersman who takes his family and goes West to open up new territory, engage in legitimate agricultural pursuits, and grow up with the country, is pretty apt to be of hardy stock and insanity, if it appears at all, comes in later generations."[23] Dr. R. Jones, superintendent of the London County Asylum in Claybury, England, had a similar view. He asserted that "With the progress of civilization, mental breakdown becomes more serious, if not more frequent, and the varieties of insanity more chronic and less curable when life was simpler and men were more content."[24] At this point in history it was apparent that mental illness was importantly related to sociocultural forces.

Current Models of Mental Illness

The Biogenic View

Today there are two major schools of thought in terms of etiological perspective: the biogenic and the environmental. These are roughly equivalent to the somatogenic and psychogenic labels used in earlier

---

[21]C. D. Hayden "On the distribution of insanity in the United States," *Third Literary Messenger*, 10 (1844), p. 178.

[22]G. A. Blumer, "The increase of insanity," *American Journal of Insanity*, 51 (1893), p. 310.

[23]W. A. White, "The geographical distribution of insanity in the United States," *Journal of Nervous and Mental Diseases*, 30 (1903), p. 267.

[24]R. Jones, "Medico-Psychological Association of Great Britain and Ireland: Presidential address on the evolution of insanity," *Journal of Mental Science*, 152 (1906), p. 632.

periods. The biogenic model, also known as the medical model or sickness model, was originally based on biological theories developed by the ancient Greeks. According to this view, mental illness is a physical disease like polio or cancer. Emphasis is placed on the recurring behavior, or "pathological symptoms," of a disease as well as "diagnosis" and "treatment." The language and concepts of the biogenic model are clearly analogous to that of physical medicine. This model has dominated twentieth century psychiatry largely because psychiatrists receive a medical school training and tend to see all problems in organic terms.[25]

Another factor leading to increased reliance on the biogenic model has been the discovery and steady expansion of psychotropic drugs which are commonly used to treat many emotional conditions. These drugs were widely employed in the 1950s and proved to be an invaluable method for giving patients relief from their symptoms. Earlier somatogenic forms of treatment had been successfully developed for psychotic patients. These approaches relied on applications of shock to the patient. Manfred Sakel developed insulin shock therapy in 1929 and used it to treat schizophrenics.[26] In 1938 Cerletti and Bini developed a technique by which the channeling of electricity into the body produced a coma followed by relief from the symptoms of manic-depressive illness. This is known as electroconvulsive therapy (ECT). Even after fifty years, however, there is no generally accepted theory which explains how either of these treatments work.

Further etiological support for the biogenic school has been offered in recent decades through studies of the frequency (concordance rate) by which both members of a pair of identical twins (monozygotic) exhibit the same abnormality. The frequency rates vary by type of mental illness and from study to study. For psychosis, the most severe kind of disorder, the rates are impressively high. These findings serve as the foundation for a particular school of biogenic thought, the *genetic* school, which holds that mental illness is transmitted through heredity.

The other major biogenic view is the *biochemical* school. These researchers consider mental illness as the result of an abnormal amount of chemicals within the body. As a relatively recent development within psychiatry, biochemical hypotheses are still being tested. Some studies have shown rather convincingly that certain types of mental illness, par-

---

[25]This is unfortunate since it hinders the development of an awareness of environmental influences on mental illness. Freud warned against the employment of medically trained people as psychoanalysts but physicians dominate that field as well mainly because of the political power which physicians wield as members of the most prestigious profession in the United States.

[26]Sakel accidentally discovered the effectiveness of using insulin shock as a means of treating schizophrenia. He had been using insulin to lower the blood-sugar level of morphine addicts. In certain cases a standard dose had too strong an effect, and the patient was thrown into a coma. Sakel noticed that this experience sometimes improved the confused mental state of his addicts so he began to apply the same treatment to schizophrenics with good results.

ticularly psychosis, involve an alteration of the normal biochemical state.

There is a third biogenic school of thought. This is the *morphological* school which holds that mental illness stems from having a certain type of body build. This position is dated and frequently ignored by contemporary psychiatric researchers who contend that mental illness is too complicated to be explained simply by body type.

The Environmental View

The environmental school actually encompasses a number of theories which are bound by a common emphasis on social and psychological factors. One theory is the *behaviorist* model which is oriented toward the study of *conscious* experience because its proponents contend that abnormal behavior is no different in origin from other behavior. The behaviorist theory posits that abnormal behavior, like other behavior, is determined largely by environmental stimuli; it is not a problem within an individual but rather the result of interaction with other people. Thus according to behaviorist spokesmen such as Watson, Pavlov, and B. F. Skinner, mental illness is a learned, or conditioned, behavior.

Another environmental theory is *psychoanalysis.* This model views mental illness as the result of an excessive use of instinctual energy at a particular stage of psychosexual development which causes an arrest, or *fixation, of personality.* Each particular type of illness is linked with impairment at a specific stage. The experiences considered capable of causing fixations are essentially social, such as difficulty in fulfilling society's demands for anal control, the absence of a warm mothering figure, rejection by one's peers, and failure to achieve the expectations of significant others. The most debilitating illnesses are considered to originate within infancy and early childhood through severe frustration of the person's needs. These early pathologic influences are well-hidden within the unconscious until they manifest themselves in the form of abnormal behaviors in later life.

A third environmental school of thought is the most recently articulated and serves as the central focus of much of this book. Known as *social psychiatry* and/or *psychiatric sociology*, it is the product of a concerted effort by socially oriented psychiatrists, sociologists, psychiatric social workers, social psychologists, and cultural anthropologists. In significant ways, it is a reaction to the failure of medical researchers to "deliver" in terms of discovering all of the causes of mental illness.

The intervention of social scientists in the field of mental illness has not been without problems. One relentless issue is the ongoing debate between the social scientists and the psychiatrists concerning the domain of the discipline. This conflict has resulted in a split between the psychiatrically-oriented and the sociologically-oriented. Those who have entered the field from psychiatry call it *social psychiatry*, a subspecialty of psychiatry to which social scientists are also called.[27] They view their function in practical ways, emphasizing service rather than research, and they consider social psychiatry as the study of methods by which society combats mental illness and of the psychiatric training given to social workers. There are differing opinions within this group regarding the magnitude of the services to be performed; some see social psychiatrists functioning only within the one-to-one therapist-patient relationship while others envisage entire societies as patients.

Sociologists who have entered the field call it *psychiatric sociology*, a term coined by Arnold M. Rose. They view the discipline in theoretical, research-oriented ways. As in the social psychiatry branch, there is differing opinion concerning the scope of the research; some concentrate on studies of the one-to-one dyad while others conduct basic etiological investigations of large populations. The most popular definition of psychiatric sociology focuses upon the role played by social factors in the causation of mental disorder. Implicit in this definition is the inclusion of epidemiological analyses which are important forerunners of etiological conclusions. In short, the major difference between social psychiatry and psychiatric sociology is that the former is service-oriented while the latter is research-oriented. Their combined efforts are responsible for forging new inroads into the origins and treatment of mental illness. This book is addressed to the literature compiled in both of these fields, particularly psychiatric sociology since its data examine a number of social aspects of mental illness beyond those encountered in treatment settings.

Plan of the Book

The chapters in this book contain the research findings of those involved in the study of mental illness over the past fifty years. It is important to note that the studies reported here have not been selected simply to support a sociological perspective. That would be unfair to the reader, irrelevant to some aspects of mental illness, and a scientific disgrace. Certainly it is not uncommon for an author to overemphasize his favorite theory while ignoring other explanations that are just as valid. In the case of mental illness, however, a purely sociological explanation will not suffice any more than a purely biogenic or psychoanalytic approach. Mental illness is a multidimensional phenomenon which must be considered from a number of different perspectives. This book is an attempt to evaluate the strengths and weaknesses of *all* of the biogenic and environmental theories—an eclectic exercise which this author believes is the most reasonable approach to a phenomenon as mysterious as mental illness presently is.

[27]For a complete elaboration of the different meanings of social psychiatry see: Leo Srole, "Social psychiatry: a case of the babel syndrome," in *Social Psychiatry*, eds. Joseph Zubin and Fritz Freyhan (New York, Grune and Stratton, 1968), pp. 56–68.

There are some aspects of mental illness that *must* be considered from a sociocultural perspective. One important issue is the question, "What is mental illness?" This is a difficult question to answer objectively because of terminological problems and because of cross-cultural differences in how abnormal behavior is defined. These issues, as well as an examination of the common definitions of mental illness, comprise the major topics of the following chapter (2).

The second part of the book deals with the symptoms and causes of some of the major types of mental illness. The research evidence favors different theories for different types of illness; for some illnesses, biogenic explanations may be most valid while other disorders appear more related to environmental forces. The fact is that the etiology of mental illness is a patchwork of limited findings and educated guesses. The second part of the book (Chapters 3 through 7) organizes and criticizes all of the etiological theories.

One aspect of mental illness which is clearly sociological is the distribution of mental illness among various social groups. If particular groups have noticeably high rates of mental illness, it can be assumed that certain social roles are more stressful than others. Are there differences between males and females? Are single people more impaired than married persons? Do members of various religious and ethnic groups have different rates of mental illness? How does migration affect mental health? Are such factors as age and sibling position related to psychological status? What is the relationship between social class position and mental illness? The research on these and other questions related to the social epidemiology of mental illness is presented in part three (Chapter 8 through 10).

The fourth part of the book examines the ways in which social factors affect a person after the onset of mental illness. Psychiatric sociologists view this as a process in which the prospective patient follows a sequence of experiences which together comprise "patienthood." The status of the mental patient is separated into three chronological components. The prepatient status, examined in Chapter 11, includes the subjective onset of pathological feelings, the reactions of family and friends, experiences associated with seeking help from physicians, ministers and the like, as well as the psychiatric and legal aspects of formal evaluation before commitment.

Chapter 12 evaluates the role of the psychiatric inpatient with an eye toward the ways in which health care delivery systems affect the patient's chances for final recovery. Research evidence clearly suggests that the organizational structure of the hospital and the interpersonal relations between staff and patients often function to worsen and extend the patient's symptoms during his hospitalization. This has led to a new movement in psychiatry, commonly known as *community psychiatry,* to treat people without hospitalizing them. The utility of both approaches is considered.

The third phase of the patient process is being released from a hospital to rejoin the outside world. This is the nexus of Chapter 13 which demonstrates that a patient's chances for permanent recovery are chiefly determined by the type of social climate to which he returns. In a nutshell, the central feature of this climate is the presence or absence of negative, primitive, and stigmatizing attitudes toward mental patients among family members, employers, and other significant associates. These are the factors that are the most important determinants of the need for rehospitalization or the resumption of a meaningful life in the outside world.

2

Concepts
of Mental Illness

The United States has witnessed many unusual and violent acts during the 1960s and 1970s. Criminal investigations have been conducted of people who appeared quite deranged, at least while they were carrying out their outrageous deeds. The saga of the Boston Strangler who committed sexually perverted homicides is a case that few will forget. The mass murders of seven student nurses by Richard Speck in Chicago shocked the country and precipitated a wave of terror among urban women. Richard Whitman used the tower of a University of Texas building to randomly eliminate a dozen people by rifle. The slayings at the home of actress Sharon Tate by Charles Manson and members of his "family" will be registered in the annals of American crime as one of the most bizarre acts ever committed. In the mid 1970s, political assassination again reared its head and the names of Squeaky Fromme and Sarah Jane Moore made headlines. Then David Berkowitz, popularly known as the "Son of Sam," went on a rampage of blasting young couples with a 44-magnum pistol in New York City.

The violent acts of these people and many others have brought questions of *legal insanity* into the public limelight. But were these people actually mentally ill? This issue, central to the legal proceedings against many of them, has proven to be an area of particular confusion since it is difficult to render completely objective psychiatric diagnoses. As one University of Chicago law professor stated: "If your psychiatric labels aren't clear and the legal standards that you use to feed them into decisions are foggy, fog times fog equals fog squared."[1] This is a problem

[1]Franklin Zimring, "Fog times fog," *Time Magazine*, October 20, 1975, p. 57.

that is not limited to the area of *legal* psychiatry. It is a pervasive weakness of many aspects of modern psychiatry because of terminological and cross-cultural factors.

Terminological Issues

Psychiatrists have had a lot of difficulty constructing a meaningful system of classifying and diagnosing mental illness. Confusions have been exacerbated recently since advancing knowledge often complicates rather than simplifies an understanding of mental health and illness. The problem of the effect of personal values on diagnoses as well as terminological problems are together responsible for leaving the scientific concept of mental illness in a shaky condition. Indeed, at meetings of some of the leading American psychiatrists, sociologists and anthropologists, the question, "What is mental illness?" is often received in silence. Some contend that mental illness is a mythical notion and can not be satisfactorily defined. Others reply that such a position is ridiculous since insane people can be clearly recognized. By any standard, psychiatric evaluation is not simple. Thus it is no mere accident that much of the psychiatric literature plainly skirts the definitional issue.

Mental illness cannot be approached in the same way as an illness of the body. The mind is an abstract concept not simply a physical entity. There exists a qualitative difference between the subject matter of psychiatry and general medicine. Psychiatry investigates the origin and treatment of abnormal behavior that cannot be measured in objective, quantitative terms as physicians approach the study of physical sicknesses. Simply stated, mental illness is an invincibly obscure concept. As Sir Aubrey Lewis, the eminent British psychiatrist, points out, attempts to define mental illness use a host of terms, undefinable in themselves: lack of joy of life, no will to live, discontentment, inability to adjust, and so forth.[2] The terms used to define mental illness are vague thus creating a jungle of difficulties. One such difficulty is with the use of the term "illness" itself. This term tends to perpetuate the belief that mental abnormality stems from physical ailments as exemplified by the following syllogism:

> Behavior disorders are mental illnesses.
> Only physicians should treat illnesses.
> Therefore only physicians should treat behavior disorders.[3]

The logic is impeccable; nevertheless the conclusion is false because in the major premise "illness" is used literally when it should be used metaphorically. The term "mental disorder" is also problematic because it is employed in a multiplicity of senses. To some it is synonymous with

---

[2]Aubrey Lewis, *Between Guesswork and Certainty in Psychiatry: The State of Psychiatry* (New York: Science House, 1967).

[3]William D. G. Balance, Paul P. Hirschfield, and Wolfgang G. Bringmann, "Mental illness: myth, metaphor, or model?" *Professional Psychology*, 1970, p. 134.

mental illness. Others, however, distinguish between mental illness and mental disorder. They treat mental disorder as covering "the whole range of abnormal conditions of the mind" including both states of psychological disorder and mental retardation while they view mental illness as a specialty including only mental retardation.[4] The terms continue to be used because no other terms convey a similar meaning to most readers. Rather than get lost in a myriad of different possible meanings, the following terms are used interchangeably throughout this book: mental illness, mental disorder, psychopathology, psychological disorder, and abnormal behavior. They are used interchangeably by many psychiatric researchers as well.

Cross-Cultural Differences

A further problem in defining mental illness stems from important cross-cultural differences in the expression and evaluation of the phenomenon. Every culture must deal with mental illness to guarantee its stability, to be sure. However, it is important to recognize that standards of mental illness are relative because the social context in which a particular behavior occurs affects whether it is adjudged normal or abnormal. Depending upon the situation, the same behavior may be considered mentally ill, criminal, or even socially acceptable. For example, an adolescent who sets fires may seek psychiatric help, be labeled mentally ill, and receive psychotherapy. The same individual may have encountered the legal authorities, be labeled a juvenile delinquent, and be jailed. Moreover, behavior which is usually considered abnormal may be accepted and even admired under certain circumstances. Examples of this are hallucinatory behavior in an LSD session or the production of unintelligible speech in a church in which speaking in tongues is common. Such practices as not wearing clothes, handling poisonous snakes, and even suicide are often positively sanctioned and honored by members of certain groups.

Beyond these differences in acceptable behavior among groups in the same society, comparisons between Western and non-Western societies demonstrate still more striking differences. In Malaya, a syndrome known as *running amok* occurs in people who go berserk with little or not warning and for no apparent reason. The amok runner usually kills several animals or people before being killed by others.[5]

Imu is an illness found mainly among the older women of the Ainu of Japan. It is frequently triggered by a sudden stimulus such as loud noises or highly feared objects including snakes, caterpillars, and snails.

---

[4]Barbara Wooton, *Social Science and Social Pathology* (London: George Allen and Unwin, 1959), p. 207.

[5]S. Arieti and J. M. Meth, "Rare, unclassifiable, collective, and exotic psychotic syndromes," in *The American Handbook of Psychiatry*, ed. S. Arieti (New York: Basic Books, 1959), pp. 543–563.

Wild, aggressive behavior results, followed by running away in panic. There is occasional loss of consciousness and the person often experiences considerable embarrassment upon recovery.[6]

Among the *Bena Bena* peoples of the Eastern Highlands of New Guinea, men are affected by day-long episodes during which they become deaf and aggressive towards clanspeople, including their wives and children. They run about randomly in circles and wield clubs and arrows in threatening gestures. Speaking is rare during these attacks. The episodes are quickly forgotten and there is no social censure. The Bena believe the attacks are the work of malevolent ghosts who are the objects of intense fear.[7]

Pibloktoq, sometimes called *Arctic hysteria,* occurs among the Polar Eskimos of the Thule District of northern Greenland. This illness follows a classic four-stage sequence. In the first stage, the victim is irritable and socially withdrawn. The onset of the second stage is sudden; the victim becomes wildly excited and may tear off his clothing, break furniture, attempt to walk on ceilings, shout obscenely, throw objects, eat feces, or perform other irrational acts such as plunging into snowdrifts or jumping off icebergs. This excitement is followed by a third stage characterized by convulsive seizures, collapse, and stuporous sleep or coma lasting for up to twelve hours. In the final stage, the victim behaves perfectly normally and has amnesia regarding the experience.[8]

The *windigo psychosis,* also known as the *whitiko psychosis,* occurs among the Ojibwa Indians of the Northeastern United States and Canada. The victim who suffers from this believes he is possessed by the spirit of the whitiko monster. Symptoms involve depression, a distaste for food, nausea, and periods of semistupor. The victim becomes obsessed with the idea of being possessed by the spirit and is subject to homicidal and/or suicidal thoughts. He perceives those around him as fat, appetizing animals which he wishes to eat. He finally reaches a stage of homicidal cannibalism and is usually killed since the Ojibwa believe that the craving for human flesh will never leave once it has been fulfilled.[9]

There is also a peculiar group of disordered reactions to minor stress which have been reported in Puerto Rico.[10] The behavior includes outbursts of verbal and physical hostility, regression to infantile behavior, forgetfulness, and loss of interest in personal appearance. Physicians there describe the outbursts this way:

[6]W. Winiariz and J. Wielawski, "Imu—a psychoneurosis occurring among Ainus," *Psychoanalytic Review,* 23 (1936), pp. 181–186.

[7]L. L. Langness, "Hysterical psychosis in the New Guinea Highlands: A Bena Bena example," *Psychiatry,* 28 (1965), pp. 258–277.

[8]Anthony F. C. Wallace, "Mental illness, biology and culture," in *Psychological Anthropology,* ed. Francis L. K. Hsu (Cambridge: Schenkman, 1972), pp. 363–402.

[9]R. Landes, "The abnormal among the Ojibwa Indians," *Journal of Abnormal and Social Psychology,* 33 (1938), pp. 14–33; S. Parker, "The whitiko psychosis in the context of Ojibwa personality," *American Anthropologist,* 62 (1960), pp. 603–623.

[10]R. Fernandez-Marina, "The Puerto Rican syndrome: its dynamics and cultural determinants," *Psychiatry,* 4 (1961), pp. 47–82.

The most outstanding reaction pattern is characterized by a transient state of partial loss of consciousness, most frequently accompanied by convulsive movements, hyperventilation, moaning and groaning, profuse salivation, and aggressiveness to self or to others in the form of biting, scratching, or striking, and of sudden onset and termination.[11]

Another culturally specific dosorder occurs among Chinese males. It is known as *shook yang* or *koro*. According to yap, koro is an " . . . acute anxiety state with partial depersonalization leading to the conviction of penile shrinkage and to fears of dissolution."[12] This exotic disorder is connected with the Chinese belief that masturbation and nocturnal emission prevent the normal change in yin and yang humors that accompanies sexual maturation. This causes an unbalanced loss of the yang-producing koro and the person fears his penis will dissolve as a consequence.

A final example of exotic illness is drawn from behavior found among Haitian peasants. The condition is known as *bouffée delirante argue*.[13] It is a confused state of mind which often deteriorates to schizophrenia. Native priests interpret the illness as a form of possession caused by an unwillingness to accept the call of the voodoo gods to join the voodoo church. Consistently, the recommended treatment is to attend church.

All of the illnesses reported here exemplify culturally specific manifestations of psychological disorder, but they do not necessarily differ from one another in etiological origin. Langness has convincingly argued that a majority of the "strange" mental illnesses reported by anthropologists are all cases of hysteria.[14] The different symptoms simply manifest culturally conditioned modes of expression and belief systems, although the psychiatric origins and processes are the same.[15] There is a general consensus among those who have researched mental illness in primitive or non-Western cultures that the same types of illnesses are found in all cultures, only the symptoms and distribution vary.[16] It is the author's opinion as well that a psychiatric equivalence underlies these

[11]M. Rubio, M. Urdaneta, and J. L. Doyle, "Psychopathologic reaction patterns in the Antilles command," *United States Armed Forces Medical Journal*, 6 (1955), p. 1768.

[12]P. M. Yap, "Koro-a culture-bound depersonalization syndrome," *British Journal of Psychiatry*, 111 (1965), p. 69.

[13]Ari Kiev, "Transcultural psychiatry: research problems and perspectives," in *Changing Perspectives in Mental Illness*, eds. Stanley C. Plog and Robert B. Edgerton (New York: Holt, Rinehart and Winston, 1969), pp. 106–127.

[14]L. L. Langness, "Hysterical psychosis: the cross-cultural evidence," *American Journal of Psychiatry*, 124 (1967), pp. 143–152.

[15]This is an argument supported by others as well. Norman Jacobs has concluded that cases of mass hysteria are similar regardless of cultural context although the context is important in defining their specific expression. See Norman Jacobs, "The phantom slasher of Taipei: mass hysteria in a nonwestern society," *Journal of Social Problems*, 12 (1965), pp. 318–328.

[16]Bruce P. Dohrenwend and Barbara Snell Dohrenwend, "Social and cultural influences on psychopathology," *Annual Review of Psychology*, 25 (1974), pp. 431–432.

externally unrelated types of illness. The dramatic nature of these disorders has distracted attention from the underlying psychopathology. The syndromes actually exemplify the ways in which disordered people in specific cultures conform to the behavioral patterns that culture expects and encourages. They are, therefore, nothing more than culturally recognized and accepted ways of becoming mentally ill. This position is strengthened by recent evidence demonstrating that people from different cultures may not exhibit the same symptoms even though they are known to have the same disorder. For example, Mexicans have been found to have more severe symptoms than Americans who have an equivalent psychopathology and are of the same socioeconomic level.[17] In addition, compared to schizophrenics from other cultures, Indian schizophrenics are unusually withdrawn and rigid, an assumed reflection of their formal, hierarchical culture which fosters introversion and emotional control. Even within the same society, the nature of the symptoms can differ sharply among people of various ethnic backgrounds. Irish male schizophrenics, for example, are typically quiet and withdrawn while their Italian counterparts are often loud and aggressive.[18]

Alternative Definitions of Mental Health

Today there is a complex philosophical debate that has resulted from the discovery of cross-cultural variations in the expression of mental illness. Given the fact that the nature of mental illness and attitudes toward it vary from one culture to another, this debate circles around the question "What is mental health?" Actually this question may not be an appropriate tool to use in defining mental illness because mental health and mental illness are not necessarily mirror opposites of each other. Nevertheless, this approach is most commonly used because it is a manageable way to deal with a very involved issue.

It is presently impossible to construct a universal definition of mental health because there is considerable disagreement regarding the components of "normal" behavior. What is viewed as normal in one cultural context may be quite unacceptable in another. This is the major barrier to objectively defining mental health, although it is by no means the only obstacle. Every attempt to define mental health has failed since " . . . there exists no psychologically meaningful and . . . operationally useful description of what is commonly understood to constitute mental health."[19]

[17]Horacio Farbega Jr. and Carole Ann Wallace, "How physicians judge symptom statements: a cross-cultural study," *Journal of Nervous and Mental Disease,* 145 (1967), pp. 486–491.

[18]M. Opler and J. L. Singer, "Contrasting patterns of fantasy and mobility in Irish and Italian schizophrenics," *Journal of Abnormal and Social Psychology,* 53 (1956), pp. 42–47.

[19]Marie Jahoda "Toward a social psychology of mental health," in *Symposium on the Healthy Personality",* ed. Milton Senn (New York: Josiah Macy Jr. Foundation, 1950), pp. 211–231.

In one approach, mental health is simply viewed as *the absence of mental disorder*. This perspective is limited for two reasons. First, while most would agree that the absence of psychopathology is a necessary condition for mental health, one must still define mental illness in order to understand, by contrast, mental health. Secondly, this approach fails to take into account cross-cultural differences in acceptable behavior discussed previously. For example, is homosexuality to be viewed as an abnormality or as a lifestyle? It was a widely accepted lifestyle among the early Greeks, and it is gaining acceptability among many people in the United States today. But these views contrast sharply with attitudes predominant among nineteenth-century Europeans who viewed homosexuality in a number of negative ways ranging from "hereditary inferiority" to the result of "masturbatory insanity."[20] So, depending on the cultural assumptions of the evaluator, the same behavior can be viewed as normal, even laudable, or it can be viewed as perverted.

Another definition of mental health holds that a *correct perception of reality* is the key to mental health. In view of the cross-cultural variations in social norms which have been discussed, this approach holds little promise. What is "correct" depends on the way in which a given people perceive the world. For example, the Kwakuitl Indians of British Columbia exhibit a perception of the world that American psychiatrists would diagnose as paranoid delusions of grandeur.[21] And the Buddhist self-absorptions of esteemed mystics in India are clinically equivalent to the withdrawn type of schizophrenia Western psychiatry has dubbed catatonia.[22]

These problems are often skirted by specifying that the correct perception of reality is the opinion of the "average person," but this fosters a belief in the "average" as correct and the "exceptional" as incorrect. The concept of averaging is unsatisfactory in defining mental health because one is then faced with a further definitional problem: "Who is average?" There are countless cases in modern society in which the opinion of a majority of people has not been linked with correctness but with ungrounded and pathological beliefs. The racist ideology of the southern states (particularly in the earlier part of this century) and Nazi Germany are cases in point. Conversely, the view of the uncommon as pathological is even less viable since it logically requires the inclusion of the great achievements of individuals as well.

A third criterion of mental health utilizes the concept of *adjustment to the environment* which is generally taken to mean that a person has established a workable arrangement between his personal needs and his social relations. The absence of such an arrangement is a definite coun-

[20]For a comprehensive survey of changing attitudes toward homosexuality over time, see Arno Karlen, *Sexuality and Homosexuality* (New York: W. W. Norton, 1971).

[21]Ruth Benedict, "Anthropology and the abnormal," *Journal of General Psychology*, 10 (1934), pp. 59–82.

[22]Otto Klineberg, *Social Psychology* (New York: Henry Holt, 1945).

terindication of mental health, to be sure. After all, mental stability cannot be enjoyed by a person who is hostile toward his everyday social environment. In this sense the "adjustment" definition is useful in separating some obviously abnormal people from the rest of the population. But this approach would include some mentally ill people in the normal category since adjustment to one's environment is not always desirable. Some people are adjusted to a *pathological* environment such as that fostered by maternal deprivation, infrafamilial disharmony, or social isolation. The individual who adjusts to these conditions must do so at considerable psychological cost. Such a view of mental health denies that life circumstances are better or worse and would dangerously conclude that a passive acceptance of all environmental conditions constitutes mental health. Without specifying what environmental conditions are considered to be pathological, the "adjustment" definition suffers the same limitations as the "correct perception of reality" approach.

Psychoanalysts have developed an interesting formula. Their definition of mental health is oriented toward a state of *intrapsychic equilibrium.* The healthy personality is one that is free from conflicts among its three constituent parts: id, ego, and superego. The person whose personality is integrated is not dominated by any one part. Thus only sensualists (id-dominated types), moralists (superego-dominated types), and those with rigid, nonadaptive egos are viewed as mentally disordered.[23] Those who do suffer from an intrapsychic imbalance are considered to have regained their health if the energies of the id become more mobile, the superego, becomes more tolerant, and if the ego becomes free from anxiety with its integrative function restored. This is a particularly useful approach to the problem of defining mental health, but unfortunately it too has a shortcoming. There are some mentally ill people whose personalities are unified but whose view of reality is distorted and highly individualistic. This is true of many schizophrenics who are self-regulated and unified but live in a fantasy world which is radically different from the world of others.

Absence of mental disorder, correct perception of reality, adjustment to one's environment, and intrapsychic equilibrium are themes that most frequently appear in attempts to delineate mental illness.

Different theoreticians stress different aspects of mental health. But after all the verbiage has been sifted, one can detect the recurrence of certain themes: personal happiness, interpersonal adjustment, and ability to adapt to change. All of these criteria, however, are impossible to assess objectively, particularly on a cross-cultural level. Many of these criteria express only the personal value judgments of their authors, rather than scientifically established facts. Of course, extreme cases do not cause difficulty when it comes to defining mental illness as in the case of "The old man who no longer knows where he is, does not recognize his wife and

---

[23]Heinz Hartmann, "Psychoanalysis and the concept of health," *International Journal of Psychoanalysis,* 20 (1939), pp. 308–321.

children, and in his nightgown runs into the street to go to 'his' store which he had sold twenty years ago—this man, everybody will concede, is ill and needs protection."[24] But a large proportion of questionable behavior is not as overtly disordered as the behavior of this hallucinatory old man. It is these less extreme cases which pose the real challenge to objective diagnosis.

Mental Illness as Myth

An interesting reaction to the slippery concept of mental illness has been the recent intervention of those who claim that mental illness is nothing but a myth. This position is part of a revolution against traditional psychiatry as well as a revolution within it. A penetrating voice from within is that of Thomas Szasz who argues that psychiatric theory rests upon unproven assumptions. G. W. Albee has stated that the biogenic model of mental illness is responsible for a gross waste of time and funds ". . . to support the urine boilers and myeline-pickers looking for the defective hormone or the twisted synapse."[25] The revolutionaries posit that mental illness is essentially a sociohistorical derivative and not a scientific concept. Their position stems from empirical evidence of the lack of reliability of psychiatric diagnosis and from a strong belief that mental illness is simply social misbehavior.

The Reliability of Psychiatric Diagnoses

Much of the literature in this area indicates that psychiatrists frequently disagree with each other regarding patients' (and pseudo-patients') diagnoses. During World War II it became apparent that it is not always possible to distinguish normal persons from mentally ill ones as evidenced by an overwhelming lack of success with psychiatric screening.[26] In 1949, Ash ran an experiment in which normal persons and mental patients were presented to a group of psychiatric diagnosticians for their evaluation. In that study, the diagnosticians agreed with each other only 45.7 percent of the time.[27] Since then, other investigators have confirmed that psychiatrists disagree with one another much more than is commonly recognized.[28] This has led some to conclude that art

[24]Felix Von Mendelssohn, "On mental illness: a review", *Psychiatric Quarterly,* 48 (1974), p. 357.
[25]G. W. Albee, "The dark at the top of the agenda", *The Clinical Psychologist Newsletter,* 20 (1966), p. 7.
[26]E. Ginzberg and others, *The Lost Divisions* (New York: Columbia University Press, 1959).
[27]P. Ash, "The reliability of psychiatric diagnoses," *Journal of Abnormal and Social Psychology,* 44 (1949), pp. 271–276.
[28]See, for example: P. Chodoff, "The problem of psychiatric diagnosis: can biochemistry and neurophysiology help?" *Psychiatry,* 23 (1960), pp. 185–191.; B. Pasamanick, S. Dinitz, and M. Lefton, "Psychiatric orientation and its relation to diagnosis and treat-

outweighs science in ascertaining the presence or absence of mental illness. Further evidence for the unreliability of psychiatric diagnosis comes from cross-cultural studies. For instance, a much higher proportion of schizophrenia compared to manic-depressive psychosis is found among hospitalized patients in the United States than in England. Consequently, it is generally assumed that the two cultures predispose their members to different types of psychotic breakdown. However, there is now evidence that much of the reported difference between American and English psychotics is the result of different diagnostic criteria employed in the two settings. When the criteria are standardized, no important differences emerge between the two countries.[29]

There is another side to the question of diagnostic reliability, however. Diagnoses by psychiatrists of the same patients are apparently more consistent when they use broad diagnostic categories such as psychosis, neurosis and normal as compared to when they are required to specify a subtype of illness. In one study in which broad categories were used, a team of psychiatrists agreed on their diagnoses 96 percent of the time.[30]

Mental Illness as Social Misbehavior

The "mental illness as myth movement" also takes issue with the psychiatric nomenclature, contending that the diagnostic labels are alarming and threatening. An example is the patient who has been labeled as an explosive personality. Members of this movement feel that a damaging stigma attaches to these labels which fosters the public belief that mental patients are not merely sick but are to be feared or scorned.

The people who have raised these criticisms usually are members of the "labeling theory school," also known as the "societal reaction perspective." They view mental illness as the result of an unfortunate experience of a socially powerless individual who committed a deviant act, much like those committed by everyone at one time or another during a lifetime. This individual, however, was caught by socially powerful others and assigned the label of mentally ill. Mental illness is thus viewed as a status with a prescribed set of role-related behaviors that are acted out by those who have been so labeled. Individuals who acquire the label have simply failed to manage their lives comfortably within the demands of their social environment. They may be irritable, bad-tempered, or aggressive, and others urge them to seek medical advice—

ment in a mental hospital," *American Journal of Psychiatry*, 116 (1959), pp. 127–132; R. J. Stoller and R. H. Giertsma, "The consistency of psychiatrists' clinical judgments," *Journal of Nervous and Mental Disease*, 137 (1963), pp. 58–66.

[29]J. E. Cooper, *Psychiatric Diagnosis in New York and London* (New York: Oxford University Press, 1972); Joseph L. Fleiss and others, "Cross-national study of diagnosis of the mental disorders," *International Journal of Social Psychiatry*, 19 (1973), pp. 180–186.

[30]N. Rosenzweig and others, "A study of the reliability of the mental status examination," *American Journal of Psychiatry*, 117 (1961), pp. 1102–1108.

especially if they are young and still at the mercy of their elders. In these cases, it is often the socially obnoxious behavior that leads to mental treatment. Simultaneously, the fact of the illness is inferred from the behavior so that the behavior itself *is* the illness. According to Thomas Szasz, the behavior, which is nothing more than "problems in living," results in conduct that violates rule-following prescriptions.[31] As long as the criteria for mental illness are conduct and personal beliefs, their evaluation by a diagnostician will always reflect his own moral, ethical, or political standards.

Sarlin argues that the concept "illness" came to include unacceptable behavior during the sixteenth century to save unfortunate people from being labeled witches.[32] It was more humane to treat persons who exhibited different kinds of misconduct as if they were ill. But what was useful in an earlier historical era has, according to labeling theorists, been continued into a harmful myth.

Labeling theorists may be admired for their philosophical arguments, but Szasz and his followers have made few converts outside of mainstream sociology. Many consider their arguments to be sophistry, even though they find it difficult to refute them on purely theoretical grounds. Others view the labeling hypothesis as titillating reading for popular magazines but uninformed by clinical experience.

If mental illness cannot be defined objectively because it is *social* misbehavior, then there is no way to separate the sick from the healthy. The truth of the matter is that there is empirical evidence to support some of the claims made by labeling theorists. The claims which have received support, however, are not directly related to the theory's central proposition that mental illness is simply the acting out of behavioral expectations associated with a particular label. Instead, peripheral issues have been tested, and evidence has been compiled demonstrating that there is indeed an important social aspect to mental illness. Some of the typical ways in which significant others react to abnormal behavior can increase both the chances of the person's becoming more disordered and of his remaining ill for a longer period of time. These social reactions can adversely affect the troubled person before, during, and after psychiatric treatment.

The central proposition raised by labeling theorists is that mental illness does not exist. Has this been proven? No, and it never will be because there are many disorders stemming from biogenic factors or deeply ingrained early pathological influences that are very real and far from mythical. It is true that social phenomena may complicate an illness. It is also quite possible that, as Movahedi contends, psychiatric dossiers of mental patients are artifacts produced by a biased sample of the patient's life events so that just as gloomy a picture could be con-

---

[31]Thomas S. Szasz, *The Myth of Mental Illness* (New York: Hoeber, 1961).
[32]Theodore R. Sarlin, "On the futility of the proposition that some people be labeled 'mentally ill,'" *Journal of Consulting Psychology,* 31 (1967), pp. 447–453.

structed about nonpatients.[33] Rosenhan clearly demonstrated that psychiatric evaluators often guess as to whether and how a person is disordered. He instructed normal people how to act psychotic. They then presented themselves at the admissions department of a number of mental hospitals around the country. All were diagnosed as psychotic and the diagnoses never changed even though they acted "perfectly normal" after admission.[34] Certainly personal and cultural values affect diagnosis, and obviously psychiatry has not developed to the point of general medicine in which diagnosis and treatment can be conducted rather objectively. These labeling theory arguments have merit since mental illness is not easily defined by scientific, monistic concepts. But to say that mental illness does not exist is as foolish as to deny that there is such a thing as cancer because it is not fully understood.

Current Psychiatric Nomenclature

Presently there is no single definition of mental health that can deal with the cross-cultural and philosophical questions discussed in this chapter. Hopefully, a universal definition will eventually be developed but it must include multiple criteria. Such an approach might consider mental health *as an integrated personality that correctly perceives the world and is adjusted to a nonpathological environment and to changes within it.* This definition draws together the most significant components of the major approaches today. However, it is not without its shortcomings, particularly with regard to the ambiguity of the word "correct" which can be clearly specified only in a culturally relativistic way; that is, with regard to the norms and values of the particular society under consideration.

Two additional points are pertinent here. First, Devereux suggests that the issue of what is normal has been overemphasized.[35] Even though certain patterns considered abnormal in one society are institutionalized in other cultures, they are not often commonly observed behaviors in these cultures. People who fill these roles are usually acknowledged to be on the periphery of the social system as in the case of witch doctors. Secondly, Kiev has stated that, although mental illnesses are viewed differently cross-culturally, they are functionally equivalent in that the patient's symptoms are either distressing to him or the group.[36] Kiev further suggests that the difficulties inherent in the cross-

[33]Siamak Movahedi, "Loading the dice in favor of madness," *Journal of Health and Social Behavior,* 16 (1975), pp. 192–197.

[34]David L. Rosenhan, "On being sane in insane places," *Science,* 179 (1973), pp. 250–258.

[35]G. Devereux, "Normal and abnormal; the key problem of psychiatric anthropology," in *Some Uses of Anthropology, Theoretical and Applied* (Washington, D.C.: The Anthropological Society of Washington, D.C., 1956).

[36]Ari Kiev, "Transcultural psychiatry: research problems and perspectives," in *Changing Perspectives in Mental Illness,* eds. S. C. Plog and R. B. Edgerton (New York: Holt, Rinehart and Winston, Inc., 1969), pp. 106–127.

cultural study of mental illness can be overcome by intensive studies of single cultures. This book is based on such an approach since it utilizes the diagnostic nomenclature painstakingly developed by the American Psychiatric Association (APA). This classification system is chosen for a very practical reason—research in the field generally employs APA terminology. The author does not have much choice in the matter since the APA's nomenclature has been used in almost every investigation of mental illness for the last three decades. This framework may be viewed by some as limiting in that the phenomenon of mental disorder is considered only within the American context. It is not the purpose of this book, however, to delineate every known way in which humans have been considered disordered or healthy. That is more appropriately the responsibility of psychiatric anthropology. It is imperative, however, to be aware of the problems encountered in such an undertaking since the American view of mental illness is not necessarily shared by others.

DSM-II

After World War II, many epidemiological studies of mental illness were conducted in various parts of the United States. From these investigations, it became clear that the existing psychiatric nomenclature was not designed for a majority of people with mental disorders. In 1952, the APA published their first *Diagnostic and Statistical Manual of Mental Disorders* (DSM-I). The manual was expanded in 1968 (DSM-II) for the purpose of providing an even broader service to American psychiatrists. The manual was authored in such a way as to "... reflect the growth of the concept that the people of all nations live in one world."[37] To achieve this end, the APA worked closely with the World Health Organization to develop uniformity in international classifications of disorders. Thus the APA appears at least overtly concerned with the problem of cross-cultural variations in acceptable behavior. The diagnostice nomenclature in DSM-II includes ten categories of mental disorders. They are:

1. *Mental Retardation.* This refers to subnormal intellectual functioning which originates during early life and is associated with impairment of either learning and social adjustment or maturation, or both. The severity of the condition is classified according to the patient's IQ score.
2. *Organic Brain Syndromes.* These result from physical impairment of brain tissue. Alcoholism, senility, intracranial infection, syphilis of the central nervous system, brain trauma, and epilepsy are some of the known causes.
3. *Psychoses Not Attributed to Physical Conditions.* This category includes those whose mental functioning is sufficiently impaired to interfere grossly

---

[37] *Diagnostic and Statistical Manual of Mental Disorders,* (Washington, D.C.: The American Psychiatric Association, 1968), p. VII. The author acknowledges that much of the specific descriptions of the various types of mental illness in this book appear in the well-worded pages of DSM-II and the preliminary draft of DSM-III.

with their capacity to meet the ordinary demands of life. The subtypes include the schizophrenias, the manic-depressive illnesses, involutional melancholia, and the paranoid states. These are known as the *functional* psychoses.

4. *Neuroses*. This category encompasses patients who suffer mainly from anxiety. Unlike the psychoses, there is no gross personality disorganization or misinterpretation of reality. The various patterns of neurosis include anxiety neurosis, hysterical neurosis, phobic neurosis, obsessive-compulsive neurosis, neurasthenic neurosis, hypochondriacal neurosis, and existential neurosis.

5. *Personality Disorders*. This group of disorders is characterized by deeply ingrained maladaptive behavior patterns that are life-long. These include the antisocial, paranoid, schizoid, explosive, obsessive-compulsive, and hysterical types. Also classified under this category are sexual deviations, alcoholism, and drug dependency.

6. *Psychophysiologic Disorders*. This group of disorders is characterized by physical symptoms that are caused by emotional factors and involve a single organ system. Included are skin disorders, gastrointestinal disorders, cardiovascular disorders, and respiratory disorders.

7. *Special Symptoms*. This category is for the occasional patient whose psychopathology is manifested by discrete, specific symptoms such as facial tics, enuresis (bed-wetting), speech disturbances, and sleep disorders.

8. *Transient Situational Disturbances*. This category is for temporary disorders of any severity that occur in individuals without an underlying psychopathology. They represent an acute reaction to an overwhelming environmental stress and are classified according to the patient's age.

9. *Behavior Disorders of Childhood and Adolescence*. These are more resistant to change than the transient situational disturbances but less so than the psychoses, neuroses, and personality disorders.

10. *Conditions Without Manifest Psychiatric Disorder and Nonspecific Conditions*. These include individuals who are normal but who have certain problems severe enough to warrant psychiatric examination. These conditions include marital maladjustment, social maladjustment, occupational maladjustment, and dyssocial behavior (criminals who are not antisocial personalities).

Obviously, some of these mental illnesses are of little relevance to the study of social influences on mental disorder. For this reason, questions raised throughout this book are specifically oriented to the functional disorders. The organic disorders are not considered since they are essentially biological phenomena, although environmental factors can affect their onset and severity. This book is limited to those disorders that occur frequently and that are commonly encountered in studies of mental illness—*the functional psychoses, the neuroses, and the personality disorders.*

These diagnostic categories are always subject to change as new information about mental illness is acquired and more refined classifications are developed. Some of the changes are the result of sociological forces which cause attitudinal changes. This is particularly likely to occur in the area of sexual deviations, a blatant example of the influence of societal opinion on the accepted view of the abnormal.

At this point, it is appropriate to stress that a behavior is considered "officially" ill in this country only if it is viewed as such by the APA. The APA makes these decisions by polling the opinions of its members and resolving issues according to the majority vote. This is not unlike the "averaging" approach to defining mental illness that was criticized earlier but at least here, the population from which the vote is taken consists of those dedicated to the study of abnormal behavior. It is certainly not the ideal foundation for objectively studying mental disorder, however. But if one becomes so concerned with scientific purism that he feels compelled to wait for value free indices of mental illness to be developed, he becomes part of a self-fulfilling prophecy. It is self-fulfilling because idle waiting can never contribute to the development of indices that are pure, refined, and objectively scientific. Such indices can be achieved only through continual effort. With these problems and limitations stated, the data and theories presented in this book should be considered as a portrayal of mental illness in the United States today, recognizing that tomorrow's knowledge will be a function of today's efforts.

DSM-II

As this book was being written, the APA Task Force on Nomenclature was working on revising DSM-II to provide more refined classifications for psychiatric diagnosis. This new edition (DSM-III) was published in 1979. Since it takes a number of years for publications of psychiatric research to adapt new classification systems, DSM-II nomenclature continued in use. The major difference between DSM-II and DSM-III is that the latter separates illnesses into more categories. DSM-III does not add any new-found illness; it simply places the DSM-II disorders into more distinct categories and changes some of the earlier terminology. An April, 1977 draft of DSM-III projected the use of seventeen categories of illness.[38] They appear below along with any changes from DSM-II:

1. Organic Mental Disorders—These were orginally called Organic Brain Syndromes.
2. Drug Use Disorders—These were classified as personality disorders in DSM-II.
3. Schizophrenic Disorders ⎫
4. Paranoid Disorders ⎪ These were all originally
5. Affective Disorders ⎬ classified as functional psy-
6. Psychoses Not Elsewhere ⎪ choses.
Classified ⎭
7. Anxiety Disorders—This is the new term for the neuroses.

---

[38]*Diagnostic and Statistical Manual of Mental Disorders* (Washington, D.C., American Psychiatric Association, April 15, 1977, draft of third edition).

8. Factitious Disorders—This is a new category for patients who *voluntarily* produce physical or psychological symptoms.
9. Somatoform Disorders—These used to be classified as anxiety neurosis or hysterical neurosis, conversion type.
10. Dissociative Disorders—These are patients with amnesia or multiple personality. They used to be classified as hysterical neurosis, dissociative type.
11. Personality Disorders—Same as DSM-II.
12. Psychosexual Disorders—These were originally classified with the personality disorders.
13. Disorders Usually Arising in Childhood or Adolescence—Same as DSM-II.
14. Reactive Disorders Not Elsewhere Classified—These are equivalent to the Transient Situational Disturbances in DSM-II.
15. Disorders of Impulse Control Not Elsewhere Classified—This category includes pathological gambling, kleptomania, pyromania, and explosive behavior.
16. Sleep Disorders—These were originally included in the Special Symptoms category.
17. Other Disorders and Conditions—This is equivalent to category ten in DSM-II.

The symptoms of the various disorders are not presented here because they are detailed in the second part of this book. While reading those chapters, the reader should refer to this section on DSM-III to become familiar with the changing nomenclature. It is important, however, to remember that terminological changes are nothing more than an attempt to constitute a more useful psychiatric language. They bear little relationships to the causes of psychiatric syndromes, the central question of the second part of this book.

Conclusions

It is exceedingly difficult to define mental illness objectively. Semantic problems are partly responsible for the problem; the alternative use of words such as insane, mental disorder, psychopathology, and particularly, mental illness, can often result in substantially different interpretations by different people. Another nagging element is the lack of a definition of mental health and illness. Often one culture's deviants are the heroes of another culture.

Attempts to define mental health and mental illness have been limited by one-sided approaches which often reflect a value only endorsed by a particular group of people. None of the more well-known definitions of mental health (absence of disorder, adjustment to environment, correct perception of reality, and unity of personality) are sufficient by themselves. Their most outstanding flaws are their inability to fit with anthropological data evidencing culturally specific expressions of disorders and a lack of reliable diagnostic techniques. The cross-cultural phenomenon may be less of a problem than originally believed since evidence now suggests that what appear to be exotic illnesses are simply reflections of different ways of exhibiting psychopathology.

The American Psychiatric Association has developed a very detailed system of classifying types of illnesses. This nomenclature is based on frequently occurring syndromes that are distinct from each other in kind and degree. Three of the major types of disorders, the functional psychoses, the neuroses, and the personality disorders serve as the focus of this book because of their relationship with sociocultural forces.

The Etiology
of Mental Illness
Biogenic
and Environmental Theories

3

Neurosis

A Theoretical Overview

The chapters in this second part of the book present the symptoms and causes of the neuroses, functional psychoses, personality disorders, and sexual deviations. This material is not directly representative of the sociology of mental illness because much of it is clinical, biogenic, or intrapsychic. However, it is necessary to understand these aspects of mental illness in order to comprehend the sociological aspects of mental illness which are presented in the last two sections of the book. Without knowing the symptoms of the different illnesses and, particularly, how they can arise in an individual, the fact that they are found (or reported) more frequently in certain social groups has little meaning. In this chapter and the following chapter, one of the most complicated and widely-researched group of disorders, the neuroses, is discussed. The neuroses, as contrasted to the psychoses, manifest neither gross distortion of external reality nor gross personality disorganization. A possible exception to this is the dissociative neurosis.

Symptoms of Neurosis

If mental illness if regarded as a continuum, neurosis falls between normal behavior and psychosis. There are many criteria that differentiate neurosis from psychosis. Psychoses are profound disturbances which involve more disorganization and misinterpretation of reality than do the neuroses. For this reason, the overt behavior of the psychotic is a more accurate manifestation of the underlying disturbance than is the neurotic's behavior. In addition, psychotics usually do not realize that they are disturbed whereas neurotics are frequently aware of their problems. Another difference between the neurotic and the psychotic is the benefit which the neurotic receives from the fact of having symptoms. This phenomenon, known as *secondary gain,* usually takes the form of sympathy from others which the neurotic exploits to his best advantage.

The neuroses are not to be confused with the personality disorders which are deeply ingrained maladaptive patterns of behavior. Personality disorders are closer to normal behavior than the neuroses on the mental illness continuum. The major difference is in degree rather than kind since many of the personality disorders are conditions which lead to neurosis. They become neuroses if the personality disorder proceeds to the point where a person loses productivity.

The major symptom of all neurotic conditions is an intense experience of *anxiety,* a feeling of subjective distress. Anxiety is similar to fear, both subjectively and in objective terms of physiological disturbance. Fear, however, is an appropriate reaction to a real danger whereas anxiety is not related to a real, external threat or is grossly disproportionate to any such threat. In essence, anxiety warns of an internal danger caused by an intrapsychic conflict. Anxiety is considered to be a normal correlate of aging and experiencing new and untried things. The child, for example, experiences anxiety on his first day in school as does the old man contemplating impending death. Pathological anxiety, on the other hand, is a response which is inappropriate to a given situation. For example, almost anyone would experience unpleasant feelings in the presence of a man-eating beast, but the neurotic would be similarly upset by a docile dog. This self-created terror is known as *pure anxiety* or *free-floating anxiety* when it is severe, persistent, and experienced directly without the use of a defense mechanism. A defense mechanism is a device used by the ego to avoid danger, anxiety, and unpleasure. If a defense mechanism is involved, the type of defense mechanism largely determines the form of the neurosis. The resulting symptoms are designed to protect the person from further danger from an internal threat, but they still involve some subjective stress.

A number of physiological alterations have been found to correlate with the onset of neurotic symptoms. Among these are trembling, increased heart rate, dry mouth, nausea, gooseflesh, hot and cold sensations, dizziness and faintness, urinary urgency, fatigue, muscular tension, restlessness, insomnia, and sexual dysfunction.

Psychological symptoms of neurosis are more varied. Most neurotics are chronically unhappy. Other common features are indecisiveness, feelings of inadequacy, hostility, guilt, hypersensitivity, rigidity, shyness, excessive concerns with physical health, and self-centeredness. Neurotics often have difficulties at work which are generally related to a fear of being rejected or humiliated. This is particularly likely in a job that does not have repetitive features since the neurotic sense of inferiority can dampen creativity required by more demanding occupations.

The central psychological symptom of neurotic anxiety is defensiveness. Because of a wide array of defense mechanisms employed in neurosis, the disorder can take a variety of seemingly unrelated forms. All of the different types of neurosis are enumerated in Chapter 4. As one author puts it, "All neurotics, to be sure, tend to be peculiar . . . But the roads to emotional perplexity are confusingly multiple. Where one neurotic has terrible fears of doing almost anything, another shows his disturbance by needlessly risking his neck every day in some dangerous enterprise. While one lies abed all day and refuses to do any work, another frantically consumes himself in a dozen violent endeavors. One disturbed woman hypochondriacally insists that she is wasting away from a score of imaginary ills, and another with a cancerous ovary insists that she is not sick, that there is no death, and that her Yoga breathing exercises will take care of all her ills."[1]

Although the onset of the neuroses is abrupt, the psychopathological process which culminates in neurotic symptoms has a long history. In fact, evidence of psychological difficulties is frequently found in the childhood histories of neurotics. These include feeding problems in early infancy, difficulties in toilet-training, nightmares, temper tantrums, bed-wetting (*enuresis*) persisting until age eight or beyond, and thumb sucking or nail biting persisting into adolescence.[2] The onset of the neurosis is usually precipitated by a stressful event. A number of such events are presented in Chapter 11. Most of these involve some type of change which the individual perceives as threatening, such as pregnancy, divorce, or even an outstanding personal achievement. Whether a particular event produces stress depends on a number of variables including how the person interprets the event as well as his coping mechanisms. Individuals predisposed toward neurosis are likely to interpret everyday events in threatening ways. Such events may be viewed by most people as inherently neutral or necessary for personal growth but to others they have become highly charged merely by conditioning through a series of encounters or because they threaten the personality with meanings hidden in the unconscious. Neuroses occur only rarely among children, but when they do, they are typically preceeded by stressful events within one month of the neurotic illness.[3] Events commonly precipitating a childhood neurosis include mild physical illness, change of school, reprimand for school performance, birth of a younger sibling, and separation or impending separation of a near relative.[4] Clearly, change—particularly change in interpersonal relationships—is the central aspect of precipitating events in childhood neurosis as it is in adult neurosis.

[1]Albert Ellis, *How to Live With a Neurotic* (New York: Crown, 1957) pp. 35–36.

[2]Merrill T. Eaton, Jr. and Margaret H. Peterson, *Psychiatry* (Flushing: Medical Examination Publishing Company, Inc., 1969), p. 172.

[3]W. H. Lo, "Aetiological factors in childhood neurosis," *British Journal of Psychiatry,* 115 (1969), pp. 889–894.

[4]Ibid., p. 892.

The Prevalence of Neurosis

Neurosis is a widespread mental disorder. In fact, neuroses are so common that many people confuse them with eccentric behavior. Books on neurosis are frequently purchased as popular reading. Questions such as how to detect a neurosis, avoid it, as well as live with it, rival issues of international news, sports, and entertainment. Undoubtedly, neurosis is part of our everyday world.

Much of the psychiatric literature suggests that suppression of instinctual drives can engender anxiety, the primary symptom of a neurotic condition. For this reason, the relationship between civilization and neurosis is fundamental; the higher the level of cultural development, the more complete is the suppression of the instincts, particularly the sex drive.[5] Simply stated, neuroses are the price man must pay for cultural advancement. Hence neuroses are not common in primitive societies which allow for the expression of innate human needs.[6] In primitive society a person is not likely to be subjected to radically different behavior standards as a child than as an adult. In civilized society, however, as an individual passes from one age group to another, permissible behaviors become forbidden and vice versa. The United States epitomizes such cultural discontinuity in development. During the twentieth century, immeasurable complexities have been added to the American cultural base. Many of these additions have come in the form of material culture, such as advances in science and technology. But these advancements have had covert impacts on interpersonal relationships by introducing competition and tension to the impersonality of urban living. This growth in cultural complexity has been accompanied by a reported increase in the prevalence of neurosis.[7]

The true prevalence of neurosis is presently beyond statistical calculation, in part because different psychiatrists use different diagnostic standards and also because different types of methods are used to collect data. For these reasons, some psychiatrists avoid the issue by saying that everyone has "neurotic potential" and will display neurotic behavior under stress.[8] More conservative opinions, however, indicate that no more than 5 to 25 percent of the population suffer neurotic symptoms. Neurotics comprise about 30 to 40 percent of patients who seek medical help from general hospitals or private physicians although most of their physical complaints are psychologically imposed.[9] Neurotic patients do not often require hospitalization, but if they are hospitalized, they are

[5]This thesis, originally developed by Freud, is also the essence of other psychoanalytic views as well. See, for example, Karen Horney, "Culture and neurosis," *American Sociological Review*, 1 (1936), pp. 221–230.

[6]Robert Bastide, *The Sociology of Mental Disorder* (New York: David McKay, 1972), p. 171.

[7]See L. C. Kolb, *Noyes' Modern Clinical Psychiatry*, (Philadelphia: W. B. Saunders, 1973), p. 127.

[8]Sol. W. Ginsburg, *A Psychiatrist's Views on Social Issues* (New York: Columbia University Press, 1963), p. 32.

[9]L. C. Kolb, *Noyes' Modern Clinical Psychiatry*, p. 404.

usually found in private rather than state hospitals. This is because higher-class neurotics can afford better treatment than lower-class neurotics who frequently receive no treatment at all unless they are severely disordered, something which rarely occurs in neurosis.

Culture influences the prevalence of neurosis beyond the primitive-civilized differences noted above. Using anxiety as an indicator of neurosis, Lynn reports a number of cross-cultural differences among civilized societies.[10] France, Austria, West Germany, and Italy are reported as high anxiety countries while Sweden, the Netherlands, and Great Britain score low on Lynn's anxiety measures. This lends support to the commonly accepted stereotype of the unemotional, phlegmatic Anglo-Saxon, the excitable French, and the volatile Italian. Lynn constructs an interesting hypothesis to account for these differences by suggesting that climate has an effect on anxiety. He points out that the high anxiety countries have warmer climates and more frequent storms, both of which have a psychologically unsettling effect on people.

Theories of Neurosis

There are a number of theoretical perspectives on the etiology of neurosis. The biogenic view postulates that neurotic anxiety stems from somatic forces. In addition, there are three major environmental theories of neurosis which locate the cause of the disorder in the person's psychosocial world. One of these is the labeling theory which holds that neurosis is a reflection of the attitudes others have toward the individual. The behaviorist theory postulates that neurosis is largely the result of interaction with others who reinforce neurotic behavior. The third environmental theory is psychoanalytic which roots neurosis in the sequential process of psychosexual development. Thus psychoanalysts consider neurosis as a reaction to some interruption in this process. Of the three theoretical perspectives, the psychoanalytic view has received the greatest amount of research attention. This is reflected by the large amount of space in this chapter that is devoted to unraveling its complexities. However, the complexity of psychoanalytic theory does not necessarily mean that it is a more accurate explanation of neurosis than other theories. Many social scientists, for instance, feel that psychoanalytic interpretations are limited by an overemphasis on intrapsychic forces and a deemphasis on social factors.

Biogenic Theories

Neurosis literally means an illness of the nerves but this is more of a medical relic than a psychiatric reality because there is limited evidence that neurosis is caused by biogenic forces. Most psychiatrists assume that neurosis is environmental in origin. However, there are a few interesting biogenic positions on neurosis that cannot be ignored.

[10]R. Lynn, *Personality and National Character* (Oxford: Pergamon Press, 1971).

Eysenck, for instance, believes that the major etiological factor in all neuroses is an inherited unstable autonomic nervous system that is expressed in emotional overresponsiveness.[11] Others consider the maintenance of anxiety to be related to the level of neural activity of the frontal lobes of the brain, the center of the sympathetic nervous system. This has been demonstrated in a number of ways including the use of the surgical procedure of prefrontal leucotomy. The operation has been reported to reduce neurotic anxiety in some instances.[12] The inference is that the frontal lobes maintain anxiety since rendering them inactive reduces anxiety. Research involving surgical alteration of the brain has rarely been attempted since the 1950s because the dangerous side effects of such surgery often outweigh any benefits. It is important to note, however, that even if the frontal lobes are involved in anxiety, it is probably because they simply provide the biological vehicle for anxiety not because they actually cause the anxiety. In support of this thesis, there is no evidence that the frontal lobes of neurotic patients are qualitatively different from those of normal persons. All that can be said is that feelings are altered when the lobes are severed. This would likely be the outcome if nonneurotics were subjected to lobe severance. Hopefully, no one will feel the need to prove this in the future.

It has been demonstrated that neurosis frequently occurs among members of the same family, even over two and three generations.[13] Furthermore, the type of neurotic pattern or "reaction" is often the same. Brown studied the prevalence of neurosis in relatives of diagnosed neurotics and found that 16.8 percent of first-degree relative (siblings, mothers, and fathers) were also neurotic. In a control group made up of nonneurotics and their first-degree relatives, concordance was only 1.1 percent.[14] Rosenthal has summarized the results of studies of dizygotic and monozygotic twins where one twin was diagnosed neurotic. Consistent with the theory of genetic transmission, there is a 40 percent concordance among dizygotic twins and a 53 percent concordance among monozygotics.[15] Obviously, genetics cannot account for all cases of neurosis since the data do not reflect anything near 100 percent concordance among identical twins. Although there is some reason to believe that genetic determinants may be involved in the etiology of neurosis, it is questionable whether they are of major etiological significance. Cases of neurosis occurring within families and across generations are generally

[11]Hans J. Eysenck, "Classification and the problems of diagnosis," in *Handbook of Abnormal Psychology*, ed. Hans J. Eysenck (New York: Basic Books, 1961).

[12]A. Petrie, *Personality and the Frontal Lobes* (London: Routledge and Kegan Paul, 1952).

[13]See, for example, Seymour Fisher and David Mendell, "The communications of neurotic patterns over two and three generations," *Psychiatry*, 19 (1956), pp. 41–46.

[14]W. F. Brown, "Heredity in the psychoneuroses," *Proceedings of the Royal Society of Medicine*, 35 (1942), pp. 414–430.

[15]D. Rosenthal, *Genetic Theory and Abnormal Behavior* (New York: McGraw-Hill, 1970).

viewed as the product of social contagion rather then genetic forces. In short, mental health experts in psychiatry and social science do not believe that a person is *born* neurotic. Disruptive early childhood experiences and interpersonal difficulties are generally considered to be the common pathways to neurosis. Of course, it is possible that innate and environmental factors merge to form neurosis. If this is true, a person could be born with neurotic potential but only become neurotic with sufficient environmental stress.

Labeling Theory

Labeling theory rests on the propositions of the classic sociological theories of personality (symbolic interactionism) developed by Cooley and Mead. Both of these men believed that one's personality is largely a reflection of how an individual interprets other people's reactions to him. More recently, Scheff and Szasz have pioneered in applying this concept to mental illness in general.

The theory has been applied to neurosis by those who hold that, if the reactions of others to a person are generally negative, and if the person perceives and accepts this negative evaluation, he suffers a high degree of anxiety and eventually develops neurosis. It is important to note that labeling theorists consider neurosis and other forms of deviant behavior to be a process by which an individual moves from *primary deviance* to *secondary deviance,* a distinction made by Lemert.[16] Primary deviance is the original deviant act which may have a wide variety of causes. Secondary deviance results from being labeled a deviant. In other words, a primary deviant act is followed by negative social sanctions which cause the deviant to be hostile and resentful toward those doing the penalizing. Then the deviant reacts to others' stigmatization and penalties, not by stopping the deviance, but by accepting the deviant status. The acceptance of a negative attitude toward oneself must occur over a period of time in order to produce neurosis. It is one's self-concept that underlies neurosis and one's self-concept depends on the attitudes that others have toward him. If others blame him, he will blame himself. If they accept him, he will accept himself. It is the *negative self-image* which creates feelings of inadequacy and forms the core of later neurosis. For example, children are likely to become neurotic if they are taught to seek perfection in themselves because they will feel compelled to spend their lives trying to achieve the unattainable and to win the approval of everyone. Ellis, for instance, reports on the case of an unusually good-looking, seventeen-year-old female, an accomplished dancer and sculptress, with a tested I.Q. of 178.[17] She considered herself ugly, untalented, and stupid. The origin of this distorted self-concept was her mother who always complained that her daughter was a failure

[16]Edwin Lemert, *Social Pathology* (New York: McGraw-Hill, 1951).
[17]Albert Ellis, *How to Live With a Neurotic,* pp. 99–100.

in school because she received a 98 in a subject rather than 100!

Criticism can also engender a negative self-image because it is often perceived as disapproval, a sign of one's worthlessness. Competitiveness can inflict the same damage as perfectionism and criticism, since by promoting the belief that a child should be better than other children, the child with average talents feels deprived relative to more talented peers.

Forcing competitiveness, criticism, and perfectionism on a child are some of the ways by which a second type of self-disparagement can occur. This is a selective process by which the individual gives the negative reactions of others prime importance while disregarding any positive evaluations because the negative reactions are consistent with a sense of self-depreciation. A person who has suffered extreme criticism or who has perfectionistic attitudes often overreacts to slight blows to his ego. Such a person goes through life preoccupied with feelings of worthlessness. These feelings grow until his perception of his own worthlessness makes him unattractive to others. It is a cycle of mounting tension that deteriorates into chronic anxiety.

Criticisms of Labeling Theory. The labeling theory explanation of neurosis clearly places the origin in disturbed interpersonal relationships and therefore points out the important effect that social forces can have on psychopathology. However, one weakness of the theory is that it is deterministic in assuming that negative evaluations by others are automatically accepted by an individual. Certainly some people ignore others' criticisms and live neuroses-free lives. What is peculiar to those who accept the label? Is there an inherited weakness or an unconscious problem that leads some to respond poorly to others' evaluations? Clearly, these questions remain to be answered.

Behaviorist Theory

The theory of neurosis put forth by behaviorists holds that the disorder results from *learning,* a change of behavior that takes place through practice or experience. Behaviorists do not differentiate the symptoms of neurosis and the underlying cause; they are considered to be one and the same. This view, championed by Dollard and Miller,[18] argues that neurosis is nothing more than a set of observable symptoms. Thus the principles of the widely researched view of human behavior, *learning theory,* can be applied to neurosis as well as normal behavior. There are three processes of learning by which neurotic anxiety can be developed: *classical conditioning, operant* (or instrumental) *conditioning,* and *modeling* (social learning).

Classical Conditioning. In classical conditioning, a stimulus generates a direct response as when a heterosexual is aroused by the sight of

---

[18]J. Dollard and N. E. Miller, *Personality and Psychotherapy* (New York: McGraw-Hill, 1950).

an attractive member of the opposite sex. Applied to neurosis, this same principle of association is at work when intense anxiety becomes improperly associated with various environmental conditions. If anxiety is experienced when there is no objective threat, the person will acquire a pathological response. Classical conditioning has mainly been applied to a particular type of neurosis, the phobic neurosis. As mentioned earlier, the phobic neurotic experiences anxiety only in the presence of a particular object or situation. Joseph Wolpe[19] and Hans Eysenck[20] have been most active in this area. Eysenck was described earlier as a biogenic theorist who believes that neurosis stems from an inherited defect of the autonomic nervous system. However, this inherited defect is not a sufficient cause of neurosis; it simply provides the *propensity* for neurosis by causing individuals to have a high degree of *conditionability*. Thus, inherited conditionability *and* the pairing between a neutral environmental condition and a threatening experience together account for a neurotic response.

Eysenck reports on Watson's famous experiment with little Albert, an eleven-month-old boy who was fond of animals.[21] Through classical conditioning Watson created a phobia for white rats in Albert by making a scary noise whenever Albert reached for the animal. Eventually Albert developed a phobia for white rats and all furry animals.

Operant Conditioning. Operant conditioning is an approach to neurosis and other forms of abnormal behavior developed by B. F. Skinner.[22] Skinner contends that learning an abnormal pattern of behavior is not acquired by the simple pairing of a stimulus with a response but by producing new responses under conditions of *reinforcement*. However, the reinforcements are contingent on what a person does. If, for instance, a child receives a reward from his parents when he exhibits excessive cleanliness or orderliness, he is likely to repeat such behaviors in the future. Over time the process continues until the behavior becomes a regularly occuring part of the person's actions which, in the example above, would approximate the obsessive-compulsive type of neurosis.

Modeling. A third variant of the behaviorist school is the process of modeling. Also known as the *social learning* approach, it has been most clearly formulated in the work of Julian Rotter[23] and Albert Bandura.[24]

---

[19]Joseph Wolpe, *Psychotherapy by Reciprocal Inhibition* (Stanford, California: Stanford University Press, 1958).

[20]Hans J. Eysenck, "Learning theory and behavior therapy," *Journal of Mental Science,* 105 (1959), pp. 61–75; Hans J. Eysenck and S. Rachman, *The Causes and Cures of Neurosis* (London: Routledge and Kegan Paul, 1965).

[21]Hans J. Eysenck, "Learning theory and behavior therapy."

[22]B. F. Skinner, *Beyond Freedom and Dignity* (New York: Knopf, 1971).

[23]Julian B. Rotter, *Social Learning and Clinical Psychology* (Englewood Cliffs, N.J.: Prentice-Hall, 1954).

[24]Albert Bandura, "A social learning interpretation of psychological dysfunctions"

They postulate that a common reason for neurotic anxiety is that the individual's environment directly encourages it. Sometimes the encouragement is quite blatant as in the case of overprotective parents who urge their children to be apprehensive and habitually on guard. It can also be seen in the case of parents who are chronically guilty themselves and thereby provide a guilty role model for their children. Another common example of direct encouragement of anxiety is the parent who creates a sense of unworthiness in the child through constant punishment. Sometimes the encouragement is more subtle as in the case of overpermissive parents who do not provide their children with a stable framework with established limits of acceptable behavior. Such a lack of guidance creates feelings of insecurity.

Criticisms of Behaviorist Theory. One problem with the behaviorist view of neurosis is that it examines only surface behaviors and may therefore ignore underlying causes. The theory holds that a specific social experience or sets of experiences cause neurotic symptoms through a learning process. A fear of being in attics, for example, is linked to an earlier experience where an attic was associated with something unpleasant or painful. But this does not elucidate the way in which the specific learning experience may be generalized to anxiety about other situations as well.

Psychoanalytic Theory

The psychoanalytic position on the origin of neurosis is not in total opposition to the labeling or behaviorist views as many believe. All three theories recognize that social factors play a role in the genesis of neurosis. However, the psychoanalytic school emphasizes the specific intrapsychic pathways by which pathogenic social influences are transformed into neurotic patterns. This is accomplished by analyzing the interaction between the three parts of the personality: the id, ego, and superego. The id is innate, unconscious, and oriented toward achieving satisfaction of two major instinctual goals. One of these, known as Eros, is the desire to attach oneself to other people and objects; in short, the desire to live and grow. This can be expressed socially by the formation of families, tribes, and even nation states. An important part of Eros is the sex instinct known as libido. In fact, libido is considered to monopolize a specific amount of the energy of Eros. This is referred to as libidinal energy, which is of major importance in the development of personality. The other instinctual urge within the id is expressed by aggressive activity, both sadistic and masochistic. This is commonly known as the death instinct, or Thanatos. This part of the id has not been as well researched as has the libidinal urge of Eros. However,

in *Foundations of Abnormal Psychology*, eds. P. London and D. Rosenhan (New York: Holt, Rinehart and Winston, 1968).

Thanatos is considered to play a role in the earlier stages of personality development.

The ego is acquired in early childhood. It functions to find specific ways of gratifying instinctual needs by transforming or delaying them so that they are alleviated in socially acceptable ways and at appropriate times. The ego acts as a mediator between the id and the world of reality. Its job is compounded by the requirement that it select activities which not only satisfy id impulses but also are ethical and moral. Moral demands emanate from the part of the ego which develops later in childhood. This is the superego, or conscience.

According to psychoanalytic theory, the personality contains two opposing parts: the selfish, pleasure-seeking id and the moral, straight-laced superego. The ego acts as an executive by mediating the needs of the instincts, the constraints of reality, and the strictures of the superego. Neurosis is considered to originate in a conflict among these interdependent parts which arises during childhood when the personality is being formed. These years are crucial because the social experiences that occur then can have lasting effects on the individual's psyche. Since psychoanalysts believe that the most important experiences are those connected with libidinal needs, their view is also known as psychosexual theory. Unlike the labeling theorists and behaviorists, the psychoanalytic theory of neurosis emphasizes unconscious mental activity and is therefore oriented toward the way in which an individual interprets an event rather than toward the external, visible aspects of the event. The theory analyzes the symptoms of neurosis in terms of the way in which these symptoms *symbolically* represent intrapsychic conflicts.

Psychoanalytic theory holds that neurosis is largely the result of the responses of the unconscious to the social experience of the individual as he seeks libidinal satisfaction. Specifically, traditional psychoanalysts believe that neurosis develops from sexual problems originating in interpersonal difficulties, particularly with the parents. But the psychoanalytic conception of sexuality differs significantly from the conventional one in that psychoanalysts do not consider "sexual" to be synonomous with "genital." "Sexual" includes a variety of drives and behaviors involving a number of bodily areas, of which the genital area is only one.

Neurosis results from a conflict between instinctual impulses arising within the id or a conflict between an id impulse and the ego or superego. Since the ego represents the external social environment and the superego represents cultural values, *neurosis is essentially a conflict between innate human needs and societal norms.* The conflict often arises from a threatening childhood experience which imposed severe stress on the ego. Typically this is a disturbed parent-child relationship. The painful early childhood experience establishes a neurotic potential in an individual. However, this experience must be reactivated in adult life if neurotic symptoms are to be manifested. How? When the individual encounters a situation in life which he perceives as similar to the earlier one, neurosis may occur. For instance, an individual may experience anxiety working within a rigid bureaucracy just as he did growing up under the domination of a strict father. The mechanisms of this process have been formalized in psychoanalytic theory under the terms *fixation* and *regression*. Fixation means that personality growth is arrested at a particular developmental stage as the result of an unresolved childhood conflict, usually with the parents. It can cause difficulties in functioning later in life because the fixation remains as a scar in the person's psychological structure. To depict the phenomenon of fixation more clearly, psychoanalysts use the analogy of an army which leaves strong garrisons behind en route to conquering new territory. This serves both to forward supplies and allow for a place of retreat in case insurmountable difficulties are met ahead. The retreat is the military parallel to the psychoanalytic concept of regression whereby the personality returns to an earlier developmental stage, the stage at which it is fixated. The specific neurotic pattern is determined by the point at which the personality is fixated; for example, in hysterical neurosis at the phallic stage and in the obsessive-compulsive neurosis at the anal stage. The specific linkages between stage fixation and different neurotic patterns are discussed in Chapter 4.

Psychoanalysts believe that it is possible for a person to undergo multiple points of fixation. In such a case, the personality first regresses to the most recently established fixation point then to fixations at lower, earlier levels. Lower level fixations (at the earliest stages of personality development) are believed to cause severe psychotic disturbances. This is why a psychopathology sometimes proceeds from a less severe, neurotic form to a more severe, psychotic type.

Freud, the founder of psychoanalysis, held that neurosis results from a "learning excess".[25] This was based on his observations that fixation was often associated with unusually harsh treatment by the parents of the neurotic. This results in an excessively severe superego which impedes the healthy gratification and development of instinctual drives. Others since Freud have supported the proposition that frustrating infantile experiences can have a traumatic effect on personality development. But harsh parental treatment and unnecessary taboos on instinctual needs are not the only pathways to neurosis; sexual abuse by adults, seduction by older siblings, and seeing or overhearing sexual play between adults may be dangerous for personality development as well.[26] In addition to frustrations, there is a minority opinion in psychoanalytic theory which holds that the opposite of frustration, namely excessive satisfaction (spoiling) of an instinctual need, can also underlie fixation.[27]

[25]Sigmund Freud, *The Problem of Anxiety* (New York: W. W. Norton, 1936).

[26]Herman Nunberg, *Principles of Psychoanalysis* (New York: International Universities Press, Inc., 1955).

[27]Otto Fenichel, *The Psychoanalytic Theory of Neurosis* (New York: W. W. Norton, 1945).

The rationale for this opinion is that childhood overindulgence makes the person unable to bear frustrations at a later age. Thus in painful frustration and pleasurable satisfaction, there is a common element; an excessive amount of libidinal energy is used at a particular stage leaving an insufficient amount for normal development through the remaining stages.[28] Both arrest personality development and the resultant "weak spot" predisposes the person toward regression later.

It is important to understand the specific nuances of each particular stage of psychosexual development since the fundamental hypothesis of the psychoanalytic theory of neurosis is that the disorder stems from a disruption of a maturational sequence during which different zones of the body and social experiences become the source of sexual pleasure. A synopsis of each stage is presented here.

The Oral Stage. The oral stage, has two phases; the *oral-erotic* and the *oral-sadistic.* The entire oral stage lasts from birth to approximately 18 months. During the first stage, the oral-erotic phase, the libido is linked with the instincts of self-preservation, especially with the drive to eat. However, the infant experiences oral stimulation which is distinct from the need for food; pleasure is derived from sucking on objects which are passively incorporated into the mouth. Thus the mouth has a dual function; it is a utilitarian organ used to satisfy the hunger drive, and it is a pleasure organ which gives libidinal satisfaction. The psychological function is illustrated in the case of thumbsucking. Here, oral pleasure is linked to stimulation of the oral mucous membrane and totally unrelated to gratification of hunger need. Oral erotic needs of this stage have their counterpart in adult life, particularly the sexual acts of cunnilingus and fellatio.[29] Smoking, overeating, kissing, and drinking are other adult examples of oral eroticism.

An important characteristic of the infant at this stage is his lack of recognition of any person or object in the outside world with the important exception of the mother. This is known as *primary narcissism* because the infant is totally engrossed in himself and is unaware of any distinction between himself and other people or things in his environment. Because the world is conceived of as if it were all a part of the infant's self (including the mother's breast), there is as yet no ability to make "self-other" distinctions. The infant exists in an "objectless" state. These narcissistic ties to the self are loosened when the ego strives toward external objects not associated with the need for food through activities such as seeing, touching, and hearing the mother. Many psychoanalysts believe

---

[28]It has also been hypothesized that sharp transitions from one developmental stage to the next may cause fixation. This is caused by forcing the developing ego into a stage before it has mastered the challenges and requirements of an earlier stage. It is usually caused by impatient parents who place difficult expectations on their children.

[29]Cunnilingus is the oral stimulation of the female genitals and fellatio is the oral stimulation of the male genitals.

that distinctions between self and other are first made when the infant's oral needs are not totally fulfilled, for instance, when the mother does not respond immediately to the infant's cry.[30] Therefore, some deprivation is needed to stimulate the development of ego functions. Too much deprivation due to the lack of maternal contact can be dangerous, however, because the infant is helpless and must be relatively satisfied by a "mother figure"[31] or he will suffer. Overprotection may be dangerous, as well, because overindulgence of oral needs may cause fixation. Overindulgence tends to be most common in societies in which extended families comprising three or more generations live in the same home.[32] Infancy indulgence is greatest there because of the large number of caretakers.

At about the time that the infant is developing self-other recognition, he begins to cut teeth. This phase is known as the oral-sadistic stage.[33] Now, the infant no longer seeks passive sucking pleasure but actively incorporates any objects available to bite and chew. The oral zone remains the center of psychic pleasure but the teeth and jaws now become of primary importance. It is a cannibalistic phase in which objects are sought after and orally destroyed. Similar drives are found in interaction between adults. Specific examples include pessimism and sarcasm, both of which are oral activities with sadistic objectives. However, the sadistic object is no longer the infant's toy or mother's breast. Instead, the person chews on other people's reputations and self-images.

The mother-infant relationship is of utmost importance during the oral stage because the infant is totally dependent on the maternal figure for the emotional warmth necessary for normal personality development. If the relationship is loving, the child can pass through the stage easily. However, if the child does not receive proper maternal attention, he will be predisposed toward the most severe mental disorders, the psychoses.

The Anal Stage.   The second period of psychosexual development is the anal stage which extends from sometime after the first year of life until about age three or four. Now the anal area becomes the source of libidinal satisfaction. More specifically, the child experiences pleasure through stimulation of the mucous membrane of the rectal tract. He is

[30]G. S. Blum, *Psychoanalytic Theories of Personality* (New York: McGraw-Hill, 1964).

[31]"Mother figure" refers to an adult who assumes responsibility for the care of the child. It need not be the biological mother. In fact, it need not even be a female although this is not common in Western societies.

[32]J. W. M. Whiting, "Socialization process and personality," in *Psychological Anthropology*, ed. F. L. K. Hsu (Homewood, Illinois: Dorsey Press, 1961), pp. 355–380.

[33]Credit for differentiating the two subphases of the oral stage is generally given to Karl Abraham who referred to them as the preambivalent (oral-erotic) and ambivalent (oral-sadistic) phases. See Karl Abraham, "A short study of the development of the libido," in Karl Abraham, *Selected Papers* (London: Institute of Psychoanalysis and Hogarth Press, 1927).

preoccupied not only with the act of elimination but also with his feces. He "loves dirt", especially his own, as expressed by the common practice of smearing the crib with diaper contents.[34] Pleasure is derived in a number of ways involving the passing and retaining of the feces as well as playing with and proudly displaying them.

The first part of the anal stage is the *anal-sadistic* (or expulsive) phase which lasts for about a year. The child is directed by an urge to pass his feces spontaneously at any time or place. Aggressive impulses are marked as evidenced by temper outbursts and other displays of destructive violence. Often aggression takes the form of stubbornness in the face of parental demands for toilet-training.

The *anal erotic* (or retentive) phase occupies the last two years of the anal stage. It results from a recognition, perhaps through learning, that the rectum can yield even greater pleasure by holding back the fecal mass rather than eliminating it. The physiological source of arousal remains the same as the anal sadistic phase but now pleasure is prolonged by delaying excretion.[35]

The normal frustration to the child at the anal stage is the confrontation with toilet-training demands. These requirements conflict with both anal-sadistic and anal-erotic drives because they impose time and place demands on the child who wishes either to eliminate spontaneously or not at all. The child strives for independence and may achieve a sense of self-assertion by defying the parent through expelling feces when he should retain them or retaining feces when he should expel them. This can arouse anger in the parents and become the focus of serious conflict. Usually the disapproval of the mother suffices to discourage the child's violation of toilet-training requirements, but sometimes parents overemphasize disapproval and produce a strict, harsh conscience in the child as a consequence.[36] If discipline is harsh, aggressive impulses are pushed into the unconscious, and the child may develop obsessive-compulsive tendencies oriented toward routine, ritual, and order. These are the same characteristics of excessive toilet-training. The onset and nature of bowel training is related to the social class of the family. For instance, middle-class mothers begin bowel training earlier than do lower- and working-class mothers who often employ more severe forms of training.[37]

It is paradoxical that the child develops a sense of self-assertion at

[34]These children are known as *anal smearers*.

[35]There is some evidence that adults who seek to prolong sexual foreplay and to postpone final orgasm are latent anal-erotics. See Otto Fenichel, *The Psychoanalytic Theory of Neurosis*, p. 66.

[36]Alfred M. Freedman and others, *Modern Synopsis of Comprehensive Textbook of Psychiatry* (Baltimore: Williams and Wilkins Co., 1972), p. 332.

[37]See Robert J. Havighurst and Allison Davis, "A comparison of the Chicago and Harvard studies of social class differences in child rearing," in *Class and Personality in Society*, ed. Alan L. Grey (New York: Atherton Press, 1969), p. 52; Martha Sturm White, "Social class, child rearing practices and child behavior," Ibid., p. 62.

the anal stage since this is the same period during which the ego develops mechanisms of self-control by postponing or permanently detering the gratification of id impulses. Toilet training accelerates the growth of the emerging ego. The ego's attempts at self-control result from a dramatic conflict between instinctual drives and the requirements of society. This is the child's first intense experience with socialization since it is his first encounter with a set of socially prescribed norms of proper behavior. In this instance, the norms take the form of demands for anal sphincter control. It is at the anal stage that a rudimentary superego appears. This serves as a foundation for the establishment of the complete superego which is developed later.

The Phallic Stage.   It is only after the oral and anal stages have been surmounted that the genital organs become the major source of libidinal satisfaction.[38] This occurs around the third or fourth year of life and lasts into the fifth or sixth. The stage is called *phallic* not only because the penis and clitoris develop as the predominant sexual zones, but also to differentiate it from mature genitality connected with mating and reproduction. There are obvious signs of increased sexual interest in the genital zone during this period. One of these is a rise in masturbatory activity among both sexes. Other signs include a heightened need for body contact with the opposite sex and exhibitionistic tendencies. For the first time, the child selects a defined sexual object, the opposite-sex parent. Although the phallic stage is fundamentally similar for boys and girls, some differences have been noted.

Psychoanalysts hold that the boy falls deeply in love with his mother and develops an intense jealousy towards his father for the special privileges he monopolizes with the mother. In short, the boy loves his mother and hates his father. The boy often openly expresses his incestuous attraction for the mother by stating that he intends to marry her when he grows up and by using every opportunity to creep into her bed when the father is not home. This is called the *Oedipus complex* after the tragic Greek hero who killed his father, married his mother, and had children with her.[39] It is a useful analogy particularly because Oedipus killed his father unwillingly. This is similar to the small boy who uncon-

---

[38]There is some mention of a period between the anal and phallic stages during which the child experiences pleasure in urination. It is referred to as *urethral eroticism* and is so closely interwoven with genital eroticism that it is rarely treated separately. It is considered to be etiologically related to enuresis. See Otto Fenichel, *The Psychoanalytic Theory of Neurosis*, p. 68.

[39]According to an ancient legend of Sophocles, an infant prince was left to die because of a prophecy that he was destined to murder his father. The prince, Oedipus, was rescued by strangers and brought up in an alien court. In his search for his real home, he got involved in a quarrel with the King of Thebes and killed him. The king was actually his father, but Oedipus did not know it. After he solved the riddle of the Sphinx and saved the Thebians from her attacks, Oedipus was declared king and given the slain king's widow as a wife. When it was eventually discovered that king and queen were actually son and mother, the queen committed suicide and Oedipus blinded himself.

sciously wishes his father dead, although he does not have a developed view of reality which would make him responsible for his wishes.

The Oedipal situation is complicated by an unconscious fear that the father will discover the boy's ambitions toward the mother and punish him with castration. This fear of losing the penis, known as *castration anxiety,* is believed to be compounded if the boy discovers that girls have no penis. Because girls are viewed as having been castrated, the magnitude of the castration threat is heightened by demonstrating that the penis can be cut off.[40] During Freud's time, castration fear was often overt since many adults would actually threaten to cut off the penis of a boy who was caught masturbating.[41] However, such severe threats are less common today although it is not unusual for parents to impose other types of threats regarding masturbation. Psychoanalysts believe these can cause emotional problems such as nightmares.[42] Such problems may not be caused by masturbation per se as earlier psychoanalysts thought.[43] Instead, they may be caused by guilt about masturbating or the fear of being discovered by punitive parents.

The phallic experiences of girls are generally equivalent to those for boys except girls undergo a more complex transition since their primary attachment to the mother is shifted to a heterosexual attachment to the father. Boys, on the other hand, do not shift from a homosexual to a heterosexual attachment. The female Oedipus complex is often referred to as the *Electra complex* after the Greek mythical figure who conspired to murder her faithless mother. Girls are not considered to suffer the threat of castration that boys undergo, however. Instead, they supposedly fantasize that they have a penis or that it has been cut off and will grow back later. This is known as *penis envy* and is considered to originate from the feeling that the girl's clitoris is inferior to the penis since the penis yields obvious advantages in both masturbatory and urinary respects. The girl feels hostility toward the mother because she is blamed for denying the girl a penis. Thus, female castration anxiety is a reaction to penis deprivation. In a sense, girls feel that they have already been castrated.

Needless to say, the notion of penis envy has not been well received by the women's liberation movement. However, the psychoanalytic view of differences between the sexes is not as condescending to women as some of the jargon may suggest. In fact, the psychoanalytic literature holds that girls undergo a *more complicated* development since they are

---

[40]The fear of castration partly emanates from the level of moral reasoning of children of this age. It functions according to the "talion principle" which is the belief in "An eye for an eye; a tooth for a tooth".

[41]Otto Fenichel, *The Psychoanalytic Theory of Neurosis,* pp. 77–78.

[42]Sidney Levin, "The relation of various affects to masturbation conflicts," in *Masturbation: From Infancy To Senescence,* eds. Irwin M. Marcus and John J. Francis (New York: International Universities Press, Inc., 1975), pp. 305–314.

[43]See Sigmund Freud, "Contributions to a discussion of masturbation," in *Standard Edition* (London: Hogarth Press, 1958), pp. 239–254.

required to give up their primary attachment to the mother and transfer it to the opposite sex.[44] This is a switch from a homosexual attachment to a heterosexual one. The boy, on the other hand, is already oriented toward heterosexual activity because his first human relationship was with the mother, a female. For this reason, the Electra complex may remain operative longer in girls than the Oedipus complex does in boys.[45] It is also important to note that the Oedipus complex is not biological destiny but culturally acquired. It is the *beliefs* about the immorality of one's incestuous feelings that are important, rather than the longing after the opposite-sex parent per se. If a particular culture does not consider incestuous feelings wicked, there is little chance that children will feel disturbed by them. In short, it is the perceived reactions of others which serve as the driving force for phallic fears. These fears are considered to be overcome as the child recognizes the futility of his incestuous wishes and finally identifies with the same-sex parent. Then the Oedipus complex is resolved and the child aspires to the role of the same-sex parent. This includes a capacity to love all opposite-sex people, not just the opposite-sex parent. When the Oedipus complex is resolved, the child internalizes the moral values of the same-sex parent, and the superego is then fully formed. Only with the resolution of the complex is the superego formed. for this reason, a number of neurotic disorders which are essentially superego defects are believed to be caused by fixation at the phallic stage.

According to psychoanalytic theory, the Oedipus/Electra complex is the most significant struggle of the child's psychic development. If it is not resolved it can form the nucleus for neurotic disturbances later. In fact, it plays such an important part in the development of neurosis that some psychoanalysts believe that it is somehow involved in every case of neurosis.[46] The role of the phallic period will become evident as the etiology of the different neurotic reactions are reviewed in chapter four.

The Latency Period.   Around the sixth year of life, psychosexual development is interrupted during the period known as *latency*. At this time, libidinal energy is "desexualized," that is, it is directed to nonsexual aims. This process is known as sublimation. Only human beings experience *biphasic sexuality* in which there is a temporary biological reduction of sexual urges. This period lasts until puberty when sexual urges again become powerful.

Actually, the latency period is interrupted periodically by sexual feelings which are usually homosexual. At this time, boys typically associate only with other boys and girls with other girls. Children strongly disidentify with members of the opposite sex and punish those who fail to avoid contact with the opposite sex as evidenced by such names as

---

[44]Otto Fenichel, *The Psychoanalytic Theory of Neurosis*, p. 89.
[45]Ruth L. Munroe, *Schools of Psychoanalytic Thought* (New York: Holt, Rinehart and Winston, 1955), p. 218.
[46]Herbert Nunberg, *Principles of Psychoanalysis*, p. 73.

"sissy" and "tomboy." It is not uncommon for children of this age to engage in limited forms of sexual activity. The most common act is mutual masturbation with a same-sex peer.

Instinctual energies are devoted to building up the ego. The child relates more to objects in the external world, particularly people outside the family. The superego is developed further by the incorporation of more sophisticated ethical standards. This *postoedipal superego* is generally what is meant by the conscience which is nurtured as the child develops social skills through interaction with peers. Social attitudes reflecting this stage include a sense of competition, fair play, altruism, and loyalty, all of which are necessary if the child is to become an integrated member of society. The child begins to behave according to the dictates of an inner mechanism, the superego, rather than out of fear of punishment from an external force such as the parents. This distinction has received independent verification by the well-known Swiss psychologist, Jean Piaget.[47] He ascertained that children younger than six are oriented toward a *morality of constraint* which simply means that they conform to "rules of the game"[48] only because they fear punishment from others. They also evaluate the actions of others by their consequences rather than by their intentions.[49] Children older than six abide by social rules out of guilt. They fear punishment from an inner mechanism, the superego, and evaluate acts by intentions, not consequences. Piaget called this stage of moral development the *morality of cooperation.*

The child who becomes predisposed to neurosis from experiences at this stage is usually the overindulged child who expects to have everything his own way. He will be frustrated when he enters the wider community of his peers and discovers that his expectations are unrealistic. The child of a domineering mother is also considered to be a likely candidate for neurosis since he is typically dependent, submissive, lacking initiative, and threatened by competitive activities. The general psychopathological risk of the latency period is the development of a sense of inferiority.[50]

Puberty and Adolescence. The latency period allows for the consolidation of the events and conflicts of the first three stages of psychosexual development. In an important way, it is the time to prepare for puberty, the last stage of development which is sometimes referred to as the *genital* stage.[51] Puberty and adolescence are initiated by

---

[47]Jean Piaget, *The Moral Judgment of the Child* (New York: The Free Press, 1965).

[48]In Piaget's research, he observed children of different ages interacting games of marbles and the like.

[49]The younger children would consider a child who, in attempting to help his mother set the table, broke six cups to have done a worse thing than another child who broke one cup while stealing cookies from a jar.

[50]Erik H. Erikson, *Childhood and Society* (New York: W. W. Norton, 1950).

[51]Some psychoanalysts think that personality development does not culminate with

the biological process of sexual maturation. At this time, the repressed sexual impulses of the latency period return. The first signs occur in prepuberty which begins around the tenth or eleventh year. Puberty itself begins around the fourteenth year and is accompanied by the appearance of secondary sexual characteristics such as orgastic potency and the onset of menstruation in females. The period ends when the adolescent becomes an "adult." This varies cross-culturally. In the United States, for instance, adolescence culminates around the age of twenty-one because of the extension of the educational process. In other countries, it occurs at an earlier age.

Adolescence is a period of storm and stress, particularly in Western cultures where there is an extension of the educational process and a heavy emphasis on occupational attainment. The adolescent finds himself in a crisis situation in which there are "sexual frustrations arising out of physical maturation and social restrictions; problems of occupational choice, difficulties in emancipation from small family groups, inconsistencies in authority relationships . . . and discontinuities in socialization patterns."[52] Tremendous battles are waged between id and superego. The id has accumulated an abundance of libidinal energy which seeks discharge. At the same time, society imposes taboos against adolescent sexuality, an important reason for the frequency of masturbation during this period.

The situation of the adolescent is complicated further by marginality; the adolescent is no longer considered a child, yet he is not accorded the privileges of an adult. Eisenstadt's labeling of the adolescent plight as a period of *role moratorium* seems strikingly fitting.[53] The frustrations of this stage often take the form of rebellion from parents and the acquisition of attitudes which counter the "adult" ideology.[54]

Gradually, the adolescent adapts to his newly formed genital sexuality and begins to establish relationships with opposite-sex peers. That is, if everything goes as society planned. If the individual at puberty does not succeed in outgrowing earlier inclinations, such as Oedipal desires, a number of sexual disturbances may arise in addition to neurotic tendencies.[55]

Criticisms of Psychoanalytic Theory. The psychoanalytic theory of neurosis (and of overall personality formation) has been criticized on a

---

young adulthood but instead is a continuous process throughout life. For a presentation of the "adulthood theory" see Erik H. Erikson, *Identity and the Life Cycle: Psychological Issues* (New York: International Universities Press, 1959).

[52]Frederick Elkin and William A. Westley, "The myth of adolescent culture," *American Sociological Review*, 20 (1955), p. 680.

[53]Samuel N. Eisenstadt, "Archetypal patterns of youth," in *The Challenge of Youth*, ed. Erik H. Erikson (New York: Doubleday, 1965), p. 32.

[54]For an elaborate description of intergenerational conflict in attitudes see: Bernard J. Gallagher III, "An empirical analysis of attitude differences between three kin-related generations," *Youth and Society* 5 (1974), pp. 327–349.

[55]Herbert Nunberg, *Principles of Psychoanalysis*, p. 78.

number of points. One problem with the theory is that it is too deterministic; it assumes that one's entire personality is chained to the past. Childhood experiences may play an important role in personality formation, but if they determine everything, there is no room left for individual growth and change. This is a very pessimistic picture that has yet to be demonstrated.

The theory has also been criticized for placing too much emphasis on the parent-child relationship. One gets the impression that full responsibility for the child's make-up falls on the parents as if other forces in the social environment play no active role. This criticism seems particularly relevant in contemporary American society where the cohesiveness of the nuclear family has been weakened by the forces of industrialization. Now the mass media and educational institutions play an important role in socialization as well as the parents.

Another criticism of psychoanalytic theory is that it ignores other personality determinants such as biogenic forces. For example, how much value can a "stage sequence" theory have if an individual was genetically programmed to be mentally ill? The theory also overlooks the effect of traumatic experiences that occur during adulthood as if the personality is hardened like concrete by that time and therefore not subject to change.

From a sociological perspective, the psychoanalytic theory of personality development and psychopathology has often been criticized for assuming that the psychosexual stages occur in an invariant order. More specifically, the theory is criticized for being oriented toward Western culture and not accounting for child-rearing practices of other societies, particularly primitive ones. Certainly the oral period is quite different when children are allowed to suckle at the breast until five or six years of age. It is also obvious that the anal phase of development takes on a different character in a society which does not stress toilet-training or perhaps does not even have toilets. And what happens to the latency phase if a child is raised in an environment in which adults encourage sexual relations between boys and girls as young as seven years old? Such societies do not fit the psychoanalytic formulae very well. This may be because the theory is limited to a particular social stratum in a specific cultural context. Much of the theory stems from the original work of Freud, and his findings were largely based on observations of middle class Europeans. Thus it is questionable whether the psychic life of these people is altogether relevant to non-Western people, particularly in regard to sexuality, an elementary factor in psychoanalytic theory.

The cross-cultural criticism of psychoanalytic theory is important but it may be overstated. For instance, some cross-cultural studies found that there exist universal regulations of eliminative and sexual functions which begin at an early age.[56] At the present time, it is difficult to mea-

---

[56]Herbert Barry III, "Cultural variations in the development of mental illness," in *Changing Perspectives in Mental Illness*, eds. Robert B. Edgerton and Stanley C. Plog (New York: Holt, Rinehart and Winston, 1969), pp. 155–179.

sure accurately the number of societies which seriously deviate from the psychoanalytic model. Some cross-cultural studies support the proposition that pathological fixation is the result of excessive deprivation at a particular stage of development.[57] However, these same studies did not find any evidence that excessive gratification has a pathological effect cross-culturally.

The cross-cultural criticism of psychoanalytic theory has limited relevance to mental illness in the United States since it is a Western society. As such, it is more important to know whether the major propositions of the theory make etiological sense. Generally speaking, there is evidence that neurosis can stem from early childhood experiences. The fact that anxiety and insecurity are noticeably greater among children raised in institutions and deprived of normal parenting demonstrates this.[58] Even those who had parents but who underwent a series of humiliating childhood experiences, such as a preference of the parents for other children, often develop deep-seated personality disturbances which are neurotic in character. Some of these disturbances manifest themselves in socially acceptable ways such as a drive for upward mobility even though the drive may be a neurotic quest for power by a vindictive person who seeks to humiliate others.[59]

Perhaps the biggest "problem" with psychoanalytic theory is that it is not very popular among social scientists because it presents mental illness as an intrapsychic phenomenon. It may be true that the theory is not consistent with a purely environmental perspective, but that does not make it invalid, only unpopular. It seems rather obvious that any discussion of the etiology of mental illness, particularly neurosis, would be incomplete without the intrapsychic perspective that psychoanalytic theory offers. For this reason, it is included (and criticized) in the relevant parts of this book.

Conclusions

There are three major etiological views of neurosis: labeling theory, behaviorism, and psychoanalysis. Labeling theorists and behaviorists are somewhat aligned in their outlooks since both hold that social factors cause neurosis. The labeling theory position on neurosis is

[57]M. G. Allen, "Childhood experience and adult personality—a cross-cultural study using the concept of ego strength," *Journal of Social Psychology,* 71 (1967), pp. 53–68; J. W. M. Whiting and I. L. Child, *Child Training and Personality: A Cross-Cultural Study* (New Haven: Yale University Press, 1953).

[58]William Goldfarb, "The effects of early institutional care on adolescent personality" in *Socialization,* eds. Sandra Scarr-Salapatek and Philip Salapatek (Columbus, Ohio: Charles E. Merrill, 1973), pp. 66–101.

[59]Evelyn Ellis, "Social psychological correlates of upward social mobility among unmarried career women," in *The Mental Patient: Studies in the Sociology of Deviance,* eds. Stephen P. Spitzer and Norman K. Denzin (New York: McGraw-Hill, 1968), pp. 147–154.

that it stems from internalizing the negative reactions of other people. The behaviorists hold that the disorder results from learning. This can occur through three processes: classical conditioning, operant conditioning, and modeling.

Psychoanalysts recognize that social forces play a role in the origin of neurosis, but they believe that the instincts and the unconscious are also involved. The central proposition of the psychoanalytic theory of neurosis is that the disorder originates from conflicts that arose during a particular stage of psychosexual development.

4

The Neurotic Reactions

Although anxiety is the central symptom of neurosis, it is not always experienced in the same way. Sometimes it is felt and expressed directly as in the case of *anxiety neurosis*. It may also be controlled by a defense mechanism which makes the anxiety more manageable. The type of defense mechanism governs the form of the neurosis. The various forms are called the neurotic reactions. The symptoms and causal theories of the neurotic reactions are presented in this chapter. Because the psychoanalytic explanation involves more detail than other perspectives, there is more space devoted to it here. This should not be taken to mean that the psychoanalytic view is more valid than other views but simply that it involves more specifications.

Anxiety Neurosis

Symptoms

Anxiety neurosis is characterized by anxious over-concern extending to panic. This may occur under any circumstances and is not restricted to specific situations or objects. In this neurosis, anxiety completely dominates the clinical picture. The anxiety is accompanied by a variety of somatic difficulties such as fatigue, insomnia, tremor, diarrhea, headache, dizziness, choking sensations, nausea, appetite disturbances, heart beat irregularities, sexual difficulties, back pain, and a desire to urinate. As anxiety increases, somatic discharge accelerates. Where one symptom occurs alone, the condition is designated *abortive anxiety*. Patients also display emotional disturbances such as irritability, expectant anxiety, a sense of weakness, a fear of impending death, and an inability to relax. Between periodic attacks, the individual may be comfortable but more often there is some degree of tension. Sometimes an anxiety attack is a precursor of a schizophrenic reaction.

The symptoms represent the patient's attempts to rid himself of anxiety by directly discharging it on to the body. In this sense, the reaction is adaptive because it acts as a safety valve, but it is a very costly form of adaptation. To suffer from an anxiety neurosis is to be constantly on guard against an unknown danger. Since patients do not recognize the linkages between their psychological distress and their bodily symptoms, they begin to doubt the soundness of their body. They often attribute their symptoms to a true organic illness and are, for example, very susceptible to suggestions of hidden illness made during public health campaigns.[1]

Anxiety is a basic component of all the neuroses. However, in this form, no defense mechanisms are employed to ward it off. Rather, the anxiety is experienced in a "free-floating" form as illustrated in the case below:

> Walter A., an American oil geologist, aged thirty-two, who had been living abroad for many years, came for diagnosis because of symptoms which he feared might mean that he was going insane. For five or six years he had been having attacks of dizziness, blurred vision, weakness, and unsteady gait. For three years he had been suffering from constant "nervous tension," irritability, fatigue, increased sex pace with incomplete satisfaction, inability to relax, poor sleep, and frequent nightmares. For a year his restlessness had grown so marked that he could scarcely stand still, sit or lie still. . . .
>
> Soon he began having frequent anxiety attacks. The first came on suddenly while he was dressing to go out for the evening. Something seemed to snap in his head, everything looked unnatural, and he felt he was fainting. He lay down for a long time, his heart pounding, his breathing labored, and with the recurring thought, "I'm dying, I'm dying." Other attacks came later. They consisted of "queer head sensations," weakness, sweating, coarse tremor, palpitation and a conviction that something terrible was happening to him.[2]

Biogenic Theories

Several biogenic theories of anxiety neurosis have been advanced, including a genetic explanation. At least one empirical study has shown that the intrafamilial pattern of anxiety neurosis is consistent with a theory of genetic transmission. Slater and Shields compared seventeen pairs of monozygotic twins in which one twin had been diagnosed as having anxiety neurosis with twenty-eight pairs of dizygotic twins in

[1] Norman Cameron, *Personality Development and Psychopathology: A Developmental Approach* (Boston: Houghton Mifflin, 1963), p. 252.

[2] From *Personality Development and Psychopathology* by Norman Cameron. Copyright © 1963 by Norman Cameron. Reprinted by permission of Houghton Mifflin Company, p. 253.

which a co-twin was so diagnosed.[3] Concordance for the neurosis occured in forty-nine percent of the monozygotic twin sets and in only four
percent of the dizygotic twin sets. However, the study did not control for
the effect of being raised by the same parents.

There is a biochemical theory of anxiety neurosis which hypothe-
sizes that this type of neurotic lives in a body which overproduces
epinephrine.[4] This chemical is known to cause an overactivity of the
central nervous system which in turn may cause the variety of somatic
symptoms described earlier.

The Behaviorist View

The environmental theories of this neurosis center around a contention between the behaviorist and psychoanalytic theories. The behaviorist theory holds that anxiety is developed through imitation; that
is, anxious parents raise anxious children. Thus the parents provide
concrete role models of anxiety, and the child reflects the parents' insecurity by internalizing their anxious behavior. Cameron, for instance,
reports the case of a woman who reacted to life situations in exactly the
same anxious ways her mother did.[5]

The behaviorist, Wolpe, holds that the cause of anxiety neurosis is
related to the external environment.[6] According to Wolpe, anxiety is a
conditioned response to external stimuli. Thus, the person who is fearful
of work and reacts with vomiting as he is being transported to work does
so because the anxiety attack is a conditioned response to the experience
of being transported to a threatening environment.

The Psychoanalytic View

Psychoanalysts consider the origin of anxiety neurosis to be a disturbance in the parent-child relationship. This disturbance is most pronounced when the parent produces a child who has an excessive and
distorted superego. This child later becomes frightened of his own sexual or aggressive impulses due to a pathological fear of punishment. The
stage is set for an anxiety attack when a situation arises in which anger or
sexual demands become threateningly intense. Some psychoanalysts believe that anxiety neurosis can be the psychological result of masturbation which generates excessive guilt.[7] Another psychoanalytic opinion

---

[3]E. Slater and J. Shields, "Genetic aspects of anxiety," in *Studies of Anxiety*, ed. M. H.
Lader (Ashford, England: Headley Brothers, 1969).

[4]Alfred M. Freedman and others, *Modern Synopsis of Comprehensive Textbook of
Psychiatry* (Baltimore: Williams and Wilkins Co., 1975), p. 333.

[5]Norman Cameron, *Personality Development and Psychotherapy*, p. 268.

[6]Joseph Wolpe, *Psychotherapy By Reciprocal Inhibition* (Stanford, California: Stanford
University Press, 1958).

[7]William Thomas Moore, "Some economic functions of genital masturbation during
adolescent development," in *Masturbation: From Infancy to Senescence*, eds. Irwin M. Marcus
and John J. Francis (New York: International Universities Press, Inc., 1975), pp. 231–276.

holds that sexual deprivation can cause anxiety neurosis since coitus interruptus, frustrated excitation, long abstinence, and the like are considered capable of producing anxiety. In each of these abnormal courses of sexual activity there is no discharge in orgasm and therefore no psychological gratification. This creates a sense of psychic helplessness which then engenders an anxiety attack.

Hysterical Neurosis, Conversion Type

Symptoms

There is some similarity between anxiety neurosis and hysterical neurosis, conversion type, also known as *conversion hysteria.* Both neurotic patterns involve a displacement of anxiety onto the body, but the conversion reaction is more striking because the special senses or parts of the voluntary nervous system lose their functions for extended periods of time. Conversion hysteria is a blatant example of the way in which social factors can affect the prevalence of mental illness. Witness the significant decline in the number of such cases over the last century. There are a few macrosocial reasons for this historical change. First of all, since psychiatrists (particularly psychoanalysts) have traditionally regarded the underlying conflict in this neurosis as sexual, it is not surprising that its frequency has declined, since modern society presents fewer demands to repress sexual impulses. Secondly, since the civilized population is more sophisticated concerning medical matters, it has become more difficult for people to convince themselves that their disabilities are organically caused. Of course, it is possible that the prevalence of conversion hysteria has not actually declined but become more difficult to detect since there may have been a shift from the predominance of one type of conversion symptom to another. Today's medically sophisticated patients may be expert simulators of pain and bodily disease whereas the "classical" symptoms of conversion hysteria are generally found only among uneducated people from rural areas.[8]

In this psychopathology, the anxiety is expressed in the form of a physical symptom involving a body part stimulated by sensory or motor nerves. The primary gain is a reduction or elimination of free-floating anxiety, but the costs are considerable. The physical symptoms often do not conform to actual neurological or anatomical conditions and frequently disappear when the individual is asleep or away from his usual environment. Certain psychological symptoms are also common in cases of conversion hysteria. These patients display a curious lack of concern about the conversion symptom and the disability produced by it. This phenomenon, known as *la belle indifference,* was first noted among para-

[8]J. J. Ziegler, J. B. Imboden, and E. Meyer, "Contemporary conversion reactions: a clinical study," *American Journal of Psychiatry,* 116 (1960), pp. 901–909.

troopers in World War II but not among those members of the air force whose code did not forbid expressing fear.[9] Some neurotic patients of this type seem to enjoy their disability. While this decreases their motivation to get well, it reflects the *secondary gains* which are found most prominently in this type of neurotic reaction. The most common of these gains are attention from others and freedom from responsibilities which the disability allows.

Biogenic Theories

At one time the only conceivable explanation of conversion hysteria was biogenic. Since the symptoms meant the loss of a body function, the disorder was believed to be the result of some lesion of the nervous system. Today, very few researchers believe this, particularly because the symptoms often do not correspond to known patterns of nerve distribution. However, there are plausible organic explanations for *some* cases involving conversion symptoms. One study which followed up persons diagnosed as suffering from conversion hysteria nine years previously discovered that a majority had developed physical diseases or had died! Undeniably, some people diagnosed as having this type of neurosis may actually be suffering from an organic disorder. It is unlikely, however, that cases of conversion hysteria originate from genetic factors since studies which have investigated concordance rates among monozygotics have found no significant genetic patterns.[10]

The Behaviorist View

The behaviorist Wolpe contends that the conversion symptom originates from features which were present in a previous disturbing experience. He reports the case of a female who displayed the hysterical symptom of "gooseflesh" in her calves in response to any rectal sensation including defecation. Years before, she had had a rectal examination while awaiting the administration of anesthesia for abdominal surgery. Thus, Wolpe considers the sensation in her calves to be a conditioned response to anal manipulation which originally developed under stressful conditions.[11]

One prominent clinical feature of this type of neurotic is a high degree of *narcissism* (self-loving). This predisposes the person to engage in dramatic and often childish self-displays. It should be noted that this may be the simple result of social imitation as some behaviorists contend. In a sense, these neurotics were prepared for conversion reactions in childhood by a narcissistic, attention-seeking mother who provided the

[9]R. R. Grinker and J. Spiegel, *Men Under Stress* (Philadelphia: Blakiston, 1945).

[10]I. Gottesman, "Differential inheritance of the psychoneuroses," *Eugenics Quarterly,* 9, (1962), pp. 223–227; E. Slatu, "The thirty-fifth Maudsley lecture: hysteria 311," *Journal of Mental Science,* 107 (1961), pp. 358–381.

[11]Joseph Wolpe, *Psychotherapy by Reciprocal Inhibition,* p. 85.

child with a model of a person dramatically preoccupied with her body.[12]

Other behaviorists give a different account of conversion symptoms. They believe that a conversion reaction is the enactment of a role which provides rewards either by reducing stress or by providing positive gains.[13] Thus, conversion symptoms provide an avenue of escape from an intolerable situation; one person develops writer's cramp while another suffers paralysis of a leg. The writer actually does not want to write and the person with the paralyzed leg can now avoid meeting a threat.

The Psychoanalytic View

One of the earliest environmental theories of conversion hysteria was voiced by Bernheim. He believed that suggestibility and hypnotizability, while normal personality attributes, are excessive in certain persons who unconsciously and automatically lose bodily functions.[14] Actually, Bernheim was not far from the psychoanalytic theories of Freud and his later followers who argued that a conflict involving sexual impulses is at the root of conversion symptoms. Specifically, if the person cannot comfortably accept genital strivings of the id, he removes these desires from his conscious awareness. They are then retained in the unconscious, but their energy is displaced on to a nonsexual part of the body. In the process, that body part becomes eroticized (in a loose sense of the word) and plays the role of a substitute genital. This process is more likely to occur in response to a sudden, identifiable stress. Freud believed that this stress involved some aspect of an unresolved Oedipus complex.

Contemporary psychoanalysts do not believe that only a sexual conflict can produce conversion symptoms. Rather, they suggest that all types of instinctual conflicts may play a role in engendering such reactions. Current psychoanalytic theories distinguish between male and female patients since a sexual conflict is believed to be more common in cases of conversion hysteria in women than in men. There is some experimental evidence to support this idea. Jordan and Kempler, for example, found that female hysterics become particularly distressed when they are approached sexually.[15] They become highly agitated by questions about their femininity. Consistent with this, Marmour argues that the "hysteric is distressed when sexuality brings advances, as she is really asking to be loved as a child and not as a woman."[16] Male hysterics,

[12]Norman Cameron, *Personality Development and Psychopathology*, p. 335.

[13]L. P. Ullmann and L. Krasner, *A Psychological Approach to Abnormal Behavior* (Englewood Cliffs, N.J.: Prentice-Hall, 1969).

[14]H. Bernheim, *Suggestive Therapeutics* (New York: G. P. Putnam's Sons, 1897).

[15]Brian T. Jordan and Bernhard Kempler, "Hysterical personality: an experimental investigation of sex-role conflict," *Journal of Abnormal Psychology*, 75 (1970), pp. 172–176.

[16]J. Marmour, "Orality in the hysterical personality," *Journal of the American Psychoanalytic Association*, 1 (1954), pp. 656–671.

on the other hand, are believed to develop conversion symptoms as a way of escaping a social challenge or some blow to their self-esteem.[17]

The psychoanalytic view also suggests why certain body parts are selected for the conversion. The chosen body part is that which is most suitable to represent the focal conflicts involved. This process is a type of body language known as *somatic compliance.* Sometimes the choice may be of a chronically weak organ such as a lame leg which suddenly goes completely numb. However, it is believed that often the conversion symptom is *symbolically* important because it allows the person to avoid something uncomfortable. Mutism in a salesman and sexual impotence in a Don Juan exemplify a desire to be something else. In addition, a paralyzed hand prevents the person from carrying out a masturbatory drive.

Not all psychoanalysts accept Freud's belief that conversion hysteria originates from phallic fixation involving an unresolved Oedipus complex. Many feel that conversion symptoms involve fixation at multiple stages of development but few would place fixation at a prephallic stage. There is little emphasis on prephallic stages because conversion symptoms involve very specific selections of body parts and the selective process is not developed in the younger child who lacks a well-differentiated view of the world. Thus the fixation is generally considered to be at a later, more sophisticated level.[18]

Hysterical Contagion

A noteworthy characteristic of this neurosis is its tendency to spread like a contagion among a group of people who have some common linkage. One group of researchers reports the spread of severe physical symptoms resulting from a supposed insect bite among sixty-two workers in a southern clothing manufacturing plant. Most of the workers either fainted or complained of severe pain, nausea, or feelings of disorientation, although none of them had actually been bitten by the insect![19] The contagious idea entered the social network of workers and was disseminated in the form of a chain reaction among those who had interpersonal ties. At the present time, there is some controversy about hysterical contagion since some researchers believe it is a reaction to increased levels of group stress, and others consider it to be a type of craze.[20]

[17]L. C. Kolb, *Noyes' Modern Clinical Psychiatry* (Philadelphia: W. B. Saunders, 1973), p. 414.

[18]For an elaboration of this argument see Ruth L. Munroe, *Schools of Psychoanalytic Thought* (New York: Holt, Rinehart and Winston, 1955), p. 284.

[19]Alan C. Kerckhoff, Kurt W. Back, and Norman Miller, "Sociometric patterns in hysterical contagion," in *Social Psychology and Everyday Life,* eds. Billy J. Franklin and Frank J. Kohout (New York: McKay, 1973), pp. 495–507.

[20]For a comprehensive review of this issue see Frieda L. Gehlen, "Toward a revised theory of hysterical contagion," *Journal of Health and Social Behavior,* 18 (1977), pp. 27–35.

Hysterical Neurosis, Dissociative Type

Symptoms

At times, anxiety may become so overwhelming that the personality is disorganized, and parts of it split off from the mainstream of consciousness. Dissociative reactions are responses to anxiety which involve massive forgetting. In dissociative hysteria, the patient copes with the anxiety by eliminating some personality functions rather than by eliminating body functions. Some believe that this psychopathology should be placed with the psychoses since it often involves gross personality disorganizations which appear psychotic. Presently these reactions are not grouped with the psychoses by convention and because the APA holds that the conflict underlying dissociative reactions is neurotic in character. That is, these patients maintain *some* personality functions whereas the true psychotic functions only through delusions and hallucinations. DSM-III deals with the controversy over classifying dissociative disorders by placing them in a category separate and distinct from the neuroses and the psychoses.

The best known of the dissociative reactions is the *dissociative personality*. It is the most dramatic of all of the dissociative disorders, has often been the star of stage and screen, and yet it is exceedingly rare.[21] In fact, it is so uncommon that only seventy-six cases had been reported up to 1944[22] and only two hundred cases up to 1966.[23] In 1978 it was estimated that there were approximately one hundred cases under treatment in the United States.[24] It is often confused by the public with schizophrenia (because of the split involved), yet it is quite different from schizophrenia. Two main varieties can be distinguished. One is the *alternating personality*. This type involves two personalities which are completely separated from one another. One system dominates the personality while the other remains inactive. Each may dominate as frequently as every day or as infrequently as once every few years. What is interesting about the alternating type of dissociative personality is that the two personalities may strongly contrast with each other as in the classic case of Doctor Jekyll and Mr. Hyde.

In the more common type of dissociative personality, the *multiple personality*, there are no real alternations. Instead, a relatively mature

---

[21]Cornelia Wilbur, "Clinical considerations in the evaluation and treatment of multiple personality" (lecture delivered at Multiple Personality Conference, Friends Hospital, Philadelphia, 1978).

[22]W. S. Taylor and M. F. martin, "Multiple personality," *Journal of Abnormal and Social Psychology*, 44 (1944), pp. 281–300.

[23]D. W. Abse, *Hysteria and Related Mental Disorders* (Baltimore: Williams and Wilkins, 1966).

[24]Patients with dissociative personalities are reportedly very bright and creative people. If they score low in I.Q. tests, it is usually because a less intelligent alternate was dominant at the time of testing; Cornelia Wilbur, "Clinical considerations in the evaluation and treatment of multiple personality."

personality dominates while one or several other personalities take over. The dominant personality is not aware of the subordinate ones. Some classic examples are Morton Prince's case of Sally Beauchamps[25] and the Southerner whose personality became dissociated into the well-known *Three Faces of Eve.*[26] More recently, there is a report from Belgium of a nun who may be afflicted with multiple personality as she regularly engaged in drug abuse, varied sexual activities, and murder.[27] And in Ohio, a man who raped a number of university coeds is reported to have ten different personalities including a sadistic lesbian personality who committed the rapes!

It is important to note how distinct the personalities are from each other. Not only do they vary from each other psychologically but there are also different physical traits exhibited by each. These include different measures of galvanic skin response, heart rate variations, brain wave alterations, as well as different body postures and even eye color![28] Needless to say, these important differences in the multiple personalities can cause enormous legal problems of responsibility if one of the personalities commits a crime.

There is a report of a multiple personality involving sixteen separate identities. This is the well-publicized case of Sybil, one of the most bizarre cases of mental illness of all times.[29] Sybil had three main personalities: Sybil herself, a timid, saintly woman who was unable to express anger; Peggy, an aggressive and uninhibited girl; and Victoria, a sophisticated woman of culture. Each of the three personalities, as well as the other thirteen that Sybil exhibited in the course of treatment, differed in speech and body movements. Each was perceived as having distinct physical characteristics as well. The list of characters even included two male identities, Mike and Sid. Each of the personalities exhibited particular talents, denied the others: Sybil was the artist, Peggy was the mathematician, Victoria was the master of cultural refinement, and so on. During the period when one particular personality was in charge, Sybil had no awareness of the others' activities. She would return to a painting she had started and find that someone else had completed it in a different style. She ran into persons who insisted they knew her although she felt certain that she had never seen them before.

The Biogenic View

The origin of dissociative reactions is a real mystery. Very little research has been done on possible biogenic causes. One loosely con-

---

[25]Morton Prince, *Dissociation of a Personality* (New York: Longmans, Green, 1908).

[26]C. H. Thigpin, H. Thigpin, and H. M. Cleckley, *The Three Faces of Eve* (New York: McGraw-Hill, 1957).

[27]"The nun's story," *Time Magazine* (March 13, 1978), p. 51.

[28]Cornelia Wilbur, "Clinical considerations in the evaluation and treatment of multiple personality."

[29]For a complete account of this case see F. R. Schreiver, *Sybil,* (Chicago: Regnery, 1973).

structed biogenic proposition suggests that these disorders may be a pathological exercise of the normal functions of the central nervous system. The distorted functions include the screening of incoming information and the control of behavioral responses to them. Presently, this can not be considered as more than an interesting hypothesis. It can be supported only when sufficient data are gathered concerning the physiology of awareness.

The Behaviorist View

Behaviorists have developed some novel etiological theories of dissociative neurosis. They have considered the causes of amnesia, for example, and have concluded that amnesia is a simple case of "deficient registration of impressions."[30] That is, a person's attention is so monopolized by unpleasant feelings of anxiety that he does not have enough attention left to register what is going on around him. From this perspective, amnesia is not pathological forgetting but the failure to record an event when it first occurs.

The behaviorist theory of dissociative reactions in general is that they are avoidance reactions which protect the person from severe stress. This theory seems particularly relevant to the dissociative personality since most of these cases involve an unbearable amount of stress. In fact, one expert reports that all dissociative personalities were battered children.[31]

Another common background feature among dissociative personalities is that they were given forbidden secrets by their parents and forced to preserve them.[32] This experience is compatible with a conditioning process whereby the personalities remain hidden from each other and have their own secret motivation.

The Psychoanalytic View

Psychoanalytic theory holds that stressful life events create such overwhelming anxiety that a dissociative reaction is employed as an adaptive method of resolution. The dissociative response acts to defend the ego against material which is perceived as dangerous by either the conscious or the unconscious. The result may appear to be crippling, but it does avoid a true disaster in the form of a psychotic break with reality. Dissociative responses bring emotional tension within manageable limits. According to Cameron, "The process is a pathological form of the common demand of many a normal harassed person who exclaims tensely, 'One thing at a time, please!' "[33] Rather than displaying emotional con-

[30] Joseph Wolpe, *Psychotherapy by Reciprocal Inhibition*, p. 94.
[31] Cornelia Wilbur, "Clinical considerations in the evaluation and treatment of multiple personality."
[32] Ibid.
[33] Norman Cameron, *Personality Development and Psychopathology*, p. 341.

flicts as in conversion hysteria, the dissociative patient tries to escape from them through the use of the defense mechanism of *isolation*. This separates threatening, painful material from the rest of the conscious.

Psychoanalysts are generally agreed on the role of the unconscious and the adaptive role of isolation in the etiology of dissociative reactions. There is some disagreement, however, regarding the stage of psychosexual development which fosters these disorders. Some believe that unacceptable sexual wishes from the phallic stage increase in strength in adulthood when the ordinary form of repression fails to work any longer. This is the traditional explanation of hysterical neurosis, both its conversion and dissociative forms. Others feel that the fixation is at the primitive, oral stage in which denial and ego-splitting are common. These techniques are utilized in the infantile years before the individual develops the more mature ability to repress threatening material.

Although the nature of the fixation point remains controversial in psychoanalytic circles, it is important to point out some of the possible unconscious functions of dissociative reactions. Since the disorder can be a denial of responsibility or a repression of stressful experiences, the dissociation is sometimes a separation from superego functions. One of Freud's cases exemplifies this; he treated a patient who tried to rip her clothes off with her right hand while simultaneously trying to keep them on with her left.[34] According to Freud, she was identifying with a man raping a victim and the helpless victim at the same time! This case demonstrates the use of dissociation, in the form of multiple identification, to live out urges unacceptable to the superego through serially acting out various roles.

Phobic Neurosis

Symptoms

Phobias—irrational fears—appear more frequently as a psychiatric complaint than as a distinct neurotic syndrome. In fact some psychiatrists feel that all psychiatric patients have phobias. This may be true, but studies of the prevalence of phobias in the general population suggest that a much more conservative conclusion is warranted. One such study done in New England estimated that phobias are found in 77 people per 1000 members of the population.[35] Most of these were mild phobias; only 2.2 per 1000 were rated as severely disabling.

---

[34]Sigmund Freud, "Hysterical fancies and their relation to bisexuality," in *Collected Papers of Sigmund Freud,* volume 2 (London: Institute of Psychoanalysis and Hogarth Press, 1924), pp. 51–58.

[35]S. Agras, D. Sylvester, and D. Olvieau, "The epidemiology of common fears and phobias," (unpublished manuscript, 1969).

Although these patients have an intense fear of some object or situation, they consciously recognize that their fear is irrational because no real danger is posed. They often say that they know what it is about the phobic object that arouses anxiety, yet they engage in ritualized ways to avoid contact with it. As long as they avoid the phobic object, no anxiety is suffered. Phobias share a characteristic with conversion reactions since both involve secondary gains. For example, a fear of trains in a traveling salesman allows him to avoid work.

A phobia should not be confused with a *natural aversion*. Many people feel uncomfortable in the presence of a vicious dog but a phobic person may become extremely frightened if a timid dog licks his hand. A phobia is also not an *avoidance reaction* which is a conditioned response whereby certain objects or environments are avoided because of some previous unpleasant experience with them.

The phobic type of neurosis provides some definite advantages over the anxiety neurosis. Since no anxiety is experienced when the phobic object is absent, the escape from anxiety is organized and controlled rather than diffused to a constant threat of catastrophe. The phobic neurotic may experience somatic symptoms such as faintness, nausea, hyperventilation, tremor, and even panic. But since these symptoms are localized to the phobic object, this type of neurotic can more easily engage in everyday activities without constant harassment from within.

Phobias are known to spread, however. If, for example, a person is terribly afraid of large groups of people, this fear may gradually extend to smaller groups to the point where the person feels comfortable only when he is alone. One "contagious" case is reported of a man who had become phobic for the number thirteen.[36] This originated from the superstitious beliefs of a promiscuous maid he knew during childhood. Eventually the patient stayed in bed on the thirteenth day of each month to avoid contact with calendar and newspaper dates. Then he began to stay in bed on the twenty-seventh day of each month when he discovered it contained thirteen letters. Eventually he avoided people entirely for fear that they would greet him with a thirteen letter statement such as "Good afternoon."

Phobias are often divided into the *simple* and the *complex*. The former covers fairly specific stimuli such as cats or dogs, while the complex phobia involves vague stimuli such as novelty or loneliness. The latter are more difficult to both define and treat.

Occasionally phobic patients have "phobic partners." These are people, generally a spouse or parent, who help the patient avoid anxiety by devising techniques to guard against contact with the phobic object.

A number of phobic objects and situations are reported in the

[36]T. A. Ross, *The Common Neuroses* (Baltimore: Wm. Wood and Co., 1937), pp. 219-223.

Table 4.1. *Common Phobias*

Phobia	Fear of	Phobia	Fear of
acrophobia	high places	nyctophobia	darkness, night
agoraphobia	open places	pathophobia	disease
aichmophobia	sharp objects	peccatophobia	sinning
ailurophobia	cats	phonophobia	speaking aloud
algophobia	pain	photophobia	strong light
aquaphobia	water	pnigophobia	choking
astraphobia	thunder and lightning	pyrophobia	fire
claustrophobia	closed places	sitophobia	eating
cynophobia	dogs	taphophobia	being buried alive
ergasiophobia	writing	thanatophobia	fear of death
hematophobia	sight of blood	toxophobia	being poisoned
lalaphobia	speaking	xenophobia	strangers
mysophobia	dirt and germs	zoophobia	animals
necrophobia	dead bodies		

clinical literature. Table 4.1 lists some of the more common ones and their technical designations.[37]

Of all the phobias, agoraphobia is the most common, constituting 60 percent of all phobias examined.[38] Social phobias are also common. In this instance, the patient is afraid to be in the presence of others. Although the onset of this phobia is considered to be during adolescence, it is questionable whether it does not often appear earlier in the form of the all-too-familiar grade school phobia. Waldfogel describes the school phobia as ". . . a reluctance to go to school because of acute fear associated with it. Usually this dread is accompanied by somatic symptoms with the gastrointestinal trait the most commonly affected . . . The somatic complaints come to be used as an auxiliary device to justify staying at home and often disappear when the child is reassured that he will not have to attend school. The characteristic picture is of a child nauseated or complaining of abdominal pain at breakfast and desperately resisting all attempts at reassurance, reasoning, or coercion to get him to school."[39] Waldfogel also states that it can last for years. This is important since school phobias may later develop into social phobias in adolescence. The author knows of a child who experienced a full-blown school phobia. During adolescence he suffered anxiety in anticipation of

---

[37]Today there is a movement away from the use of the Greek prefix. Instead, the phobia is simply described in plain English, such as fear of heights, fear of death, and so forth.

[38]Gerald C. Davison and John M. Neale, *Abnormal Psychology: An Experimental Clinical Approach* (New York: Wiley, 1974), p. 134.

[39]S. Waldfogel, "Emotional crisis in a child," in *Case Studies in Counseling and Psychotherapy,* ed. A. Burton (Englewood Cliffs, N.J.: Prentice-Hall, 1959), pp. 35–36.

social events, particularly dating. The underlying threat emanated from a fear of failure in front of others. In childhood, vomiting was the typical beginning of a school day. This was also the major somatic symptom in adolescence. What is remarkable about this case is that the patient chose college teaching as an occupation. Vomiting continued to be the normal order of events before each lecture. After many years of hell, the phobia eventually subsided.

One of the most famous cases of phobia occured in a five-year-old boy who refused to go into the streets because of a fear of being bitten by horses which pulled the street cars in Vienna of the early 1900s. This is the case of Little Hans who was reported by Freud.[40] Freud interpreted Hans's fear of the horse as a displacement of the boy's fear of his father. Hans's fear of his father reportedly originated in castration threats which are common during the phallic stage. Freud held that the horse came to represent his father for a number of reasons; the father had played "horsie" with Hans, the horse's bridle reminded Hans of his father's moustache, and so on. It was the analysis of this case which helped to develop the psychoanalytic theory of phobic neurosis. Of course, it is also quite possible that Hans had had a frightening experience with horses and therefore was conditioned to avoid them. It would be interesting to know how the case would have been interpreted had Freud been a behaviorist and not been predisposed to look for unconscious factors.

Other famous cases of phobia include Augustus Caesar who was afraid to sit in the dark. King James I of England feared the sight of an unsheathed sword; his contemporary King Henry III of France was afraid of cats. Daredevil Evel Knievel reportedly has a phobia about planes, while Alfred Hitchcock, the master of movie terror, admits a fear of policemen. The late Howard Hughes suffered from a morbid dread of germs carried by people around him.

The Biogenic View

There is very little evidence that phobias are caused by biogenic factors. No studies have been done to assess the rate of phobias among relatives to ascertain the effects of genetic influences. There are only infrequent suggestions in the literature that people who develop pathological fears may be constitutionally predisposed to do so. Lacey, for instance, theorized that in such people the autonomic nervous system is easily aroused by environmental stress.[41] This hypothesis remains to be tested, however.

[40]Sigmund Freud, "Analysis of a phobia in a five-year-old boy," in *Collected Papers*, volume 10 (London: Hogarth Press, 1957), pp. 5–149.

[41]J. I. Lacey, "Somatic response patterning and stress: Some revisions of activation theory" in *Psychological Stress*, eds. M. H. Appley and R. Trumbull (New York: McGraw-Hill, 1967).

The Behaviorist View

The established theories of phobic neurosis are environmental. However, there is considerable disagreement as to which environmental theory is most valid. The debate centers around differences between the psychoanalytic and behaviorist theories. The psychoanalysts consider phobias to have unconscious symbolic significance while the behaviorists contend that phobias arise from unpleasant experiences with the phobic object or situation. The debate is somewhat senseless because the two positions are really not analyzing the same psychiatric phenomenon. The psychoanalysts study true phobias—irrational fears of an object that have no apparent explanation. The behaviorists, however, concentrate their research on the origin of strong fears of objects or situations which the person has actually encountered in some threatening way. Technically, these are not phobias but avoidance reactions which are quite rational, compared to the neurotic cases which psychoanalysts examine. This is not to say that behaviorist theory is less valid than psychoanalytic theory because the latter has concentrated on the irrational type of fear. On the contrary, avoidance reactions can be just as debilitating as phobias. The point is that the behaviorist - psychoanalytic debate exists largely because the two schools concentrate on different types of psychiatric fears.

According to behaviorists, the etiology of phobias does not involve any type of intrapsychic conflict or any belief that the phobic object *symbolizes* a more deep-seated fear. This school of thought stresses simple learning by association which is held to be the basis for selecting the phobic object. The model holds that phobias develop after a noxious experience with the phobic object or through the process of imitating a phobic parent.[42]

There have been attempts to test the behaviorist theory of phobias experimentally. Some of these experiments have not been successful in demonstrating that fear is acquired through conditioning.[43] However, one major experimental study did demonstrate the influence of modeling on the development of fear.[44] In this study, subjects watched others experience pain when a buzzer sounded. Eventually the observer expressed a negative emotional response to the sound of the buzzer alone. Of course, it is questionable whether this experiment actually demonstrated the genesis of a phobia based on conditioning since it did not analyze an *irrational* fear but an avoidance reaction. However, since

[42]See O. H. Mowrer, "On the dual nature of learning—a reinterpretation of 'conditioning' and 'problem-solving,'" *Harvard Educational Review,* 17 (1947), pp. 102–148.

[43]See, for example, H. B. English, "Three cases of the 'conditioned fear response,'" *Journal of Abnormal and Social Psychology,* 34 (1929), pp. 221–225; E. L. Thorndike, *The Psychology of Wants, Interests and Attitudes* (New York: Appleton, Century, 1935).

[44]A. Bandura and T. L. Rosenthal, "Vicarious classical conditioning as a function of arousal level," *Journal of Personality and Social Psychology,* 3 (1966), pp. 54–62.

people with both types of fears seek psychiatric help, this distinction is largely theoretical, especially in light of the fact that behaviorists have been very successful in eliminating debilitating fears through the principles of conditioning. Thus, from a practical perspective, the etiology of these conditions may not be as important as how to effectively treat them.

The Psychoanalytic View

According to psychoanalytic theory, the emotion associated with an unconscious conflict is *displaced* on to the phobic object which comes to symbolize the conflict. The anxiety generated by the conflict is substituted for by fear of a specific object. The specificity of the displaced anxiety on to a particular object makes the anxiety more manageable; that is, if the person avoids the object, he also avoids anxiety. Thus, threatening forces from the unconscious are alleviated by an act of camouflage. The phobia is a compromise between wishes that are repressed in the unconscious and the inhibiting forces that repressed the wishes. The person actually both wants and fears the phobic object at the same time or, more appropriately, he wants that which the object symbolizes. Psychoanalysts contend that a phobic neurotic is not really afraid of the phobic object per se; he is afraid of the wish for what the object *symbolizes*. The fear simply prevents the forbidden wish from being fulfilled. Therefore, the mother who has a phobia that she will harm her child, unconsciously wants to do exactly that. The person who is irrationally afraid of dirt, actually desires to be dirty but finds such anal-erotic temptations upsetting. Or the person who has a phobia about knives is actually tempted to harm himself.

At one time, psychoanalysts believed that each type of phobia had a distinct etiology. Now the psychoanalytic theory of phobias has become less specific; all phobias are considered to develop in response to conflicts with unconscious impulses. These are not necessarily just conflicts involving sexual and aggressive impulses but can be any "out of control" impulses such as drives for power or the need to maintain self-esteem.[45] It is not always possible to specify the nature of the conflict only by knowing the phobic object because personal experience and cultural influences affect the meanings of symbols. Two patients with a morbid fear of cats, for instance, may suffer different underlying conflicts. To one patient the cat may symbolize aggressive behavior and therefore be related to a fear of his own aggressive wishes. To another patient, the cat may symbolize sexuality and thus represent the patient's fear of his own sexual desires. Both of these are believed to be common fears among patients who have zoophobias. Animals are feared because they are sexually uninhibited, unpredictably violent, and openly violate a number of human taboos such as incest and cannibalism.[46]

[45]Leon Salzman, *The Obsessive Personality* (New York: Jason Aronson, 1973), p. 129.
[46]Norman Cameron, *Personality Development and Psychopathology*, p. 293.

Although it is impossible to know the origin of the anxiety by knowing only the phobic object, certain themes reportedly appear frequently among patients with particular phobias. Claustrophobia, for example, is commonly interpreted by psychoanalysts as a fear of being left alone with one's own impulses and fantasies.[47] Such a situation supposedly tempts the person to embark on secretive sexual adventures. This phobia may originate in the experience of being locked in one's room as a child. In that situation, the child can ease the pain of loneliness through masturbation and other forms of erotic play. At the same time, the child suffers considerable guilt over the sexual activity. From the original guilt comes the negative response to the opportunities of being alone in a confined space later. Some cases of claustrophobia occur in a confined space with others, such as in an elevator. Here, the etiology is considered to be different. The person with an elevator phobia is not afraid of physical harm if the elevator falls but feels threatened by being in close proximity to strangers. He views strangers as unpredictable and tries to avoid confrontations with them but in an elevator they can not be avoided. This is particularly threatening to people who become anxious in social situations.

Cases of school phobia have common characteristics according to psychoanalytic researchers. The child almost always become anxious when he is separated from the mother. Some feel that this implies a fault in the mother's relationship with her husband, since a mother in a satisfying marriage is not likely to have such a symbiotic relationship with her child.[48]

Other phobias have recurring psychoanalytic themes as well. Acrophobia, for example, is not a fear of a physical fall but of a social fall and the loss of self-esteem that accompanies it.[49] Sleep phobias are interpreted as fears of unconscious wishes that may arise during sleep.[50] The fear of sleep is therefore a fear of dreams in which repressed material emerges. Fears of darkness are believed to be the result of witnessing the primal scene.[51] The darkness triggers memories of the conditions in which the scene was observed. A fear of being away from home is interpreted as a fear of one's voyeuristic impulses; the person is afraid that he may see something which is forbidden.[52] Stage fright evokes underlying exhibitionistic desires or, in some cases, the feared desire to express hostility openly to others.[53] Fears of high places engender feelings of

---

[47]Ibid., p. 289.

[48]Leon Eisenberg, "School phobia: Diagnosis, genesis and clinical management," in *Sourcebook in Abnormal Psychology*, eds. Leslie Y. Rabkin and John E. Carr (Boston: Houghton Mifflin, 1967), p. 429.

[49]Norman Cameron, *Personality Development and Psychopathology*, p. 280.

[50]Otto Fenichel, *The Psychoanalytic Theory of Neurosis*, p. 190.

[51]Ibid., p. 206.

[52]Ibid., p. 72.

[53]Merrill T. Eaton, Jr. and Margaret H. Peterson, *Psychiatry* (Flushing: Medical Examination Publishing Company, 1969), p. 163.

sexual arousal because of their unconscious connection with an erection.[54] There are other recurring psychoanalytic themes reported in common phobic objects, such as the association of snakes with the penis, spiders and cats with the female genitalia, and rats and mice with children, especially younger siblings.[55] Of course, many of these associations may just be educated speculations.

Obsessive-Compulsive Neurosis

Symptoms

Obsessive-compulsive traits are common in normal persons. Many people have their favorite way of arranging their bureaus or closets or organizing their study habits. Others employ their own sleep-inducing gadgets as a nightly bedtime preparation. A certain degree of obsessive-compulsive drive adds a desirable quality to the individual and is partly responsible for the organization necessary to accomplish a diversity of tasks. The obsessive-compulsive neurotic, however, has a pathological exaggeration of these traits. He is not free to lead a normal life because he is excessively preoccupied with such concerns as cleanliness or the irresistable urge to perform daily tasks in certain ways. Some of these persons suffer from *obsessions* which are recurring, unwanted thoughts that cannot be excluded from consciousness. Other persons are dominated by *compulsions* which are recurring needs to perform a certain act. A compulsion is, in effect, an obsession put into action.

A central symptom of this disorder is constant doubting; the person must check and recheck the front door lock, the jets on the stove, the contents of his pockets, his answer on an exam, or rewash his hands to guarantee their cleanliness. Freud aptly called this neurosis a "private religion" because it is often characterized by elaborate ceremonies, self-denials, penances, and ruminative thoughts about sin.

The symptoms of this disorder may be meaningless to an observer, but they are aggravating rituals to the person since they must be completed to avoid anxiety. Therefore, although the obsessive-compulsive does not want to act upon his urges and even feels a need to resist them, he has to act or suffer worse consequences. Because these persons experience their urges as being foreign to themselves, they are classified as *ego-alien* symptoms.

Kolb differentiates three major types of obsessive-compulsive symptoms: *Folie du Doute, compulsive acts,* and *phobias with compulsions.*[56] Folie du Doute is persistent doubting and indecision which leads to repetitive acts (compulsions) intended to dispel the irrational doubts.

[54]Ibid., p. 163.
[55]Ibid., p. 163.
[56]L. C. Kolb, *Noyes' Modern Clinical Psychiatry,* pp. 425–428.

Common acts include the "checking-rechecking" syndrome described above. Compulsive acts are symbolic rituals which psychoanalysts believe serve as a sort of self-punishment and atonement for unacceptable urges. Phobias with compulsions are exemplified by the common combination of a fear of dirt and repeated handwashing (*washing mania*). The handwashing ritual is undertaken to alleviate the fear of contamination (*mysophobia*). This phenomenon is sometimes referred to as the "Pontius Pilate Complex." Mysophobia may also be alleviated by opening doors with one's elbows or handling all articles while wearing gloves. The famous millionaire, Howard Hughes, suffered from mysophobia. He insisted that everything be handled by Kleenex and even made his barber use different scissors for different parts of his head to avoid germ build-up. In one case a woman, every Saturday, washed the church pew she expected to occupy on Sunday![57]

The obsessive thoughts of these neurotics have magical aspects in that they feel that they can cause something to happen just by thinking about it. This belief, coupled with the fact that the content of the thoughts often involves repugnant ideas, makes this neurosis a painful one which is not reduced by any type of secondary gain. Obsessive thoughts often involve the expression of sexual and aggressive impulses such as destructiveness, dirtiness, and crude, violent sexuality. One extreme example is *Giles de la tourette's syndrome* which is an irresistible urge to scream obscenities. This usually involves facial tics as well. This particular syndrome has received more attention recently since there has been an increase in the number of people who report their lives to be miserably disrupted by these uncontrollable urges. Some stay at home rather than risk public exposure, while others spend part of their lives alleviating their urges in the privacy of others' bathrooms.

Obsessive thoughts vary from trivial acts, such as saying a word or phrase over and over or counting (*arithomania*), to more complex procedures such as reassembling the letters in words according to private equations. One such "word game" consists of spelling a word according to the alphabetical ordering of its letters. In another type of obsession the person spends hours brooding about an abstract topic, usually religious or philosophical, to the exclusion of other interests. This is known alternatively as the *thinking compulsion,* the *obsessive-ruminative state,* and *Gruebelzwang.*[58]

Ritualistic compulsions, which are undertaken to dispel obsessive thoughts, may be nonspecific and appear as qualities in all of the patients' behavior. This type of compulsive performs daily activities according to a rigid sequence. Other compulsives have more specific drives which can be dangerous such as an impulse to jump off a high building, to leap in front of an approaching subway, or to act defiantly toward authorities. Some researchers have suggested the existence of a compul-

[57]Ibid., p. 427.
[58]Otto Fenichel, *The Psychoanalytic Theory of Neurosis,* p. 290.

sive drive toward eating which they consider to be a factor in some cases of obesity.[59] Sometimes compulsions can lead to socially undesirable acts such as compulsive promiscuity, arson, and shoplifting (*kleptomania*).[60]

Obsessive-compulsives suffer from a deep fear of not being able to control their environment completely. This may be the reason for the development of phobias in so many of these patients.[61] Like the phobic neurotic, the obsessive-compulsive feels that he would be in perfect control of the world were it not for the phobic object. Thus, the phobic object serves to capsulize their fundamental fear of losing control. Examples of this fear of loss of control abound; many obsessive-compulsives have difficulty in falling asleep because they are no longer in command while sleeping.[62] These patients are also frequently incapable of expressing affection toward others because of a perceived danger in committing themselves to other people who are not entirely under their control.[63] This is not to say that they shy away from sex as well. On the contary, they often approach sex as a personal challenge to their endurance. Some male obsessive-compulsives, for instance, believe it is a failure not to prolong intercourse by maintaining a limitless erection.[64] Salzman reports a case of a man who tried to achieve orgasm in a woman who had never been able to have one.[65] When he failed, he blamed himself!

The obsessive-compulsive neurosis is one of the most severe neurotic reactions. It offers a poor prognosis; the patient usually worsens as he grows older, and he may break down when stressful events occur such as an accident, disease, or any abrupt change in lifestyle.[66] When this occurs, depression with suicidal tendencies is a frequent outcome.[67] This type of neurotic may also develop an addiction to alcohol or drugs if he realizes that he cannot completely control his environment. The addiction represents the discarding of all controls and a movement to the opposite extreme—the binge.[68]

Not all cases end in such disaster. Some, in fact, develop to the point where the patient develops unusual skills as exemplified in the case below:

> Jonathan G., a 28 year-old professional, often occupied his consciousness with obsessive thoughts. As a child, he used to count the number of letters in words. However, in an effort to make every word balanced, he would add vowels to the words at preconceived points so that the letters of each

[59]Merrill T. Eaton, Jr. and Margaret H. Peterson, *Psychiatry*, p. 166.
[60]Ibid., p. 166.
[61]Leon Salzman, *The Obsessive Personality*, p. 16.
[62]Ibid., p. 62.
[63]Ibid., p. 40.
[64]Ibid., p. 29.
[65]Ibid., p. 29–30.
[66]Leon Salzman, *The Obsessive Personality*, p. 148.
[67]Merrill T. Eaton, Jr. and Margaret H. Peterson, *Psychiatry*, p. 167.
[68]Leon Salzman, *The Obsessive Personality*, p. 166.

word added to a number divisable by 4.[69] Sometime in adolescence this process was altered in a more sophisticated way when he began to juxtapose the letters in words so that they were arranged alphabetically. By young adulthood, Jonathan was so well versed in this mental game that he could put a word in its alphabetical ordering before the average person could spell it in its normal form. He kept the whole thing a secret until he saw a celebrity attempt to "alphabeticize" on national television. This served to legitimize his obsession and allowed Jonathan to freely express his "talent" in front of others.

The Biogenic View

The obsessive-compulsive neurosis is the most complicated of all neuroses not simply because its origin is not entirely known but also because of the complexity of the pathways between the origin and the symptoms. Very little has been said concerning biogenic causes. In the nineteenth century, there was mention of a possible defect in intellectual functions which in turn was considered to cause a distorted preoccupation with unimportant ideas. This view, however, simply reflects the somatogenic orientation of that time and has been discarded long ago. There are reports of the neurosis occuring among many members of the same family. One such report documents the presence of the neurosis in fourteen relatives over three generations.[70] Although it is theoretically possible that gene-controlled variables may contribute to the obsessive-compulsive neurosis, few researchers consider it likely. Cases of the disorder occuring among relatives are interpreted as the result of disturbed interpersonal relationships which are perpetuated by social contagion.

The Behaviorist View

The behaviorist school of thought considers obsessions and compulsions to be learned and repeated over time because they are reinforced by their positive consequences.[71] The obsession is a conditioned stimulus to feelings of anxiety, and a compulsive act is undertaken when the patient realizes that that act can reduce the anxiety attached to the obsessive thought. Eventually, the act becomes a fixed pattern of behavior. Sahakian summarizes the behaviorist theory in the following way:

> An obsessional neurosis develops as the result of a mental conflict in which the neurotic vainly resists an overwhelming drive—not once, but

[69]Obsessive-compulsives typically have favorite numbers which are even. Psychoanalysts consider this to be a symbolic attempt at balancing the demands of id and superego. See Otto Fenichel, *The Psychoanalytic Theory of Neurosis,* p. 288.

[70]Jan Ehrenwald, "Neurosis in the family: a study of psychiatric epidemiology," *Archives of General Psychiatry,* 3 (1960), pp. 232–242.

[71]U. Meyer and E. S. Chesser, *Behavior Therapy in Clinical Psychiatry* (Baltimore: Penguin Books, 1970).

repetitively—if not invariably, then at least with a degree of regularity. Actually, he is undergoing a state of conditioning of which he is not aware, amounting to the establishment of a mental habit of doing things that he chooses not to do.[72]

According to this position, the source of the original anxiety is relatively unimportant compared to understanding the pattern by which ritualistic actions are developed. However, this is not true for all behaviorist researchers. Some research on conditioned rituals addresses the etiological question more directly by including traumatic events in adulthood which can produce the neurosis. Kardiner, for example, reports a case of a patient who could not sleep at night until he performed an elaborate ceremony consisting of lying flat on his stomach with his nose in the pillow.[73] He also held his face in his hands and held his breath as long as possible. This ritual was a reenactment of a battlefield experience during which he desperately tried to protect himself from an enemy attack at night. The enemy used gas as a weapon and the patient made constant adjustments of his gas mask.

Wolpe reports the case of a man with a strong compulsion to strike people.[74] This reportedly developed when the patient was in the military service and was unjustly imprisoned. When he resisted the military police, he was sent to a psychiatrist who pronounced him well. A sense of helpless rage increased to the point where he struck a military policeman. The compulsion to strike people reappeared eleven years later when he was again jailed. Then it began to recur frequently and under a variety of conditions.

The major thrust of the behaviorist argument is that the origin of the obsessive-compulsive behavior need not be in childhood or, if it is, it is not necessarily connected with sexual experiences as psychoanalysts hold. Washing mania, for instance, may yield a direct reassuring effect to a person simply because in childhood it reassured him against being criticized by his mother for having dirty hands.

The Psychoanalytic View

Freud viewed the obsessive-compulsive disorder as a defense against guilt from the incestuous wishes of the phallic stage. He believed that this forced a regression to a prephallic period, specifically the anal stage, as an unconscious flight from Oedipal threats. This position is no longer accepted in psychoanalytic circles, at least not entirely. Contemporary psychoanalytic theory holds that obsessive-compulsive behavior originates in fixation at the anal stage without any phallic complications.

[72]William S. Sahakian, "A social learning theory of obsessional neurosis," *Israel Annals of Psychiatry and Related Disciplines*, 7 (1969), pp. 70–75.

[73]A. Kardiner, *The Traumatic Neuroses of War* (New York: Hoeber, 1941), pp. 15–20.

[74]Joseph Wolpe, *Psychotherapy by Reciprocal Inhibition*, p. 92.

The foundation of this theory was the recurring observation that neurotics of this type exhibit two key features of the anal-sadistic stage: ideas associated with dirt and aggressive behavior. A preoccupation with dirt signifies anal tendencies because these impulses are normally modified in the remaining stages of development. However, in many obsessive-compulsives they remain as an ingrained part of the emotional make-up. This is considered to be the result of unresolved conflicts during the anal stage, conflicts involving order and disorder, cleanliness and soiling.

Psychoanalysts consider the neurosis to arise from the anal-sadistic stage rather than the anal-erotic stage because sadism, in the form of painful impulses, comes closer to breaking through in the obsessive-compulsive neurosis than in any other neurosis.[75] The ego attempts to manage the sadistic impulses which were energized by fixation at the anal-sadistic level. In the process, the superego becomes cruel, aggressive, and excessively demanding.[76] The fixation is believed to be the result of toilet-training that was begun too early or conducted in too demanding a way by the parents. This causes the child to become anxious. He tries to control the anxiety by rigid performance standards which translate into ritualistic patterns.[77] The child who initiates such patterns is unable to please his parents by living up to their demands for sphincter control. Consequently, he is left with feelings of doubt and uncertainty, symptoms which frequently appear among obsessive-compulsive adults. The type of parents who are likely to bring about anal-sadistic fixation in their children are well-known. They simply cannot tolerate soiling by their child or any stubborn attempts by the child to maintain his autonomy.[78] The mothers are rigid and compulsive themselves. This may be one reason why the disorder frequently appears among members of the same family.

There is an overt relationship between the symptoms of the obsessive-compulsive neurosis and an underlying conflict stemming from the anal stage. These persons are extremely neat, clean, and orderly. They tend to be stingy, often in the handling of money. They frequently experience constipation and diarrhea. Most importantly, they have difficulty accepting authority figures who attempt to control their external behavior. This last symptom is consistent with the theory that these patients have fears of not being able to fulfill expectations placed on them by others because they were unable to live up to their parents' toilet-training demands in early life.[79] Just as the child viewed these demands as arbitrary rules, so the neurotic adult invokes similar rules to ward off anxiety. And the rules take the form of obsessions and compulsions.

[75]John C. Nemiah, *Foundations of Psychopathology*, (New York: Aronson, 1973), p. 110.

[76]Ibid., p. 279.

[77]Leon Salzman, *The Obsessive Personality*, p. 47.

[78]Norman Cameron, *Personality Development and Psychopathology*, p. 409.

[79]Leon Salzman, *The Obsessive Personality*, p. 90.

Psychoanalytically, the symptoms of this neurosis are considered to represent a compromise between aggressive impulses in the unconscious and the defense mechanisms employed by the ego against them. There are a number of such defenses in this neurosis.[80] *Isolation* is involved because an unacceptable impulse from the anal-sadistic period is separated from its memory origin. *Reaction formation* also takes place; the ritualistic activity is the opposite of the unacceptable impulse, for example a washing ritual in a person who wishes to be dirty. *Undoing* occurs as well since the ritual functions as atonement for the unacceptable impulse. *Displacement* is another defense mechanism involved in the obsessive-compulsive neurosis. Through this process, the conflict which contains forbidden wishes is displaced on to something harmless such as rechecking door locks. All of these defenses are utilized to manage the great struggle between the contradictory demands of id and superego. In some cases, these defenses break down, and the ego becomes effectively eliminated. When this happens, the disorder can develop into a full-blown psychosis.

Psychoanalysts believe it is the harsh superego of the obsessive-compulsive that causes the heightened sense of self-criticalness frequently found in these people. This can result in what Nunberg described as "those wrecked by success."[81] If they achieve a long-cherished objective, they become depressed. They cannot enjoy success because their superego ". . . only permits them to await happiness but never to enjoy its fulfillment."[82] There are many people who have attained highly prized positions (perhaps partly due to their obsessive-compulsive tendencies), but are saddened immediately afterwards. This is not uncommon among graduate students who have just completed the formal requirements for the Ph.D. In graduate school circles, this is known as the "Post-Doctoral Syndrome." In its more general form, Maslow refers to it as the "Jonah Syndrome" and he explains it as an incapacity of obsessive-compulsives to enjoy peak experiences for an extended time because of a fear of losing control and being shattered.[83]

Hypochondriacal and Neurasthenic Neuroses

Symptoms

The hypochondriacal neurotic is dominated by a preoccupation with the body and with a fear of presumed diseases of various organs. The condition differs from conversion hysteria in that there are no

---

[80]Otto Fenichel, *The Psychoanalytic Theory of Neurosis*, p. 292.

[81]Herbert Nunberg, *Principles of Psychoanalysis* (New York: International Universities Press Inc., 1955), p. 315.

[82]Ibid., p. 316.

[83]Abraham H. Maslow, "Neurosis as a failure of personal growth" in *Psychopathology Today: Experimentation, Theory and Research,* ed. William S. Sahakian (Itasca, Illinois: F. E. Peacock Publishers, Inc., 1970), pp. 122–130.

actual losses or distortions of function. This neurotic category is controversial because some claim that these people exhibit symptoms which actually arise from another neurosis, chiefly either the anxiety neurosis or the obsessive-compulsive neurosis. However, it is a separate diagnostic entity in DSM–II. These persons are morbidly preoccupied with their physical or emotional health. Some of them complain of vague illness symptoms. Others complain of organ-centered problems which are usually abdominal, although the chest and head are frequently involved as well. When they do have normal body ailments, their complaints are entirely out of proportion to their actual physical condition as the person who thinks that his headache stems from a brain tumor.

Many of these persons are addicted to reading medical journals and other health-related literature. Some are "food faddists" who rush to purchase new foods which reportedly aid health. Their preoccupation with their body prevents them from attending to their underlying problems. Consequently, they do most of the talking when examined by a physician, and give a too-detailed, technical account of their symptoms. Because they are hypersensitive to criticism, they may shift from physician to physician as each in turn recommends psychiatric evaluation.

Closely related to hypochondria is a neurosis characterized by chronic weakness, easy fatigue, occasional exhaustion, and band-like headaches. This is known as the neurasthenic neurosis. Until recently it was classified as a psychophysiologic disorder. Some now consider it to be a type of hypochondriacal neurosis.[84] Both hypochondria and neurasthenia offer useful secondary gains. Because these people lack attention from others, their symptoms meet an attention-getting need. Their symptoms also serve to rationalize any inadequacies and allow them to avoid undesired responsibilities. The following case exemplifies a hypochondriacal reaction to anxiety:

> A 50 year old man suffered from the fear that his heart would stop beating, that his limbs would fall off, and the like. He was unable to sleep, for he awoke every few minutes in order to check whether he still had all of his limbs. He suffered from real sensations which he perceived as painful ones in the region of the heart, the extremities, and the nose. All of these complaints culminated in the fear that he would die of "arteriosclerosis." He had heard something about arteriosclerosis as appearing at his age and now imagined that his vessels, which he thought of as some kind of tubes, would become obstructed so that some parts of his body would have to fall off. He . . . connected his suffering with his irregular sexual life. For years he had practiced coitus interruptus. He felt that this had harmed him; he had pains in his genitals and his head . . . At last, he was overcome by the fear that the semen held back during intercourse would stop up his penis . . .[85]

[84]See Theodore Millon and Renee Millon, *Abnormal Behavior and Personality* (Philadelphia: W. B. Saunders, 1974), p. 304.
[85]Herman Nunberg, *Principles of Psychoanalysis,* pp. 183–184. By permission of publisher.

The Behaviorist View

Little etiological research on hypochondria and neurasthenia has been undertaken. Biogenic theories are nonexistent and environmental theories are sketchy. This paucity of research is probably due, at least in part, to two factors; first, as stated earlier, many consider these reactions to be idiosyncratic symptoms of other neuroses, and secondly, the hypochondriacal and neurasthenic reactions are not very common.

Behaviorists stress the influence of social learning in hypochondria. They believe the disorder is caused by overprotective parents who display an exaggerated concern over their child's health. They do not differ from other parents in warning about sitting in a draft or having enough clothes on to go outside, but they differ in their constant and overdramatic warnings about such things.[86]

The Psychoanalytic View

Psychoanalysts have treated these reactions as separate neurotic entities each with a specific etiology. The hypochondriacal behavior is considered to be the result of the renunciation of masturbation. Hypochondria is said to replace masturbation because the cessation of masturbation results in a "damming up" of libidinal energy. The person, in turn, deals with the resultant anxiety by displacing it on to imaginary body difficulties.

Neurasthenia received attention from early psychoanalysts who believed it resulted from excessive masturbation. They held that the masturbatory activity taxed the psychic system to such a degree that the person's libidinal energy was reduced and consequently caused fatigue. Some research suggests that these people do experience frequent conflicts about masturbation. They tend to be compulsive masturbators or "masturbation addicts," particularly when they experience stress.[87] The ways in which masturbation causes neurasthenic symptoms are not yet clear, however. It has been suggested that the linkage may not be purely physiological but may possibly be a psychic consequence of guilt over masturbating.[88]

Existential Neurosis

Symptoms

The existential neurosis is the most recent neurotic reaction to be recognized. Many of the biogenically-oriented researchers consider this

[86]Louis P. Thorpe, *The Psychology of Mental Health* (New York: Ronald Press, 1960), p. 155.

[87]Otto Fenichel, *The Psychoanalytic Theory of Neurosis*, p. 191.

[88]See William Thomas Moore, "Some economic functions of genital masturbation during adolescent development," p. 232.

diagnostic category to be of little importance. On the other hand, sociologically-oriented researchers contend that this disturbance is quite real and a predictable consequence of the quality of life in modern, industrial society. Although this disorder is not listed in DSM–II, it entails a set of known symptoms which are described elsewhere.[89] The central symptom is the belief that one's life is meaningless. Consequently, apathy, boredom, and an inability to believe in values such as truth and importance are also involved. Like the neurasthenic neurosis, a sense of listlessness is experienced, but in this case, it is a cognitive rather than a somatic disability. It is considered to be different from a depressive state because the complaints center about the purpose of life. Perhaps this neurosis is simply a specific type of depression which increases as society becomes more fragmented.

The Sociocultural View

The major etiological perspective on the existential neurosis is sociological. The neurosis is not considered to arise from such factors as instinctual conflicts or conditioning but is viewed as a consequence of sociocultural situations. Specifically, it has been argued that anxiety among adults can arise when the basic values and purpose of a society begin to disintegrate.[90] Such conditions pose a real threat in the United States today since increasing technology, mass production, and urbanization contribute to a sense of anonymity. The individual feels a loss of a sense of community (*Gemeinschaft*) and is forced to live in a social system that thrives on competition and impersonality (*Gesellschaft*). People no longer interact with each other through a diversity of roles. Instead, they know each other only in a particularistic way such as occupationally. The furthering of mechanization and automation requires that people suffer the dehumanization and alienation engendered by occupational specialization.

The institutions of the family and the church have traditionally functioned to link the individual with society. But in today's industrial age they are disappearing or have, at least, been rendered impotent. Melvin Tumin claims that economic concerns have become so important in the United States that values formerly confined to the occupational sphere have "invaded" the family.[91] Parents, for instance, compete among themselves for distinction in terms of the material goods which they buy for their children; children are awarded affection on the basis of their achievements in school and athletics; spouses judge each other

[89]Salvatore R. Maddi, "Existential neurosis," *Journal of Abnormal Psychology*, 72 (1967), pp. 311–325.

[90]See S. Kirson Weinberg, "Social psychological aspects of neurotic anxiety," in *The Sociology of Mental Disorders: Analyses and Readings in Psychiatric Sociology*, ed. S. Kirson Weinberg (Chicago: Aldine, 1968), pp. 143–149.

[91]Melvin Tumin, "Some dysfunctions of institutional imbalance," *Behavioral Science*, 1 (1956), pp. 218–223.

by their "breadwinning ability." All of these shifts threaten social cohesion and produce psychological strain on the individual. Because the links between the individual and society have been ruptured, some people seek an irrational attachment to the security and purpose of past life by disidentifying themselves from present society. Thus, the crisis of the existential neurosis is a microcosm of a societal crisis.[92]

In addition to growing social decay, the sense of meaninglessness which is central to the existential neurosis can be incurred through more individualistic precipitating stresses that can make a person feel shallow or superficial. Maddi discusses three of these.[93] One is any gross disruption of the social order, such as war or economic depression. This type of rapid change can lead to disintegration of social roles and can spread a crippling sense of anomie among the populace. A second source of a sense of purposelessness is the threat of imminent death followed by unexpected recovery. If the threat of death disconfirmed one's previous identity, the individual has no real identity left. Thus the person undergoes psychological death and feels that his life has lost its meaning. Finally, Maddi holds that the existential neurosis can be brought about when a person continuously interacts with others who point out his failures and weaknesses. Thus, the disorder can originate from labeling.

Conclusions

It is appropriate here to consider a central etiological issue regarding neurosis; namely, "What governs its form?" To be sure, different neurotics react to anxiety in specific ways. Some reduce anxiety by direct discharges of anxiety on to the body (anxiety neurosis). Some lose a special sense or body function (conversion reaction). Other neurotics undergo alterations in consciousness or identity (dissociative reaction). Phobic neurotics have an intense fear of an object or situation. Obsessive-compulsive neurotics engage in ritualistic behavior. Hypochondriacs and neurasthenics experience a felt reduction in physical health and strength, and finally, some neurotics complain of a lack of meaning in life (existential neurosis).

The specific neurotic syndrome is not a "choice" made by a person with unmanageable anxiety. According to psychoanalytic theory, it is the consequence of the composition of the patient's personality which was formed from interpersonal experiences during childhood. From this perspective, the mechanisms of defense utilized by neurotics represent ways of alleviating unconscious conflicts originating from a traumatic period of earlier life. Thus, for instance, reaction formation may play a role in the mind of the obsessive-compulsive neurotic who retains unac-

---

[92]Roy D. Waldman, "Neurosis and the social structure," *American Journal of Orthopsychiatry,* 38 (1968), pp. 89–93.

[93]Salvatore R. Maddi, "Existential neurosis," pp. 318–319.

ceptable desires to soil in defiance of earlier toilet-training experiences that infringed on pleasure impulses. In conversion hysteria, sexual conflicts are believed to be managed by displacing them on to a substitute body organ, and so on for the rest of the neurotic types.

The behaviorist theory of neurosis emphasizes conscious forces in the neurotic's social circle that prompted particular neurotic behavior. Thus, parents who are suggestible and reward the child for showing off predispose the child toward hysterical symptoms. Those whose parents made a big fuss over health-related matters were being guided toward hypochondria at the same time, and so on.

The existential neurosis clearly demonstrates the role of social forces on mental health since this anxious state of personal meaninglessness has increased in frequency as industrial society has become more fragmented. However, in all major theories of neurosis, there is a crucial role played by social factors. The major difference between the theories is the significance each accords to hidden, unconscious origins since these are vital issues only in psychoanalytic theory.

5

The Functional Psychoses

Psychosis: An Overview

The psychopathological conditions known as the functional psychoses or "major psychoses" include the most severe and bizarre mental aberrations: schizophrenia, the manic-depressive psychoses, involutional melancholia, and the paranoid states. These disorders are presented here in terms of their prevalence, clinical symptoms, and etiology. Together, the functional psychoses account for a major portion of the hospitalized mentally ill in the United States today. Other functional psychoticlike states exist but are not considered here because they are uncommon and, in some instances, unclassifiable. Some of these, such as pibloktoq and running amok, were discussed in chapter two. In addition to these conditions, which appear to be culturally specific, there are other psychotic states which have been noted in the literature.[1] For example, some people develop the belief that a person, usually a relative, has been replaced by a double. This is known as the *Capgras syndrome*. In the *Couvade syndrome*, husbands, during their wives' pregnancies, suffer symptoms which are ordinarily associated only with pregnant women. In addition, there is also what is known as *voodoo death* or *Thanatomania*. Here the person actually dies after transgressing a taboo or from the fear of being bewitched.

[1]For a more complete description of the uncommon psychotic syndromes see; M. D. Enoch, W. H. Trethowan and J. C. Barker, *Some Uncommon Psychiatric Syndromes* (Bristol: John Wright, 1967); S. Arieti and J. M. Meth, "Rare, unclassifiable, collective, and exotic psychotic syndromes," in *American Handbook of Psychiatry*, ed. S. Arieti, vol. 1 (New York: Basic Books, 1959).

Regardless of whether a particular syndrome is exotic or common, it is considered to be a psychosis if it involves a loss of contact with reality. In psychosis the person replaces reality with a world of fantasy. The symptoms of the functional psychoses are often bizarre, but they have been fully delineated. The epidemiology of these illnesses has also been well studied. There is some patterning to the occurrence of these disorders; some appear most frequently among lower class people, some among males, and some among certain age groups. What is less well-documented is their etiology. A wealth of causal theories exists, however. Some theories, especially those with empirical support, are more compelling than others but no one theory can presently account for all cases of any particular psychosis. Some of the material in this chapter deals with the clinical aspects of psychosis as well as etiological theories that do not involve environmental factors. This information is vital to *all* students of psychiatry, including students of psychiatric sociology, since it allows for a fuller understanding of the sociology of mental illness.

The biogenic approach to the etiology of functional psychosis has relied partially on the measuring of the coincidence (concordance rate) of a disorder among family members in an effort to pinpoint the role of genetic agents. This family method suffers serious methodological biases because it overlooks the contribution of common environmental experiences among members of the same family. To mitigate the effect of this factor, some studies have limited their samples to identical and fraternal twins. A genetic hypothesis is then supported when a disorder is shared more often between identical twins than between fraternal twins. However, it assumes that both types of twins have different environmental experiences. This is a questionable assumption since identical twins often cling together and are treated more similarly by their parents and others than are fraternal twins. Thus only those studies of identical twins raised in different environments allow for a *pure* assessment of genetic forces. Unfortunately such studies are rare.

There are also biogenic theories of psychosis that are biochemical. These theories postulate a relationship between psychosis and an abnormal state of body chemistry, such as unusual agents in the blood, irregularities in metabolism, or a disruption of the nervous system. A third biogenic approach to the etiology of psychosis is morphological; it stresses the influence of body type or physique. This approach used to be populr during the ealrier part of this century but it has few supporters today becuase it is generally viewed as unscientific.

The environmental theories of psychosis include a variety of approaches. Some of these are purely social while others are intrapsychic. Included in the socially-oriented approaches are those that stress the causal influence of threatening life changes such as the shrinking of one's social circles, retirement, or divorce. The need for social mobility and concomitant status approval is another explanation which is particularly appropriate to capitalistic societies such as the United States which employ individual economic mobility as an indicator of personal worth. Other socially-oriented theories emphasize a linkage between the onset of psychosis and living in a deprived, threatening environment such as that fostered by social isolation. In addition, there are theories which locate the origin of the disorder in the structure of the family.

The intrapsychic environmental theories are largely psychoanalytic. This school views psychosis as the result of a severely deprived childhood resulting in fixation. Psychosis, then, is considered to be a regression to the childhood stage at which the patient is fixated. Typically, these are the earliest stages of psychosexual development, stages in which the child's mind is normally full of fantasy as is the mind of the adult psychotic. Additionally, psychoanalytic interpretations of psychosis suggest that some of these mental conditions are the result of the repression of socially unacceptable sexual orientations. But even here a social factor is involved since the disorder could not develop without the existence of negative attitudes in society toward certain sexual urges.

There are other intrapsychic theories which are not purely psychoanalytic. Some of these view psychosis as an extreme response to the loss of a highly prized person, or love object. Other theories place the origin of psychosis in the specific ways in which people in different sibling positions are socialized, particularly in large families.

Both biogenic and environmental theories are presented in this chapter since it would be unwise to discount any explanation while the origins of psychosis remain such a mystery. However, there are psychotic syndromes, namely the paranoid states, in which there is very little evidence of biogenic causation. For this reason, possible biogenic factors appear only in the sections on schizophrenia, the manic-depressive psychoses, and involutional melancholia.

Schizophrenia

Prevalence

Estimates of the prevalence of schizophrenia in the United States range up to 1 percent of the population. Approximately 34 percent of all admissions to mental hospitals are diagnosed as schizophrenics, but because of their relatively poor chances for recovery, these patients tend to remain institutionalized for long periods, particularly in state hospitals.[2] Thus they constitute 50 to 60 percent of the state hospital population. However, some have charged that the prevalence of schizophrenia is typically overestimated because of broad diagnostic standards and misdiagnoses.[3] It is certainly difficult to know the true extent of schizophrenia since there may be as many schizophrenics outside of hospitals as

---

[2]Nadine Myers, *HEW News Release,* National Institute of Mental Health, Alcohol, Drug Abuse, and Mental Health Administration, November 1, 1977.

[3]Michael Alan Taylor and Richard Abrams, "The prevalence of schizophrenia: a reassessment using modern diagnostic criteria," *American Journal of Psychiatry,* 135 (1978), pp. 945–948.

there are inside of them. Such *outside* schizophrenics are usually referred to as *ambulatory schizophrenics.*

Schizophrenia is primarily a disorder of the young. It begins early in life, often during adolescence. Admission rates for schizophrenia are concentrated in the age range of twenty to forty years, with most cases occurring between twenty-five to thirty-four years. The disorder is also known to be heavily concentrated among lower class people.

General Symptoms

To many, schizophrenic reactions are the most fascinating of all psychopathologies. Over fifteen thousand professional articles and books have been written about them, evidencing that schizophrenia is the subject of lively controversy and much speculation. Part of this fascination lies in the bewildering variety of symptoms exhibited by schizophrenics. Schizophrenia is considered to be chiefly expressed through *disordered thought processes* which in turn lead to difficulties in communication, interpersonal relationships, and in reality testing. As a consequence of these difficulties, the schizophrenic withdraws from social participation and retires into the private world of his thoughts and fantasies. In addition to the common features of disordered thought processes and social withdrawal, there are more specific symptoms commonly known as the "four A's" of schizophrenia. The first "A" is an *Affective disturbance* which usually takes the form of a flatness of affect, a lack of outward display of emotion. This may be manifested by an apparent dissociation between affect and thought content as when a patient laughs when describing a tragedy. The second "A" is *looseness of Association* which refers to a lack of continuity of ideas and to an inability to move orderly from one group of thoughts to another. For example, the schizophrenic, when asked how old he is, may respond with a completely irrelevant answer, such as "a colonial home." *Autism* is the third "A." This refers to a self-centered type of thinking which is filled with fantasy. Schizophrenic humor is often autistic; no one gets the joke besides the patient himself. The fourth "A" of the schizophrenic syndrome is *Ambivalence.* This refers to having two opposite feelings or emotions toward the same object (person, situation, goal) at the same time. This in itself may not be abnormal since most people experience a number of ambivalent feelings. However, the schizophrenic is ambivalent toward everything, and his ambivalent feelings tend to be half positive and half negative. Beside the "four A's," there are other symptoms which frequently appear in schizophrenia. Included are the following "accessory symptoms": *sensitivity* (hyperawareness to stimuli coming from the environment), *loss of ego boundaries* (misidentifying others in the environment and the feeling of being controlled by external boundaries), *hallucinations, magical thinking* (thoughts are not differentiated from actions), *neologisms* (creation of new verbal expressions that have no meaning to others), *echolalia* (repetition of another's words), *verbigeration* (repetition of the same word over and over again), *echopraxia* (imitation of the gestures of a person whom the patient is observing), *perseveration* (use of the same word to name different objects).

Schizophrenic Types

The general symptoms of schizophrenia are found in many different combinations. However, there are certain groupings of symptoms that appear regularly. These groupings constitute the seven major schizophrenic types. The *simple* type of schizophrenia is characterized by a gradual withdrawal from outside interests, impoverished interpersonal relations and mental deterioration. This type is less dramatically psychotic than other forms of schizopohrenia. In the *hebephrenic* type, for example, the psychosis is characterized by primitive, uninhibited behavior which is best described as "silly" since it usually involves unpredictable grinning and giggling. There are two types of *catatonic* schizophrenia. The *catatonic excited* patients manifest excessive and sometimes violent motor activity. They often talk continually in incoherent streams of speech. They can be destructive and assaultive and for that reason are frequently regarded as dangerous. By contrast, the *catatonic withdrawn* patient is inhibited and manifests stupor, mutism, a refusal to eat, and an attempt to retain feces. These patients will often maintain uncomfortable physical positions for an extended period of time regardless of whether they assume these positions themselves (*posturizing*) or are placed there by others (*waxy flexibility*). The *paranoid* form of schizophrenia is characterized primarily by the presence of persecutory or grandiose delusions, often accompanied by hallucinations. The patient's attitude is frequently hostile, and his behavior is consistent with the delusions. Excessive religiosity is sometimes present.

There are other forms of schizophrenia as well. One category includes patients who show a mixture of schizophrenic symptoms and mood swings. This is the *schizo-affective* type. In addition, there is a special category for cases in which the symptoms appear before puberty, the *childhood* type, often incorrectly referred to in the popular literature as the autistic child. Many schizophrenic patients exhibit symptoms that are a mixture of other types. These cases are designated as *chronic undifferentiated*, a label which is frequently used. Some feel that this schizophrenic label is simply a diagnostic wastebasket. Below are two cases that represent the hebephrenic and catatonic withdrawn types respectively.

Greta S., a twenty-two-year old single woman who displayed an avoidant pattern ever since early adolescence. She was shy, somewhat fearful of all people, even those she had known all her life, and preferred to spend her days at home helping her mother cook and clean for her father and younger brothers. One morning she became "silly and confused," began to talk "gibberishly," as her mother put it, became incontinent, grimaced and giggled for no apparent reason. When the family physician arrived, he noted that Greta placed herself into a series of contorted positions on the floor, sang incoherent songs and cried fitfully for brief periods.[4]

Arnold N., a twenty-eight-year old married man was found one morning by his wife to be "staring in a funny way" outside his bathroom window. Not only did he refuse to reply to her concerned questions regarding his health, but he remained in a rigid position and refused to budge; no amount of pleading on her part was adequate to get him to relax or lie down. A physician was called to examine him shortly thereafter, but he was equally unable to penetrate Arnold's mutism or to alter his taut and unyielding physical posture. Although Arnold did not resist being carried into an ambulance, he refused to change the body position in which his wife found him that morning.[5]

The Biogenic View of Schizophrenia

Research into the etiology of schizophrenia is extensive but, in many ways, contradictory; nearly ten distinct explanations have been proposed as sufficient causes of the disorder. Some researchers have attempted to order the different theories by noting common themes among them and then creating workable subgroups. Siegler and Osmond, for instance, developed a theoretical framework consisting of "models" of schizophrenia.[6] They describe six models: medical, moral, psychoanalytic, family interaction, conspiratorial, and social. Soskis uses a similar approach by dividing the causal hypotheses into the genetic, psychodynamic, family-learning, social, biochemical or neurological, and existential.[7] However, many of these overlapping perspectives fail to deal realistically with a long-lived controversy—the debate between those who contend that schizophrenia is caused by biogenic forces and those who stress the impact of environmental influences.

The biogenic theories of schizophrenia include those that consider genetic forces, biochemical imbalances, as well as the influence of body type. The presence of various biological abnormalities in the schizophrenias has not been fully confirmed. Since hypotheses concerning the existence of such abnormalities are far from proven, few investigators regard schizophrenia as exclusively biological although evidence supporting biogenic explanations is growing.

---

[4]Reprinted from Theodore Millon and Reneé Millon, *Abnormal Behavior and Personality: A Biosocial Learning Approach* (Philadelphia: W. B. Saunders Company, 1974), p. 337. By permission of publisher.

[5]Reprinted from Theodore Millon and Reneé Millon, *Abnormal Behavior and Personality: A Biosocial Learning Approach* (Philadelphia: W. B. Saunders Company, 1974), pp. 340–341. By permission of publisher.

[6]M. Siegler and H. Osmond, "Laing's models of madness," *British Journal of Psychiatry*, 115 (1969), pp. 947–958.

[7]D. A. Soskis, "Aetiological models of schizophrenia: relationships to diagnosis and treatment," *British Journal of Psychiatry*, 120 (1972), pp. 367–373.

Genetic Theory

Genetic research has been the major focus of biogenic attention throughout this century. The preferred method is the study of concordance rates for schizophrenia in monozygotic and dizygotic twins. The concordance rates in the several studies of monozygotic twins range with great variability from zero to 86.7 percent. The rates of concordance for the dizygotic twins range from 2 to 14 percent. The fact that concordance is much greater among monozygotic twins than among dizygotic twins strongly suggests the influence of genetic factors. However, genetic transmission does not comprise the complete picture. If it did, the concordance rates would never be less than 100 percent among identical twins. By their own assumptions, the genetic studies have forced the conclusion that schizophrenia involves more than genes, although genes may well be contributing factors. In fact, most genetic researchers feel that their findings indicate that both genetic and environmental factors are significant in schizophrenia.[8] In addition, studies of the rate of schizophrenia among identical twins do not always provide a vehicle to directly test the contribution of genes because the twins are not always identical; they do not always equally share the placenta as indicated by differing birth weights.[9]

The most widely cited of the genetic investigators is F. J. Kallman, the researcher who found a concordance rate of 86.7 percent among monozygotics.[10] He pointed out that this concordance was an *average* over monozygotic twins who had not lived together for some years as well as for those who had not been separated. In the nonseparated group, the concordance rate was 91.5 percent but it dropped to 77.6 percent in the separated group. In other words, concordance decreased when the social environment was changed.

Recent studies were designed to counter the criticism of genetic studies by environmentalists who found them to be confounded by a confusion of genetics and environment. Heston followed up forty-seven people who were born to schizophrenic mothers in state mental hospitals.[11] The infants were separated from their mothers at birth and raised in foster homes. This group was compared to fifty control subjects who were also residents of the foster homes. Psychiatric diagnoses were made on members of each group. None of the control subjects was diagnosed schizophrenic, but 16.6 percent of the offspring of schizophrenic

---

[8]See: Martin Gallen, Stephen Cohen, and William Pollin, "Schizophrenia in veteran twins: a diagnostic review," *American Journal of Psychiatry,* 128 (1972), pp. 939–945.

[9]James R. Stabenau, "Schizophrenia: a family's projective identification," *American Journal of Psychiatry,* 130 (1973), pp. 19–23.

[10]F. J. Kallman, *Heredity in Health and Mental Disorder* (New York: W. W. Norton, 1953).

[11]L. L. Heston, "Psychiatric disorders in foster home reared children of schizophrenic mothers," *British Journal of Psychiatry,* 112 (1966), pp. 819–825.

mothers were so diagnosed. Other studies of the adopted-away offspring of schizophrenics also support the idea that there is a *vulnerability* to schizophrenia which is transmitted genetically.[12] Since there is only a significant tendency for schizophrenia to frequently occur among children born of schizophrenic mothers and not an invariant relationship, it is likely that a vulnerability to schizophrenia is inherited rather than schizophrenia per se. The vulnerability must be mixed with sufficient environmental stress to produce schizophrenia. This is the position taken by well-known genetic researchers. Paul Meehl, for instance, considers an inherited brain defect to be the necessary but not sufficient cause of schizophrenia.[13] According to Meehl, a person with this defect displays only mild schizophrenic symptoms (*schizotaxia*) and will not decompensate into schizophrenia unless the psychosocial environment is stressful.

Research by Gottesman and Shields has resulted in an important refinement in the assessment of the role of heredity.[14] They divided fifty-seven monozygotic twins into four categories graded in terms of degree of concordance with respect to severity of schizophrenic symptoms. They uncovered a significant direct relationship between concordance and severity of symptoms which suggests that only severe cases of schizophrenia are attributable to a genetic defect while milder forms of the disorder may not be attributable to genetic factors at all. Many more refinements of the role of heredity in schizophrenia are to be derived from future studies. One such refinement is the determination of the way in which schizophrenia is actually transmitted genetically. Currently there are several positions on this issue, some favoring a dominant gene, others a recessive gene, and still another that favors the operation of different genetic mechanisms for each of the schizophrenic types.

Biochemical Theories

A second perspective within the biogenic school postulates that schizophrenia is a result of abnormal functioning of the central nervous system caused by a biochemical imbalance. Research in the 1950s with mescaline and LSD yielded some insight into the nature of the chemical alterations possibly involved with the schizophrenic state.[15] Both of these

[12]See: Seymour S. Kety, and others, "Mental illness in the biological and adoptive families of adopted schizophrenics," *American Journal of Psychiatry,* 128 (1971), pp. 302–306; David Rosenthal and others, "The adopted-away offspring of schizophrenics," *American Journal of Psychiatry,* 128 (1971), pp. 307–311. Norman Garmezy, "New approaches to a developmental overview of schizophrenia," (paper presented at the annual meeting of the American Psychological Association, Toronto, 1978).

[13]Paul E. Meehl, "Schizotaxia, schizotypy, schizophrenia," *American Psychologist,* 17 (1962), pp. 827–838.

[14]I. I. Gottesman and J. Shields, "Genetic theorizing and schizophrenia," *British Journal of Psychiatry,* 122 (1973), pp. 15–30.

[15]See M. Rinkel, "Experimental psychiatry II: clinical and physio-chemical observations in experimental psychosis," *American Journal of Psychiatry* (1955), pp. 881–895.

drugs were found to produce temporary schizophrenic symptoms in normal people. Experimental subjects underwent considerable turmoil and confusion and experienced marked disturbances of thinking, perceiving, and feeling. Some subjects showed catatonic reactions; others hallucinated or exhibited paranoid suspiciousness, while several subjects reported losing their sense of personal identity and experiencing their bodies in peculiar ways. All subjects suffered a loss in sociability. The psychotic-like episode lasted for only a few hours and normal subjects seemed none the worse for their brief visit to the schizophrenic state. The specific linkages between the components of these chemicals and their effects on the brain remain uncertain. Research in this area has been hampered by society's attitudes toward LSD and mescaline, both of which symbolize to the public the countercultural movement of the 1960s.

Today there are a number of specific chemicals considered to cause schizophrenia if they are present in abnormal amounts. One such chemical is *serotonin.* Wooley and Shaw postulate that schizophrenia stems from a cerebral serotonin hormone deficiency resulting from metabolic failure.[16] A clue to the importance of serotonin came from the discovery that LSD blocked its normal effects on the involuntary muscles.[17] It was hypothesized that drugs whose effects mimicked schizophrenia did so by inhibiting the action of serotonin.

In the late 1950s a second biochemical hypothesis was generated by Heath and his associates at Tulane University.[18] They found a protein substance, *taraxein,* in the blood serum of schizophrenics and claimed that it was responsible for their mental condition. Taraxein was said to interact with other bodily substances to produce a toxic chemical which resembled a copper-containing globulin. This disturbed neural functioning in the septal area of the brain, the region which controls pleasure and pain responses. Heath isolated taraxein from the blood and administered it to nonschizophrenic prison volunteers. All the subjects developed schizophrenic symptoms.

In 1967 Heath and Krupp reported finding taraxein in the cells of the septal regions of the brains of schizophrenic patients who had died.[19] The substance was present in amounts which correlated strongly with the severity of the psychosis preceding death; the more taraxein present, the more serious the psychotic symptoms had been. Heath argued that taraxein produces symptoms closer to schizophrenia than those reported for LSD which were more akin to the delirious states found in

[16]D. W. Wooley and E. Shaw, "A biochemical and pharmacological suggestion about certain mental disorders," *Science,* 119 (1954), pp. 587–588.

[17]D. W. Wooley and E. Shaw, "Some serotoninlike activities of lysergic acid diethylamide," *Science,* 124 (1956), pp. 121–122.

[18]R. G. Heath and others, "Effect on behavior in humans with the administration of taraxein," *American Journal of Psychiatry,* 114 (1957), pp. 14–24.

[19]R. G. Heath and I. M. Krupp, "Schizophrenia as an immunologic disorder," *Archives of General Psychiatry,* 16 (1967), pp. 1–33.

organic psychoses produced by toxic agents. Some researchers have been unable to isolate taraxein in schizophrenic patients, leaving Heath's results not completely verified.[20] However, more recent findings on the role of copper in certain schizophrenic patients supports the taraxein theory.[21]

Recently, a third biochemical hypothesis has been put forth which links schizophrenia with excessive amounts of *dopamine*.[22] This theory stemmed from the observation that antipsychotic drugs produce side effects similar to the physical problems found in patients with Parkinson's Disease. Parkinson's Disease is caused by too little dopamine in the brain. Thus is was inferred that antipsychotic drugs work with schizophrenics by blocking the effects of excessively large amounts of dopamine.

At the present time, the role of biochemical abnormalities in schizophrenia is not completely known. It is possible that such abnormalities may not be of etiological significance since they may be simply the effects of schizophrenia rather than the cause. It seems logical to expect a disordered state of mind to be accompanied by a chemical abnormality since mental or emotional activities can engender changes in the biochemical process. This is a particularly important criticism in light of recent findings that schizophrenia can be effectively treated without drugs.[23] However, there is also new evidence that strengthens the position of the biochemical school such as the use of vitamins and urine dialysis as therapies as well as speculation that some cases of schizophrenia may be linked to opiate-like chemicals manufactured in the brain.

Morphological Theory

A third perspective within the biogenic school originated with the research of Ernst Kretschmer and deals with physical constitution.[24] Kretschmer frequently observed an association between people of certain body types and particular forms of mental disorder. He categorized individuals according to their physique and reported a marked association between schizophrenia and the slender, fragile build which he called *asthenic* or *leptosome*. In a comparable schema of body types developed by

---

[20]See H. Hoagland, "Biochemical aspects of schizophrenia," *Journal of Nervous and Mental Disease,* 126 (1958), pp. 211–220; M. Siegel and others, "Taraxein: fact or artifact?" *American Journal of Psychiatry,* 115 (1959), pp. 819–820.

[21]Carl C. Pfeiffer, "Does acid well water erode plumbing, vessels, and sanity?" *The Journal of Applied Nutrition,* 27 (1975), pp. 43–49.

[22]Steven W. Matthysse, "Current status of biochemistry in schizophrenia" (paper presented at the annual meeting of the American Psychological Association, Toronto, 1978).

[23]William T. Carpenter, Jr., Thomas H. McGlashan, and John S. Strauss, "The treatment of acute schizophrenia without drugs: an investigation of some current assumptions," *American Journal of Psychiatry,* 134 (1977), pp. 14–20.

[24]Ernst Kretschmer, *Physique and Character* (New York: Macmillan, 1936).

Sheldon, the same physique is called *ectomorphic* which he related to what he termed a *cerebrotonic* temperament.[25] Sheldon's conception of cerebrotonic people includes traits related to schizophrenic behavior.

Kretschmer's and Sheldon's morphological theory offers little empirical evidence in support of their assertions. Consequently, few researchers take this theory seriously. It does not explain why one individual of a particular physique is prone toward schizophrenia while a similarly built individual remains normal. Although more recent investigations of body type and schizophrenia have concluded that a relationship exists between schizophrenia and ectomorphy,[26] such a relationship can be explained through environmental interpretations as well since environmental influences affect both behavior and physique. For example, economic deprivation may give rise to self-consciousness, social withdrawal, and nutritional deficiencies which then lead to ectomorphic qualities in physique. Social stereotypes and role expectations of individuals with certain physiques can cause them to actually develop the characteristics of that stereotype. In addition, physical structure can either encourage or limit the kinds of behaviors an individual will learn. For example, a frail ectomorph is not likely to have his aggressive efforts rewarded and consequently he becomes withdrawn. All of these examples demonstrate that an association between morphology and abnormal behavior is more likely due to social learning rather than to a purely biogenic cause.

The Environmental View of Schizophrenia

Psychoanalytic Theory

Freud attempted to bring schizophrenia into consonance with the concept of regression. In different patients, the regression may have had different causes, but Freud held it always reached back to earlier times when the ego first came into existence. Specifically, psychoanalytic theory holds that the schizophrenic has regressed to a state of *primary narcissism,* a phase in the early oral stage before the ego has differentiated from the id. The differentiation of the ego coincides with the discovery that the self is distinct and separate from objects in the outside world. Therefore, the following etiological formulae of psychoanalysts mean one and the same thing: the schizophrenic's ego has broken down; the schizophrenic has regressed to narcissism; the schizophrenic has parted with reality. Through such regression, the schizophrenic has effectively lost contact with the real world. Psychoanalysts believe the schizophrenic regression is caused by the patient's personality being severely fixated at the oral stage either because he underwent frustrating

---

[25]W. H. Sheldon and S. S. Stevens, *The Varieties of Temperament* (New York: Harper and Row, 1942).

[26]See L. Rees, "Constitutional factors and abnormal behavior," in *Handbook of Abnormal Psychology,* ed. H. J. Eysenck (New York: Basic Books, 1961).

weaning experiences or was denied the comfort of a warm, mothering figure. These experiences leave the personality in an unbalanced state since the unfulfilled id impulses are highly intense, resulting in a poorly formed ego which eventually dissolves entirely or partly into the id. The regression is manifested through social withdrawal, a major symptom of schizophrenia. Also, resemblances between schizophrenic thought processes and those of children are striking in that both are simplistic, concrete, and weakly governed by principles of relevance.[27] As the schizophrenic patient regresses, he revives fears, conflicts, and fantasies which he experienced during the earliest phase of psychosexual development. In other words, he lives in a dream world in which people and things lose their distinct identities and appear to merge.

Because of the regressive nature of schizophrenia, psychoanalytically-oriented researchers view it as the royal road to the unconscious since its study can yield information about the make-up of the unconscious as well as information about the dynamics of early childhood. In fact many fruitful hypotheses concerning the early infantile period have been derived from the study of deeply regressed schizophrenic adults. Some feel that such research is speculative and without empirical support. However, while it is true that many psychoanalytic propositions are difficult to assess, there is some evidence which suggests that the schizophrenic mind is structurally equivalent to the fantasy-filled mind of the infant.[28]

Cognitive Theory

The cognitive approach emphasizes man as an information processor and utilizes various aspects of cognition in attempting to explain schizophrenia. Some of these theorists focus on associations while others focus on concepts. It has been clearly demonstrated that schizophrenics experience disturbances in both of these areas. In recent years, researchers who view schizophrenia as a cognitive dysfunction have increasingly endorsed the notion that *attention* is the key problem in schizophrenia. Research in this area has been carried out by Shakow and, most notably, McGhie and Chapman.[29] The basic assumption of these researchers is that schizophrenia is the result of an inability to select, focus on, and regulate incoming information. Because the schizophrenic cannot cope with elements in his environment, he be-

---

[27]For further elaboration of the resemblances between schizophrenic thinking and that of young children, see A. E. Goldman, "A comparative-developmental approach to schizophrenia," *Psychological Bulletin,* 59 (1962), pp. 57–69.

[28]See Samuel F. Klugman, "Differential preference patterns between sexes for schizophrenic patients," *Journal of Clinical Psychology,* 22 (1966), pp. 170–172.

[29]D. Shakow, "Psychological deficit in schizophrenia," *Behavioral Science,* 8 (1963), pp. 275–305; A. McGhie and J. Chapman, "Disorders of attention and perception in early schizophrenia," *British Journal of Medical Psychology,* 34 (1961), pp. 103–117.

comes perplexed and disorganized. The psychotic symptoms are considered to stem from the cognitive problems.

The weakness of the cognitive approach is that it may simply be *describing* the altered mental state of schizophrenia rather than explaining its origin. Indeed, this approach appears to be more of an elaboration of the cognitive state which occurs in schizophrenia than of its cause.

Behaviorist Theory

There are a number of environmental theories which are essentially social. Many of these theories point to the family unit as the agent responsible for the schizophrenic breakdown. One such view is a behaviorist theory which contends that schizophrenia is the result of mentally disturbed parents raising children. Because the parents are disturbed, their children are considered to learn disordered behaviors through the normal process of imitation. Such parents deviate seriously from usual child-rearing patterns and breed psychopathology in their children in an emotionally bizarre and deprived familial context. In such settings the child is often subjected to rejection, hostility, and social and emotional abuse.

Through studies of schizophrenic patients and their families, Lidz and his colleagues concluded that schizophrenic patients virtually always emerge from homes marked by serious parental strife or eccentricity.[30] Lidz contends that it is not the characteristics of a single parent but rather the disorganization fostered by an irrational strife between the parents which creates a family climate unfavorable to child rearing. The Lidz's studies classify types of intrafamilial structures and then correlate those structures with the incubation of schizophrenia. Two family types have been observed. One is the *schismatic* family which is divided into two antagonistic and competing factions. The other is the *skewed* family in which the serious personality disturbance of one parent sets the pattern of family interaction.[31] In either case schizophrenia is the product of the family's failure to provide the psychosocial climate necessary for normal personality development.

Others who support the "socialization by the mentally disordered" theory have concentrated on the pathological traits of specific parents rather than their interactive effect. Studies of socially withdrawn children indicate that they are frequently raised by mothers who are demanding, interfering, and overwhelming.[32] These disordered mothers

---

[30]Theodore Lidz and S. Fleck, "Schizophrenia, human integration, and the role of the family," in *The Etiology of Schizophrenia*, ed. D. D. Jackson (New York: Basic Books, 1960).

[31]Theodore Lidz, "Schizophrenic patients and their siblings," *Psychiatry*, 26 (1963), pp. 1–18; Theodore Lidz, S. Fleck, and A. R. Cornelison, *Schizophrenia and the Family* (New York: International Universities Press, 1965).

[32]L. Nagelburg, H. Spotnitz, and Y. Feldman, "The attempt at healthy insulation in the withdrawn child," *American Journal of Orthopsychiatry*, 23 (1953), pp. 238–252.

are not merely overprotective or rejecting, rather they tend to be both simultaneously. Thus, the child is socialized in an environment characterized by changing and often contradictory pressures. The mothers are tense, anxious people who communicate these feelings to their children. This situation engenders a cycle of mounting tension. The child's only escape is withdrawal. The fathers often add to the emotional chaos through threatening and brutal behaviors directed toward both the mother and the children.

Double Bind Theory

Bateson and his colleagues described the intrafamilial origins of schizophrenia more specifically through the advancement of their *double bind hypothesis*.[33] These researchers believe that schizophrenic thought disorder develops through the constant subjection of a child to contradictory messages from the parent(s). Of prime importance is the fact that the child can neither comment on the mutually contradictory messages, nor ignore the messages, nor can he withdraw from the situation. One message is often verbal and the other nonverbal. An example of such messages is beckoning someone to come through gestures and saying "Go away" at the same time. Such contradictory communications are particularly dangerous to children because the parent threatens the child, often in subtle ways, with rejection or disapproval if the child fails to respond to both messages. Escape is impossible since an infant or a small child has nowhere to go. Simply stated, they are damned if they do and damned if they don't.

Bateson and his associates contend that enough childhood double bind experiences can cause the person to perceive the total environment in double bind patterns, to the point that any part of what appears to be a double bind sequence is met with fear and rage.

In a study comparing schizophrenic patients with their nonschizophrenic siblings, Lu uncovered a recurring form of the double bind pressure.[34] The parents' relationship with the preschizophrenics was significantly different from the way they interacted with their other children. The parents expected a higher degree of obedience, submission, and dependence from the preschizophrenic than from the nonschizophrenic child. Yet, while they expected the preschizophrenic child to be more dependent, they simultaneously entertained the conflicting expectation that the preschizophrenic should assume responsibility for achievement and perfection. The preschizophrenics were thereby involved in a stressful dilemma by being expected to play the contradictory roles of dependence and responsibility at the same time. The di-

[33]Gregory Bateson and others, "Toward a theory of schizophrenia," *Behavioral Science*, 1 (1956), pp. 251–264.
[34]Yi-chuang Lu, "Contradictory parental expectations in schizophrenia: dependence and responsibilities," *Archives of General Psychiatry*, 6 (1962), pp. 219–235.

lemma was heightened after the preschizophrenic was confronted with two social situations which precipitated the actual schizophrenic breakdown. The first situation was a sudden, explicit expression by the parents that the child should assume concrete adult responsibility.[35] The second situation was the loss of intimate relations with persons on whom the children depended for emotional support. Together, these two experiences traumatized the preschizophrenic by placing him in a position of independence without the support of others—a position threateningly different from the way he was raised.

There is an additional aspect of the double bind theory of schizophrenia which includes the effect of being the last born child in a large family.[36] The youngest, by being allotted the special affections and privileges due to the family "baby," has difficulty acquiring the skills required for independent behaviors and is thus particularly prone to dependency. This hypothesis is consistent with the dependency facet of the Lu theory and is also supported by data demonstrating a higher rate of schizophrenia among last-borns.[37]

Social Class Theory

One theory of schizophrenia holds that the disorder is the result of belonging to the poorest socioeconomic class. It would be an oversimplification to say that poverty causes schizophrenia but the fact is that schizophrenia is much more common in the lower class than in the working, middle, or upper classes. There are several explanations for the observed relationship between social class and rate of schizophrenia. Some believe that being a member of the lower social class may itself cause schizophrenia. Lower class people frequently experience stressful situations in the form of broken homes, degrading treatment by others, the lack of opportunity for education, inability to achieve cultural goals, and the overall miserable conditions of deprived life circumstances.[38] The desire to escape these stressful life conditions can cause a lower class person to break with reality altogether in search of relief.

Another explanation of the preponderance of schizophrenia in the lower class is that schizophrenics *drift* into poverty from higher social classes. That is, those who are already disordered lose their ability to function successfully in their occupations and eventually *skid into* the lower class, rather than being born in it. Some studies indicate that

---

[35]Yi-chuang Lu, "Mother-child role relations in schizophrenia: a comparison of schizophrenic patients with nonschizophrenic siblings," *Psychiatry*, 24 (1961), pp. 133-142.

[36]H. Barry and H. Barry, "Birth order, family size and schizophrenia," *Archives of General Psychiatry*, 17 (1967), pp. 435-440.

[37]Bruce P. Dohrenwend and Barbara S. Dohrenwend, "Stress situations, birth order, and psychological symptoms," *Journal of Abnormal and Social Psychology*, 71 (1966), pp. 215-223.

[38]Melvin Kohn, "Social class and schizophrenia: a critical review and reformulation," *Schizophrenia Bulletin*, 7 (1973), pp. 60-79.

schizophrenics are downwardly mobile[39] although other studies evidence that this is not the case.[40] The question of class-caused schizophrenia has also been addressed by determining whether the fathers of schizophrenics are from the lower class. If they are, this would support the theory that lower class life itself is conducive to schizophrenia. If the fathers are not from the lower class, the *drift* hypothesis would then be supported. A study conducted in England and Wales,[41] as well as one conducted in the United States,[42] found that male schizophrenic patients tended to be employed in lower class occupations but that their fathers held more prestigious occupations. These data lend support to the theory that schizophrenia precedes social class rather than the reverse. Further support of this proposition comes from a related set of data demonstrating that schizophrenics exhibit significant discrepancies between their status aspirations (supposedly developed through socialization in a higher class) and their actual accomplishments (lower class status).[43] Such a discrepancy is consistent with the experience of skidding into the lower class.

The high frequency of schizophrenia in the lower social class has also been explained ecologically as the result of living in a socially isolated environment.[44] There is ample evidence that schizophrenics do live in such conditions since they frequently reside in the socially disorganized areas of cities. The relationship between social class and mental disorder is etiologically important. It is also highly complex and impossible to delineate in a few paragraphs. For these reasons, the question is dealt with more thoroughly in Chapter 10.

Existential Theory

There is also a theory of schizophrenia which is existential. According to this view, schizophrenics are persons devoid of the freedom they

[39]See M. M. Lystad, "Social mobility among selected groups of schizophrenics," *American Sociological Review*, 22 (1957), pp. 288–292; R. J. Turner and M. O. Wagonfeld, "Occupational mobility and schizophrenia," *American Sociological Review*, 32 (1967), pp. 104–113.

[40]See J. A. Clausen and M. L. Kohn, "Relation of schizophrenia to the social structure of a small city," in *Epidemiology of Mental Disorder*, ed. B. Pasamanick (Washington, D.C.: American Association for the Advancement of Science, (1959); W. H. Dunham, *Community and Schizophrenia: An Epidemiological Analysis* (Detroit: Wayne State University Press, 1965).

[41]E. M. Goldberg and S. L. Morrison, "Schizophrenia and social class," *British Journal of Psychiatry*, 109 (1963), pp. 785–802.

[42]R. J. Turner and M. O. Wagonfeld, "Occupational mobility and schizophrenia."

[43]See C. Bagley, "The social aetiology of schizophrenia in immigrant groups," *International Journal of Social Psychiatry*, 17 (1971), pp. 292–304; S. D. Eitzen and J. H. Blau, "Type of status inconsistency and schizophrenia," *Sociological Quarterly*, 13 (1972), pp. 61–73.

[44]R. E. Faris, "Cultural isolation and the schizophrenic personality," *American Journal of Sociology*, 40 (1934), pp. 155–164.

once possessed. The schizophrenic has lost his "will-to-meaning"[45] and his purpose in life. The psychosis is considered to be solely the result of being unable to find meaning for one's existence. Ronald Laing is the most well-known existential psychiatrist who believes that schizophrenia is a *strategy* adopted as a means of escaping the reality of an unlivable world. He states that ". . . the experience and behavior that gets labeled schizophrenic is a special sort of strategy that a person invents in order to live in an unlivable situation . . . the person has come to be placed in an untenable position. He cannot make a move or make no move without being beset by contradictory pressures both internally, from himself, and externally, from those around him. He is, as it were, in a position of checkmate."[46]

Laing's ideas are clearly in line with a labeling theory perspective. Thus he is quite popular among those who feel that both society and the mental health establishment are laden with hypocrisies. However, it seems that the existential school is of little *etiological* value since it appears to be oriented toward creating a sympathetic understanding of schizophrenics rather than developing a causal theory based on empirical evidence.

The Status of Present Research

At the present time, the causes of schizophrenia are still not clearly known. Researchers have expended considerable energy investigating possible origins, but not one of today's theories of schizophrenia is capable of explaining all cases of the psychosis. Schizophrenia appears to be a disorder that can be caused in a variety of ways, probably through the complex interplay of many factors. Recent studies have attempted to assess the relative importance of the major theories of schizophrenia by polling the views of psychiatrists. Two such studies in this country produced conflicting results. One was undertaken by Soskis who uncovered a preference for biogenic theories among psychiatrists in his sample.[47] However, the findings of that study have limited application because the sample was drawn from a census of psychiatrists practicing in a specific county of New York state. The findings may well be nothing more than a by-product of the local-minded setting in which the study was conducted. A more comprehensive study was undertaken by Gallagher[48] who randomly sampled members of the APA and derived a final sample that was representative of psychiatrists from all geographical areas, in various types of treatment settings (private practice, state hospital, and

[45]V. E. Frankl, *The Will to Meaning* (New York: World Publishing, 1969).

[46]R. D. Laing, "Is schizophrenia a disease?" *International Journal of Social Psychiatry*, 10 (1964), p. 186.

[47]D. A. Soskis, "Aetiological models of schizophrenia."

[48]Bernard J. Gallagher III, "The attitudes of psychiatrists toward etiological theories of schizophrenia," *Journal of Clinical Psychology*, 33 (1977), pp. 99–104.

so forth), and of different theoretical learnings (psychoanalytic, behaviorist, and so forth). He discovered that most psychiatrists are quite uncertain about the causes of schizophrenia and consequently are reluctant to endorse any particular etiological theory. However, those theories that were most frequently endorsed by psychiatrists were environmental.

The Manic-Depressive Psychoses

Prevalence

The manic-depressive psychoses are fundamentally severe disorders of *mood* (affect). They are more frequently treated in private hospitals which cater largely to wealthier families who are more prone toward the disorder than the poor. A majority of manic-depressive attacks occur between the ages of thirty-five and sixty. The manic form occurs primarily in the younger age group; the depressed type, in older persons.

The rate of the manic-depressive psychoses appears to have decreased considerably in the United States during this century. This may be due to a tendency among American psychiatrists to give the manic-depressive diagnosis less frequently. In New York state, for instance, the rate diminished from 177 per 100,000 in 1920 to 71 in 1950.[49] Because of this decline, research in this area is on the wane.

Symptoms

Toward the middle of the last century, it was recognized that mania and melancholia (depression) should be classified within the same type of disorder. Thus, the disorder was originally designated *cyclical insanity.* Some researchers question the use of the term psychosis here because manic-depressives do not always seriously lose contact with reality. This occurs only in severely depressed states and highly manic states. There is also considerable disagreement among psychiatrists as to whether the less severe cases should be termed mild psychosis. Unlike schizophrenia, in which there is always a sharp break with reality, the manic-depressive illnesses vary in degree of impairment from person to person. The number of attacks is variable also. One person may have only one episode in a lifetime while another individual may have numerous attacks. The nature of the episodes also varies; an individual may have alternating episodes of depression and mania or recurrent episodes of depression or mania only. Perhaps as many as 20 percent have only one attack. However, those who do have a second attack typically experience recurrences throughout their lives. The attacks are separated by periods rang-

---

[49]L. C. Kolb, *Noyes' Modern Clinical Psychiatry* (Philadelphia: W. B. Saunders Company, 1973), p. 366.

ing from a few months to several years, but the duration and the frequency of attacks tend to increase as the patient grows older. Attacks of all types begin quite suddenly with little warning.

The depressive phase is characterized by feelings of worthlessness, hopelessness, and guilt. In about half of the cases, there are delusions and hallucinations which have traits consistent with the depression. Often these patients feel better in the evening than in the morning. The mildest form of the depressed phase is called *simple retardation*. The most severe is referred to as *depressive stupor* which typically includes psychomotor retardation such as slow reaction time and underproductive speech. The depression often involves preoccupation with death, sleep and appetite disturbances, as well as somatic difficulties. The following case description gives a common picture of depression.

> Mr. J. was a fifty-one-year old industrial engineer who, since the death of his wife five years earlier, had been suffering from continuing episodes of depression marked by extreme social withdrawal and occasional thoughts of suicide. His wife had died in an automobile accident during a shopping trip which he himself was to have made but was unable to because professional responsibilities changed his plans. His self-blame for her death which was present immediately after the funeral and regarded by his friends and relatives as transitory, deepened as the months, and then years, passed by. He began to drink, sometimes heavily, and when thoroughly intoxicated would plead to his deceased wife for forgiveness. He lost all capacity for joy—his friends could not recall when they had last seen him smile. His gait was typically slow and labored, his voice usually tearful, his posture stooped. Once a gourmet, he had lost all interest in food and good wine, and on those increasingly rare occasions when friends invited him for dinner, this previously witty, urbane man could barely manage to engage in small talk. As might be expected, his work record deteriorated markedly, along with his psychological condition. Appointments were missed and projects haphazardly started and then left unfinished. When referred by his physician for psychotherapy, he had just been released from a hospital following a near-fatal and intentional overdose of sleeping pills. Not long afterward, he seemed to emerge from his despair and began to feel like his old self again.[50]

Manic reactions are mood disorders, accompanied by delusions, which are exaggerations of normal elation and are often initially mistaken for happiness. These patients appear restless and overactive and usually do not realize that they are in an abnormal state. They speak rapidly and jump quickly from one idea to another (*flight of ideas*). In addition, they often joke and tease others. However, they may suddenly become insulting and sarcastic. They behave in a grandiose manner, are invulnerable to reason and logic, frequently allude to outstanding personal achievements, and bend every circumstance to the service of self-

[50]Reprinted from Gerald C. Davison and John M. Neale, *Abnormal Psychology: An Experimental Clinical Approach* (New York: John Wiley, 1974). By permission of publisher.

aggrandizement. The milder cases are called *hypomanic* and the most severe cases are known as *acute mania* or *delirious mania*.

Occasionally, manic patients may experience a transitory breakthrough of depressed feelings. Some researchers suggest that this is because the mania acts as a substitute method of working through problems which threaten to precipitate depression. From this perspective, the *latent* content in mania is deeply depressive although the *manifest* content is superficially boastful, happy, and overactive. Cameron has compiled some evidence to support this position. He found that depressive and manic states are very much alike at the biological level when measures such as basal metabolism, blood pressure, blood sugar level, and rate of blood flow are compared.[51]

The following case exemplifies the behavior of a manic-depressive patient with moods alternating between mania and depression, the *circular* type, which is also known as the *bipolar affective disorder*.

> Mrs. M. was first admitted to a state hospital at the age of 38, although since childhood she had been characterized by swings of mood, some of which had been so extreme that they had been psychotic in degree. At 17 she suffered from a depression that rendered her unable to work for several months, although she was not hospitalized. At 33, shortly before the birth of her first child, the patient was greatly depressed. For a period of four days she appeared in a coma. About a month after the birth of the baby she "became excited," and was entered as a patient in an institution for neurotic and mildly psychotic patients. As she began to improve, she was sent to a shore hotel for a brief vacation. The patient remained at the hotel for one night and on the following day signed a year's lease on an apartment, bought furniture, and became heavily involved in debt. Shortly thereafter Mrs. M. became depressed and returned to the hospital . . . After several months she recovered and . . . remained well for approximately two years.
>
> She then became overactive and exuberant in spirits and visited her friends to whom she outlined her plans for reestablishing different forms of lucrative business. She purchased many clothes, bought furniture, pawned her rings and wrote checks without funds. She was returned to a hospital. Gradually her manic symptoms subsided, and after four months she was discharged. For a period thereafter she was mildly depressed. In a little less than a year Mrs. M. again became overactive, played her radio until late in the night, smoked excessively, took out insurance on a car that she had not yet bought. Contrary to her usual habits, she swore frequently and loudly, created a disturbance in a club to which she did not belong, and instituted divorce proceedings. On the day prior to her second admission to the hospital, she purchased 57 hats.[52]

[51]Norman Cameron, "The place of mania among the depressions from a biological standpoint," *Journal of Psychology*, 14 (1942), pp. 181–195.

[52]Reprinted from L. C. Kolb, *Noyes' Modern Clinical Psychiatry* (Philadelphia: W. B. Saunders Company, 1973), p. 376. By permission of publisher.

The Biogenic View of Manic-Depression

There is a growing acceptance that biogenic factors play a role in the origin of manic-depression. Evidence for this comes, in part, from comparisons of psychotic depressives with those suffering from less severe depression. The psychotic depressives respond much more favorably to somatic treatments including electroshock and antidepressant pharmaceuticals, particularly lithium carbonate. The most widely researched biogenic theories are genetic, biochemical, and morphological. Other theories exist but are not reported here because of their questionable nature. One such theory contends that the psychosis is related to the processes that in lower animals are involved in hibernation since the disorder seems to occur more frequently in the spring!

Genetic Theory

One study of genetic factors measured the concordance among known manic-depressives and their first-degree relatives.[53] The data from that study indicated that such relatives are about ten times more likely to be diagnosed as manic-depressive than are members of the general population. This would mean that the psychosis appears in about 5 percent of those who have a manic-depressive, first-degree relative and in about .05 percent of the general population. Another study found a particularly high risk for the manic-depressive disorder among first-degree relatives where the disorder appears early in life (early onset).[54]

The rates of manic-depression among monozygotic and dizygotic twins whose co-twins are diagnosed manic-depressive are revealing. It has been well-documented that the concordance rate in dizygotic twins is approximately 13 percent, while the concordance rate in monozygotic twins is over 60 percent.[55] The fact that the pathology is substantially higher among relatives of manic-depressives than in the general population, and that it increases as genetic similarity increases, lends support to a genetically-oriented explanation. Of course, these findings are subject to the same criticism as are the genetic studies of schizophrenia, namely that the similarity of the social environment is also greater among members of the same family (particularly identical twins) than among members of the general population.

[53]D. Rosenthal, *Genetic Theory and Abnormal Behavior* (New York: McGraw-Hill, 1970).

[54]Sue A. Marten and others, "Unipolar depression: a family history study," *Biological Psychiatry*, 4 (1972), pp. 205–213.

[55]E. S. Gershan, S. D. Targum, and L. R. Kessler, "Genetic studies and biologic strategies in the affective disorders," *Progress in Medical Genetics*, 2 (1977), pp. 103–125.

Biochemical Theories

One biochemical hypothesis postulates that mania and depression stem from autonomous fluctuations in the metabolic system. This idea was triggered by the observation that the person's mood shoots up or down as if he had taken a strong drug or a strong drink. The theory goes beyond this analogy, however, since metabolic dysfunction is suggested by a variety of somatic disturbances found among manic-depressives. These include loss of appetite, insomnia, cessation of menstruation, heart rate and circulatory alterations, skin difficulties, and gastrointestinal disorders. These symptoms appear because the autonomic nervous system is operating in a deranged manner. In turn the adrenal glands are not stimulated normally which results in an abnormal production of epinephrine. Depression is considered to be caused by a deficiency of epinephrine and mania by an excess of the same substance. Schildkraut has compiled indirect evidence for this position by noting such effects in persons receiving drugs known to cause abnormal production of epinephrine.[56]

A related biochemical hypothesis involves electrolyte metabolism. Two of the electrolytes, sodium and potassium chloride, play an important role in the functioning of the nervous system. Alterations in the distribution of sodium and potassium affect the excitability of the nerve cell. The level of intracellular sodium has been found to be elevated in manic-depressives.[57] Of course, these biochemical theories are subject to the criticism that observed metabolic fluctuations may not be autonomous occurrences but simply biochemical responses to psychological stress.

Morphological Theory

A third biogenic theory of the manic-depressive psychoses is morphological. Such "body-type" theories were criticized earlier on the grounds that much of the relationship between physique and mental illness can be explained through environmental factors. Nevertheless, research in this area has provided some intriguing speculations. Kretschmer, for example, detected a relationship between manic-depression and his so-called *pyknic* type of physique.[58] The pyknic constitution is equivalent to Sheldon's *endormophic* physique which is the short, stout, body-type, with a great deal of fat and a rotund face.[59] The theory has received some support from Rees,[60] but most research in this

[56]J. J. Schildkraut, "The catecholamine hypothesis of affective disorders: a review of support evidence," *American Journal of Psychiatry*, 122 (1965), pp. 507–522.

[57]A. Coppen, "The biochemistry of affective disorders," *British Journal of Psychiatry*, 113 (1967), pp. 1237–1264.

[58]Ernst Kretschmer, *Physique and Character*.

[59]W. H. Sheldon and S. S. Stevens, *The Varieties of Temperament*.

[60]L. Rees, "Constitutional factors and abnormal behavior."

area is plagued by poorly designed studies and consequently is not given widespread serious consideration.

The Environmental View of Manic-Depression

Psychoanalytic Theory

According to classical psychoanalytic theory, the potential for manic-depressive behavior is created in early childhood, specifically during the first two years of life, the oral stage.[61] During this period the infant's oral needs are insufficiently gratified. This causes fixation at the oral stage and a dependency on the instinctual needs that are peculiar to it. Such individuals remain excessively dependent on others, particularly for feelings of self-esteem. In manic-depressives, ordinary personality defenses fail to keep feelings of dependency and helplessness in the unconscious. As a result, these feelings eventually reemerge and cause the personality to regress to the state of helplessness found in infants.

The precipitating factor in the psychosis is the loss of an important love object such as a parent. This the individual cannot tolerate. The loss does not have to be experienced early in life, however. It may be the loss of a loved one through death or desertion in adult life as well. The precipitating event may also be a *perceived* loss, such as an imaginary cooling of interest on the part of a person's spouse. Whatever the nature of the loss, it is significant to the individual for it reanimates the childhood experience of separation from the mother or her affection. The manic-depressive behavior is considered to be a cry for love and a display of helplessness that is an appeal for lost affection and security. The loss is considered to be particularly important because it is perceived by the person as rejection which, in turn, causes anger. The feeling of anger cannot be tolerated, and it is turned inward onto the self in the form of self-blame and causes the person to feel unworthy and depressed. This sequence of events is highly likely to occur in dependent personalities and is fostered by traumatic infantile experiences. These individuals cannot loosen their emotional bonds with the lost love object, and they castigate themselves for the loss. Depression, then, is anger turned against oneself, according to psychoanalytic theory.

Those who have researched the etiology of the manic-depressive psychoses have not treated mania and depression separately because there is general agreement among psychoanalysts that mania is a reflection of an underlying depression. The manic's behavior is considered to be a way of defending against depression by denying its existence. Although he may appear self-confident, the manic is basically dependent on others. He denies the existence of every fact and thought that engen-

---

[61]Sigmund Freud, "Mourning and melancholia" in *Collected Papers* (London: Hogarth Press and the Institute of Psychoanalysis, 4, 1950).

ders depressed feelings and behaves in a way which is the exact opposite of his real feelings. This defense mechanism, known as reaction formation, is often found in a variety of situations involving depression. In tragic bereavement, for example, some people immediately immerse themselves in work and even amusements to convince themselves that they are not grief-stricken over a person's death. Thus, the manic state has an adjustive purpose in affirming that all is well. Depressed states, on the other hand, do not involve any such struggle to rectify the situation. Both mania and depression are considered equivalent psychologically. For this reason, psychoanalysts believe that discoveries about the origin of depression simultaneously shed light on the origin of mania.

The central proposition of psychoanalytic theory is that manic-depression has infantile origins. There is some evidence for this. Spitz has described depressive reactions in infants who experience a loss or reduction of the "emotional supplies" that had been provided by the mother.[62] When removed from a mothering environment, the children showed signs of social withdrawal, loss of appetite, difficulty in sleeping, and a slowdown of mental development. All of these symptoms parallel features of the adult manic-depressive syndrome and suggest that in infancy the stage is set for later depressive reactions. However, early parental loss may not necessarily mean eventual manic-depression but may, as some suggest, create a personality weakness that is *conducive* to manic-depression.[63]

Cognitive Theory

The cognitive theory of manic-depression emphasizes the effect of the person's thought processes on his emotions. This is a reverse of the psychoanalytic contention that the emotional condition of the person affects his beliefs. The cognitive theory thesis is that individuals suffer depression because they commit *errors of logic*. This theory is chiefly advanced by Beck who noted that his manic-depressive patients tended to distort normal experiences in the direction of self-blame.[64] From Beck's view, the manic-depressive operates within a set of logical principles that dispose him to conclude that he is a fool whose life is hopeless. These persons tend to draw sweeping conclusions on the basis of a single, often trivial, event (*overgeneralization*), to see themselves as losers in spite of a series of achievements (*minimization*), and to draw conclusions on the basis of one minor, negative element in a situation (*selective abstraction*).

The basic assumption of Beck's theory is that thoughts determine

---

[62]R. Spitz, "Infantile depression and the general adaptation syndrome" in *Depression*, eds. P. H. Hoch and J. Zubin (New York: Grune and Stratton), pp. 93–108.

[63]A. T. Beck, B. B. Sethi, and R. W. Tuthill, "Childhood bereavement and adult depression," *Archives of General Psychiatry*, 9 (1963), pp. 295–302; M. J. Abrahams and F. A. Whitlock, "Childhood experience and depression," *British Journal of Psychiatry*, 115 (1969), pp. 883–888.

[64]A. T. Beck, *Depression: Clinical, Experimental and Theoretical Aspects* (New York: Harper and Row, 1967).

emotions rather than the reverse. Although this is difficult to prove, there is some relevant evidence from experimental psychology. In one study of normal people, it was discovered that individuals become less fearful when they are led to believe beforehand that they will experience pleasure even when this belief is not confirmed.[65] However, at the present time, there is no empirical evidence that directly shows that the manic-depressive's emotions follow from his illogical thought patterns. Certainly manic-depressives exhibit a very negative view of the world, but this could well be the result of a psychological abnormality rather than the cause of it. In fact, Beck himself suggests that childhood experiences, such as the loss of a parent, establish the potential for the depressive's illogic.[66]

Behaviorist Theory

The behaviorist theory of manic-depression holds that the loss of accustomed positive social reinforcements is responsible for depression. Once a person loses an important source of rewards, he begins to behave differently, and this new type of behavior, that is, depression, may itself be reinforced by others. When for example, a depressed person receives sympathy and special dispensations from others, he may continue to feel depression long after it is appropriate because of the rewarding secondary gains.

According to this perspective, depression need not be preceded by the loss of a loved one, although such a loss is one common way in which a person's positive social reinforcements may be cut off. Thus, this theory is not inconsistent with the psychoanalytic theory; it is simply more general in that it interprets loss in a less specific way than psychoanalytic theory. The loss which engenders depression may be the loss of a job or of one's credit standing as well as of a loved one.

It is very difficult to assess this theory empirically since one would have to keep records of the number of social reinforcements depressed people receive each day. These data would then have to be compared with the number of social reinforcements received during the pre-psychotic state. This would be very difficult to do. Some studies, however, do partially confirm the behaviorist hypothesis that depression is caused by low levels of positively reinforced behavior. But there is presently no specific evidence that clearly demonstrates that a depression in mood is the simple result of low social reinforcement.

Family Structure Theory

There is also an environmental theory of manic-depression that centers on the family. It has been documented that the families of manic-

---

[65] J. H. Geer, "Reduction of stress in humans through nonveridical perceived control of aversive stimulation," *Journal of Personality and Social Psychology*, 16 (1970), pp. 731–738.

[66] Maria Kovacs and Aaron T. Beck, "Maladaptive cognitive structures in depression," *American Journal of Psychiatry*, 135 (1978), pp. 525–533.

depressives are unusually concerned about social approval.[67] The heads of these families have often failed to reach their desired status level, and consequently they place expectations on one of their children to change this through achievement. Case histories do frequently reveal that the manic-depressive's family was set apart, usually economically, from other families in the community.[68] The manic-depressives' families felt this difference keenly and reacted to it through attempts to raise the family's prestige in the community by excessive adherence to conventional standards of proper behavior.

The family structure theory helps to explain why only one of the children in these families developed manic-depression. This was the child who occupied a special place among his siblings; that is, he was designated as the one who should raise the family's prestige. He was often the best-endowed member of the family and was given great responsibility to achieve.[69] He felt different and alone because his special position exposed him to the envy of his siblings. To counteract this hostile envy, the future manic-depressive developed a pattern of belittling himself to conceal his real abilities. According to this theory, depression is the result of a belittling process.

The Status of Present Research

At the present time, the causes of the manic-depressive psychoses have not been entirely determined. There is considerable evidence that it can be caused by biogenic factors or environmental factors, or both. The only conclusion that can be drawn from the evidence that exists is that manic-depression, like schizophrenia, is a multicausal phenomenon. Hopefully, future research will elaborate the specific developmental process of the psychosis as well as assess the relative importance of each causal factor.

Involutional Melancholia

Prevalence

Kielholz found this psychosis to occur three times more frequently among women than among men.[70] He also observed that the condition

---

[67]See, for example, P. H. Lewinsohn and J. M. Libet, "Pleasant events, activity schedules and depressions," *Journal of Abnormal Psychology,* 79 (1972), pp. 291–95; J. M. Libet and P. H. Lewinsohn, "The concept of social skill with special reference to the behavior of depressed persons," *Journal of Consulting and Clinical Psychology,* 40 (1973), pp. 304–312.

[68]R. W. Gibson, M. B. Cohen, and R. A. Cohen, "On the dynamics of the manic-depressive personality," *American Journal of Psychiatry,* 115 (1959), pp. 1101–1107.

[69]L. C. Kolb, *Noyes' Modern Clinical Psychiatry,* pp. 378–379.

[70]P. Keilholz, "Diagnosis and therapy of the depressive states," *Docum. Geigy Acta Psychosom,* 1 (1959), p. 37.

occurs most frequently in women between fifty-one and sixty years of age and in men between the ages of sixty-one and sixty-five. Its onset in women is typically between three to seven years after menopause. Rates are highest among the lower social classes, the widowed and divorced, and urban dwellers.

Symptoms

An involutional psychotic reaction is one which appears for the first time in middle or late life, known as the involutional period. At this stage of life, the psychosis is most likely to be depressive or paranoid and is rarely manic or schizophrenic. Involutional paranoid reactions are not treated separately here but instead are grouped with other paranoid reactions presented at the end of this chapter.

The involutional period is associated with important biological changes. This is the period in which the activity of the endocrine and reproductive glands decreases which in turn, causes extensive changes in the metabolic and vegetative functions of the body. Such changes are known to produce an increased irritability of the nervous system. These physiological changes are doubly important because of their psychological implications in terms of a *perceived* loss of youth. Because of the special physiological and psychological features of involutional melancholia, it is not considered to be a modified manic-depressive reaction although depression is common to both disorders. Therefore, the diagnosis of involutional melancholia is not made for those with a history of a previous manic-depressive reaction.

The main symptom is agitated depression, that is, hyperactivity and quick body movements in addition to feelings of worthlessness, helplessness, and a lack of self-esteem. The onset of involutional melancholia is more gradual than in manic-depression. In most cases, several weeks elapse between the first symptoms and the fully developed disorder. These patients develop hypochondriacal fears, suffer from insomnia, and are given to spells of weeping. They often have delusions of sin and become preoccupied with impending death. In no other disorder is the risk of suicide so great. The following case exemplifies involutional melancholia in a male.

Mr. J., a 65-year-old man, was admitted to the hospital complaining of loss of appetite, insomnia, weight loss, depression, and constipation. His illness began six months earlier when he was retired from his job as a shop foreman. He had always enjoyed good physical health and never had emotional illness previously. He had no interests aside from his work and was described by his family as serious, conscientious, rigid, and hard-working. On admission he was obviously depressed and cried frequently. He showed psychomotor retardation, complained of difficulty in thinking, and was preoccupied with his symptom of constipation, believing that his bowels had dried up because he had no bowel movements. He was self-deprecatory and at times did not wish to eat because he thought he was unworthy.[71]

The Biogenic View of Involutional Melancholia

Because involutional melancholia occurs most frequently in women about the time of menopause, biogenic theorists propose that the disorder is a response to endocrine changes. If these changes do play a part in etiology, the specific pathological chemical pathways have not yet been identified. Instead, the biogenic school has focused its attention on the loss of physical appearance and bodily functions. The woman's loss of her childbearing ability is often experienced as the loss of her most fundamental of functions. Coupled with this loss is the concomitant decline of the woman's physical attractiveness and sexual desirability that reportedly occurs during this time of life.

Biological changes during this period affect men as well as women. The hair becomes sparse with age; the skin becomes dry and wrinkled. There is a tendency to fatigue more easily and to recover from exertion slowly. Visceral disturbances are also common, particularly gastrointestinal and urinary problems.

The feared loss of sexual function and sexual desire during the involutional period is not exclusively female. Men fear a loss of potency at this time also. It is doubtful, however, that men go through a structured sequence of hormonal changes comparable to menopause, which some have labeled a *male climacteric*. It is known, however, that the average frequency of sexual activity of fifty-year-old men is about half that of twenty-year-old men. While the sexual activity of males decreases with age, it is possible that it may be simply the male's response to the female's changed behavior. This is an interesting hypothesis in light of the fact that men do not usually lose procreative ability at this time of life, yet they often experience some of the same reactions as women.

If involutional melancholia is simply a psychiatric reaction to hormonal losses and metabolic changes which naturally occur at this time, it is logical to assume that the symptoms of the disorder should be eliminated by therapy which replaces the lost hormones. Such therapy has no influence at all on the disorder, however.[72] On the basis of this observation, the illness is generally considered to be environmental in origin. The disorder may be *associated* with biological changes, but there is no biogenic theory which satisfactorily explains the psychiatric response. The response must, therefore, be elicited by environmental factors.

---

[71]Reprinted from Clarence J. Rowe, *An Outline of Psychiatry* (Dubuque: William C. Brown Company, 1975), p. 190. By permission of publisher.

[72]A. M. Freedman and others, *Modern Synopsis of Comprehensive Textbook of Psychiatry* (Baltimore: Williams and Wilkins Co., 1972), p. 259.

The Environmental View of Involutional Melancholia

Sociocultural Theory

The involutional period of life is particularly threatening since many of the person's qualities which had determined their social status are suddenly lost. The loss has a powerful impact, especially on those who do not easily adjust to new situations and circumstances. Particularly vulnerable is the woman who is attractive to others largely because of her appearance and figure which she finds are suddenly giving way to wrinkles and middle age spread. This woman will be more threatened by these changes than will the woman who sees herself as admired for her intellect and occupational successes. The man who views himself as oriented toward physical strength and competition in athletics will suffer a greater blow to his self-image than the man who values maturity and judgment. The Don Juan, who sees himself mainly in terms of his abilities as a stud, will be particularly crushed when he enters a period in which there is decreased sexual activity. Such a person is likely to prove his continued attractiveness and ability by engaging in extramarital relationships. These affairs are usually doomed to failure because they were undertaken for the wrong reasons. In fact, they can often add to the trauma by introducing guilt and fears of getting caught.

To a woman, menopause can be a source of disappointment because she wants to have children and no longer can. This wish can be either conscious or unconscious but it is caused largely by the structure and limitations of the female role in the United States. This role has traditionally dictated that women are to find identity through experiences related to the child-bearing and child-rearing functions. Because the lives of American women are narrowed to such a limited set of fulfilling experiences, it is to be expected that they will become depressed during menopause since the menopause period signifies the loss of their major social function. In other words, the *social significance* that American culture attaches to menopause is itself pathological. Women who have not based their lives on their procreative and nurturing abilities are much less likely to be affected by involutional changes since other channels, such as a career, continue to yield satisfying rewards.

Involutional depression is also affected by cultural attitudes and behaviors which exalt youth and shun the aged. In this sense, the disorder represents a rebellion against aging. But the process of becoming old in America is threatening for reasons aside from the cultural idealization of youth. The problem is compounded by the fact that the aging person's view of the world is no longer appropriate in a society which has changed drastically over the individual's lifetime.[73] This results in a feel-

---

[73]For an empirical description of specific differences between the attitudes of younger and older Americans see Bernard J. Gallagher III, "An empirical analysis of attitude differences between three kin-related generations," *Youth and Society*, 5 (1974), pp. 327–349.

ing of having lost the roots of one's beliefs as well as having lost other people who share those beliefs. As if these problems were not enough, one's social circles begin to shrink through the death of friends and family which gives rise to a sense of social isolation. In addition, children begin to move away from home, causing elders to feel they are no longer needed or wanted. The loss of significant others is a major reason for the high suicide rate among aging people. Emile Durkheim explains this type of suicide as a response to a diminished sense of belonging in which people no longer feel needed by others.[74] *Egoistic suicide* is Durkheim's term for suicides which result from a person becoming alienated from others and lonely.

The psychotic melancholic state occurs later in men than in women because the common precipitating factor in men is the loss of one's job through retirement which usually occurs around age sixty-five. Retirement requires a renunciation of long-cherished interests and closes a major channel through which psychic energy had been expended. The individual's socioeconomic status is also jeopardized because the loss of a job usually means the loss of financial independence and social prestige, two important mechanisms for maintaining one's social integrity. Retirement is especially problematic for the man who has no outside interests to substitute for the job since he soon finds himself in the position of a bored husband at home disturbing the routines of his wife. Retirement can entail an even greater blow to independence and self-esteem for the person who must suffer living in the home of a child who does not want him and often treats the dependent parent with motives of revenge. The sudden shift from high prestige to low prestige is particularly difficult for men of this age to accept. Cameron explains that, "One of the chief obstacles in the way of adaptation to reduced power and prestige is that the same qualities of domination and possessiveness which helped a person to achieve and hold his position in life may now prevent his accepting any compromise in which domination and possession are minimal."[75]

The overriding factor in the etiology of involutional melancholia, in both men and women, is the recognition that the zenith of life has passed and earlier ambitions are not likely to be achieved. Combined with this is institutionalized prejudice against the aging person. This phenomenon, known as *ageism*, takes the form of stereotyping, myth-making, distaste, and/or avoidance of the aging person.[76] Much of ageism is fostered by some of society's inaccurate attitudes towards various parts of the aging process. For example, the considerable amount of misinformation which circulates concerning menopause causes some

[74]E. Durkheim, *Suicide* (New York: The Free Press, 1951), chapters 2 and 3.

[75]Norman Cameron, *Personality Development and Psychopathology,* (Boston: Houghton Mifflin, 1963), p. 633.

[76]Robert N. Butler, "Thoughts on aging," *American Journal of Psychiatry,* 135 (1978 Supplement), pp. 14–16.

women to fear its onset. A woman need not lose her sexual attractiveness or suffer the discomforts of menopause that old wives' tales describe, yet an adherence to these mythical beliefs tends to be self-fulfilling. Many women experience just what they fear and expect from menopause, including hot flashes and impending madness. Therefore, a labeling theory approach to involutional melancholia appears to be the most realistic since the disorder exemplifies the acting out of a socially prescribed role.

Psychoanalytic Theory

From a psychoanalytic point of view, the origin of involutional melancholia is equivalent to that of manic-depression except that involutional melancholia occurs at a later age. In both psychopathologies, the depression is considered to arise from feelings of grief and anger to a real, anticipated, or imagined loss. Therefore, it is not surprising that the psychosis is precipitated by such disturbing experiences as the breaking up of the home, particularly through the death of one's spouse or the loss of one's occupational position.[77] Other less common types of losses also drastically increase the probability of psychotic depression among people at the involutional stage. Among these are mutilating surgery, such as radical mastectomy, or the abrupt reduction in one's strength that often follows an illness or accident. All of these exacerbate the situation by adding physical and interpersonal chaos to a person who already feels helplessly unwanted in a society in which he had once occupied a useful position. Involutional melancholia clearly illustrates the negative effects of social factors on mental health.

Paranoid States

Prevalence

Some researchers contend that there are no reliable statistics concerning the prevalence of paranoid states. This lack of data exists for two reasons. First, paranoid reactions are common in the general population and occur in otherwise normal people without disabling them. Secondly, the nature of the disorder itself prevents many from seeking help and thus from being diagnosed as paranoid cases.

There is some evidence from records of those who do seek treatment that the rate of the disorder is not the same for all groups. Paranoia is infrequent in youth and occurs chiefly in the fourth, fifth and sixth decades of life. Rarely does it occur before the age of thirty. Paranoid states are more common among urban dwellers than among those from rural areas. They also appear more frequently among

---

[77]L. C. Kolb, *Noyes' Modern Clinical Psychiatry,* pp. 360–361.

divorced or separated persons. Additionally, paranoia is more common among those who have migrated from one part of the country to another and, in particular, among those who have left their native countries to live in another. Furthermore, it has been noted that paranoids are often people of superior intellectual endowment.

Symptoms

True paranoia is manifested by a *single delusional system* which is logically consistent within itself, that is, the delusion makes sense if one accepts the original premise, which is false. Paranoid impulses include suspiciousness, jealousy, hostility, and a tendency to accuse others of evil acts or intentions. These symptoms may occur in a variety of mental disorders, particularly schizophrenia, but the classification of paranoid states refers specifically to those patients whose central abnormality is some type of delusion. Given this definition, pure paranoid states are rare.

Paranoid persons usually remain in good contact with reality, much better than schizophrenics. Because of this contact, paranoid states are considered by some to occupy a position between the psychoses and the neuroses. Aside from true paranoia, another category is reserved for paranoid patients who are middle-aged. This is called the *involutional paranoid state.*

The symptoms of paranoia are described in terms of various delusional systems. The most common are *delusions of persecution.* A delusion of persecution is a belief that a person is the victim of some organized conspiracy or the prey of a particular person, usually of the same sex. The "enemy" is believed to be damaging the person's reputation, keeping him from attaining a goal, or even threatening him with physical harm.

Closely related to persecutory delusions are *delusions of jealousy.* Here the individual becomes overwhelmingly suspicious about a spouse or lover who is believed to be in love with someone else or to be promiscuous. This delusion, sometimes referred to as the *Othello syndrome,* typically deteriorates into persecutory ideas that the loved person is spying on or secretly attempting to kill the paranoid.

Paranoid *delusions of grandeur* are less common than persecutory beliefs. These persons believe that it is their mission to achieve great fame and success. Common cases include those who insist that they are the heir to a large fortune, or that they are God or some well-known important figure, such as Napoleon or Hitler. Other recurring grandiose delusions include the belief that one is the mastermind of a new scientific theory or invention. One type of grandiose delusional system includes erotic features and is most common among females. In this instance, the person is certain that someone of the opposite sex is trying to seduce her. The seducer is usually someone who is famous and extremely attractive but one with whom the person is not even acquainted. This is known as *erotomania*, or *De Clerambault's syndrome*, and is sometimes expressed by a belief that many people are overcome by the patient's charm.

In most of these delusions, the person recognizes that others see his ideas as ungrounded, but he is not influenced by their opinions. There is, however, a rare paranoid condition in which another person shares the identical delusion. This is known as *folie à deux* and is also referred to as *double insanity* or *psychosis of association*.[78] The two people are usually closely related, often members of the same family, who live in close, intimate association. One of the two is a dominant paranoid with the delusions while the other is a dependent, suggestible type who takes on the dominant one's delusions while in his company. Typically, the dominant individual is intellectually brighter, and the submissive individual incorporates the other's delusions because he identifies with the other's greater abilities. Most frequently, folie à deux involves a husband and wife, mother and daughter, or two sisters. It usually occurs in a setting where the two persons live in seclusion. For this reason, it occurs more frequently among women who are isolated within their homemaking roles and thus limited in their opportunities to pursue outside interests.

The following case presents many of the characteristics of paranoia, in this instance the individual suffered from persecutory delusions.

> Charles G., a bachelor of 49, became involved in a furious quarrel with bookies, men who place bets on racehorses. They insisted that he had not put money on a certain winning horse, which had unexpectedly won, and he insisted that he had. He was superficially a pleasant, reserved person, but on this occasion he worked himself into a towering rage. Fortifying himself with a few drinks at a nearby tavern, he returned to the bookies, demanding the payoff, shouting threats and insults at them and inviting them into the street to fight. When he found that this was ineffective, he returned to the hotel where he lived, still furious.
>
> Later on, as he pondered over the injustice and his rage, Charles began to worry over the possibility of retaliation against him. He recalled that bookies were supposed to have gangster protection. With these thoughts his fury changed to fright, and his recklessness changed to vigilance. The next day he noticed strangers loitering about the hotel lobby. They seemed to be watching him and making little signs which referred to him. An automobile full of men stopped in front of the hotel entrance. He now felt sure that he would be kidnapped, tortured, and killed. He barricaded himself in his room and arranged by telephone with a relative to flee the city the next morning. His relative accepted the patient's fears as facts.
>
> As Charles thought over his plans that evening, he suddenly "realized"

[78]Recently, the psychopathological state in which two persons share the same delusion, has been extended to include clinical reports of groups of people exhibiting such behavior. One researcher has noted that the phenomenon has occurred among whole households, apartment buildings, and neighborhoods. See Roger Bastide, *The Sociology of Mental Disorder* (New York: David McKay Co., 1972).

that the telephone wire had probably been tapped by the gangsters. So he fled alone in his car during the night to outwit the imagined pseudo-community . . .

In his long flight across the country he kept seeing signs that he was being trailed. He could not possibly doubt them. He decided that he would never be caught alive. When he reached the home of relatives a thousand miles away they at first believed his story. When, however, they found poison and a razor concealed in his clothing, and he admitted that he was planning suicide, they brought him to a psychiatric hospital to preserve his life.

Charles was courteous and pleasant in the hospital, but he always chose solitude when he could. Although he obviously wanted to confide in his therapist, and several times started to do so, he could never bring himself to talk about anything but trivialities and the plot. He persuaded a local pastor to visit him in the clinic. He then arranged a later meeting which was to be kept secret from the clinic. There was something in his past, he said, that he wanted to confess. As soon as the pastor had gone, however, Charles "realized" that he had made a terrible mistake. The pastor was dark-skinned. Therefore he must be a foreigner and a gangster in disguise. Charles made a suicidal attempt and when this was unsuccessful, he insisted upon transfer to a Veterans Hospital . . .[79]

The Environmental View of Paranoia

Paranoia clearly exemplifies the impact of social psychological factors on psychopathology. Unlike some of the other functional psychoses, the etiological factors involved in the paranoid states are entirely environmental. Genetic inheritance and other biogenic factors appear to play no part in the development of the disorder. Instead, etiological theories emphasize such causes as defenses of the personality against impulses unacceptable to society, traumatic life experiences, and exclusion of the individual by others.

Psychoanalytic Theory

The original psychoanalytic theory developed by Freud holds that paranoid delusions result from homosexual urges which are repressed in the unconscious but which strive for expression and satisfaction.[80] Much anxiety is generated by the threat of their expression. The anxiety is managed through the use of the defense mechanism of *projection*. The central feature of projection is attributing to other people socially unacceptable wishes that actually reside within the person himself. There is some controversy within psychoanalytic circles regarding the nature of

[79]From *Personality Development and Psychopathology*, by Norman Cameron. Copyright © 1963 by Norman Cameron. Reprinted by permission of Houghton Mifflin Company, pp. 488–489.

[80]Sigmund Freud, "A case of paranoia running counter to the psychoanalytical theory of the disease" in *Collected Papers*, Volume II, (London: Hogarth Press, 1959), pp. 150–161.

the repressed wishes. Alfred Adler, for example, contended that they were feelings of inferiority, not homosexuality. Perhaps both positions are valid. If so, the type of repressed wish may vary from patient to patient while the use of the projection mechanism remains constant. It is also possible that homosexual feelings and inferiority feelings coexist within the same person. If so, the inferiority would be the consequence of the person's homosexual orientation since society regards homosexuals as deviants.

Classical psychoanalytic theory holds that delusions of persecution originate from the homosexual thought, "I, a man, love him." This unacceptable feeling is converted into the opposite feeling of "I do not love him, I hate him." This is a reaction formation. Hating the other person of the same sex is also not acceptable so it is projected onto the other person and results in the belief that "I don't hate him, he hates me and persecutes me." Delusion of grandeur require an additional step involving *rationalization*. Rationalization is a defense mechanism whereby a person substitutes contrived reasons for the real reasons behind a belief or action. In this instance, the rationalization results in a grandiose delusion by offering the justification, "He hates me because I am someone very important."

Erotomania also fits with the psychoanalytic proposition that paranoia emanates from repressed homosexuality. Here, the unacceptable homosexual impulse is converted into the belief that the person is attracted to members of the opposite sex as society dictates. But this feeling still produces discomfort and is projected into the belief "I, a woman, do not love him, he is trying to seduce me."

If, in fact, homosexuality forms the basis of paranoia, society must then be considered partially responsible for the disorder because of the negative, stigmatizing way in which homosexuality is viewed. If psychoanalytic theory is correct, paranoia could never develop among people living in a society in which homosexuality is an acceptable style of life. What evidence is there for homosexuality being etiologically related to paranoia? One supporting fact is that an unusually high percentage of paranoids are single or divorced. Divorce or never marrying at all is a logical choice for those who are not oriented toward heterosexuality. But it is also possible that since paranoids are prone to be hostile and angry, others see them as undesirable partners. If they do marry, their marital life is usually so full of disharmony that it ends in divorce. There is also evidence for the homosexual thesis in the form of clinical reports stating that paranoids have disturbed sexual development that rarely result in mature heterosexual behavior.[81] In addition, it is reported that the person seen as a persecutor by the paranoid is, as a rule, a person of the patient's own sex who was previously loved.[82]

[81] Norman Cameron, *Personality Development and Psychopathology*, p. 479.
[82] H. Nunberg, *Principles of Psychoanalysis* (New York: International Universities Press, 1955), p. 218.

Parental Treatment Theory

There is another theory of paranoia that is also psychoanalytic but places a greater emphasis on parental treatment of preparanoids than on sexual impulses. From this view, paranoia is essentially a lack of basic trust in others that stems from an early childhood which was filled with tension and anxiety. The feeling of trust allows an infant to feel confident that someone (usually the parent) will relieve intolerable frustrations. This was often not the experience of paranoids, however. They were frequently raised by parents who were authoritarian, harsh, and cruel and who rejected them. This created feelings of inadequacy and a self-image of a "bad" child, both of which are difficult to accept. The feelings are projected onto others who are seen as sadistic persecutors because the patient's own sadism is denied and projected. Where does this unusually high sadistic drive come from? It originates within the childhood situation; the paranoid's parents raised a baby who was over-stimulated, aggressive, and angry. The parents allowed the infant to freely express the rage and anger which they themselves created by their indifference to his needs. In short, the paranoid patient was treated sadistically in infancy and reacted with an uncontrollable fury which the parents often enjoyed.

The sadistic treament of the child may not be limited to physical abuse. Often it encompasses more than that because a variety of experiences, such as maternal coldness, belittling, or teasing, may *seem* cruel to a child. Teasing is particularly threatening at the age when a child is facing the demands of toilet-training. At this time, a parent can easily push the child into temper tantrums by mocking his shortcomings. Such traumatic experiences often arrest the child's personality development at a period during which he is under parental control. For this reason, others are seen as criticizing and threatening figures just as the parents were in earlier years.

Labeling Theory

There is an alternative etiological view which considers paranoia to be a problem within others rather than in the individual. This perspective is fostered by labeling theorists who feel that paranoid persons are not in fear of imagined conspiracies but are reacting to actual rejection by others.[83] Furthermore, this school contends that psychosexual needs or early childhood traumas do not account for the main features of paranoia because the individual is not the primary framework for the study of paranoia. Rather, society is.

The person who becomes known as paranoid is simply an individual who cannot be trusted by others because he threatens to expose

---

[83]For a lucid presentation of this view see E. M. Lemert, "Paranoia and the dynamics of exclusion," *Sociometry*, 25 (1962), pp. 2–20.

secrets. Thus, many people consider the paranoid person "dangerous." The paranoid process begins with interpersonal difficulties between the individual and his family, neighbors, fellow workers, or others in the community. Frequently, these difficulties arise from a bona fide issue which involves an important loss of status for the individual, such as the loss of a job or even a series of failures. Others fear retaliation from the paranoid person. This situation lays the groundwork for a conspiracy among those seeking to oust him. The conspiracy is integrated by a common commitment against the individual, and it demands secrecy and loyalty from its members.

Labeling theory contends that any supposed delusions exhibited by paranoid people are realistic reactions to actual social exclusion. The paranoid then plays the role of the mistrusted person. This becomes a way of life that provides him with an identity he may not otherwise have had. There is evidence that, at times, paranoid persons who claim they are being harassed by others may be reporting facts, not delusions. This evidence takes the form of factors known to precipitate paranoid reactions. In many cases, the precipitating situation involved some threat to the person's social role, such as the end of a husband-wife relationship or the loss of other sources of emotional gratification. However, it seems unlikely that *all* cases of paranoia result from exclusion by others, simply because such a view fails to explain why one individual reacts with paranoia while another remains unchanged by the same experience.

Conclusions

The functional psychoses involve a variety of symptoms that are only matched by the diversity of opinion about their causes. The most common psychosis in the United States is schizophrenia, a severe alteration of thought that has a number of subtypes. There is considerable evidence that schizophrenia is biogenic in origin and there are also many data pointing to environmental determinants. The biogenic theories are threefold; first, there is the proposition that the disorder is genetic as evidenced by a marked concordance among monozygotic twins; second, there is the biochemical argument that schizophrenia results from an abnormal production of body chemicals that in turn disturb the central nervous system; third, there is the morphological approach that considers schizophrenia to result from a physical constitution with slender, fragile body traits.

Environmental theories of schizophrenia are numerous. According to psychoanalytic theory, severe fixation at the oral stage of psychosexual development is the cause of schizophrenia. This results in a regression to the infantile stage at which the individual does not yet have the ability to differentiate between self and other. This same weakness is considered to be the central symptom of schizophrenia in which the individual's fantasies constitute reality. The cognitive explanation of schizophrenia appears to be more descriptive of the mind-altering nature of the disorder than a causal theory. Cognitive theorists see schizophrenia as a breakdown in communicative abilities without really explaining what caused the breakdown.

There are a number of theories of schizophrenia that emphasize the social environment. Behaviorists, for example, hold that the disorder is the result of being socialized by mentally disturbed parents. Other intrafamilial theories include the double bind hypothesis which holds that schizophrenia is fostered by parents that treat their children in inconsistent and mutually exclusive ways. For instance, they expect their children to develop feelings of autonomy, yet they expect the children to be overly dependent on them at the same time. Some hold that this experience is particularly likely to happen to those born last in a large family. The theory linked with macrosocial forces is the social class hypothesis which views schizophrenia as the result of living under the miserable conditions of socioeconomic deprivation. There is a significant proportion of the schizophrenic population with lower class status but it remains unclear whether membership in the lower class preceeded schizophrenia or whether an underlying schizophrenic proneness causes one to drift into the lower class. Existentialists see schizophrenia resulting from insurmountable life conditions which are more likely to occur among the socially and economically deprived.

Manic-depressive psychoses, psychotic alterations of mood, also have different subtypes and a number of etiological theories. Most of these theories, however, consider depression, not mania, to be the fundamental problem. There is impressive evidence for the role of genetic forces in the development of this disorder since concordance rates among monozygotic twins are rather high. Biochemical hypotheses postulate the existence of a metabolic dysfunction producing an abnormal amount of body chemicals. The morphological school considers the disorder to originate from personalities doomed to live in a fat body.

Environmental theories of the manic-depressive psychoses involve a number of positions. The psychoanalysts' theory is similar to their theory of schizophrenia in that fixation at the oral stage is believed to lay the foundation for manic-depressive reactions later in life. But the nature of the fixation varies in the two disorders. The manic-depressive's fixation results in a sense of dependency on others that is normal for infants but pathological for adults. This orientation toward dependency, coupled with the loss of an important love object later, engenders a manic-depressive reaction. The cognitive school holds that manic-depressives are individuals who commit logical errors that force them to conclude that they are worthless people. The behaviorist school contends that manic-depression is a reaction to a loss of rewarding reinforcements. Thus this proposition is not inconsistent with the psychoanalytic one since both consider a loss to be etiologically essential. There is also a family-related theory of the manic-depressive psychoses. According to this view, manic-depressives are those who had unrealistic expectations placed on them by their parents. Often this resulted from an excessive concern with status attainment by the parents who failed to achieve their aspirations and placed the burden of the accomplishment on one of their children instead.

The key to the causes of involutional melancholia is in its epidemiology since it is most common among men and women when each group is most vulnerable to an important social loss. This is menopause for women and forced retirement for men. The disorder is a blatant example of the negative influence of societal attitudes on mental health. Essentially, the inappropriate attitudes toward aging that are fostered by American culture are responsible for the high rate of psychiatric response to social experiences that signify growing old.

The paranoid states are environmental in origin. According to psychoanalytic theory, paranoia is the projection of unacceptable motives within a person onto others. Since the unacceptable wishes are typically considered to be homosexual, social attitudes are important contributory factors because of negative, stigmatizing attitudes toward homosexuality in American society. The parental treatment theory describes paranoia rising from sadistic child-rearing practices producing a negative self-image which is in turn projected onto others. The labeling theory perspective postulates that paranoia was created by others, not the individual. In short, labeling theorists view paranoia as a realistic response to actual rejection by others who have formed a conspiracy against a person.

6

Personality
Disorders

An Overview

The APA defines personality disorders as a "... group of disorders ... characterized by deeply ingrained maladaptive patterns of behavior that are perceptibly different in quality from psychotic and neurotic symptoms. Generally, these are life-long patterns, often recognizable by the time of adolescence or earlier."[1] These patients are considered to be different from psychotics and neurotics because they do not have symptoms in the usual sense of the word; their problems are not experienced subjectively but as problems in living resulting from their maladaptive behavior. Typically, their actions are self-defeating and center around their pursuit of instinctual drives, their adjustment to society, or relationships with other people. In a nutshell, personality disorders refer to patients who are free of neurotic and psychotic symptoms but who behave pathologically. However, while this may be the official designation of these conditions, it is not a realistic one because this category includes miscellaneous disturbances whose common grouping has caused much confusion. Many of the disorders in the personality disorder category differ importantly from one another. DSM–II states that these patients experience minimal subjective anxiety yet certain of these disturbances are preneurotic conditions characterized by much anxiety.[2] In addition,

---

[1]*Diagnostic and Statistical Manual of Mental Disorders,* 2nd ed. (Washington: D.C.: American Psychiatric Association, 1968), p. 41.

[2]Merrill T. Eaton, Jr. and Margaret H. Peterson, *Psychiatry* (New York: Medical Examination Publishing Company, Inc., 1969), p. 121.

a number of disorders in this category are known to be antecedents of a psychotic breakdown.

To alleviate some of this terminological confusion, personality disorders are divided here into three types: *prepsychotic states, preneurotic states,* and *pure personality disorders.* The sexual disorders are also considered to be personality disorders in DSM–II although they are classified separately as *psychosexual disorders* in DSM–III. Here they are treated separately in Chapter 7.

The prepsychotic states differ from the functional psychoses chiefly in degree; they are less severe, less disabling, and do not involve the total personality as the psychoses typically do. In short, prepsychotic persons do not present the gross disturbances of mood or thought of psychotics. The prepsychotic states include the *schizoid personality* (preschizophrenic), the *cyclothymic personality* (premanic-depression), and the *paranoid personality* (preparanoid state).

Neurosis is distinguished from the preneurotic state in that the neurotic conflict is more overt in neurosis. Like the neurotic, the preneurotic suffers personality distortion, but he manages to achieve a stable life style which incorporates the distortion because he is not compelled to use the exaggerated defenses of the neurotic. The difference between the two, then, is more a matter of degree than kind. The same underlying conflict can cause differing degrees of impairment in different individuals. The reason for this differential impairment is not yet known, although some have suggested that preneurotic states become neuroses when the person encounters threatening stresses such as those discussed in Chapter 11.[3] The preneurotic states include the *hysterical personality* (pre-hysterical neurosis), the *obsessive-compulsive personality* (preobsessive-compulsive neurosis), and the *asthenic personality* (preneurasthenic neurosis).

The pure personality disorders generally do not develop into other psychopathologies. They do not involve anxiety but external problems in living. For this reason, they are often referred to as "acting out" conditions. Most of these disorders condemn the person to repeated violations of society's norms. It is these disorders that are consistent with the DSM–II definition—maladaptive, lifelong, and with few subjective symptoms. They include the *antisocial personality,* the *explosive personality,* the *passive aggressive personality,* and the *inadequate personality.*

Since there is a general etiological equivalence between the preneurotic states and neuroses and the prepsychotic states and psychoses, they are not considered here in any great detail to avoid repetition. This chapter is devoted mainly to the pure personality disorders, particularly the widely researched, antisocial type. Etiological theories of pure personality disorders are largely environmental. Biogenic theories exist, but they have generally failed to produce confirming evidence. The ac-

[3]See Salvatore R. Maddi, "The existential neurosis," *Journal of Abnormal Psychology,* 72 (1967), pp. 311–325; Norman Cameron, *Personality Development and Psychopathology: A Dynamic Approach* (Boston: Houghton Mifflin, 1963), p. 641.

cepted theories frequently emphasize the causal role of childhood events, such as identification with a significant person who displays similar personality traits or other experiences which encourage maladaptive behavior.

The Antisocial Personality

Symptoms

Perhaps no other disorder is more clearly related to society than is the antisocial personality. This type of person suffers from a weak or absent superego, the intrapsychic representative of society. DSM–II reserves the term for individuals who are basically unsocialized and whose behavior repeatedly conflicts with society's expectations. These conflicts ensue because the demands of the person's instincts have not been adjusted to the demands of society.

The central symptom is a defect in the conscience, technically known as *superego lacunae*. This allows the person to pursue a lifestyle that regularly opposes the laws and mores of society. Typically, immoral behavior is exhibited in many aspects of life although, as children, antisocial personalities may have been immoral only in particular areas.[4] They may have been thieves, but not truants, or they may have set fires but behaved normatively otherwise. At that age, the superego appears to be "punched out" with regard to certain norms. Because these persons lack a well-developed conscience, they can freely pursue antisocial activities without the pain of guilt. Psychiatrists typically report that antisocial individuals *act* as if they are indifferent to the social impact of their behavior. The truth is they are not acting, they really are indifferent.

Since the superego defect causes antisocial personalities to be callous to societal norms, they live by the pleasure principle; their primary concern is immediate gratification of instinctual impulses. Freud recognized this personality type and referred to it as the "erotic type" because such people seek only pleasure regardless of the welfare of others.

Since antisocial individuals persistently violate the laws and mores of society, it is other people who suffer, rather than the violators themselves. The fact that they have no remorse for the harm they do others exacerbates the problem further. In fact, they have an inner conviction that they are special people who are immune to society's rules and, in a sense, they are, for they have no internalized element of society. These attitudes, combined with a superego defect and an extreme sense of narcissism, render antisocial personalities dangerous people. When they are frustrated, they can spontaneously commit a number of offenses including robbery and rape. This is the type of person who could be-

---

[4]Mary E. Giffin, Adelaide M. Johnson, and Edward M. Litin, "The transmission of superego defects in the family," in *A Modern Introduction to the Family,* eds. Norman W. Bell and Ezra F. Vogel (New York: The Free Press, 1968), pp. 670–682.

come a profit murderer or "hit man" because he feels no guilt in committing such crimes. Rarely does he take his own life through suicide simply because he is in love with himself.

The antisocial individual does not experience any subjective discomfort from his condition as the neurotic does. His only anguish stems from the fear of getting caught and being punished for moral or legal violations. If he is punished, he is likely to repeat his behavior. He does not learn from experience since punishment can not create a conscience.[5] When he does get into trouble, he usually projects all blame on to others. Unreliability and chronic lying are also common features.

If the antisocial person has any goals, they are immediate and directed toward self-aggrandizement, the acquisition of money, and the use of others for pleasure. Using others is a particular skill of the antisocial person since he is often a gifted, intelligent individual with superficial charm.[6] These skills, along with an attractive physical appearance, make it easy for him to carry out his plots adeptly. If the antisocial individual is questioned about moral and legal principles, he can verbalize all the correct rules, but he does not really understand them or believe them in the way that others do. Cleckley calls this verbal facade the "mask of sanity."[7]

Diagnostic Problems

This psychopathology has had a unique history in psychiatry. The antisocial personality was originally called *moral insanity* by Prichard in 1835. This label was later changed to avoid a moral issue which is foreign to modern psychiatry.[8] In the latter part of the nineteenth century, the disorder was called *constitutional psychopathic inferior,* a reflection of the somatogenic orientation of the time. Other terms that have been used are *anethopathy, semantic dementia,* and, more recently, *psychopathic* and *sociopathic.* They all refer to the personality disorder which is now classified as antisocial.

The label for this condition continually changes, in part, because there is confusion regarding the personalities which should be included within the category. Some feel that so many different types of personalities can be considered antisocial that the term has become a diagnostic wastebasket.[9] This is true to an extent since individuals with any of a number of disorders may engage in occasional antisocial behavior as occurs among those with organic brain syndromes and schizophrenia. In these instances, however, the antisocial behavior is only a consequence of

[5]Michael Croft, "The meanings of the term 'psychopath,'" in *Psychopathic Disorders,* ed. Michael Croft (Oxford: Pergamon Press, 1966), p. 4.

[6]David Abrahamsen, *The Psychology of Crime* (New York: Columbia University Press, 1967), p. 135.

[7]H. Cleckley, *The Mask of Sanity* (St. Louis, Mo.: Mosby, 1964).

[8]Karl Menninger, *Whatever Became of Sin?* (New York: Hawthorn Books, Inc., 1973).

[9]Cason claims that there are 202 variations of the antisocial diagnosis. See H. Cason, "Psychopath and psychopathic," *Journal of Criminal Psychopath,* 4 (1943), p. 522.

a qualitatively different condition. Other cases involving antisocial behavior and an additional disorder are more difficult to unravel. For example, many antisocial individuals indulge in alcohol and narcotics.[10] It is generally considered that the antisocial condition establishes a predisposition for drug abuse, but it is also possible that chronic drug intake can generate a disregard for social laws and customs.

A further example of a possible overlap between the antisocial diagnosis and another condition is the so-called *ganser syndrome*. This is a psychotic-like state that occurs among hardened criminals. The central symptom is a dissociation from the social environment which typically occurs in a prisoner who has received a long term sentence. This is a temporary condition, however, and usually occurs when the antisocial individual feels doomed.

The most common difficulty in diagnosing the antisocial disorder involves the recognition that not all criminals are antisocial. Since the antisocial label is applied from the viewpoint of the host culture, behavior which is acquired in a deviant subculture is sometimes confused with the antisocial condition. Actually many members of deviant subcultures, particularly delinquents, are conforming to the criminal norms of their subculture, just as conventional people conform to the norms of mainstream society.[11] The activity of such people who follow criminal pursuits but who are psychiatrically normal is called *dyssocial behavior*. This is a personality type that is different in important ways from the antisocial type since the dyssocial person can form stable relationships with others although they may be members of a crime gang. In addition, the dyssocial person can defer pleasure, learn from experience, and feel guilt.[12] None of these qualities exist within the antisocial personality.

A further classification problem involves separating some types of neurotics from antisocial personalities. This seems to contradict the usual portrayal of the neurotic as an anxious, guilt-ridden person who internalizes conflicts. Generally, this is true, but some neurotics "act out" their conflicts by expressing their psychopathology antisocially. However, the antisocial personality and the "acting out" neurotic are mirror opposites in terms of superego strength. The antisocial individual's superego is weakly formed, and this permits a guiltless pursuit of unconventional activities. The "acting out" neurotic, on the other hand, is driven by a harsh superego which burdens him with excessive guilt. In this instance, the neurotic desires to be apprehended and caught to relieve an unconscious sense of guilt.[13] In short, he seeks punishment.

The psychiatric concept of the antisocial personality is much nar-

---

[10]David Abrahamsen, *The Psychology of Crime,* p. 139.

[11]S. Kirson Weinberg, "Social psychological aspects of acting-out disorders and deviant behavior," in *The Sociology of Mental Disorders,* ed. S. Kirson Weinberg (Chicago: Aldine, 1967), pp. 150–158.

[12]Merrill T. Eaton, Jr. and Margaret H. Peterson, *Psychiatry,* p. 257.

[13]L. C. Kolb, *Noyes' Modern Clinical Psychiatry* (Philadelphia: W. B. Saunders, 1973), p. 506.

rower than is the concept of delinquency. This is evidenced in a national study of crime which concluded that most delinquents operate in the company of their peers.[14] That study estimated that between 60 and 90 percent of all delinquent acts are committed with companions. The fact that group support is so common to delinquent activity signifies that many criminals are not antisocial since, by definition, antisocial personalities are incapable of having group ties.

Legal Issues

Other definitional issues regarding antisocial behavior involve the question of criminal intent and mental illness. These concepts are incompatible in the United States. If a bank has been robbed or a woman brutally raped, legally there is no criminal act unless the perpetrator of the act is adjudged mentally responsible. The decision is often a function of the particular social circumstances involved in the case. For example, if each of two women is booked for her fourth shoplifting offense within a year's time, the court decisions about the two cases may be quite different. If one woman was on welfare with a large family, her shoplifting is seen as a rational act, and she becomes criminally responsible. She will be pronounced guilty and be fined or sentenced to jail. If the other woman is married to a rich physician, she is not considered to be in need and therefore must have shoplifted because of an "unreasonable need." The judge finds it impossible to perceive any criminal intent. The woman is "clearly" ill and is committed to see a psychiatrist once a week as an outpatient.

Certain laws are designed to separate mentally ill people who commit criminal acts from mentally competent people who do so. One such law is the well-known M'Naghten rule. It provides that a person may establish a defense of insanity if he did not know that he was doing something wrong in the eyes of society. A major difficulty with this principle is that it excludes those with antisocial personality disorders since they know that others disapprove of their behavior. This is an inappropriate way to define mental illness because many disturbed people are adjudged to have criminal responsibilities and are then punished with a jail term. The psychiatric reality is that they often have a superego defect which requires psychiatric help. However, since the M'Naghten rule is not sophisticated enough to detect various types of disturbances, antisocial personalities are sent to prison rather than a psychiatric facility where they might be helped. In prison their condition usually deteriorates since they are placed with other criminals with whom they exchange tricks of the trade in "factories of crime."

The "right-wrong" concept of the M'Naghten rule is currently the most prevalent ruling even though more realistic decisions have been

[14]*The Challenge of Crime in a Free Society,* Report by the President's Commission on Law Enforcement and Administration of Justice (Washington, D.C.: Government Printing Office, 1967), p. 66.

made. The Durham test of sanity is closer to psychiatric reality than the M'Naghten rule. According to this test, a person is not criminally responsible if his unlawful act was the product of a mental illness. Mental illness is determined by psychiatrists' evaluations conveyed to the court. This approach has also proven difficult since psychiatrists often disagree regarding the mental status of the accused. Some psychiatrists find very few accused criminals to be abnormal, while other psychiatrists report severe abnormalities in almost all of the accused people they examine.[15]

The American Law Institute proposed its own guidelines on criminal responsibility in an effort to specify the M'Naghten and Durham rulings.[16] According to these proposals, a person is not criminally responsible for his conduct if he has a mental illness which inhibits his understanding of the wrongfulness of his behavior. This approach is also problematic since it can be argued that the antisocial individual does understand the wrongfulness of his acts, as evidenced by the fact that he tries to avoid getting caught. To be sure, there is a wide gap between the APA's guidelines of mental disorder and what the court system is willing to officially designate as legal insanity. Consequently, many mentally ill people are sent to prison just as they were centuries ago.

Prevalence

It is impossible to ascertain the real number of antisocial personalities in the United States because they are not the type of patients who seek treatment on their own. If they are treated, it is usually after having been caught by authorities and referred for psychiatric evaluation. Thus those antisocial personalities who are never arrested go unrecognized. Additionally, those who were arrested but not adjudged in need of psychiatric care are also overlooked because of the unrealistic legal guidelines which determine criminal responsibility. Apparently the rate of this disorder is rising if the national crime rate can be used as a rough barometer. Crime is dramatically increasing in the United States although some of it is carried out by normal people.[17]

From records of diagnosed antisocial personalities, it is reported that most come from lower class families living in slum areas. The prevalence by sex is predominantly male. Estimates are that five to ten times as many males as females are diagnosed as antisocial.[18] The condition occurs more frequently in males with muscular, athletic builds, the mesomorphic physique.[19] Typically, the antisocial behavior is manifested

[15]G. D. Gulevick and P. G. Bourne, "Mental illness and violence," in *Violence and the Struggle for Existence*, eds. D. N. Daniels, M. F. Gilula, and F. M. Ochberg (Boston: Little, Brown, 1970).

[16]American Law Institute, "Model penal code: proposed official draft," (Philadelphia: The American Law Institute, 1962).

[17]Marshall B. Clinard, *Sociology of Deviant Behavior* (New York: Holt, Rinehart and Winston, 1974), pp. 264–265.

[18]Alfred M. Freedman and others, *Modern Synopsis of Comprehensive Textbook of Psychiatry*, (Baltimore: Williams and Wilkins, 1972), p. 368.

before the age of fifteen. There is also a high rate of antisocial personality types reported among adopted children.[20]

The Biogenic View of Antisocial Behavior

EEG Abnormalities

There have been a number of attempts to demonstrate that the antisocial disorder is caused by biogenic factors. Some researchers note that criminal antisocials frequently have a history of head injury or epilepsy.[21] The relationship between antisocial behavior and brain tissue impairment has been further demonstrated by a number of studies using electroencephalographic (EEG) procedures to record the electrical activity of the brain. In thirteen of fourteen such studies, antisocial individuals showed some form of EEG abnormality.[22] The proportion of subjects with abnormal patterns of brain activity ranges from 31 to 58 percent in various studies. In this connection, one report further finds that EEG abnormalities vary with type of antisocial traits; fire-setting is associated with high EEG abnormality, while stealing is associated with low EEG abnormality.[23] However, it is questionable whether the EEG procedure is a valid way of assessing those activities of the brain that are related to thought and behavior since it records only a small sample of activity from the brain surface.

Genetic Theory

Toward the end of the nineteenth century, long before any speculation on EEG brain patterns, Cesare Lombroso tried to apply Charles Darwin's theory of evolution to the antisocial personality. He theorized that the disorder was genetically inherited, in short, that a person was born with delinquent inclinations, or what some call a "bad seed." This theory was popularized in the early 1900s through two alarming studies of antisocial behavior among relatives. One of these was the study of the Juke family.[24] The original Jukes were a "socially incompetent" couple who procreated many descendants. More than 700 of their descendants were traced over five generations. Only a handful had become socially acceptable members of society.

---

[19]S. Glueck and E. Glueck, *Physique and Delinquency* (New York: Harper and Row, 1956).

[20]Nathan M. Simon and Audrey G. Senturia, "Adoption and psychiatric illness," *American Journal of Psychiatry*, 122 (1966), pp. 858–868.

[21]Michael Croft, "The causation of psychopathic disorder" in *Psychopathic Disorders*, p. 62.

[22]R. J. Ellingson, "Incidence of EEG abnormality among patients with mental disorders of apparently nonorganic origin: a criminal review," *American Journal of Psychiatry*, 3 (1954), pp. 263–275.

[23]David Abrahamsen, *The Psychology of Crime*, pp. 138–139.

[24]Richard L. Dugdale, *The Jukes: A Study in Crime, Pauperism and Heredity*, 4th ed. (New York: Putnam, 1910).

A more famous study was of the Kallikak family.[25] Martin Kallikak married a feeble-minded woman. Only 46 of 480 of their descendants were normally competent members of society, as defined by the investigators. Later Martin married a respected woman. Only 3 of the 496 descendants of the second marriage were said to be "somewhat degenerate." Many of the others were in prominent social positions.

Very little can be concluded from these two early studies of antisocial behavior because they were filled with methodological problems. They failed to differentiate antisocial behavior from mental retardation. Furthermore, they did not *directly* measure the association between antisocial disorder and genetic factors since they studied only family members, not twins.

In the 1930s, more sophisticated studies of hereditary influences were done using monozygotic twins. Lange found thirteen antisocial criminals in Germany each of which had an identical twin. Ten of the thirteen twins were antisocial themselves.[26] However, a study of nineteen monozygotic twin pairs in the United States did not support a genetic explanation of the antisocial disorder.[27] The twins in the United States' study had been separated at an early age and raised separately. No significant concordance for the antisocial disorder was demonstrated, leaving the theory of genetic transmission open to question. The results of another German study, this one by Kranz, also points toward the importance of environmental factors.[28] Kranz found a 54 percent rate of concordance among fraternal twins of the same sex but only a 14 percent rate among fraternal twins of the opposite sex. The marked difference between concordance rates of same-sex fraternal twins and opposite-sex fraternal twins is critical because it demonstrates the greater effect of differing child-rearing practices over genetic similarity.

Since the heredity transmission theory has been laid to rest, a new genetic theory of antisocial behavior has appeared. The central thesis of this theory is that antisocial persons, who are usually males, have an extra male (Y) chromosome. This chromosomal abnormality (XYY) is believed to cause aggressive behavior which can lead to antisocial acts. However, the XYY pattern, considered to produce "supermales," does not account for many cases of antisocial disorder. Rosenthal has noted that only about 1.5 percent of antisocial criminals have this chromosomal make-up.[29] In fact, any link-up between the antisocial diagnosis and the XYY pattern may be due to the physical traits exhibited by these men; they are frequently large and riddled with acne, both of which may predispose evaluators to see them as deviants.

---

[25]Henry H. Goddard, *Feeblemindedness: Its Cause and Consequences* (New York: Macmillan, 1923).

[26]J. Lange, *Crime as Destiny* (London: George Allen, 1931).

[27]H. H. Newman, F. N. Freeman, and K. J. Holzinger, *Twins: A Study of Heredity and Environment* (Chicago: Chicago University Press, 1937).

[28]H. Kranz, *Lebenschicksale Krimineller Zwillinge* (Berlin: Springer-Verlag, 1936).

[29]D. Rosenthal, *Genetic Theory and Abnormal Behavior* (New York: McGraw-Hill, 1970).

Biochemical Theory

There is an additional biogenic aspect to antisocial behavior which is biochemical. Lykken has demonstrated that antisocial personality types experience less anxiety about socially unpleasant situations than do normal people.[30] It is possible that antisocial individuals are less sensitive to social mores due to a defect in the autonomic nervous system that in turn reduces arousal levels. If this is true, then they should act like normal people in their response to socially unpleasant situations when their anxiety levels are increased. This hypothesis was tested by Schachter and Latone who injected a group of antisocial personalities with adrenalin, a chemical agent which stimulates the autonomic nervous system.[31] Under the influence of the adrenalin, individuals in the group exhibited increased anxiety in response to socially unpleasant situations. It is possible that their thirst for excitement and their inability to deal with boredom and routine may be the result of a biochemical state of lowered arousal. In this view, then, their "thrill-seeking" behavior may be an attempt to increase their level of arousal to a normal state. It has been demonstrated experimentally that antisocial people perform less well than do normal people in tedious, monotonous tasks,[32] and studies show also that they clearly prefer novel situations over familiar ones.[33] It is clear that antisocial people do not have the same emotional make-up as most people do since they feel no anxiety in response to behavior which normally elicits guilt. It is unclear, however, whether this is a direct result of a neural dysfunction. If it is, the specific biochemical alterations have yet to be uncovered. It is more likely that any abnormalities in their nervous systems are in response to pathologic factors in the psychosocial environment since there are simply too many common family background features among antisocial individuals to justify a purely biochemical theory.

The Environmental View of Antisocial Behavior

Psychoanalytic Theory

Psychoanalytically, antisocial behavior is viewed as the improper response of the ego and superego to id impulses, resulting from a poorly formed superego which leaves the ego at the mercy of the instincts.

[30]D. T. Lykken, "A study of anxiety in the sociopathic personality," *Journal of Abnormal and Social Psychology,* 55 (1957), pp. 6–10.

[31]S. Schachter and B. Latone, "Crime, cognition, and the autonomic nervous system," in *Nebraska Symposium on Motivation,* ed. D. Levine, vol. 12 (Lincoln: University of Nebraska Press, 1964).

[32]J. B. Ovvis, "Visual monitoring performance in three subgroups of male delinquents" (unpublished master's thesis, University of Illinois, 1967).

[33]G. J. Skrzypek, "The effects of perceptual isolation and arousal on anxiety, complexity preference and novelty preference in psychopathic and neurotic delinquents," *Journal of Abnormal Psychology,* 74 (1969), pp. 321–329.

Consequently, the ego is not able to tolerate instinctual tension or to postpone instinctual gratification.[34] Since the superego is defective, there is no inner mechanism to regulate life activities according to moral principles or social norms. Antisocial personalities have only an "external superego," that is, a fear of being caught by the law. Because they lack a healthy superego, these people are constantly overwhelmed by the need for pleasure. This is the psychoanalytic explanation of their "thrill-seeking" behavior. Consistent with this theory, one researcher estimates that 90 percent of antisocial males are driven by sexual tension.[35] What causes the superego defect? The common psychoanalytic explanation is that, as a child, the antisocial person was denied the normal opportunity to form a close relationship with a parental figure. Thus, the individual never incorporates the set of moral standards which usually result from normal phallic experiences and from identification with the same-sex parent. Numerous situations can create this type of deprivation. For example, when a child is repeatedly moved from one foster home to another, he is not provided with any stable parental figure after which to model himself. This kind of parental deprivation appears quite frequently in antisocial personality types. In fact, one study revealed that 60 percent of a sample of antisocial personalities had lost at least one parent during childhood.[36]

Secondly, a superego defect can result when a child is raised by parents who do not offer him a stable model of security. Such parents are usually cruel, neglectful, indifferent, or inconsistent in their treatment of the child. In all cases, the child has no example to follow and therefore does not develop an ability to differentiate right from wrong. Some view the resultant unsocialized behavior as a search for the attention and affection that was withheld by the parents.[37] Others see the antisocial behavior as a creative way to avoid psychosis.[38] But the residues of survival under such extremely deprived familial circumstances are a sense of cunning and a set of techniques for exploiting others without regard for their feelings.

Psychoanalysts believe improper parenting is the primary cause of the antisocial disorder. Some research does report a marked association between the disorder and a lack of parental affection. One such study compared attitudes of antisocial boys and normal schoolboys toward their fathers.[39] A significantly larger number of the antisocial boys

[34]Herman Nunberg, *Principles of Psychoanalysis*, (New York: International Universities Press, 1955), p. 309.

[35]Clinton T. Duffy, "Sex as the cause of most crime," in *Sex: Male/Gender: Masculine: Readings in Male Sexuality*, ed. John W. Petras (Port Washington, N.Y.: Alfred Publishing Co., 1975), pp. 38–45.

[36]S. Greu, "Study of parental loss in neurotics and sociopaths," *Archives of General Psychiatry*, 11 (1964), pp. 177–180.

[37]Clarence J. Rowe, *An Outline of Psychiatry* (Dubuque: Wm. C. Brown Company, 1973), p. 89.

[38]Leon Salzman, *The Obsessive Personality* (New York: Aronson, 1973), p. 186.

[39]R. G. Andry, *Delinquency and Parental Pathology* (London: Methuen, 1960).

felt that their fathers were disinterested in them. Further evidence suggests that the antisocial individual is often a child born to parents who did not want him.[40] He is frequently either an illegitimate birth or a child born to parents with a bad marriage. As a result, he is often passed between a series of temporary "caretakers" or institutionalized.

In psychoanalytic circles, there is a minority opinion which holds that antisocial behavior originates in deprivation at the oral stage of psychosexual development since the narcissistic, pleasure-seeking make-up of the antisocial is closely linked to the normal tendencies of young infants. This argument runs deeper than simply positing that the antisocial has an infantile emotional make-up. The antisocial individual is viewed as a masochist who thrives on painful experiences stemming from a denial of his emotional needs during the oral period.[41] He derives masochistic gratification through his perpetual rebelliousness which brings him repeated negative sanctions from society. From this perspective, he is the rebel who *has* a cause.

Parental Hypocrisy Theory

A second environmental theory consists of both psychoanalytic and behaviorist concepts. The central proposition of this theory is that children learn antisocial behavior from parents who encourage and reward it. In this sense, the disorder develops through conditioning and positive reinforcement. The other side of the theory is that parents who encourage antisocial behavior do so unconsciously for they achieve vicarious gratification of their own forbidden, repressed impulses through their child's acting out behavior. Therefore, the latent antisocial parent produces the manifest antisocial child. This theory assumes that the superego develops through the incorporation of the parents' covert behaviors as well as their manifest behaviors. For example, the parent who immediately checks to see that a child has followed an order and who constantly warns of dire consequences, simultaneously conveys an unstated alternative to the order, namely disregard for authority.[42] Thus, it is parental hypocrisy that corrupts the superego. The parents condemn antisocial behavior overtly while they simultaneously encourage it covertly. One team of researchers states, "It is possible in every case adequately studied to trace the specific conscience defect in the child to a mirror image of similar type and emotional charge in the parent."[43] The same researchers cite some common examples of the ways in which the parents of antisocial individuals encourage immorality such as, " 'Here is an extra quarter, but don't tell your father; 'You can get into the movie

---

[40]L. C. Kolb, *Noyes' Modern Clinical Psychiatry,* p. 496.
[41]Walter Bromberg, "Psychopathic personality concept evaluated and reevaluated," *Archives of General Psychiatry,* 17 (1967), pp. 641–645.
[42]Mary E. Griffin and others, "The transmission of superego defects in the family."
[43]Ibid., p. 671.

for half-price, since you certainly don't look 12 years old'; 'Fires are dangerous but if you must get it out of your system, then we'll set some in the yard'. . . . Children hear their parents gloating about shortchanging the grocer; naturally they sense the parental pleasure."[44]

Clinical observations of antisocial children who are being treated together with a parent support the theory of parental hypocrisy. In some cases the parent showed unmistakable joy while his child was telling the therapist about his misdeeds. Immediately after the report, however, the parent became moralistic and condemned the child's behavior.[45] In other instances, the parent encouraged the child to relate his misdeeds in graphic detail, provided missing pieces of information himself, and openly enjoyed the lawbreaking of the child.

It is not difficult to understand how parental hypocrisy can foster a defective superego. Parents who verbally support one set of values but who act according to another can not hope that their children will respect moral principles. A father who lectures on honesty while bragging about an ability to evade income taxes or a mother who appears to be astounded when she hears a four letter word but who promiscuously performs the act it symbolizes is likely to raise children who harbor resentment toward authority figures.

The psychoanalytic parental rejection theory seems to be a useful explanation of antisocial behavior in the lower classes in which there are entire families of antisocial personalities. The parental hypocrisy model, however, may be more appropriate to the etiology of the disorder in middle and upper class families where often only one sibling in a family manifests the disorder, while other siblings are well-adjusted.[46] This may be the result of one child being selected as the scapegoat for the parents' own forbidden desires. This explanation makes particular sense in light of the high rate of antisocial behavior among adopted children. The attitudes which parents manifest toward adopted children are likely to be quite different from their attitudes toward their natural children.[47] Such parents are often hostile toward each other as well. This hostility may either lead to childlessness or be the consequence of it. In either case, an adopted child can not overcome the problem of childlessness since he does not verify the biologic and sexual identity of the parent. Rather, the child serves as a living reminder of the parent's own inadequacies. Small wonder that he is often not cared for lovingly.

Labeling Theory

Labeling theory posits that the behavior of the antisocial personality is fashioned by the attitudes of significant others toward him. If the

---

[44]Ibid., p. 675.
[45]Norman Cameron, *Personality Development and Psychopathology*, p. 654.
[46]L. C. Kolb, *Noyes' Modern Clinical Psychiatry*, p. 504.
[47]Nathan M. Simon and Audrey G. Senturia, "Adoption and psychiatric illness."

child is rejected by his parents or by the community, he may live up to the bad name given him by others. This serves to establish some sort of identity for the child, although it is a negative one. Labeling theorists do not believe that the family experience is the complete cause since many children who are raised by rejecting or inconsistent parents do not become antisocial. Furthermore, they contend, the family is not the exclusive source of social norms but part of the larger community whose norms it reflects. Children who are reared in the slum of a city are raised in a community which rewards crime and pleasure-seeking while ignoring ethical standards of the larger society. Since there is a high rate of antisocial behavior among poor people living in slum areas, this theory certainly has some value. Some antisocial people may be simply acting out a role rewarded by their community. This argument is even more compelling when the city slum is contrasted with life in an entirely different setting. The religious sect of the Hutterites provides such a contrast. The Hutterites are an isolated Anabaptist sect who live a simple, rural life in the midwestern United States. The children are raised with strict discipline, suffering penalties for any infringement of moral law. Among these people there is a complete absence of antisocial personalities.[48] This suggests that the moral fibre of the community in which the child is socialized may be an important etiological factor.

Excessive Moralism Theory

A superego defect may be caused by parents who are consistent but who are unduly moralistic. These parents establish unreasonable standards of moral conduct for their children. If these standards are in sharp opposition to the child's instinctual needs, a severe intrapsychic conflict may result. While this battle may end in the defeat of the id, it may also defeat the developing conscience through a reaction formation.[49]

Prognosis

The antisocial disorder begins in early childhood during which time a number of indications of the psychopathology appear. These children are emotionally immature and often react to small frustrations with violent temper tantrums. They are frequently deceitful, boastful, destructive, quarrelsome, and defiant. Their condition reaches a peak in adolescence and typically subsides in the late twenties.[50] There are only a few older antisocial individuals in society. This occurs for one of two reasons. First, many have been placed in prisons or mental hospitals

---

[48]Joseph Eaton and Robert J. Weil, "The mental health of the Hutterites," *Scientific American*, 189 (1953), pp. 31–37.

[49]Merrill T. Eaton, Jr. and Margaret H. Peterson, *Psychiatry*, p. 249.

[50]David Abrahamsen, *The Psychology of Crime*, p. 138.

before they reach middle age, and second, for unknown reasons, some "level off" or "burn out" in later life and cease to exhibit antisocial behavior. In general, however, the chances for recovery are very poor because these patients are particularly difficult to treat. For this reason, many hospitals avoid admitting antisocial people. If they are admitted, hospitals are unwilling to treat them for long periods of time because they upset other patients.[51] In the literature there are only scattered reports of successful treatment of antisocials. Those who do report success typically use a therapeutic approach involving discipline and punishment.[52]

The Explosive Personality

Symptoms

The chief symptoms of the explosive personality, also known as the *epileptoid personality disorder,* are gross outbursts of rage or of verbal or physical aggressiveness. These outbursts contrast with the person's usual behavior and he may regret them afterwards. In some cases, uncontrollable bursts of rage may result from epilepsy rather than a psychologically maladaptive pattern, but these are cases of organic brain disorder and not instances of explosive personality.

Megargee differentiates two types of explosive personality: the *undercontrolled aggressive type* and the *chronically overcontrolled type.*[53] The undercontrolled aggressive personality has low inhibitions against aggressive behavior and usually responds to frustration with aggression. The chronically overcontrolled type has strong inhibitions against aggression, and his aggressive tendencies accumulate over time. The chronically overcontrolled type is more dangerous and more closely resembles the description of the explosive personality presented in DSM-II. A greater amount of research has been conducted on the overcontrolled type, partly because the undercontrolled aggressive type is frequently an antisocial personality as well.

Prevalence

Little is known about the prevalence of this disorder. However, if homicide can be used as a rough barometer of explosive tendencies, the condition is more prevalent in the United States than in other countries since the United States has the highest homicide rate in the world.[54]

---

[51]H. B. Kidd, *Violence and the Mental Health Services* (London: L.A.M.H., 1962).

[52]Frederick C. Thorne, "The etiology of sociopathic reactions," in *Sourcebook in Abnormal Psychology,* eds. Leslie Y. Rabkin and John E. Carr (Boston: Houghton Mifflin, 1967), pp. 276–282.

[53]Edwin I. Megargee, "Undercontrolled and overcontrolled personality types in extreme antisocial aggression," *Psychological Monographs,* 80 (1966), no. 611.

[54]David Abrahamsen, *The Psychology of Crime,* p. 180.

However, many murders in this country are motivated by some rational purpose, such as the man who kills for personal gain or in retaliation. The explosive murder, on the other hand, is an open expression of primitive violence with no apparent motive. For example, Satten and his colleagues report a thirty-one-year-old chief petty officer who was talking casually to the nine-year-old daughter of one of his superior officers.[55] Suddenly he grabbed the child, choked her, and held her head under water until she was dead. The same team of investigators also report the case of a forty-three-year-old soldier who was being taunted and seduced by a prostitute. He killed her with a tire jack and then mutilated and dismembered her body.

Of course, it is not necessary to search the psychiatric literature for examples of explosive behavior, for they are commonplace in the news. One famous case involved two housemaids who were sisters. They became known as the "Maids of Le Mans". In France, in 1933, they hacked their employers to death for no apparent reason, inflicted multiple wounds and cuts on the bodies, plucked out the victims' eyes, and knocked all their teeth out. More recently, an eleven-year-old Phoenix boy, described as being extremely polite, stabbed his brother thirty-four times with a steak knife. In New York, an eighteen-year-old unemotional youth, planning a career in the ministry, strangled a seven-year-old girl and burned her body in a church furnace. In San Francisco a man known as the "Paper Bag Killer" would approach an old man on the street, pull a gun out of a paper bag, and shoot him to death.

Etiology

What causes these seemingly senseless outbursts? Unfortunately, very little is known about the origins of the explosive personality. There is some biogenic evidence that the condition is the result of abnormal brain activity as evidenced by EEG measures.[56] However, these findings probably represent organic cases of epilepsy which also involve unprovoked assault, rather than a real personality disorder.

Satten and his colleagues discovered that explosives have "... a longstanding, sometimes life-long, history of erratic control over aggressive impulses."[57] They also found that explosive persons have poor self-images and consider themselves to be weak and inadequate. Perhaps the explosive behavior serves to compensate for this weak self concept.

The most widely accepted theory of explosive behavior involves the family dynamics of the preexplosive's childhood years. Parents who themselves are extremely violent tend to produce explosive children.[58]

[55]Joseph Satten and others, "Murder without apparent motive: a study in personality disorganization" in *Sourcebook in Abnormal Psychology*, pp. 283–287.
[56]Alfred M. Freedman and others, *Modern Synopsis of Comprehensive Textbook of Psychiatry*.
[57]Joseph Satten and others, "Murder without apparent motive: a study in personality disorganization," p. 284.
[58]Ibid., p. 284.

Explosive behavior may also develop in children whose parents, while not necessarily violent themselves, permissively allow their children to be aggressive.[59] Parents who use physically punitive discipline also increase the likelihood of the disorder in their children. All of these socialization experiences are considered to cause explosive behavior through behaviorist principles of modeling and reinforcement. However, there is a psychoanalytic aspect to the disorder as well; these forms of parental treatment are particularly dangerous to the child's personality development during the anal-sadistic stage when the child's normal rage can be compounded by parentally imposed sadism.[60] Not all parents of explosive people act as models or promoters of violence. A majority of parents in one study discipline their children in an erratic fashion; the child is severely punished for a certain action at one time and allowed to perform the action at other times.[61]

Psychoanalytic interpretations of explosive behavior stress fantasied, rather than actual, violence in the childhood background. Satten and his colleagues infer from their data that explosives perceive the primal scene as overwhelmingly violent and sadistic. They state further that, "That history relating to *extreme* violence, whether fantasized, observed in reality, or actually experienced by the child, fits in with the psychoanalytic hypothesis that the child's exposure to overwhelming stimuli, before he can master them, is closely linked to early defects in ego formation and later severe disturbances in impulse control."[62]

Another factor frequently found in the childhood history of explosives is stuttering.[63] Early speech difficulties can increase explosive potential because they make it difficult for the child to express feelings verbally.

There is empirical evidence for the behaviorist theory that explosive tendencies originate in parents who, in various ways, are violent themselves. However, it would be naive to dismiss the operation of unconscious motives in explosive personalities. Upon closer scrutiny, apparently senseless murders may not be so purposeless since there is evidence that these acts occur when the victim-to-be is perceived as a threatening figure from the past, thus activating a murderous response.[64] In such a "surrogate murder," the actual victim is a substitute for the intended one. The real reason for the murder remains hidden from the explosive person himself because it is linked to a repressed

[59]R. R. Sears, E. E. Maccoby, and H. Levin, *Patterns of Child-Rearing* (New York: Harper and Row, 1957).

[60]Herman Nunberg, *Principles of Psychoanalysis*, p. 305.

[61]William McCord, Joan McCord, and Alan Howard, "Familial correlates of aggression in nondelinquent male children," *Journal of Abnormal and Social Psychology*, 62 (1961), pp. 79–93.

[62]Joseph Satten and others, "Murder without apparent motive: a study in personality disorganization", p. 284.

[63]Ibid., p. 285.

[64]Ibid., p. 286; See also, David Abrahamsen, *The Psychology of Crime*, p. 185.

hatred for someone known during childhood. Thus, a bellhop is murdered because he resembles someone's father.

The Passive-Aggressive Personality

Symptoms

This disorder is usually subdivided into three types: the *passive-dependent*, the *passive-aggressive*, and the *aggressive*. The passive-dependent acts like a helpless, grown-up baby who frighteningly looks to others for direction. This is the "clinging vine" who can never assume responsibility for his own actions. This behavior may not be disabling; it may even be socially useful. There are many employers, for instance, who seek employees who ask for orders and follow them out. The person, in turn, is content as long as he is not promoted.

The passive-aggressive type, as the name implies, is aggressive in a passive way. He is stubborn and very uncooperative toward authority figures who are perceived as domineering tyrants. In school, this person may not openly refuse to do an assignment, but he grudgingly complies, all the while complaining and procrastinating. Pouting is also common. This type is attracted to such passive-aggressive activities as sit-down strikes. This is a disabling psychopathology as evidenced by its frequent role in educational, occupational, and marital failure.[65]

The aggressive type is overbearing, rude, sarcastic, and argumentative. Temper outbursts are common, and this person can become destructive with little provocation. Some of these cases overlap with antisocial and explosive behavior.

Etiology

Persons with the passive-aggressive disorder show both aggressive and dependent behavior in different circumstances. For this reason, the underlying problems of the different types are considered to be the same. It is very difficult to estimate the prevalence of this psychopathology but some experts contend that it is the most common psychiatric disorder.[66] It only stands to reason that the number of disorders involving aggressive activity is rising as modern society increasingly restricts open expressions of aggression. In the process, the instinctual need for aggressive outlets is directed into covert pathological channels. Typically, the problem is compounded by a deep sense of resentment toward an unsatisfactory relationship, such as a marriage, or toward an institution, such as one's employer.

---

[65]Merrill T. Eaton, Jr. and Margaret H. Peterson, *Psychiatry*, p. 124.
[66]Ibid., p. 121.

The Inadequate Personality

Symptoms

This person is inadequate in all facets of life. He gives ineffectual responses to emotional, social, intellectual, and physical demands. The inadequate person is often good-natured, but he constantly exhibits poor judgment and a lack of physical and emotional stamina. However, performance in standardized tests indicates no actual physical or mental deficiency. The inadequate person is permanently disabled for work and is usually considered to be suffering from an untreatable condition.

Etiology

This disorder poses an etiological mystery. Biogenic factors are believed to be operative but none have yet been identified. The literature is ambiguous, citing such possible causes as abnormalities in family structure or the crushing of childhood impulses by inhibiting mechanisms, the results of which extend to all aspects of life. Another etiological suggestion is that the person has a poor self-concept derived from childhood failures to live up to parental demands. Another possibility is that inadequate personalities were overprotected children who were treated as if they could not do anything for themselves. Thus, the pathological result is self-fulfilling.

Conclusions

Many of the conditions designated as personality disorders are simply prepsychotic or preneurotic states. They differ from psychoses or neuroses only in degree. The schizoid, cyclothymic, and paranoid personalities parallel schizophrenia, manic-depression, and the paranoid states respectively. The hysterical, obsessive-compulsive, and asthenic personalities are early forms of the hysterical, obsessive-compulsive, and neurasthenic neuroses respectively.

The "pure" personality disorders include the antisocial disorder, a condition which blatantly demonstrates the role of the intrapsychic agent of society, the superego. Antisocial personalities have a superego defect which allows them to violate other people and suffer no remorse. Although this disorder is considered terminal, it is possible that it could be prevented and cured. If so, society has failed miserably to deal with it. This is partly due to laws which do not segregate antisocial individuals from others who commit crimes. As a result, these people often end up in jail where their condition worsens.

There is only a limited amount of evidence that the antisocial disorder is caused by biogenic factors. Psychoanalysts consider this pathology to originate in parental rejection and the concomittant lack of opportunity to form a normal superego through identification. Behaviorists stress the etiological influence of parents who encourage immoral behavior in their children. Labeling theorists explain antisocial behavior as a response to the countercultural standards of lower class life in the slums.

The explosive personality has been explained by two major etiological theories. The behaviorists propose that the disorder is the imitative result of having been raised by violent parents. Psychoanalysts theorize that there is an unconscious factor at work, specifically the repression of a violent experience at a young age.

The passive-aggressive personality is a reflection of the restrictions which modern society places on acceptable forms of aggressive behavior. Because there are fewer opportunities to alleviate the aggressive instinct in a rational, orderly, rule-oriented society, these people do not function well interpersonally since they are beset by a chronic sense of hostility.

The inadequate personality is an etiological puzzle. At present, the only plausible explanation is that it stems from a poor self-image that was fostered by demanding or overprotective parents.

7

The Sexual
Disorders

Sexual Disorder: An Overview

It is difficult to discuss the nature of sexual disorder and be scientifically objective at the same time because there is much disagreement concerning exactly what a disorder is. Sexual disorders are universal and have been practiced in all ages. Many of the behaviors included in the list of common disorders are nothing more than exaggerations of popular sexual activity. But we live in an age of moral ambiguity in which there is no "correct" way of differentiating normal and abnormal sexual behavior. Each group in society has its own set of standards. Even if there were a universal set of norms that proscribed certain sexual acts as deviant, the problem of objectivity would still remain because social standards are often quite divergent from people's actual sexual behavior. For example, if certain state laws were used to establish a code of acceptable activity, an enormous amount of the everyday sexual life of Americans would be adjudged abnormal. The only form of sex that is legally acceptable in every state of the United States is heterosexual intercourse between a husband and wife, at night, in bed, in an upper room, with the lights out, and in the missionary style position (man on top of woman). Certainly this guideline is inconsistent with the everyday lives of many Americans, but such laws remain on the books because the orderly continuation of civilized society apparently requires that people pay *verbal* homage to puritanical ideals. In that way "uncomfortable" conversations about premarital sex, extramarital sex, homosexuality, masturbation, and oral sex, to name a few, can be avoided for the same reason that a behavior such as necrophilia (intercourse with a corpse) is condemned;

all are violations of a moral code. Unfortunately, these attitudes have hampered scientific investigations of human sexuality. In fact, it was not until 1948 that Alfred C. Kinsey and his colleagues published the first study of the sex lives of Americans. It showed many people that their secret sexual desires and acts were shared by others.[1] For many Americans it must have been a relief to discover that they were not the only ones who masturbated or had a lover of the same sex. This landmark work paved the way for subsequent investigations of human sexual behavior. In 1975 *Redbook Magazine* financed a survey of the sex lives of 100,000 American women which uncovered an extraordinary change in sexual values.[2] In the study 90 percent of the women who were under 25 had had premarital intercourse. In Kinsey's study, only 33 percent of the women reported that they had done so. The *Redbook* study also reported some startling information about the sex lives of married females; almost 40 percent of women married more than ten years reported having sexual relations with men other than their husbands.

The topic of sex is finally "out of the closet" but the closet door did not open on well-oiled hinges. Now there is a real problem in developing guidelines for determining which types of sexual behavior indicate psychological abnormality. The conservative position is that any violation of a legal code is a disorder. This is of little value to science because it represents only a reflection of the narrow-minded views of certain lay groups. The liberal position contends that no sexual act is a disorder as long as it occurs between consenting adults and no one is physically harmed. The moderate position is that a sex act becomes a disorder if it is preferred to, or takes the place of, heterosexual intercourse. Most mental health professionals subscribe to the moderate view, although they make certain exceptions. For example, the person who is segregated from the opposite sex for long periods of time and seeks sexual gratification in other ways is not considered abnormal. "Situational homosexuality" among prison inmates illustrates this. The person who may enjoy deviant inclinations on occasion but who is not obsessed with them is not disordered either. Thus there is an important difference between a person who uses field glasses to look in the windows of the women's dorm as a pastime and the Peeping Tom who is excited *only* when climbing fire escapes.

Sexual deviants perform a variety of activities. Some may find complete gratification in acts that are part of foreplay in conventional intercourse. Others may become excited only at the sight of a certain object, such as a shoe. There are also those who have a preference for children as sex partners, as well as those who can make love only to a cadaver. Some persons like to watch others nude while others are pleased if they are being watched. Certain persons can achieve pleasure

---

[1]Alfred C. Kinsey, Wardell B. Pomeroy, and Clyde E. Martin, *Sexual Behavior in the Human Male* (Philadelphia: W.B. Saunders, 1948).

[2]Robert J. Levin, "The Redbook report on premarital and extramarital sex: the end of the double standard?" *Redbook Magazine* (October, 1975), pp. 38–192.

only if sex is mixed with violence, while others enjoy sex only when human excrement is present. The list of sexual disorders is indeed quite lengthy. Perhaps the best way to order these different behaviors is according to whether the behavior involves a deviant *type* of sexual object, a deviant *mode* of gratification, a gender *identity* or role disorder, or a deviation in the *intensity* of the sexual drive.

Deviations in *type* of object include *pedophilia* (child partner), *fetishism* (inanimate object), *incest* (family member), the *excretory perversions* (feces or urine), *necrophilia* (corpse), *bestiality* (animal) and *pyromania* (fire).

Deviations in *mode* of gratification include *exhibitionism* (displaying one's self), *voyeurism* (watching others), *sadism* (inflicting pain), *masochism* (receiving pain), *rape* (forcing a person to be a sex partner) and *frotteurism* (rubbing).

Gender *identity* or role disorders include *transvestism* (dressing in the clothes of the opposite sex) and *transsexualism* (persistent wish to be rid of one's own genitals and to live as a member of the opposite sex).

Deviation in *intensity* of desire includes two conditions: *nymphomania* (excessive desire for coitus in a female) and *satyriasis* (excessive desire for coitus in a male).

This list of disorders may offend many readers who see some of their own behaviors included. Here a word of caution is in order. Some of these activities are quite common. It is not the content of an act itself that makes it abnormal but the way it is viewed by the person who performs the act. It is also important to note that this list includes all known forms of human sexual activity. As such, it is a useful paradigm and not necessarily a list of pathological symptoms. All of the activities on the list are considered in this chapter. Some sexual activities have not been included because they do not indicate a definite abnormality. Homosexuality is an example of this. For this reason, it is best considered to be a "sexual variation" rather than a "sexual disorder." The remaining activities on the list more clearly represent a real disturbance. Of course, much of this breakdown is based on opinion. Some will feel that the author is running liberal risks by considering homosexuality as a lifestyle variation, rather than a disorder. The fact is that homosexuality can be either a lifestyle or a disorder depending on how the person deals with being gay. Others will argue that the breakdown conservatively includes as disorders certain acts which do not indicate sickness. Certainly it is impossible to please everyone. The matter rests there.

Before proceeding to specifics, some general comments about the epidemiology and etiology of sexual disorders is in order. One commonly asked question is "Do all sexual deviants suffer from another disorder as well?" There is no black or white answer to this question. Some feel that a sexual disorder and a neurosis stem from the same instinctual impulse but that the neurosis is simply the "negative of the perversion."[3] The neurotic and the sexual deviant both experience

[3]Herman Nunberg, *Principles of Psychoanalysis* (New York: International Universities Press, Inc., 1968), p. 263.

internal conflict; the sexual deviant "acts out" the conflict whereas the neurotic hides it in some way. In other words, the sexual deviant may have a neurosis, a personality disorder, or the sexual disorder alone. The APA considers a sexual disorder to be a type of personality disorder although they place sexual disorders in a separate category because of the ambiguous nature of the concept. In short, a sexual disorder can be found alone or it can be either a cause or a consequence of another condition.

Homosexuality

Attitudes Toward Homosexuality

The American View. Homosexuality is a topic about which most Americans are quite ignorant. Consequently, this sexual variation is as much a social problem as it is a sexual problem. The myths that have been created about gay persons are problems themselves because they create inappropriate, negative, and stigmatizing attitudes toward homosexuality. A number of such myths are in current circulation. One is that a homosexual has specific physical attributes. Even some psychiatrists foster this belief. For instance, one psychiatrist, describing a "typical homosexual" states, "He is thin and has slender limbs; his cheeks are flushed, his face soft, and his appearance and manners pleasant. Hair on the chest, axilla, and pubes is scarce. He behaves like a girl, walks like a girl, and smiles like a girl. He may like to cook and sew."[4] Nothing could be further from the truth. The homosexual athlete will attest to that. A British study of male homosexuals found that most homosexuals are indistinguishable from other people; only 17 percent had slight or pronounced feminine characteristics.[5] Yet these misconceptions are propogated, even by some supposed "experts" on the topic, and they are often accepted as fact by the public.

Surveys indicate that approximately two-thirds of the American people feel that homosexuals are "harmful" to society and regard homosexuals with "disgust, discomfort, or fear."[6] One study revealed that Americans consider the homosexual person as "deviant" more frequently than other persons.[7] In the same study, people categorized homosexuals, in order, as "sexually abnormal," "perverted," "mentally ill," "maladjusted," and "effeminate." Undoubtedly, Americans have many misconceptions about gay people. This results in an ungrounded fear of homosexuals, a condition known as *homophobia*.

[4]David Abrahamsen, *The Psychology of Crime* (New York: Columbia University Press, 1967), p. 169.

[5]Gordon Westwood, *A Minority: A Report on the Life of the Male Homosexual in Great Britain* (London: Longmans, Green and Co., Ltd., 1960), p. 62.

[6]Marshall B. Clinard, *The Sociology of Deviant Behavior* (New York: Holt, Rinehart and Winston, 1974), p. 547.

[7]J. L. Simmons, "Public stereotypes of deviants," *Social Problems*, 13 (1965), pp. 223–332.

Because of the negative, stigmatizing way that gay people are viewed by a majority of Americans, it is no small wonder that the typical reactions to individuals who are first perceived as homosexual are disapproval and withdrawal.[8] Of course, this is not true of all Americans. Some openly affirm the right of the homosexual to live his or her own life, and they do not let their subsequent relationship with the gay person change after discovery of his or her homosexuality.

Many Americans regard the sexual preference of homosexuals as an overriding factor in understanding the entire personality of the gay person.[9] For instance, a gay interior designer is assumed to have chosen that occupation because of his homosexual qualities. On the other hand, a heterosexual in the same line of work is considered to be simply pursuing an intrinsic interest.

It is clear that many homosexuals with psychiatric difficulties have them because of the way they are treated by others, not because homosexuality itself is a psychiatric condition. In the 1960s, this issue reached the public forum through the actions of various groups commonly referred to as the "gay liberation movement." Several gay activists persuaded mental health professionals to consider the issue of whether homosexuality should be considered a mental illness or simply a normal variant of sexual behavior. Since there is no evidence indicating that homosexuals are more emotionally disturbed than heterosexuals, the APA considered the issue and concluded that homosexuality should no longer be listed as a mental disorder in its then official nomenclature, DSM–II.[10] In a 1973 press release, the Trustees of the APA (by a unanimous vote) stated that it is not scientifically valid to consider homosexuality a psychiatric disorder since, in and of itself, it implies no impairment. However, those homosexuals who were troubled by or in conflict about their sexual orientation, to the point where their social functioning is impaired, were classified as having a *sexual orientation disturbance*. The DSM–III term for this condition is *dyshomophilia* a type of *paraphilia*. These people experience their homosexuality as "ego-alien" and not as "ego-syntonic" since they can't accept themselves because of society's attitudes toward homosexuality, not because of some inherent disinclination toward being gay.

There are several reasons for the APA's decision to drop homosexuality per se from its official nomenclature. One reason is that a majority of homosexuals are satisfied with their sexual orientation. A second reason is that they frequently show no signs of psychopathology. A third

---

[8]John I. Kitsuse, "Societal reaction to deviant behavior: problems of theory and method," in *The Mental Patient: Studies in the Sociology of Deviance,* eds. Stephen P. Spitzer and Norman K. Denzin (New York: McGraw-Hill, 1968), pp. 40–51.

[9]J. H. Gagnon and W. Simon, *Sexual Conduct: The Social Origins of Human Sexuality* (Chicago: Aldine, 1973).

[10]Before this decision, the American Psychological Association openly supported the position of gay groups.

reason is that it is unreasonable to consider homosexuality to be a psychiatric disorder simply because of a failure to function heterosexually. If failure to function optimally in some area of life is sufficient to indicate a psychiatric disturbance, then other conditions would also have to be added to the psychiatric nomenclature, such as celibacy (failure to function optimally sexually), religious fanaticism (rigid adherence to religious doctrine), and vegetarianism (unnatural avoidance of carnivorous behavior). If optimal functioning were used to ascertain acceptable sexual behavior, then value judgments would determine how everyone should act.

In the same news release, the APA cried out against discriminatory practices in employment, housing, and licensing. The APA also urged the repeal of all laws against homosexual acts performed by consenting adults in private. The penalties for such acts are severe. In most states the punishment is five years imprisonment. In a large number of states, the penalty ranges from ten years to life imprisonment. Illinois, Connecticut, Hawaii, Colorado, and Oregon have been the first states to eliminate such antiquated legislation. Approximately fifteen other states followed. However, in 1978 there was a backlash movement to rescind prohomosexual laws.

Cross-Cultural Views. Throughout history, some societies have maintained very positive attitudes toward homosexuality. It was practiced extensively by ancient Babylonians and Egyptians, the first civilized men. A number of important historical figures engaged in homosexuality including Plato, Sappho, Alexander the Great, Socrates, Virgil, and Julius Caesar. In ancient Greece, male homosexuality was widely practiced and accepted. This may have been partly the result of the practice of young men having older men as mentors as well as the fact that male children were often brought up by male slaves.

In non-Western societies today, homosexuality is often considered to be a normal part of life. Ford and Beach investigated seventy-six such societies and discovered that homosexuality is considered normal and socially acceptable in forty-nine (64 percent) of them.[11] They found two broad patterns of accepted homosexuality: the institutionalized homosexual role and relations between men and boys who are otherwise heterosexual. Among the Siwans of North Africa, males of all ages are expected to perform homosexual acts. In fact, the Siwans consider it abnormal for a man not to have homosexual experience! In New Guinea, Keraki bachelors universally engage in anal intercourse (*sodomy*). The Keraki view anal intercourse as a necessary part of the puberty rites of young boys who need the experience for growth. After a year of playing the passive (recipient) homosexual role, the Keraki male

---

[11]Clellan S. Ford and Frank A. Beach, *Patterns of Sexual Behavior* (New York: Harper and Row, 1951).

spends the remainder of his bachelorhood actively administering anal intercourse to the newly-initiated. Some of the other societies in which homosexuality is accepted are the Mohave Indians of California and Arizona, the Aranda of Central Australia, and many Moslem societies, to name a few.

In most Western European societies, homosexual acts carried out in private between consenting adults are not considered crimes. These laws arose from a liberalization of legal attitudes which were greatly influenced by the French Revolution and the Napoleonic Code which followed. Although the general attitudes of Western peoples toward homosexuality are not as liberal as are those of non-Western peoples, there is a great divergence among the legal positions held by different Western societies toward homosexual acts. Very few European countries consider homosexual acts to be criminal acts. In the United States, on the other hand, homosexual acts are often met with harsh legal reprisals.

The Mental Status of Homosexuals

Americans exhibit strongly negative attitudes toward homosexuals. This is largely the result of ignorance and misunderstanding which cause a "devil effect," a negative evaluation of all facets of an individual on the basis of one personality trait. In short, the homosexual's sex object choice dominates others' total imagery of him. Consequently, he is not seen as a person comprised of various parts but as a person who is abnormal in every way. Are there any areas in which homosexuals are qualitatively different from heterosexuals? The few differences that do exist are largely the result of their living in a society which condemns homosexuals. Some gays, for instance, find sex partners in public toilets and engage in totally impersonal sex.[12] In the same vein, many heterosexuals visit prostitutes for anonymous pleasure as well.

The lifestyle of homosexuals is different from that of heterosexuals. Societal rejection pushes homosexuals to form their own distinctive subculture. Within the subculture homosexuals often occupy certain slices of cities, speak a special language, and have their own social centers, most notably the so-called "gay bar." All of this alienates them from the dominant culture. Because of this alienation, some homosexuals never declare themselves and lead secret, painful lives in straight society. If they do decide to "come out of the closet," they usually enter the homosexual community through certain social channels. Gay bars, gay parties, and frequenting parks are some of the means of entrance into the gay community.[13] In addition, several formal voluntary organizations can help the person learn about the homosexual community, such as Gay Activists Alliance, Society for Individual Rights, and the

[12]There is evidence that venereal disease is an unfortunate complication of homosexual intercourse. Estimates are that 14 percent of all new cases of V.D. occur in homosexuals. See John Randell, *Sexual Variations* (Westport, Conn.: Technomic Publishing Company, Inc., 1976), p. 42.

[13]Barry M. Dank, "Coming out in the gay world," *Psychiatry,* 34 (1971), p. 194.

Matlachine Society. They organize various activities and furnish a number of services to homosexuals, including counseling. If present trends continue, one can expect the development of homosexual organizations to represent gays from all walks of life. Perhaps someday even the Teamsters will have a gay chapter!

The critical question is whether the psychological profiles of homosexuals are inferior to those of heterosexuals. The popular belief is that they are since many consider healthy psychological adjustment and homosexuality to be mutually exclusive. Some mental health experts believe this too, but only a few empirical studies support them. Cattell and Morony, examining only sixteen male homosexuals, report that their psychological profiles are similar to those of neurotics.[14] Kenyon reports the same result for lesbians.[15] Saghir and others conclude that male homosexuals are more disturbed than are male heterosexuals, but their measures of psychopathology are highly questionable.[16] They used drug abuse, attempted suicide, and use of a psychotherapist as measures of disturbance. Obviously, these measures may simply reflect the homosexual's despair over a world that rejects him. Personal unhappiness is particularly great among aging male homosexuals who have fewer sociosexual contacts and are more likely to be living alone than are younger homosexuals.[17]

The *sophisticated* analyses of the psychological status of gay people demonstrate that homosexuality is not a pathological syndrome always associated with neurotic patterns. Evelyn Hooker reports that three psychologists who examined the performance of thirty male homosexuals and thirty heterosexuals on standardized psychological tests (including the Rorschach Ink Blot Technique) agreed that two-thirds of the homosexuals were average to superior in adjustment.[18] Despite the many obstacles society creates for lesbians, Hedblom, after conducting in-depth interviews with sixty-five exclusively homosexual females, found no indication of psychopathology.[19] Other studies also find no differences between lesbians and female heterosexuals.[20] In fact, one study re-

---

[14]Raymond Cattell and John H. Morony, "The use of the 16 PF in distinguishing homosexuals, normals, and general criminals," *Journal of Consulting Psychology,* 26 (1962), pp. 531–540.

[15]F. Kenyon, "Studies in female homosexuality," *British Journal of Psychiatry,* 114 (1968), pp. 1337–1350.

[16]M. Saghir and others, "Homosexuality," *American Journal of Psychiatry,* 126 (1970), pp. 1079–1086.

[17]M. S. Weinberg, "The male homosexual: age-related variations in social and psychological characteristics," *Social Problems,* 17 (1970), pp. 527–537.

[18]Evelyn Hooker, "Symposium on current aspects of the problems of validity: what is a criterion?" *Journal of Projective Techniques,* 23 (1959), pp. 278–286.

[19]J. H. Hedblom, "The female homosexual: social and attitudinal dimensions", in *The Homosexual,* ed. James A. McCaffrey (Englewood Cliffs, N.J.: Prentice-Hall, 1972).

[20]See U. Armon, "Some personality variables in overt female homosexuality," *Journal of Projective Techniques,* 24 (1960), pp. 292–309; J. Hopkins, "The lesbian personality," *British Journal of Psychiatry,* 115 (1969), pp. 1433–1436; M. Siegelman, "Adjustment of

ports lesbians to be less neurotic than heterosexuals.[21] Clearly, the APA made an appropriate decision in designating homosexuality as a psychopathology only if the person's sexual orientation makes it difficult for him to adjust to a heterosexual society. Psychological tests indicate that homosexuals lead ordinary lives and have the same everyday concerns that others have, although they may become disturbed as a consequence of social harassment. Social harassment almost always stems from the bigoted and the ignorant. For example, the movement to repeal equal rights laws for homosexuals proclaims the danger of homosexuals mixing with children. However, a recent study of children *raised* by homosexual parents found that the children were not dramatically affected and, in fact, were heterosexually oriented.[22]

Fetishism

Symptoms

Fetish, a term derived from the Portuguese word *feitico,* for "charms," is frequently used to refer to a special object viewed as magical by primitive people who employ it in their religious rituals. As a sexual disorder, it refers to the use of a body part or inanimate object to achieve orgasm. Fetishism is reportedly peculiar to men, and it usually appears in adolescence.

Men with fetishes are involuntarily and irresistibly stimulated by articles of clothing, inanimate objects, or parts of the body not generally experienced as erotic, such as feet. Many men, of course, have fetishistic tendencies which are considered normal. This type of fetishism is known as *partialism.* It develops through cultural influences and personal tastes which render particular physical attributes especially arousing. Thus many men term themselves "breast men" or "leg men." Also common is the pleasure many men experience by looking at a female in some particular state of undress. These men are not pathological relative to those who can achieve orgasm only by masturbating in the presence of the fetish object. Some men with fetishes can have sexual intercourse without the fetish, but they must force themselves to do so, and they usually fantasize about the fetish during intercourse.[23] The fetish may dominate much of the person's life, as in the case of the man who is so enthralled with women's underwear that he goes into the lingerie business.

----

homosexual and heterosexual women," *British Journal of Psychiatry,* 120 (1972), pp. 447–481.

[21]M. Wilson and R. Greene, "Personality characteristics of female homosexuals," *Psychological Reports,* 28 (1971), pp. 407–412.

[22]Richard Green, "Sexual identity of 37 children raised by homosexual or transsexual parents," *American Journal of Psychiatry,* 135 (1978), pp. 692–697.

[23]M. E. Romm, "Some dynamics in fetishism," *Psychoanalytic Quarterly,* 18 (1949), pp. 137–153.

Sometimes the fetish object is an article of clothing having certain characteristics; it may be soiled, stolen, or owned by a particular person. Often the fetish is an object related to skin, especially odiferous skin.[24] The choice of fetish object is heavily influenced by cultural factors. In ancient China, for instance, foot-binding was the social norm. This practice developed into a fetish as some men experienced sexual arousal while viewing the bound feet of women[25] and today in Great Britain increasing numbers of men are reportedly becoming sexually aroused at the sight of baby carriages![26]

Types of Fetishes

Randell offers a useful classification of forms of fetishism.[27] One form is *adherent fetishism.* Here the fetish object is worn and, in some instances, makes contact with the genitals. *Olfactory fetishism* involves the smell of rubber, leather, or other substances. Where the preferred scents are rank odors, such as those from soiled garments or unclean bodies, the variation is called *osphresiolagnia.* Another form of fetishism is *acoustic fetishism* in which sexual arousal is experienced by listening to dirty stories or bathroom sounds. *Beast fetishism* refers to the use of fur or animal skins. Closely linked to this is a preoccupation with women who have long hair, braids, or pigtails. When such coiffeurs are in fashion, some men feel compelled to cut the girls' hair. Men with this type of fetishistic need are known as *braid cutters.* A final form of fetishism is *pygmalionism* in which there is an attraction to statutes or life-sized rubber doll versions of women, such as are commonly advertised in pornographic magazines.

Societal Effects

Societal attitudes toward men with fetishes range from humor to disgust. However, few people recognize that some fetishistic preoccupations can proceed to the point at which society becomes a victim. One seventeen year-old student, for example, committed three brutal murders only because he was caught in the act of burglarizing women's apartments to steal their underwear.[28] Another example is John George Haigh, a man of outward charm, who was actually the notorious English murderer of the late 1940s, known as the "acid-bath blood drinker."

[24]C. W. Socarides, "The development of a fetishistic perversion," *Journal of the American Psychoanalytic Association,* 8 (1960), pp. 281-311.

[25]V. W. Grant, "A case study of fetishism," *Journal of Abnormal and Social Psychology,* 48 (1953), pp. 142-149.

[26]Gerald C. Davison and John M. Neale, *Abnormal Psychology: An Experimental Clinical Approach* (New York: John Wiley, 1974), p. 273.

[27]John Randell, *Sexual Variations,* p. 85.

[28]F. Kennedy, H. R. Hoffman, and W. H. Haines, "A study of William Heirens," *American Journal of Psychiatry,* 104 (1947), pp. 113-121.

Haigh's fetishistic thirst for blood was relieved only by shooting a victim through the nape of the neck, making an incision in an artery, and drinking a few inches of blood in a glass. He later disposed of the body by dissolving it in acid. And who knows how much misery Boston would have been spared if the Boston Strangler had not been fetishistically motivated to cut out his victim's sexual organs and hang pieces of their flesh on picturenails on the walls?

Etiology

Of course, most people with fetishes are not driven to such macabre actions as in the cases above. The typical fetishist alleviates his sexual urges in secretive ways without bothering others. What is behind this strange hook-up between the sex drive and inanimate objects or body parts? Actually, very little is known about the origin of fetishes, as is true for most of the sexual disorders. However, some intriguing speculations have been offered. Freud believed that in such cases the male's sex drive was frustrated during infancy, and he had to settle for a *symbol* of sexual fulfillment, rather than a complete sex object. The fetish need, therefore, is a defense against normal sexual contacts. The fetish is not only a substitute for a sex partner, but it is also a replacement that makes no demands and poses none of the threats that a human can. Psychoanalysts link fetishism, as well as many other sexual behaviors, with castration anxiety. The fetish serves to deny the genital difference between the sexes by symbolizing a female penis. Therefore, long hair, earrings, or the foot or shoe of a woman function to restore a relationship with a missing object whose absence evokes fear.[29] The fetishist thus avoids homosexuality because the fetish object gives the woman a penis, which makes her acceptable as a sex partner. Of course, the question remains of how castration anxiety can lead to fetishism or some other sexual behavior. Here psychoanalytic theory is ambiguous, suggesting that the fetishist can not accept the fact that women have no penis without really explaining why.[30]

Psychoanalysts also have a theory concerning the *choice* of the particular fetish object. The fetish is believed to be an object which was part of the environment in which the child first saw the penisless female genitals. This theory is consistent with the position originally developed by Binet in 1888. He considered that the choice of a fetish was largely the result of accidental circumstances. Certain objects were unintentionally present during periods of sexual excitement in childhood. Over time, the child masturbated in the presence of the fetish object to the point

[29]There are other possible symbolic meanings of common fetish objects. Some psychoanalytically-oriented theoreticians believe a shoe fetish expresses a masochistic desire to be stepped on, and others of the same ilk believe braid-cutters have a sadistic drive to symbolically castrate the female. See Norman Cameron, *Personality Development and Psychopathology: A Dynamic Approach* (Boston: Houghton Mifflin, 1963), p. 668.

[30]M. Katon, "Fetishism, splitting of the ego, and denial," *International Journal of Psychoanalysis,* 49 (1964), pp. 237–245.

where the fetish acquired the power to evoke sexual excitement by itself.

One experiment lends some support to a behaviorist proposition. In this study, men were shown slides of attractive females interspersed with slides of women's boots.[31] Eventually, the men became aroused by the sight of the boots alone. The weakness of this particular experiment, as well as the behaviorist theory of fetishism in general, is that both fail to demonstrate that behaviors acquired in adulthood through conditioning are also acquired in childhood in the same way.

There must be some mechanism by which certain objects become linked with sexual excitation aside from the mere fact that they were present at a sexually traumatic scene. The recurrence of particular objects such as a foot or shoe suggests that hidden dimensions of the unconscious are at work. Perhaps, however, the etiology of fetishism is related neither to unconscious conflicts nor to conditioning experiences. It may be, as Nagler suggests, an attempt to escape from the demands of the male role which are increasingly threatening in today's competitive society.[32]

Pedophilia

Symptoms

Pedophilia is a pathological sexual interest in prepubescent children of the same or opposite sex. The popular opinion is that this is limited to homosexual activity such as anal intercourse between men and boys (*pederasty*). However, although most pedophiles are men, their acts are directed to children of both sexes. Because of the great potential for psychological and physical harm to the child, this disorder has more serious social consequences than most forms of deviant sexual behavior.

The age of the victim presents a problem in ascertaining whether a person is a pedophile. In those cases in which the child is prepubescent, pedophilia has certainly occured. However, not all sexual acts with people under the age of consent constitute pedophilia from a psychiatric perspective although they may constitute legal pedophilia.[33] If the victim has fully developed secondary sexual characteristics, the act may indicate poor judgment, but it does not necessarily demonstrate psychosexual pathology. Pedophilia should also not be confused with *gerontophilia,* which is the classical *Lolita* or *sugar daddy* situation in which a man, usually fifty-five or older, forms an attachment to a young, but fully developed, girl.[34]

---

[31]S. Rachman, "Sexual fetishism: an experimental analogue," *Psychological Record,* 16 (1966), pp. 293–296.

[32]S. H. Nagler, "Fetishism," *Psychiatric Quarterly,* 31 (1957), pp. 713–741.

[33]The most common age of consent for a female in the United States is 16. At this age a woman can have sexual intercourse without her male partner being subject to a charge of statutory rape.

[34]Occasionally the sex roles in this pattern are reversed as when a young boy is in a sexual association with an older woman. This is known as the *gigolo situation.*

Societal Attitudes

It is important to note that attitudes toward sex between adults and children vary cross-culturally. In contrast to the United States, the Lepcha of India believe that girls can not mature without sexual intercourse. Consequently, it is socially acceptable for older men to copulate with girls as young as eight years of age. This is also true for the Trobriand Islanders who live off the coast of New Guinea. However, in the United States and other Western societies, such practices are severely condemned. For this reason, reliable data on the prevalence of pedophilia are difficult to obtain. Such data as are available do indicate, however, that fellatio and masturbation of male infants by nurses and mothers are not rare.[35]

Types of Pedophiles

Cavanagh classifies pedophiles into two groups: the *tender type* and the *aggressive type*.[36] The tender type is usually homosexually directed toward young boys whereas the aggressive type is more frequently oriented toward eight- to ten-year-old girls. The aggressive type may physically harm the child and may even panic and kill. Surprisingly, both types of pedophiles tend to be rigidly religious and moralistic.[37] Heterosexual offenses frequently occur in the home of the pedophile or the victim because they often know each other. In fact, one study estimates that 27 percent of pedophilic acts are simultaneously incestuous acts.[38] The physical acts may be as simple as stroking the child's hair but usually the pedophile attempts to manipulate the child's genitals or encourages the child to fondle his. Heterosexual pedophiles rarely attempt coitus but 50 percent of homosexual pedophiles try to reach orgasm by fellatio, masturbation, or anal intercourse.[39]

Etiology

Little research has been done on the etiology of homosexual pedophilia but some information is available concerning heterosexual

---

[35]Alfred M. Freedman, Harold I. Kaplan, and Benjamin J. Sadock, *Modern Synopsis of Comprehensive Textbook of Psychiatry* (Baltimore: The Williams and Wilkins Co., 1975), p. 423.

[36]John R. Cavanagh, *Counseling the Invert* (Milwaukee: The Bruce Publishing Company, 1966), pp. 97–98.

[37]Gerald C. Davison and John M. Neale, *Abnormal Psychology*, p. 277.

[38]L. Frisbie, "Treated sex offenders and what they did," *Mental Hygiene*, 43 (1959), pp. 263–267.

[39]David Lester, *Unusual Sexual Behavior: The Standard Deviations* (Springfield, Illinois: Charles C. Thomas, Publisher, 1975), pp. 146–147.

pedophilia. Some of these men molest children due to an organic brain syndrome; this type represents a minority of cases and will not be discussed here. The typical pedophile is an impotent or senile man who has lost the ability to perform the sex act. As a consequence, he turns to children who do not place expectations of performance on him.

As children and as adolescents, pedophiles engaged in normal sex play, but they often failed to participate in adult sexual behaviors.[40] Clinical studies have shown that pedophiles frequently experienced early infantile deprivation and lacked the courage to approach mature females.[41] The mental status of heterosexual pedophiles reportedly varies according to age. One team of investigators found that pedophiles cluster into three age groups: adolescence, mid to late thirties, and mid to late fifties.[42] The adolescent pedophiles lack sexual experience with people of their own age and do not desire such experience. The largest group of pedophiles are in their thirties. They are severely socially maladjusted and are frequently intoxicated during the sex act. The pedophiles in their fifties suffer from loneliness and isolation and prefer younger children who can relieve these feelings. Of course, it is possible that the mental status of pedophiles may change as they grow older. If this is true, the cross-sectional study discussed above may be overlooking longitudinal changes which occur as part of an aging process.

Age may be a more important index of the degree of mental disturbance when examined in terms of the age of the victim rather than that of the offender. Younger victims are chosen by men with more deeply-ingrained pedophilic tendencies.[43] This is not surprising since older children are more mature sexually and may even play an active role in the act. In fact, in one study of female victims, 60 percent participated in the initiation of the act.[44] As expected, the participant girls were older and more often knew the male. In these instances, it is questionable whether a pedophilic act actually occurred in a psychiatric sense. Freund and others argue that most males generalize their sexual desires to younger females particularly if no older partners are available.[45] Therefore, not all men who are legally labeled as pedophiles are really sexually disordered. In support of this, it is reported that the offenders who use

---

[40]Theodore Millon and Reneé Millon, *Abnormal Behavior and Personality: A Biosocial Learning Approach* (Philadelphia: W.B. Saunders, 1974), p. 178.

[41]M. Kurland, "Pedophilia erotica," *Journal of Nervous and Mental Disease,* 131 (1960), pp. 394–403.

[42]J. W. Mohr, R. E. Turner, and M. B. Jerry, *Pedophilia and Exhibitionism* (Toronto: University of Toronto Press, 1964).

[43]David Lester, *Unusual Sexual Behavior,* p. 153.

[44]J. Weiss, and others, "A study of girl sex victims," *Psychiatric Quarterly,* 29 (1955), pp. 1–27.

[45]K. Freund, and others, "The female child as a surrogate object," *Archives of Sexual Behavior,* 2 (1972), pp. 119–133.

no violence with older children are relatively healthy in comparison to those who exploit young children.[46]

Psychoanalysts have constructed a few propositions concerning the origin of pedophilia. Freud called it the act of weak and impotent persons.[47] However, this only describes the disorder; it does not pinpoint its cause. Other psychoanalysts have been more explicit. Cassity believes that the *aggressive type* of pedophile was denied maternal warmth as an infant.[48] This sense of deprivation causes hostility toward maternal figures which is then displaced onto small children by treating them abusively. Thus, the pedophilic relationship is a simulation of an earlier unsatisfactory mother-son relationship in which the son takes on the role of the mother vis-a-vis the small child. The *tender type,* on the other hand, is theorized to have had an excessively satisfying relationship with his mother that resulted in an overidentification with her. Consequently, the pedophile is attracted to children who give him the opportunity to reenact his pleasurable memories. This psychoanalytic explanation suffers from the fact that it resembles that used to account for other forms of sexual behavior. The psychoanalysts have yet to refine their general theory of sexual deviation to delineate the mechanisms by which the same experience (excessive mothering) can create different sexual behaviors.

The sociological view of pedophilia holds that the condition stems from a person's feeling of failure in the adult world. It has been suggested that these men feel deficient in their performances as males so they turn toward children who are not likely to ridicule them.[49] The failure is not always sexual but may be social and occupational as well.

Psychological Harm to the Child

It was mentioned earlier that pedophilia can cause psychological harm to the child involved. This is not always the result of the pedophile's act itself. The harm is often unintentionally inflicted by the child's parents who react with frightening alarm to the act and thus cause the child to react similarly. Sometimes it is best not to discuss what has happened with the child, especially a very young child to whom the man may have appeared like a friendly father or grandfather. It may be wiser to leave such an image intact rather than transform it into a threatening experience through parental outbursts which themselves can cause psychological scars.

[46]David Lester, *Unusual Sexual Behavior,* p. 155.

[47]Sigmund Freud, *Three Contributions to the Theory of Sex* (New York: E.P. Dutton, 1962), pp. 13–14.

[48]J. Cassity, "Psychological considerations of pedophilia," *Psychoanalytic Review,* 14 (1927), pp. 189–199.

[49]S. B. Kopp, "The character structure of sex offenders," *American Journal of Psychotherapy,* 16 (1962), pp. 64–70.

Incest

Definition

Incest refers to sexual relations between members of the same family, such as between a parent and child or a brother and sister. When it occurs between a parent and child, it is a form of intrafamilial pedophilia. The legal definition of incest varies from one state to another. In some states incest is equated with sexual relations between cousins. In Ohio, however, incest laws include relatives who are related only by marriage.

The Incest Taboo

Incestuous desires are apparently not limited to a select number of people. On the contrary, incestuous feelings are said to be commonplace possibly because humans are especially attracted to similar others. Yet, while incestuous desires are widespread, so also are strong defenses against them. These defenses are usually referred to as the *incest taboo*. The taboo against incest is one of the few human behaviors that transcends time and culture. With the possible exception of murder, no other act has been condemned by members of practically all societies. There are, however, some important exceptions. Inbreeding was characteristic of all classes in ancient Egypt, particularly among the Pharoahs who married their sisters and infant daughters.[50] Since inheritance was matrilineal in Egypt at that time, this allowed the Pharoahs to preserve their power. A similar situation existed among the royalty in Hawaii hundreds of years ago. Other groups reportedly lacking incest regulations include those who lived in old Iran[51] as well as the Mormons in the United States.[52]

A number of explanations of the incest taboo have been offered.[53] One theory suggests that prohibition of incest is instinctive. If this were true, then societies would not need to create strong laws against incest since people would have a natural aversion toward sex with close relatives. Another weakness with the "instinct theory" is that the definition of incest varies cross-culturally and intraculturally. Therefore, the instinct would logically have to vary along these cultural lines as well and, of course, instincts do not recognize cultural dictates.

[50]R. Middleton, "Brother-sister and father-daughter marriage in ancient Egypt." *American Sociological Review*, 27 (1962), pp. 603–611.

[51]J. S. Slotkin, "On a possible lack of incest regulations in old Iran," *American Anthropologist*, 49 (1947), pp. 612–617.

[52]T. Schroeder, "Incest in Mormonism," *American Journal of Urol Sexol*, 11 (1915), pp. 409–416.

[53]For a lucid analysis of the various explanations of the incest taboo see Leslie A. White, "The definition and prohibition of incest," *American Anthropologist*, 50 (1958), pp. 416–435.

A second theory of the origin of the incest taboo is that inbreeding causes biological degeneration. Actually inbreeding does not necessarily cause degeneration. It simply intensifies the inheritance of traits, both desirable and undesirable. The major problem with the "degeneration theory" is that there are groups of people, such as the Trobriand Islanders, who are unaware of the reproductive process. In fact, they do not evidence any knowledge of a connection between sexual intercourse and pregnancy. Therefore, if they do not even understand the biological aspects of reproduction, they certainly could not have established an incest taboo to prevent any undesirable results of inbreeding.

Freud theorized that the incest taboo originated from an early stage of human society during which everyone lived in small groups dominated by a powerful male, the father.[54] He called this social unit the "primal horde." The father monopolized all the females in the group and drove his sons away to avoid sharing the women with them. The sons rebelled and killed the father. However, rather than enjoy their father's women, they made a pact not to touch them as atonement for the murder. In this way the practice of *exogamy* (marrying outside of one's family) was begun. This is an interesting thesis but it is difficult to prove historically.

One of the more compelling arguments for the origin of the incest taboo was advanced by Tylor in the nineteenth century.[55] He claimed that exogamy resulted from the economic pressures that threatened primitive man. Mutual aid and cooperation between members of different families was accomplished by an incest taboo which created a wider network of social ties than would have existed if people married only members of their own families. Thus, the taboo originated in a choice between "marrying-out and being killed out."

Another theoretical perspective on the incest taboo was developed by Fox who postulates that sex is aversive between people who live together.[56] This "indifference theory" is consistent with the interpersonal patterns reported in college dormitories where men and women reside together. In these settings, relations between men and women are more fraternal and less romantic than relations between male and female students living separately.

Prevalence

Statistics on the prevalence of incest are extremely difficult to collect since most cases go unreported. Weinberg collected data on prosecuted incest participants and reported that each year there are one to

[54]Sigmund Freud, *Totem and Taboo* (New York: W.W. Norton, 1950).

[55]E. B. Tylor, "On a method of investigating the development of institutions: applied to laws of marriage and descent," *Journal of the Anthropological Institute,* 18 (1888), pp. 245-269.

[56]J. R. Fox, "Sibling incest," *British Journal of Sociology,* 13 (1962), pp. 128-150.

two cases per million members of the United States population.[57] According to these figures, incest is rare but the statistics are based only on subjects who were brought to court. The Kinsey studies include more reliable data on incest. In those investigations of a noncriminal sample of almost 12,000 persons, there were five cases of incest reported for every 1,000 persons. Even the Kinsey figures probably underestimate the true prevalence of incest because they are based on self-reports. A later survey in the United States reported that 3.9 percent of the normal population and 13.1 percent of a prison population have experienced incest.[58] Apparently, the true prevalence figures are just beginning to be uncovered. The most commonly mentioned incestuous pattern is that between a father and daughter. Brother-sister incest occurs especially in lower class families where siblings share the same bed. Mother-son incest is reportedly rare. Now it seems that father-son incest is more common than was thought previously.[59]

Etiology

What causes incest? Some researchers, particularly psychoanalysts, believe that the appropriate question is why it does not happen more frequently. Lindzey has been outspoken in this regard.[60] He cites the psychoanalytic assumption that powerful incestuous impulses are present in all humans. In addition, he stresses that homogamous need matching and geographical proximity have a powerful effect on mate selection patterns.

Perhaps the psychoanalysts are right in their argument that incest is a highly attractive act to all persons. Nonetheless, there are specific attributes which characterize the families in which incest is known to have occurred. Research in this area has concentrated on families in which the incestuous relationship involved a father and daughter. The prominent etiological view is the "mother substitute theory" which holds that the mother relegates her role as central female of the family to a daughter, usually the oldest one.[61] This may be a conscious act as when a wife, unable or unwilling to meet her husband's sexual needs, deliberately steers him into it. In this way she keeps her husband in the family rather than losing him to a mistress. However, the "mother substitute

[57]S. K. Weinberg, *Incest Behavior* (New York: Citadel, 1955).

[58]P. H. Gebhard and others, *Sex Offenders* (New York: Harper and Row, 1965), pp. 230-271.

[59]Katharine N. Dixon, L. Eugene Arnold, and Kenneth Calestro, "Father-son incest: unreported psychiatric problem?" *American Journal of Psychiatry,* 135 (1978), pp. 835-838.

[60]Gardner Lindzey, "Some remarks concerning incest, the incest taboo, and psychoanalytic theory," *American Psychologist,* 22 (1967), pp. 1051-1059.

[61]Irving Kaufman, Alice L. Peck, and Consuelo K. Tagiuri, "The family constellation and overt incestuous relations between father and daughter," in *A Modern Introduction to the Family,* eds. Norman W. Bell and Ezra F. Vogel (New York: The Free Press, 1968), pp. 599-609.

theory" runs deeper than this. The mother's desire to put her daughter into the maternal role unconsciously stems from the unsatisfactory relationship she had with her own mother. She was rejected or neglected by her mother so she gives the daughter her responsibilities so that she can become a daughter again herself and act out the role of daughter as she wishes it had originally occurred. In effect, the mother and daughter switch roles. If this is true, then one reason why wives do not usually report incest between their husbands and daughters is because they actually condone it.

Incest usually begins when the father and daughter feel that the mother has abandoned them; both need love that the mother cannot or will not give them.[62] The girl accepts the father's sexual advances because she interprets them as signs of needed affection. She sees the mother as cruel and unjust. Thus the incest serves as a means of getting revenge against the mother as well as receiving affection.[63] In fact, one team of researchers discovered that in terms of initiating and maintaining the relationship, the girl takes an active role in about 60 percent of the instances.[64] The girls may feel guilty about any disruption of the home which results from the incestuous relationship, but they do not feel guilty over the incest itself.

The psychological status of the fathers has been evaluated. Although they are depressed, anxious, and confused about sex,[65] they are also moral men who are fundamentalistic in their religious beliefs.[66] The coexistence of religiosity and incest appears to be a blatant contradiction. However, father-daughter incest frequently occurs within a family comprised of a denying wife and a seductive daughter so perhaps many of these fathers simply succumb to frustration and temptation. Consistent with this, Lester, reviewing the literature on incest participants, reports that such men are not usually psychiatrically disturbed.[67]

Exhibitionism

Symptoms

The exhibitionist is a person who displays his sex organs to strangers who are usually of the opposite sex. The typical exhibitionist does not want actual sexual contact with the "victim." Instead, he achieves gratification simply through drawing attention to his exposed genitals. It is questionable whether this is only a disorder of the sex instinct since not

---

[62]Ibid., p. 608.

[63]David Lester, *Unusual Sexual Behavior,* p. 133.

[64]J. Weiss and others, "A study of girl sex victims."

[65]Irving Kaufman and others, "The family constellation and overt incestuous relations," p. 600.

[66]P. H. Gebhard and others, *Sex Offenders.*

[67]David Lester, *Unusual Sexual Behavior,* p. 142.

all exhibitionists have an erection during the act of exposure. Oliven suggests that there is a compulsive type of exhibitionist who does not seek erotic pleasure from exposing himself but acts to relieve a state of inner pressure from abnormal discharges in the temporal lobes of the brain.[68] However, this does not apply to all exhibitionists since some do have an erection and experience orgasm through masturbation after the exposure. A few have a spontaneous orgasm while exposed. Other exhibitionists expose themselves after sexual intercourse with their wives.[69]

The exhibitionist's behavior is stereotyped. He often returns to the same place to commit the offense. Usually this is a public place such as a street, train, or elevator, although some exhibitionists display their penis from a window of a house. Others drive around in cars with their pants pulled down and lure victims close by asking for directions. The timing of the act is also ritualized since they frequently expose themselves at the same time of day. The number of offenses increases noticeably in summer. Another stereotyped aspect of the exhibitionist's behavior is his dress. Many of these men wear a special outfit known as "flasher's gear." This consists of a long coat. Underneath the man is nude from the waist down, his pants secured above the knee by elastic. It is reported that only 7 percent undress completely.[70]

Closely related to the exhibitionist is the obscene phone caller. Usually this person randomly selects a female's number from the phone book and masturbates while making an obscene statement. Many obscene phone callers also have histories of exhibitionistic behavior.[71] The dynamics of this disorder are presently unclear. In fact, some consider the obscene phone caller to be a type of auditory voyeur.

Prevalence

It is impossible to measure the true prevalence of exhibitionism since many incidents are not reported. However, it *is* one of the most common sexual disorders that ends in arrest, constituting one third of all sexual offenses.[72] The disorder is reportedly found only among men who are typically between fifteen and thirty years old. In half the cases they are married, but they have unsatisfactory sexual relations with their wives.[73]

It is questionable whether the psychiatric literature is accurate in insisting that there are no female exhibitionists. This statement may simply reflect the American view of sex-appropriate behaviors. Certainly it is more socially acceptable for women to dress in ways that seductively

[68]John F. Oliven, *Clinical Sexuality* (Philadelphia: J.B. Lippincott, 1974), p. 469.
[69]J. W. Mohr and others, *Pedophilia and Exhibitionism.*
[70]J. M. Macdonald, *Indecent Exposure,* (Springfield, Illinois: Thomas, 1973).
[71]R. P. Nadler, "Approach to the psychology of obscene telephone calls," *New York State Journal of Medicine,* 68 (1968), pp. 521–526.
[72]J. M. Macdonald, *Indecent Exposure.*
[73]J. W. Mohr and others, *Pedophilia and Exhibitionism.*

exhibit their secondary sex characteristics. This reaches an extreme in the case of the woman who consciously undresses in front of an open window or the strip teaser who titillates a large audience. Yet in American society, it is the audience that is considered pathological not the undressed female. Davison and Neale suggest that there is a sex role bias here since "... a man surreptitiously looking at a nude woman is a voyeur, but ... a woman looking at a naked man is watching an exhibitionist."[74]

Etiology

Psychiatry is still in the dark about the origins of this disorder although there is no dearth of theories. All theories relate to functional exhibitionism, not the indecent acts of those with organic problems such as the senile old man who forgets to fasten the fly of his pants or the epileptic who unintentionally exposes himself during a temporal lobe seizure.

The main psychoanalytic theory holds that the exhibitionist suffers from unconscious fears of castration. He overcomes these feelings by showing his penis to assert its existence. These persons are not satisfied with a nonchalant response from their victim, however; they want to elicit a *shocked* response. Psychoanalysts believe that this is related to the exhibitionist's need for others to reassure him against castration. The greater the victim's response, the more the person is reassured. Some psychoanalysts contend that by his behavior, the exhibitionist is suggesting that the woman exhibit herself. In effect, he is saying, "I show you what I wish you could show me." Thus he seeks evidence that the woman has a penis to alleviate his castration anxiety. If castration anxiety is the core of the problem, this explains why the disorder may be so rare in women since they obviously have no such fear. Psychoanalysts believe that the exhibitionist is fixated at the phallic stage. There is some supporting evidence for this stage-specific proposition. First, during this stage many boys manifest exhibitionistic pleasure by showing their penises to others. Secondly, the phallic stage of development commonly includes sexual conflicts. Such conflicts are evident among exhibitionists, many of whom have the urge to expose themselves after an argument with a female.[75] Usually the conflict is with the mother during adolescence and with a wife or fiancée in adulthood.

Behaviorists view exhibitionism as the result of social learning. They believe the urge to expose originated during earlier experiences in which nudity was either a natural part of the home environment or pleasurably linked with an accidental happening. One theory suggests that free genital exhibition stems from a lack of privacy during childhood.[76] The prominent behaviorist theory, however, contends that the

---

[74]Gerald C. Davison and John M. Neale, *Abnormal Psychology*, p. 280.
[75]J. W. Mohr and others, *Pedophilia and Exhibitionism*.
[76]R. Zechnich, "Exhibitionism," *Psychiatric Quarterly*, 45 (1971), pp. 70–75.

person has a history of preadolescent, unplanned, but titilating exposures to females. One team of researchers reports the case of two boys who were surprised during urination by the entry of a woman. Later they masturbated while fantasizing about the experience and eventually began to exhibit.[77] Other accounts describe the continuation of exhibitionistic games such as "doctor and nurse" which some children play. It is interesting to note that the exhibitionist usually has a greater-than-average number of sisters.[78] Thus, his first audience may well be intrafamilial. This also helps to explain why the most common victims of exhibitionists are children and adolescent girls; they were present in the original setting in which the habit developed.

Other theories of exhibitionism are not very well developed. One suggests that since the exhibitionist seems to like to shock women, his behavior is an expression of hostility toward females. Two other theories are mutually exclusive. One contends that exhibitionists suffer extreme narcissism since they want to show off their bodies. The other theory postulates that exhibitionists dislike themselves and have a masochistic need to be caught and punished for their actions. Interestingly enough, it *is* a fact that exhibitionists often declare that they are relieved when they are finally caught.[79]

Regardless of the cause of the disorder, exhibitionists suffer from more than a problem with sexual orientation. Researchers consistently describe them as having great difficulty forming adequate interpersonal relationships. One team of researchers found 72 percent of the exhibitionists they evaluated to be neurotic.[80] Psychopathology may be even more severe among obscene telephone callers who often display schizoid and depressive qualities.[81] They suffer special anxiety generated by face-to-face confrontation. Telephoning prevents such contact and protects the obscene callers from acting out their rage-filled fantasies.

Voyeurism

Symptoms

Closely allied to exhibitionism is voyeurism. The voyeur, or *Peeping Tom*, derives sexual pleasure by looking at a member of the opposite sex in some state of undress, in a sexual act, or in the act of excretion. Such behavior is considered a pathology when it is the person's preferred

[77]R. J. McGuire, J. M. Carlisle, and B. G. Young, "Sexual deviations as conditioned behavior: a hypothesis," *Behaviour Research and Therapy*, 2 (1965), pp. 185–190.
[78]Cited in John R. Cavanagh, *Counseling the Invert*, p. 45.
[79]John Randell, *Sexual Variations*, p. 115.
[80]A. Ellis and R. Brancale, *The Psychology of Sex Offenders* (Springfield, Illinois: Thomas, 1956).
[81]R. P. Nadler, "Approach to the psychology of obscene telephone calls."

sexual activity or when it is undertaken at serious risk. The voyeur is usually a timid, inadequate person who is sexually inhibited and often impotent. He is nearly always a heterosexual and a habitual masturbator. He is not interested in spying on his wife or girlfriend. In 95 percent of reported incidents, he observes strangers in situations in which his risk of being caught is great.[82] There is mixed opinion about the dangers that voyeurs pose to others. Most researchers describe them as withdrawn persons who do not graduate to other forms of sexual disorder. However, some evidence suggests that one particular type of voyeur (the one with impulse-ridden, antisocial traits) can become tomorrow's rapist.[83]

Prevalence

Like exhibitionism, voyeurism is said to be common among men, but it is questionable whether this simply reflects behavior allowed males through their sex roles or whether there actually are other differences between the sexes in regard to sexual pleasure derived through watching. Certainly men act as if they are more aroused through sexual watching than women do. However, not all sexual watching (*scopophilia*) is pathological; a number of socially acceptable activities feed voyeuristic impulses in normal people. Pornographic material, pin-ups of females (or males), and all-nude girlie shows are commonly available for the "average citizen." Sexual looking is also a normal precursor of adult sexual intercourse. In fact, some couples prefer watching one another throughout the act and employ special lighting or mirrors to enhance their pleasure.

Etiology

The true voyeur is interested only in watching whereas for normal men, watching only supplements the pleasure they achieve through intercourse. The psychodynamics of this perversion are similar to those of exhibitionism except that the etiology has presently been sketched out only in psychoanalytic terms. Like the exhibitionist, the voyeur is considered to be fixated at the phallic stage of development. This fixation is typically the result of experiences involving parental sexual activity which aroused anxiety. A primal scene, such as the witnessing of parental intercourse or the sight of adult genitals, may cause an unusual preoccupation with the visual aspects of the human body as well as its sexual or excretory functions. Psychoanalysts believe the scene frightens the child and paves the way to adult voyeurism. Thus, the adult voyeur attempts to deny his fright by repeating the alarming scene.[84]

[82]H. A. Katchadourian and D. T. Lunde, *Fundamentals of Human Sexuality* (New York: Holt, Rinehart and Winston, 1972), pp. 288–289.

[83]John F. Oliven, *Clinical Sexuality*, p. 492.

[84]I. D. Yalom, "Aggression and forbiddenness in voyeurism," *Archives of General Psychiatry*, 3 (1960), pp. 305–319.

The voyeur spies on strangers to avoid the complications of sexual involvement with a lover which would be particularly threatening to a psychosexually immature person. In addition, many voyeurs reportedly use strangers to satisfy their sadistic needs since they unconsciously feel that they are punishing women by viewing them without their knowledge.[85]

It is important to note that the frequency of voyeuristic acts is affected by pornography laws. Pornography is a safety valve which allows the draining off of voyeuristic impulses.[86] The person who uses visual material as a masturbatory stimulant need not resort to peeping from the fire escape of a girls' dormitory. The relationship between voyeurism and the sociology of pornography has received empirical verification. In Denmark, for instance, there was a significant decline in voyeurism following the liberalization of pornography laws.[87]

Sadism and Masochism

Symptoms

The sadist is sexually aroused by inflicting pain on, restricting, or humiliating another person, usually a masochist. Sadism is a term derived from the Marquis de Sade, a novelist who was afflicted with the disorder himself. He catalogued 600 different varieties of inflicting pain. A common form of sadism is beating prostitutes who offer such services at extra cost. The most extreme form of sadism is the sex killer (*necrosadist*) who derives erotic pleasure from killing his victims. Some necrosadists multilate the body after the murder, a practice known as *necrostuprum*. Jack the Ripper was afflicted with such drives. Other sadists derive pleasure from deliberate cruelty to animals. Clyde Chestnut Barrow, the male half of the notorious Bonnie and Clyde bank robbing duo, was an animal sadist among other things. As a child he enjoyed wringing a chicken's neck almost to the point of death or breaking a bird's wings and mocking its attempts to fly.

It is impossible to know how many Americans have such impulses, but it is interesting to note that pornographic films involving lust murder ("snuff films") command a sizeable audience in this country. The least severe form of sadism is *moral sadism*. These people have a need to discharge their aggression against society, and they express these aggressions through verbal humiliation of others rather than through physical attack.

---

[85] Ibid.

[86] Ned Polsky, "On the sociology of pornography," in *Hustlers, Beats and Others,* ed. Ned Polsky (Chicago: Aldine, 1967), pp. 186–202.

[87] B. Kutchinsky, *Studies on Pornography and Sex Crimes in Denmark* (Copenhagen: New Social Science Monographs, 1970).

The masochist obtains orgastic gratification by receiving pain. Masochism is a term derived from the Austrian novelist, Leopold von Sacher-Masoch, a masochist himself, who wrote a number of stories depicting men being brutally beaten and humiliated by women. Some masochists like to be whipped or beaten. Others like to wear uncomfortable garments. *Bondage* is a variant of masochism. In this practice, a willing victim is constrained by ropes, chains, or handcuffs and then placed in vulnerable positions. Often he is beaten as well. Masochists requiring rectal stimulation insert various objects into their rectums and enjoy erotic pleasure from the resultant pain. Most male masochists are impotent unless they are tortured.[88]

There are varying degrees of masochism as there are degrees of sadism. On the milder side is the *moral masochist* who seeks humiliation, hardship, and failure rather than physical abuse. An example is the meek, henpecked husband who enjoys his position or the man who loves a cruel woman all the more when she rejects him. Another behavior which may be considered mildly masochistic is the penance (such as scourging or the wearing of hair shirts) required by some religious groups. In its extreme forms, masochism may lead to serious injury and even death. There are reports, for example, of young men who hang themselves to achieve erection and orgasm[89] and of females who increase their sexual pleasure by partially suffocating themselves.[90]

Prevalence

Freud considered sadism and masochism to be paired instinctual components because they often appear in the same person. This disorder is referred to as *sadomasochism*. For such people, the sadistic and masochistic acts are often a prelude to sexual intercourse. In its pure form, sadism is held to be most common among men, while masochism usually occurs among women. This distinction is, in part, the consequence of American sex roles. Men are expected to be domineering and aggressive; women are expected to be passive and submissive. Most men and women live out these cultural expectations, but sadism and masochism are pathological extensions of the sex-appropriate behaviors.

The true extent of these disorders is not known. The prevalence of sadism and masochism can not be inconsequential, however, as evidenced by the increasing number of sex shops catering to the needs of these deviants. Alfred Kinsey launched the only attempt at assessing prevalence in his studies of male and female sexuality. He estimated that 3 percent of women and 10 percent of men are sexually responsive to

---

[88]R. Litman and C. Swearingen, "Bondage and suicide," *Archives of General Psychiatry*, 27 (1972), pp. 80–85.

[89]H. Resnick, "Erotized repetitive hangings," *American Journal of Psychotherapy*, 26 (1972), pp. 4–21.

[90]A. Weisman, "Self-destruction and sexual perversion," in *Essays in Self-destruction*, ed. E. Shneidman (New York: Science, 1967), pp. 265–299.

sadomasochistic stimuli. Age does not appear to be directly related to this disorder since some persons have masochistic needs that remain latent until a crisis occurs during the middle-age years.

Etiology

As with most of the sexual disorders, the causes of sadism and masochism are not entirely clear. Psychoanalysts believe that there is a process by which pain can be connected with sexual gratification. This linkage probably occurs during childhood when the sexual instinct is highly plastic. Any number of experiences can connect sex with pain. Social scientists have long been warning about the danger posed by television shows which contain inordinate amounts of sex and violence. Such entertainment may not jeopardize the mental health of adults but the developing personalities of children are much more vulnerable since children often interpret what they see in literal terms. Therefore, if sex is presented as a brutal attack, then sex and brutality can become synonymous in the child's mind.

Psychoanalysts believe that those adults who connect sex with pain were children who directly observed a primal scene and concluded that sex *is* pain. Not all children who view a primal scene associate pain with sexual gratification. The interpretation depends on a number of factors which Meyers has summarized.[91] The age of the child is important; the younger child, with fewer verbal and cognitive skills, is more subject to confusion about the experience. Another factor is the exact nature of the observation(s). Such ingredients as the presence or absence of lighting and the type of sexual activities witnessed affect the child's reaction. The frequency of the exposure(s) is also related to the final outcome; chronic exposure to the primal scene is more psychologically dangerous and potentially traumatic than is a single exposure. Usually parents who habitually expose their children to the primal scene were so exposed by their own parents.[92] Another factor is the immediate response of the parents to the episode(s). If the child is spanked by a guilty parent, painful elements are added to whatever misconceptions of the sexual act the child already has.

Psychoanalysts consider sadism in men to emanate from a misinterpretation of the male role by the child who witnessed adult intercourse. He perceived it as a violent attack on a woman. If he also has Oedipal problems which cause him castration anxiety, he is even more likely to seek pleasure by hurting another. In this way, castration fear is reduced by doing to the woman that which he is afraid might be done to him. Thus he assures himself of his strength and masculinity by sadistically dominating another person.

[91]Wayne A. Meyers, "The primal scene: exposure to parental intercourse," *Medical Aspects of Human Sexuality*, 8 (1974), pp. 156–163.
[92]Ibid., p. 161.

A violent interpretation of the primal scene and castration fear are the two leading psychoanalytic hypotheses concerning sadism in men although other suggestions have been advanced as well. According to one other perspective, if the person has been raised to view sex as dirty, he is unconsciously driven to degrade and torture his partner before intercourse because he feels extreme contempt for the person who willingly engages in this forbidden behavior.

Rape

Definition

Rape is a sexual disorder in which force is used to obtain sexual pleasure from an unwilling partner. Actually rape is a legal term which does not fit into a meaningful psychiatric category because force can be present in some sex acts which do not involve rape. It is not rape, for instance, if a husband forces himself upon his wife because she has given her body to him under the terms of their marriage contract. Presently, some states are considering legislation which would extend the definition of rape to a husband and wife. Another terminological problem is the distinction between *statutory rape* and *forcible rape*. In the former, the female may have been a willing partner but if she is under the legal age of consent, her lover is considered to have raped her. Statutory rape occurs more frequently than forcible rape, or at least it is reported more frequently.[93] Legal penalties are most severe when aspects of statutory and forcible rape are combined. Such is the case when a man forcibly rapes a girl under sixteen.

Because of American sex role definitions, it is rare for a woman to rape a man. If a woman uses force on a man or boy, the act is legally designated as indecent assault, not rape. However, a female can be charged with rape if she assists a man who is raping another woman.

Prevalence

Rapes by total strangers occur but frequently the rapist and victim are acquainted in some way. It is difficult to estimate the actual prevalence of rape since many cases go unreported, often due to women's fears of public censure and stigma. However, some studies have attempted to characterize the typical rape on the basis of available data. In one such study of forcible rapes in Philadelphia, 19 percent of the rapes were reportedly precipitated by the victim.[94] In the same study, most of the rapists were lower class males, aged fifteen to twenty-five, who lived in slum areas. Most of the rapes were planned attacks involv-

[93]N. S. Goldner, "Rape as a heinous but understudied offense," *Journal of Criminal Law and Criminological Police Science*, 63 (1972), pp. 402–407.
[94]M. Amir, *Patterns in Forcible Rape* (Chicago: University of Chicago Press, 1971).

ing physical force but brutal beating or choking occurred in only 35 percent of the cases. Based on reported cases, rape is more common among blacks than whites. Rapists also tend to attack women of their own race. In another study of rapists in Boston and Los Angeles, the typical offenders were found to be young married men with physical handicaps.[95]

Etiology

Etiological theories of rape are quite similar to theories of other sexual disorders, most notably sadism and antisocial behavior. Like sadism, rape is a mixture of sex and aggression. The major difference between the rapist and the sadist is that the rapist does not seek out a willing partner. This is probably due to a weakly constructed superego which permits the rapist to exploit a female victim without a sense of guilt. Because rapists have a dehumanized approach to people, there is considerable overlap between the rapist personality and the antisocial personality disorder discussed earlier.[96]

Rapists are often reared by cruel, sadistic mothers who beat them.[97] In the process, the mothers give their sons the unconscious impression that women must be taken by force. In fact, some rapists are totally impotent unless a woman resists them.[98] This may be related to a desire to dominate women in order to satisfy deep-seated hostility toward them or to quell castration anxiety.

The wives of rapists are often part of a pattern as well. Despite the social disgrace of repeated offenses, they usually remain with their husbands because they fear being beaten or killed if they leave. Often the wives' fathers were sexually aggressive individuals like the rapists.[99] This suggests that the wives cling to their husbands and replay a masochistic pattern learned in childhood. These women are frequently frigid. Consistently, a rape is often precipitated by a long period of sexual abstinence.

Aside from family patterns, other social factors contribute to the rape count. One of these is a subcultural setting in which violence is common, as is often the case in slum areas of a city. It has also been hypothesized that rape is more common in highly civilized societies which impose rigid restrictions on sexual behavior.[100]

[95]D. Chappel and others, "Forcible rape," in *Studies in the Sociology of Sex*, ed. J. Henslin (New York: Appleton, 1971), pp. 169–190.

[96]E. F. Hammer and I. Jacks, "A study of Rorschach flexor and extensor human movement responses," *Journal of Clinical Psychology*, 11 (1955), pp. 63–67.

[97]David Abrahamsen, *The Psychology of Crime* (New York: Columbia University Press, 1967), pp. 162–163.

[98]John Randell, *Sexual Variations*, p. 105.

[99]R. Palm and D. Abrahamsen, "A Rorschach study of the wives of sex offenders," *Journal of Nervous and Mental Disease*, 119 (1954), pp. 167–172.

[100]D. Chappel and others, "Forcible rape".

One variant of rape is the *gang rape* in which a number of men assault one woman. Usually a leader organizes the activities. The gang members have been described as gratifying homosexual inclinations by sharing the same sexual object.[101]

Social Implications

Rape is a serious social problem because it often permanently scars the victim psychologically. Even if there is no psychological damage, a series of humiliating events invariably follow the rape report. These include gynecological investigation, police interrogation, and public testimony in court which has involved questioning about the victim's past sex life. In addition, some women are not able to return to the relationships they had with their husbands or lovers. Sometimes this occurs because the woman has uncomfortable feelings toward sex following the attack, but often it is because the husband or lover can not accept a "stained" woman. The public certainly needs to be educated about rape. Presently, many rapes go unreported because of the stigma attached to being a rape victim. However, some groups, such as Women Against Rape (WAR), are working to alleviate these problems.

Transvestism

Symptoms

The transvestite achieves sexual gratification by wearing clothing associated with members of the opposite sex. Less often transvestism involves a wish to be viewed and accepted as a person of the opposite sex. Female impersonation is sometimes called *drag* which stands for *dr*essed *a*s a *g*irl. Transvestism is often confused with other sexual orientations such as transsexualism, fetishism, and homosexuality.

The question of whether transvestism symbolizes homosexual feelings has not been answered. It is true that some homosexuals cross-dress but it is uncertain whether cross-dressing among homosexuals is used for its own pleasure or as a means toward homosexual ends. Available evidence indicates that transvestism and homosexuality are not usually found in the same person. A number of studies, including the Kinsey reports, found transvestites to have engaged in very little homosexual behavior.[102] Those studies maintain the typical transvestite is a married male with children, and he is exclusively heterosexual. Many cross-dress and masturbate. Others cross-dress before they have relations with their

[101]W. H. Blanchard, "The group process in gang rape," *Journal of Social Psychology*, 49 (1959), pp. 259–266.
[102]P. M. Bentler, R. W. Sherman and C. Prince, "Personality characteristics of male transvestites," *Journal of Clinical Psychology*, 126 (1970), pp. 287–291; H. T. Buckner, "The transvestic career path," *Psychiatry*, 33 (1970), pp. 381–389.

wives. Randell's study of 160 male transvestites did not support others' reports of exclusive heterosexuality; 49 percent of Randell's subjects were homosexual, and 51 percent were heterosexual.[103] Presently, the question of the prevalence of homosexuality among transvestites has not been resolved. Another unanswered question is whether this disorder is as rare among women as it is reported to be. It is quite possible that transvestism is as common among women as it is among men but is simply less noticeable because it is socially acceptable for women to wear men's clothes in American society.

Some cross-dressers are disordered in other ways as well. For instance, some voyeurs dress up like women and enter ladies' rest rooms in disguise. There are also reports that some masochists cross-dress and then hang themselves to obtain sexual pleasure from partial strangulation.[104]

The true transvestite is often weak in all kinds of sexual behavior.[105] He usually masturbates while fantasizing being of female gender. His prime source of pleasure seems to be the sexual disguise itself. Therefore, his satisfaction is more emotional than orgasmic. In fact, after the practice has continued for some time, it may no longer produce a sexual response but simply a feeling of contentment.[106]

Life Style

Sometimes out of guilt, the transvestite decides to give up the practice and discards his wardrobe. Invariably he returns to cross-dressing and purchases new outfits. Most male transvestites like to appear as a female of approximately thirty-five to forty years of age. In a rare form of transvestism, known as *infantosexual transvestism,* the person dons the clothes of an infant or small child.

Although cross-dressing often begins in early childhood, it may not become manifest until young adulthood. Many wives of transvestites do not discover the truth about their husbands until well after the wedding. Their reaction varies. Some leave their husbands immediately. Others stay as long as they do not have to see their husbands dressed like women. Others become supportive of their husbands' habits and aid them with useful tips on feminine dress, walk, and make-up. Some couples may even live together as two females and call one another by female names. In cases in which the children find out, there are reports that they prefer the father in female attire because he treats them better in that condition.[107] This probably reflects his greater peace of mind while cross-dressed.

---

[103]John Randell, *Sexual Variations,* p. 56.
[104]H. Resnick, "Erotized repetitive hangings."
[105]Arno Karlen, *Sexuality and Homosexuality: A New View* (New York: W. W. Norton, 1971), p. 356.
[106]John Randell, *Sexual Variations,* p. 58.
[107]Ibid., p. 61.

Etiology

Most psychiatrists agree that the transvestite does not have a well-established sense of gender identity, but they do not yet know how this problem originates. Behaviorists believe that parental pathology is the cause since there are a number of case histories of transvestites who were cross-dressed in childhood with the knowledge and approval of the parents.[108] There are reports that transvestites had fathers who cross-dressed.[109] Thus the origin may lie in the positive reinforcement or modeling of cross-dressing which then became habitual. In fact, some of the mothers of transvestites gave extra love to a son when he dressed as a girl, even to the point of complimenting him for looking so "pretty." This is most likely to occur when the parents would have preferred a child of the opposite sex. Their disappointment is expressed by treating the son as if he were a girl. Perhaps this explains the frequency of transvestism among first-borns; the parents may have had their hearts set on a child of the opposite sex and were particularly disappointed when their wishes were not granted.[110]

Psychoanalysts consider the transvestite male to suffer from castration anxiety which is alleviated by the belief that the female has a penis. Thus he identifies with the phallic woman by cross-dressing. He feels that he gains the rights and privileges of a woman by simulating her appearance. Therefore cross-dressing may serve as a refuge from the traditional roles of males in society.

Another etiological theory holds that transvestism is a particular type of fetish that develops as does any attachment for a fetish object. In this instance, however, the process may begin with a fondness for a particular item of clothing, such as silk panties, but it multiplies to the point where all feminine clothing yields pleasure and satisfaction.

Transvestites have been studied through the use of standard personality tests. The results clearly indicate that they are not grossly disturbed individuals, although compared to a control group of normal people, they are less impulsive, more socially inhibited, and more independent.[111] It seems safe to assume that a transvestite is narcissistic and

[108]Norman Cameron, *Personality Development and Psychopathology: A Dynamic Approach*, p. 670; Alexander C. Rosen, "The inter-sex: gender identity, genetics, and mental health," in *Changing Perspectives in Mental Illness*, eds. Stanley C. Plog and Robert B. Edgerton (New York: Holt, Rinehart and Winston, Inc., 1969), pp. 654–671.

[109]David W. Krueger, "Symptom passing in a transvestite father and three sons," *American Journal of Psychiatry*, 135 (1978), pp. 739–742.

[110]In one study of the family background of transvestites some 50 percent were firstborn. See: V. Prince and P. Bentler, "Survey of 504 cases of transvestism," *Psychological Reports*, 31 (1972), pp. 903–917.

[111]P. M. Bentler and C. Prince, "Personality characteristics of male transvestites: III," *Journal of Abnormal Psychology*, 74 (1969), pp. 140–143; P. M. Bentler and C. Prince, "Psychiatric symptomatology in male transvestites," *Journal of Clinical Psychology*, 26 (1970), pp. 434–435; P. M. Bentler, R. W. Shearmen, and C. Prince, "Personality characteristics of male transvestites," *Journal of Clinical Psychology*, 26 (1970), pp. 287–291.

enamoured of himself since, for example, the typical transvestite likes to view himself as an attractive girl while gazing in a mirror. Consistent with this, one research team found that nearly 80 percent of transvestites feel that they are a different person when cross-dressed.[112]

Transsexualism

Symptoms

The transsexual has a total aversion to his (or her) biological sex although he is physically normal. From early childhood onward, he has had a strong desire to change his sex.[113] Some eventually undergo sex change surgery, and others assume the identity of the opposite sex without any surgery. A transsexual should not be confused with a *hermaphrodite* who is a person born with the physical attributes of both sexes.[114] Transsexuals *wish* that they had the physical features of members of the opposite sex, but they do not.

Although the transsexual may have been arrested as a transvestite or homosexual, he is neither. He may don female clothes, but unlike the transvestite, he does not do it for a specific thrill; he truly believes that he is a female inside a male body. If he engages in homosexual relations with other men while he is still a man himself, he considers his behavior to be heterosexual. If another man shows interest in his penis, he is not stimulated because he is interested in the man as a heterosexual partner.

Prevalence

The number of transsexuals in the United States is unknown, but in Great Britain it is estimated that there are about 30,000 male transsexuals.[115] Female transsexuals exist, but they comprise only a small fraction of the transsexual population and are less often married than are male transsexuals.[116]

---

[112]C. Prince and P. Bentler, "Survey of 504 cases of transvestism," p. 909.

[113]Pauly, in a study of one hundred male transsexuals, reports that, by the age of five, two-thirds of the men felt certain that they were girls. See: I. Pauly, "Male psychosexual inversion," *Archives of General Psychiatry*, 13 (1965), pp. 172–179.

[114]Rosen reports some cases of hemaphroditism. One is an individual born a normal genetic and biological male. At puberty, he began to develop breasts and a characteristic female body structure. Another case is a person who was identified as a girl at birth. She possessed a large, rubbery organ which appeared to be a clitoris. It was removed but later a medical examination showed that she was a biological male who had been mistaken for a female because of the anomalous genital which was really a bound-down penis. See Alexander C. Rosen, "The inter-sex: gender identity, genetics and mental health".

[115]John Randell, *Sexual Variations*, p. 65.

[116]C. Hamburger, "The desire for change of sex as shown by personal letters from 465 men and women," *Acta Endocrinology*, 14 (1953), pp. 361–375.

Sex Change Surgery

When they request surgery, most transsexuals come cross-dressed. The males may have had their facial hair removed through electrolysis and may be taking estrogen, the female hormone that lowers the male sex drive. The females often bind their breasts flat. Usually a transsexual asks a number of surgeons for a sex change operation and is refused. He will continue to be miserably unhappy until he is able to obtain the treatment. Sex change surgery is difficult to get in the United States. Some psychiatrists fear that the operation will transform a delusion into reality; surgeons fear malpractice suits; hospital board members often oppose such operations on moral and religious grounds. In addition, many applicants forego surgery when they find out that they will have to undergo psychiatric evaluation to confirm their suitability for the sex change.

The male-to-female surgery involves removing the scrotum and penis (*penectomy*). A vagina is created from a loop of intestine or a plastic pouch (*vaginoplasty*). The Adams apple is shaved down. Female hormones are administered to stimulate breast development and to reduce hair growth. Silicon injections are used to enlarge breasts, buttocks, and hips.

The female-to-male surgery is much more complex. It requires a number of operations and may take as long as six months to a year. The breasts and internal sex organs are removed. Labial tissue is used to make a scrotum. A penis is devised by grafting skin onto a tube that encloses an artificial urethra. Then the clitoris is embedded in the artificial penis to retain orgasmic capacity. The patient is also administered androgen which produces facial hair and causes a weight increase.

Etiology

The causes of transsexualism are not entirely known. It appears, however, that it is not of biogenic origin since there are no cases of abnormal chromosomal make-up reported in the literature, nor is there any evidence linking transsexualism with biochemical factors. One group of psychiatrists is convinced that transsexuals are not rational. If they were, they would not insist that they are members of the opposite sex. Actually, most transsexuals do not actually believe themselves to be members of the opposite sex in a physical sense. They simply feel that they have the psychological make-up of an opposite-sex person. They want a sex change operation so that their bodies will complement their emotional make-up. Randell examined 640 cases of transsexualism. He found that true psychosis of the paranoid and/or schizophrenic types is rare

[117]John Randell, *Sexual Variations,* p. 75.

among transsexuals.[117] Only three persons in his sample were psychotic. Transsexuals are reportedly not as narcissistic as transvestites are. One study of male transsexuals revealed that their verbal and penile responses to pictures of other people are more intense than are their responses to pictures of themselves nude or in female attire.[118]

The psychoanalytic theory of transsexualism suggests that the disorder begins in early childhood through pathological parenting. Like the male homosexual, the male transsexual frequently had an unusually close relationship with a domineering mother and has had a father who was either physically absent or psychologically distant. Thus the son did not have a model for male identification. Stoller presents the most comprehensive analysis of the intrafamilial dynamics of the transsexual's childhood.[119] He has found that the transsexual boy first exhibited feminine behavior at three to five years of age. He was not cross-dressed by his mother although he sat to urinate and often asked when his breasts would grow. The mother was usually confused about her own sexual identity. She led the child to overidentify with her through constant physical contact to the point where the boy was unable to develop his own identity separate from that of his mother. Thus the boy's childhood was a continuation of his intrauterine life; he felt himself to be one with the mother, both emotionally and physically. Stoller's theory is not completely satisfying, however, because many mothers maintain skin-to-skin contact with their children for years, yet they do not produce transsexual sons. Therefore, there must be factors other than physical contact involved in the development of transsexualism. One possibility is that the mother may transmit her confused self-image to her son. In fact, Stoller found that often the mother of the transsexual had almost become a transsexual herself. She was labeled a tomboy and wanted to become a male, but her body developed in the wrong direction at puberty. She then repressed her hope of being a male but was able to fulfill that wish unconsciously through her long lasting intimacy with her son's body. Thus, the motivation and intensity of this type of mother may be what differentiates her from the normal mother who also engages in warm physical contact with her son.

Stoller also investigated the childhood backgrounds of female transsexuals and found that their mothers were often physically weak or ineffective. In addition, the father was often absent from the family. The daughter took on the responsibilities that the father normally would have assumed. She cared for the mother as the father should have, and in the process she developed a masculine identification which her mother encouraged.

[118]K. Freund, and others, "The transsexual syndrome in homosexual males," *Journal of Nervous and Mental Disease,* 158 (1974), pp. 145–153.
[119]Robert J. Stoller, *Sex and Gender* (New York: Science House, 1968).

Hypersexuality

Symptoms

Hypersexuality is excessive sexual desire that can not be satisfied. The sexual preoccupation may be confined to a single partner but typically it is manifested through a series of affairs with a diversity of people. The latter is termed *promiscuity*. It is difficult to say how many Americans are hypersexual because most cases go unreported and untreated. It is also impossible to ascertain the prevalence of hypersexuality by sex because of biased stereotypes of "normal" sexual conduct of men and women. The man who beds every woman he approaches may well be afflicted with some psychopathology, yet his friends envy his great "talent" with women. On the other hand, the woman who is not sexually monogamous may be branded "promiscuous." Largely because of these narrow conceptions of appropriate sex-role behaviors, no objective data are available on the true epidemiology of hypersexuality.

Hypersexuality among females is known as *nymphomania*. Typically, the nymphomaniac dislikes foreplay and wishes only for intercourse, but often the act does not produce orgasm. If orgasm is achieved, the desire for further intercourse usually returns within minutes. *Satyriasis* (old goat) is the term for the insatiable male who feels compelled to have intercourse with every female he sees. This is the *Don Juan*, also known as the *compulsive womanizer*. As soon as he "conquers" a woman, his thoughts turn to the next potential partner. Hypersexuality in men and women can be the source of many problems, particularly when the person feels guilty about his or her behaviors. Hypersexuality can also cause a number of social problems including venereal disease, unwanted pregnancies, and an increase in marital break-up.

Hypersexuals are emotionally immature adults who are usually incapable of forming lasting relationships because many of them are antisocial personalities whose feelings toward others are largely exploitative. They are typically compulsive masturbators. In fact, some psychiatrists consider intercourse by the Satyr male as the equivalent of compulsive masturbation *in vaginam*.

Etiology

The cause of hypersexuality may be a biochemical imbalance producing excessive amounts of male or female sex hormones. It may also be caused by abnormal brain activity, alchoholism, or drug use. However, the most common etiological theories in the psychiatric literature are environmental. Some theories describe hypersexuality as the result of a permissive superego or as a form of compulsive behavior.

Nymphomania reportedly can be caused by traumatic childhood sexual experiences such as sexual play with the father. This establishes within the girl a perception of sex as something to be used to obtain affection. There is evidence that a significant number of women who were molested as children develop promiscuous tendencies while others become professional prostitutes.[120] Nymphomania can also develop from social learning through imitation. This can happen in a family in which the mother has a number of affairs with strange men or where the mother uses sex to seductively manipulate her husband. Some believe that nymphomania can develop within a family in which the parents are extremely moralistic and strictly forbid sex as well as any physical expression of affection. Children in such families require outlets for their unsatisfied emotional needs. Thus they may seek relationships which are the opposite of the counter-erotic home environment.

Theories of satyriasis are mainly psychoanalytic. According to some psychoanalysts, the Satyr male suffers from an unresolved Oedipus complex which leads him to an endless search for his mother in all women. Other psychoanalysts consider satyriasis as a defense against a latent homosexual orientation while still others believe that the Satyr male *fears* sex so he reassures himself of his own potency by having repeated intercourse.

Miscellaneous Disorders

Other sexual abnormalities occur, although little is known about their epidemiology or etiology. However, in an effort to be complete, they are described here.

Frotteurism is a disorder in which a male rubs his penis against the fully clothed body of a strange female. These acts usually occur in crowded places, particularly buses, subways, and elevators. The frotteur is usually a passive, isolated person who relies on rubbing as his source of sexual gratification.[121] Sometimes the contact is maintained until ejaculation occurs. It is probable that frotteurism is linked with satyriasis and exhibitionism. Some psychoanalysts consider it to be an extension of the infant's desire to rub against his mother.

The *excretory disorders* consist of *coprophilia* and *urolagnia*. Coprophilia refers to sexual pleasure attained through defecating on a partner or being defecated upon. *Coprophogia* is an extremely rare disorder involving the eating of excretement. Some psychiatrists feel that coprophilia in adults occurs only among very disturbed psychotics. It may be associated with anal fixation since fecal play is a common practice among children at the anal erotic stage. Fenichel theorizes that coprophilia occurs among males with severe castration fear.[122] He postulates that the

[120]Harold Greenwald, "The call girl," in *Deviant Behavior and Social Process,* ed. William A. Rushing (Chicago: Rand McNally, 1969), pp. 194–200.

[121]Alfred M. Freedman and others, *Modern Synopsis of Comprehensive Textbook of Psychiatry,* p. 424.

[122]Otto Fenichel, *The Psychoanalytic Theory of Neurosis* (New York: W. W. Norton, 1945), pp. 349–350.

perverted act allows the male to experience sexual pleasure without being reminded of the physical difference between the sexes, particularly the female's missing penis. Therefore the female's feces are perceived as a symbol for the penis.

Urolagnia is sexual pleasure derived from urinating on a partner or from being urinated upon. It is also known as *Undinism* after Undine, the water spirit of mythology. Only a few sketchy statements about the etiology of urolagnia have been advanced. One proposition maintains that this disorder is a form of urethral eroticism which may stem from an overprotective mother.

Necrophilia is sexual gratification obtained from intercourse with a corpse. For obvious reasons, this disorder is only found among males. They obtain cadavers in various ways. Some choose occupations that give them easy access to dead bodies such as graveyard attendants, undertakers, and hospital personnel. Some are forced to rob graves to satisfy their needs while others murder victims. Necrophilia is fantasied as well as overtly practiced. For instance, some prostitutes provide specific services for necrophiliacs by cooling their skin and lying still in a coffin. The origin of this bizarre practice remains a mystery. It may be the act of a psychotic mind. It seems clearly related to feelings of masculine inadequacy since these persons derive satisfaction from a dead vagina which can neither engender castration fear nor demand a skilled performance.

Some persons obtain sexual gratification through intercourse with a living animal. This is known as *bestiality* or *zoophilia*. It is most common among adolescent boys who live in rural areas. In fact, Kinsey found that one-third of males in rural areas have had intercourse with animals. Goats, sheep, and dogs are usually involved but there are also case reports of sexual acts with horses, ducks, and even crocodiles. Some consider this disorder to result from a scarcity of human love objects in underpopulated rural areas, but the official APA definition holds that an animal is preferred, no matter what other forms of sexual outlet are available.

Another unresearched disorder is *pyromania*. The pyromaniac derives sexual pleasure from starting and watching fires. Often he obtains particular stimulation from seeing the fire extinguished. For this reason, there is probably an inordinate number of these people among the ranks of firemen. Pyromania differs from *arson*; both the pyromaniac and the arsonist deliberately set fires, but only the pyromaniac does so for sexual reasons. Fenichel has advanced an etiological proposition concerning this disorder. He proposed that pyromania is a form of urethral eroticism.[123] If this is the case, the link between urinary pleasure and flames has yet to be established.[124]

[123]Ibid., p. 371.

[124]Actually Freud first postulated a hook-up between sexual pleasure and fire. He believed that a tongue of flames symbolizes the penis. Thus, putting out a fire, especially by micturating, is "... a kind of sexual act with a male, an enjoyment of sexual potency in a homosexual competition." See Sigmund Freud, *Civilization and Its Discontents* (New York: W. W. Norton), p. 37.

Conclusions

Only recently has sexual behavior become the subject of scientific inquiry. As a consequence, many of the sexual practices of humans have not been fully delineated. In fact, there is no sense of agreement about which practices are normal and which are disorders. The evidence available does demonstrate, however, that homosexuality is not indicative of an underlying disturbance. For that reason, it is classified here as a sexual variation rather than a sexual disorder.

The attitudes held by many Americans toward homosexuality illustrate that it is a social disease rather than a sexual one. Contrary to popular belief, gay people are not harmful to society, have no abnormal physical characteristics, and do not necessarily play masculine or feminine roles with a partner. Some gays develop psychological problems because of the stigmatizing attitudes of others, not because their sexual orientation per se is a psychopathology.

It seems clear that an individual's preferred form of sexual gratification is linked with social psychological factors active during childhood. The exact process by which particular disorders develop is less clear, however. The etiological theories of sexual disorder are simply not well-developed. In fact, only the psychoanalytic school of psychiatric thought has devoted a significant amount of research attention to etiology, but the psychoanalysts account for different disorders using the same theory. Castration anxiety, for instance, is considered to be the central cause of a number of disorders including fetishism, pedophilia, exhibitionism, voyeurism, and transvestism. How is it that castration anxiety leads to an urge to exhibit in one individual and to a desire to cross-dress in another? The answer is simply not known because the origins of the sexual disorders are a mystery. In fact, the origins of all sexual orientations, including homosexuality and heterosexuality, are not yet known with any degree of certainty.

The only clear-cut aspect of the sexual disorders is their symptoms. But descriptions do not yield much insight into the psychodynamics of a condition. Knowledge of the way in which a disorder develops and what groups of people are likely to have that disorder are the pressing issues. Epidemiological data on the sexual disorders are highly suspect for a number of reasons. First, most cases go unreported, making prevalence estimates nothing more than guesses. As social attitudes toward reporting change, more reliable figures should be available. This is presently happening in regard to rape and incest. A second problem with the epidemiological data on sexual disorders is that the data are contaminated by sex-role stereotypes. A majority of disorders are supposedly found only among men. However, it may very well be that women are as likely to develop these behaviors as are men, but they are simply not recognized as such among women. Thus, the cross-dressed or partially-clothed female is not questioned while her male counterpart faces the disgust, contempt, and rejection of society.

III

The Social
Epidemiology
of Mental Illness

Patterns
of Mental Illness
Sex, Marital Status, Religion, and Ethnic Membership

Prevalence: An Overview

A useful test of the influence of social and cultural factors on mental illness is the epidemiological approach. Epidemiology is the study of the distribution of an illness within a carefully delimited area or population group. This is the type of investigation most frequently undertaken by psychiatric sociologists who, by measuring the occurrence and distribution of mental illness, uncover important clues about the role of social and cultural factors in etiology. The most common epidemiological study involves measurement of the total number of psychiatric cases in a given population. This measurement is known as a *prevalence* rate. The other type of epidemiological study involves measuring the *incidence* of mental illness, that is the number of new cases during a specified time period. Incidence studies are rare because it is very difficult to determine retrospectively when an illness began. The prevalence studies work on the assumption that if there is a difference in prevalence between different population groups, then the social factors that differentiate the groups may be related to etiology. If, for example, prevalence rates are different between males and females, then sex roles may be an etiological factor. Or, if married people have lower impairment rates than single people, this indicates that there is something about married life that is conducive to mental health. Additionally, if members of the lower social class are more frequently impaired than people from higher classes, this suggests that lower class life is a mental health hazard.

In this chapter and the two that follow, the major findings of epidemiological research conducted since the turn of the century are reviewed. These include studies of the relationship between rates of mental illness and such demographic factors as sex, marital status, religious membership, ethnicity, race, migration, place of residence, age, family size, birth order, adopted child status, social class, and social mobility. Some of these demographic groupings have been investigated more thoroughly than others; social class, for example, has been the focus of considerable research while relatively few studies have examined the effects of religious affiliation.

Methodological Problems with Epidemiological Studies

One inconsistent aspect of epidemiological studies is the diversity of procedures used by different investigators to measure prevalence. Some studies use hospitalization records. Others use evaluations by psychiatrists of people in the community on the assumption that not all mentally ill people are or have been hospitalized. Both types of studies have been criticized on the grounds that psychiatric diagnosis can not be made objectively because there are still many unsolved questions about the nature of mental illness. Thus, two sets of research findings may differ from each other simply because the investigators have different concepts of mental illness or use different methods to detect it. This criticism is valid to some extent. However, the data drawn from studies using hospitalization as the criterion of mental illness are less useful than those using a psychiatric evaluation of community members because the hospitalization definition is based on the shaky assumption that treatment rates evidence the amount of mental disorder in the general population. The fact is that impaired people who are *treated* are only a part of the entire population of people with mental disorders.[1] Consequently, figures based on treatment rates do not provide a satisfactory estimate of the real prevalence of mental illness in a society. A number of studies have demonstrated that treatment rates are a function of the availability of treatment facilities, public awareness of the facilities, public attitudes toward their use, the attitudes of the providers of psychiatric treatment as well as administrative factors.[2] Studies of patient records suffer further from the fact that they frequently do not include patients treated in private facilities. Typically, state mental hospital records

---

[1]Bruce P. Dohrenwend and Barbara Snell Dohrenwend, *Social Status and Psychological Disorder: A Causal Inquiry* (New York: Wiley-Interscience, 1969), p. 6.

[2]See, for example, E. M. Brooke, "International statistics," in *Roots of Evaluation: The Epidemiological Basis for Planning Psychiatric Services*, eds. J. K. Wing and H. Hafner (London: Oxford University Press, 1973); R. Fink and others, "The 'filter-down' process to psychotherapy in a group practice medical care program," *American Journal of Public Health*, 59 (1969), pp. 245–257; B. Kaplan, R. B. Reed, and W. Richardson, "A comparison of the incidence of hospitalized and nonhospitalized cases of psychosis in two communities," *American Sociological Review*, 21 (1956), pp. 472–479; M. Kramer, "Statistics of mental disorders in the United States: current status, some urgent needs and suggested solutions," *Journal of the Royal Statistical Society*, 132 (1969), pp. 353–407.

are used since this is one source that has been readily available over the years. The use of state hospital populations may bias results since admission rates to these facilities vary across social classes. The higher social classes, for instance, are better able to afford private hospitals or private practitioners. Another general handicap in using admission records is that they often record only the total number of admissions. Thus the researcher frequently has no way of knowing whether a single person is admitted three times or three persons are each hospitalized once. At this point, it should be emphasized that the numerous problems with prevalence studies make it difficult to draw inferences with any degree of certainty. Thus *the research reported in these chapters on epidemiology should be interpreted with caution.*

Studies of Nonhospitalized Populations

The type of epidemiological study that evaluates psychiatric impairment among members of a nonhospitalized population gives a clearer picture of real prevalence by seeking information about the "hidden part of the iceberg," rather than just the "tip." The investigators who collect data detect more cases, as would be expected. Based on these studies, the estimate of "one in ten" is most often used to refer to the number of mentally ill persons in the United States population. Compared to the alarmingly high rates of well over 50 percent reported in some studies, that figure is a rather conservative estimate.

Because of methodological differences between studies, various investigators report findings that are radically diverse. Since this has caused much confusion, two epidemiologists, Bruce P. Dohrenwend and Barbara Snell Dohrenwend, have spent a considerable amount of time painstakingly trying to impose order on a disorganized body of literature. They report that about sixty different investigators or teams of investigators have attempted to count treated and untreated cases in over eighty studies since the turn of the century. These attempts to measure both treated and untreated cases are known as *true prevalence* studies. They have been conducted all over the world—in North America, South America, Europe, Asia, and Africa. The range in overall rates of functional psychiatric disorder is presented in Table 8.1.

The rates are quite varied; in some communities rates of one percent and less are reported and in others the rates exceed 50 percent. Some of these differences are the result of different data collection techniques and contrasting conceptions about the definition of mental illness. However, one consistent result is that only a minority of the cases have ever received treatment. This is painfully clear in two famous studies done in North America. One of these measured the prevalence of mental illness in a random sample of residents of Midtown Manhattan.[3] The other used a similar approach among residents of rural Ster-

[3]Leo Srole and others, *Mental Health in the Metropolis* (New York: McGraw-Hill, 1962).

Table 8.1. *Medians and Ranges of Percentages of Total Cases of Functional Psychiatric Disorder According to Geopolitical Area and Rural Versus Urban Study Site*

Site		North America	South America	Europe	Middle East	Africa	Asia	Australia
Rural:	Median	17.3	—	11.9	9.9	40.0	1.0	—
	Range	1.7–69.0	—	1.1–28.6	4.5–14.9		0.4–54.0	5.4–6.8
	Number of Studies	12	0	15	3	1	14	2
Urban:	Median	21.0	18.4	15.5	—	—	1.8	25.9
	Range	1.8–32.0	17.5–29.8	1.0–33.0	47.4	11.8–45.0	0.8–3.0	25.4–29.4
	Number of Studies	12	4	5	1	2	3	3

Bruce P. Dohrenwend and Barbara Snell Dohrenwend, "Social and cultural influences on psychopathology," *Annual Review of Psychology*, 25 (1974), p. 423. Reproduced, with permission, from the *Annual Review of Psychology*, Volume 25, Copyright © 1974 by Annual Reviews, Inc. All rights reserved.

ling County in Nova Scotia.[4] Both the Midtown study and the Sterling County study concluded that there is a great unmet need for psychiatric treatment since a considerable portion of the untreated residents of both communities were evaluated as impaired to some degree. The interview and questionnaire data that were compiled on the 1,660 residents of Manhattan revealed that ". . . less than one-fifth of the population is well, about three-fifths exhibit subclinical forms of mental disorder and . . . 23.4 percent exhibit some impairment in life functioning."[5] The Sterling County study estimated that about 50 percent of the population is psychiatrically impaired.

Changes in Prevalence Over Time

It is important to note that, among those studies which evaluated a nonhospitalized population, there is a substantial difference in results between the studies published before 1950 and those published in 1950 or after. The later studies show an average prevalence rate about seven times greater than those published before 1950.[6] This finding led some to what seemed to be an obvious conclusion—that there is an increasing amount of strain in modern life. However, the conclusion is not actually that simple since psychiatric diagnostic procedures and forms of treatment have changed considerably since 1950. One such change has been an alteration in the concept of what constitutes a case of mental illness. On the basis of psychiatric screening experiences during World War II, there was a great expansion of the psychiatric nomenclature as exemplified by DSM-I. In short, the new nomenclature was based on a much broader definition of mental illness. Consequently, a greater proportion of test subjects were rated as impaired in the post-1950 studies. In addition, there have been notable changes in psychiatric diagnosis since the 1950s; the proportion of patients with depressive and schizophrenic disorders has increased while the proportion of patients diagnosed neurotic has significantly declined.[7] This may be due to shifts in the patient population, increased treatment of neurotic patients on an outpatient basis, changes in diagnostic categories due to increased clinical knowledge, or an increase in diagnoses more consistent with somatic treatment.

The introduction of tranquilizers, antidepressants, and other forms of chemotherapy, as well as an increase in out-patient facilities, have reduced the length of stay in mental hospitals and allowed many people to be treated in the community who at one time would have been

[4]D. C. Leighton and others, *The Character of Danger* (New York: Basic Books, 1963).

[5]T. S. Langner and S. T. Michael, *Life, Stress and Mental Health* (New York: Free Press, 1963), p. 76.

[6]Bruce P. Dohrenwend, "Sociocultural and social-psychological factors in the genesis of mental disorders," *Journal of Health and Social Behavior*, 16 (1975), p. 368.

[7]Jeffrey D. Blum, "On changes in psychiatric diagnosis over time," *American Psychologist*, 33 (1978), pp. 1017–1031.

institutionalized. Yet, while the proportion of the total population that is hospitalized at a given time has dropped steadily since 1950, the rate of admission has been increasing since the same year. The upturn in admission rates is the result of a growing tendency to label behavior as mentally ill which was formerly unrecognized or designated as eccentric or criminal. In addition, blacks and the poor who previously went untreated are now being admitted to hospitals and clinics.[8] Because the rate of discharge has crept ahead of the rate of admission, the overall size of the mental hospital population has declined since the early 1950s.

Cross-Cultural Differences

One important way to determine the effect of cultural factors on mental health is to compare the prevalence of mental illness in different societies, particularly societies that are quite divergent from one another. A comparative analysis of differences between industrial and primitive societies can provide such a perspective. Unfortunately, epidemiological studies of primitive cultures have been uncommon as a result of the once popular belief that mental illness is so different in primitive areas that the psychiatric nomenclature of industrial, Western societies is inapplicable. This belief has been contradicted by recent psychiatric research of anthropologists and sociologists in primitive societies.[9] In fact, the research that has been done on primitive societies has generated some interesting hypotheses. Weinberg, for example, holds that mental illness is less common among homogeneous, primitive cultures than in heterogeneous, technologically complex industrial societies.[10] Linton, on the other hand, believes that the prevalence of mental illness is consistent throughout the world, but the symptoms are shaped by the customs of each culture.[11] Linton is partially correct; culture can affect the symptoms of mental disorder, but it can also affect prevalence. As the Dohrenwends have noted, the lowest reported rates of mental illness occur in primitive societies: 0.8 percent in two isolated aboriginal groups in Taiwan[12] and 5.4 percent and 6.8 percent in two studies of aboriginal groups in Australia.[13] The American Indians appear to be an exception

[8]James H. Parker, "The urbanization-mental illness hypothesis: a critique," *Journal of Human Relations*, 20 (1972), pp. 190–195.

[9]Bruce P. Dohrenwend and Barbara Snell Dohrenwend, "Social and cultural influences on psychopathology," p. 431.

[10]S. Kirson Weinberg, *Society and Personality Disorders* (New York: Prentice Hall, 1952).

[11]Ralph Linton, *Culture and Mental Disorders* (Springfield, Illinois: Thomas, 1956).

[12]H. Rin and T. Lin, "Mental illness among Formosan aborigines as compared with the Chinese in Taiwan," *Journal of Mental Science*, 108 (1962), pp. 134–146.

[13]M. A. Kidson, "Psychiatric disorders in the Walbiri of Central Australia," *Australia and New Zealand Journal of Psychiatry*, 1 (1967), pp. 14–22; M. A. Kidson and I. H. Jones, "Psychiatric disorders among aborigines of the Australian western desert," *Archives of General Psychiatry*, 19 (1968), pp. 413–417.

since they have the highest rate reported in any study to date—69 percent in one group in the northwestern United States.[14] However, the American Indians no longer exemplify a culturally homogeneous, nonindustrialized group. On the contrary, they are a people who have been uprooted by what has become their host culture, the highly industrialized United States. The elevated rate of mental disorder among the American Indians is probably indicative of the disruptive impact of contact with industrialization. At the present time, available evidence suggests that mental illness is less frequent among people living in an uncomplicated, primitive society than among those living in a complex industrial society.[15] However, this must remain a hypothesis until more research can be conducted since one study of Yoruba villages in Nigeria found prevalence rates of about 40 percent, much higher than would be expected if the mere fact of living in a primitive culture immunized people against mental disorder.[16]

The data in Table 8.1 indicate that there is a wide disparity in prevalence of mental illness in different parts of the world. The median rate in rural Asia, for example, is 1.0 percent, considerably less than the 17.3 percent median rate in North America. Even in cultural areas where the rates are more similar, such as those in urban North America (21.0 percent) and Europe (15.5 percent), there are often important differences in the *types* of mental illness to which members of different cultures are susceptible. As was mentioned on pages 26 and 27, there is a preponderance of schizophrenic psychotics in the United States, but in England the manic-depressive psychoses are more common.

Another noteworthy aspect of the cross-cultural epidemiology of mental illness is the unusually high rate of alcoholism among the Irish. No one has satisfactorily explained this phenomenon to date. Some feel that because Ireland offers little social life other than the pub, alcoholism inevitably results. Others believe that the epidemiology of mental illness in Ireland is similar to that of other countries but that nonalcoholic disorders go unrecognized because they are masked by more visible drinking problems. A third explanation, and perhaps the most useful, suggests that alcoholism is so common among the Irish because they are one of the most sexually repressed groups of people in the world. Indeed, empirical data demonstrate an unusually high rate of celibacy among the Irish population[17] which is probably due to the ability of the Roman Catholic church to control the personal lives of the Irish. The

---

[14]J. H. Shore and others, "Psychiatric epidemiology of an Indian village," *Psychiatry*, 36 (1973), pp. 70–81.

[15]The reader is reminded of Lynn's finding that anxiety levels vary between industrial societies. The countries with the greatest preoccupation with industrial growth, such as Germany and Japan, have the most anxious populations. See R. Lynn, *Personality and National Character* (Oxford: Pergamon Press, 1971), pp. 94–95.

[16]A. H. Leighton and others, *Psychiatric Disorder Among the Yoruba* (Ithaca: Cornell University Press, 1963).

[17]R. Lynn, *Personality and National Character*, pp. 91–92.

Catholic teachings on sex have been interpreted by the Irish in very rigid ways as evidenced by a censorship on sexually arousing literature and a ban on the sale of contraceptives.

Differences Between Males and Females

In 1969 the Dohrenwends reported that studies of differences between male and female patterns of mental illness were inconclusive since eighteen studies reported higher rates for females and twelve reported higher rates for males.[18] The difference did not seem large enough to establish a clear trend. However, a more recent tally by the same researchers demonstrated that rates of mental illness are higher for females; in sixteen studies men show higher total rates of disorder, while in twenty-seven studies women show higher rates.[19] This came as no surprise since earlier research indicated that females expressed more distress than men in many areas of behavior including phobias, constant worrying, concern over an impending "nervous breakdown," and a desire to seek help with a personal problem.[20] Analyses of hospitalization records support the "greater illness among females" hypothesis; for example, in the United States 125,351 more females than males were hospitalized in the period from 1964 to 1968 alone.[21] Female patients also outnumber males in private treatment. In fact, a greater proportion of females than males are said to be mentally ill, as indicated by first admissions to mental hospitals, psychiatric treatment in general hospitals, outpatient clinics, private outpatient treatment, and mental illness treated by general physicians.[22] More relevant to estimates of *true prevalence*, community surveys of nonhospitalized populations found higher rates of psychiatric impairment among females. These surveys include both the Midtown Manhattan and Sterling County studies as well as a number of other similar investigations.[23] Although studies of the prevalence of mental illness by sex examined by the Dohrenwends were conducted in North

[18]Bruce P. Dohrenwend and Barbara Snell Dohrenwend, *Social Status and Psychological Disorder*, p. 13.

[19]Bruce P. Dohrenwend and Barbara Snell Dohrenwend, "Social and cultural influences on psychopathology," p. 437.

[20]G. Gurin, J. Veroff and S. Feld, *Americans View Their Mental Health* (New York: Basic Books, 1960).

[21]U.S. Department of Health, Education and Welfare, *Selected Symptoms of Psychological Distress* (Washington, D.C.: U.S. Department of Health, Education and Welfare, Public Health Services, and Mental Health Administration, 1973).

[22]W. Gove and J. Tudor, "Adult sex roles and mental illness," *American Journal of Sociology*, 78 (1973), pp. 812–835.

[23]See, for example: James Davis, *Stipends and Spouses* (Chicago: University of Chicago Press, 1962); Thomas Langner and Stanley Michael, *Life, Stress and Mental Health*; Derek Phillips, "The 'true prevalence' of mental illness in a New England state," *Community Mental Health Journal*, 2 (1966), pp. 35–40.

America and Europe, investigations of other cultural areas also find greater prevalence among females.[24]

Historical Changes

Females have not always had higher recognized rates of mental illness. In 1850, Edward Jarvis published a report on 250 hospitals in the United States and Europe.[25] He found that men were more prone to mental disorder than women, and he believed that this occurred because men experienced more stress than did women. Jarvis' findings do not stand alone; in a majority of prevalence studies published before 1950 (usually referred to as the "pre-World War II studies" because of the gap in publication between 1943 and 1950) the overall rates were higher for males. These findings contrast sharply with the post-World War II studies which report higher rates among females. Table 8.2 summarizes the studies reporting rates of psychiatric disorder for men and women according to publication date.

The reported growth in rates of mental illness among women since World War II has been interpreted in a number of ways. One interpretation is that females have become increasingly ill since World War II because ". . . women find their position in society to be more frustrating and less rewarding than do men and . . . this may be a relatively recent development."[26] In other words, there have been important changes in the female role during the post-World War II period, and these changes have created increased stress for women. Accordingly, more women than men now become mentally ill. The Dohrenwends, on the other hand, do not believe that the dramatic reported increase in mental illness among women should be taken at face value. They argue that much of this change is due to differences in methodology between the two groups of studies and not to an actual increase in mental illness among females.[27] The studies published prior to 1950 relied on official records, particularly police files, to identify psychiatric cases. These types of records are most likely to record antisocial behavior, alcoholism, and drug

[24]Investigations in Mexico have shown that Mexican females report significantly more symptoms than Mexican males. See: H. Farbega Jr., A. J. Rubel and C. A. Wallace, "Working class Mexican psychiatric outpatients: some social and cultural features," *Archives of General Psychiatry*, 16 (1967), pp. 704–719; T. S. Langner, "Psychophysiological symptoms and the status of women in two Mexican communities," in *Approaches to Cross-Cultural Psychiatry* eds. J. M. Murphy and A. H. Leighton (New York: Cornell University Press, 1965), pp. 360–392; J. G. Manis and others, "Estimating the prevalence of mental illness," *American Sociological Review*, 29 (1964), pp. 84–89.

[25]E. Jarvis, "On the comparative liability of males and females to insanity, and their comparative curability and mortality when insane," *American Journal of Insanity*, 7 (1850), pp. 142–171.

[26]W. Gove and J. Tudor, "Adult sex roles and mental illness," p. 369.

[27]Bruce P. Dohrenwend and Barbara Snell Dohrenwend, "Sex differences and psychiatric disorders."

Table 8.2. *Number of European and North American Studies Reporting Higher Rates of Psychiatric Disorder for Men or for Women According to Publication Prior to 1950 or in 1950 or Later*

Date of Publication and Type of Psychopathology	Studies in Which Rate is Higher for (N)	
	Males	*Females*
Before 1950:		
All types	7	2
Psychosis	3	3
Neurosis	1	2
Personality disorder	3	0
1950 or later:		
All types	2	22
Psychosis	5	10
Neurosis	0	15
Personality disorder	11	3

From Bruce P. Dohrenwend and Barbara Snell Dohrenwend, "Sex differences and psychiatric disorders," *American Journal of Sociology,* 81 (1976), p. 1449. By permission of publisher.

addiction, the types of mental illness more frequently found among men. At the same time, such data sources are not likely to identify the more private neurotic problems which are disproportionately found among females. The later investigations use more inclusive data collection techniques, such as interviews with community residents. These are likely to uncover the neurotic illnesses of women. Thus, the increase in rates of mental disorder among women may be the result of changes in methods for defining a psychiatric case rather than the result of stress-inducing changes in the female role.

Theories of Sex Differences in Prevalence

The controversy continues to rage over whether women are really more frequently impaired or whether this statistical finding is simply an artifact of biased techniques of data collection. On one side, such researchers as Gove, Tudor and Clancy argue that there are real differences in levels of mental illness between the sexes.[28] They note that the high concentration of reported illness among females is consistent

[28]W. Gove and J. Tudor, "Adult sex roles and mental illness"; K. Clancy and W. Gove, "Sex differences in mental illness: an analysis of response bias in self-reports," *American Journal of Sociology,* 80 (1974), pp. 205–215.

regardless of who is doing the selecting—". . . that is, women have higher rates when the patient is selecting, as with private outpatient care; when others in the community are selecting, as with most admissions to public mental hospitals; and when a disinterested researcher is selecting, as is the case in community surveys."[29]

On the other side, Phillips and Segal contend that the higher reported rates of mental illness among women reflect the fact that it is more acceptable in American society for women to express their problems. Consequently, women are more likely than men to *admit* to feelings and behaviors that may lead to a psychiatric diagnosis.[30] Men in Western society are generally reluctant to admit to unpleasant feelings whereas Western women enjoy much greater freedom in expressing their feelings and in seeking help in dealing with perceived emotional problems.[31] Women are also more likely to play the role of "emotional monitor" for their families by going to help sources for family problems of which they are only a part. Thus, by seeking help for others, they are mistakenly confused with the disturbed conditions of other people.[32] These sex differences are consequences of the socialization process. Males are socialized to ignore symptoms, while females are taught to be more sensitive to personal discomforts and to report their symptoms rather than overlook them.[33] Some women—in particular housewives—also have fewer time constraints than do most men since they spend less time in the labor force. Thus, non-working women have more opportunity to bring their problems to the attention of a help source. In addition, the rates of mental illness among women may be artificially inflated due to the fact that women are more cooperative during health interviews and are better able to recall their symptoms than are men.[34]

Another factor involved in sex differences in rates of mental illness is the heavy negative sanctions that men receive for abnormal behaviors. Studies utilizing case descriptions of disordered people have found that the male version of the case is rated as being more mentally ill than is the female version of the same case, regardless of whether the evaluators are men or women.[35] Since men suffer more stigmatization than women do,

[29]K. Clancy and W. Gove, "Sex differences in mental illness," p. 206.

[30]Derek L. Phillips and Bernard E. Segal, "Sexual status and psychiatric symptoms," *American Sociological Review*, 34 (1969), pp. 58–72.

[31]Ruth Cooperstock, "Sex differences in the use of mood-modifying drugs: an explanatory model," *Journal of Health and Social Behavior*, 12 (1971), pp. 238–244.

[32]Saundra Gardner Atwell and Gerald T. Hataling, "Sex differences in help-seeking behavior: a test of three perspectives" (paper presented at the annual meeting of the Society for the Study of Social Problems, San Francisco, California, 1978).

[33]P. Chesler, *Women and Madness* (New York: Avon, 1972); David Mechanic, "Perception of parental responses to illness," *Journal of Health and Social Behavior*, 6 (1965), pp. 253–257.

[34]Lois M. Verbrugge, "Females and illness: recent trends in sex differences in the United States," *Journal of Health and Social Behavior*, 17 (1976), pp. 387–403.

[35]Derek L. Phillips, "Rejection of the mentally ill," *American Sociological Review*, 29 (1964), pp. 679–687; Sherman Eisenthal, "Attribution of mental illness in relation to sex of

it is to be expected that they will admit to fewer psychological difficulties and therefore be underreported in epidemiological studies. The culturally defined male role tolerates less mentally ill behavior than does the female role. Females recognize, admit, and seek help more frequently than males because they are granted greater emotional indulgence than men who are expected to be more self-reliant. For this reason, males, particularly psychotic males, experience a prompter and more severe reaction from others than females do.[36] This runs counter to the labeling theory proposition that persons of low status and little power are most likely to be labeled deviant. If that were true, mentally ill females (in a sexist society such as the United States) would experience a more severe social reaction than their male counterparts. These sex role biases are found not only among members of the general population; they are also common among clinicians who are said to have significantly lower standards of mental health for women.[37] This double standard among clinicians appears in a number of studies which demonstrate that mentally ill males are hospitalized earlier than females and also spend more time in the hospital.[38] As sex roles continue to change, these prejudiced views of men and women should diminish in future generations as will the reported relationship between sex and mental illness. In the future, males may be much less hesitant to admit to psychological problems if the current standards of masculinity are altered.

Sex Differences in Type of Mental Illness

Although it is difficult to determine whether the reported higher rates of mental illness among women reflect real differences in *true prevalence* by sex or nuances of sex roles that permit women to freely express emotional difficulties and require men to camouflage their problems, there is little doubt that the two sexes differ in the *type* of mental health impairments that they experience. One researcher states that:

> Men's anxieties revolve around actual or threatened failure in creative work, inability to find a meaningful type of vocation, or difficulty in mastering the increasingly complex world of modern technology. Women's worries center around lack of competence in interpersonal relations, in-

---

respondent and sex of rated stimulus person," *Psychological Reports,* 28 (1971), pp. 471–474.

[36] Jeannette F. Tudor and Walter R. Gove, "The effect of sex role differences on the social control of mental illness," *Journal of Health and Social Behavior,* 18 (1977), pp. 98–112.

[37] I. K. Broverman and others, "Sex role stereotypes and clinical judgements of mental health," *Journal of Consulting and Clinical Psychology,* 34 (1970), pp. 1–7.

[38] P. L. Hurley and M. Conwell, "Public mental hospital release rates in five states," *Public Health Reports,* 82 (1967), pp. 49–60; B. Z. Locke, "Outcomes of first hospitalization of patients with schizophrenia," *Public Health Reports,* 77 (1962), pp. 801–805; A. Raskin and R. Golob, "Occurence of sex and social class differences in premorbid competence, symptom and outcome measures in acute schizophrenia," *Psychological Reports,* 18 (1966), pp. 11–22.

ability to achieve intimacy with a man, personality flaws, lack of a positive self-image, and insufficient approval, encouragement, and reassurance from others. With regard to family interaction, women's worries concern unsatisfactory fulfillment of the roles of homemaker and mother, anger and loss of temper in contact with the children, and lack of recognition and praise for successful role fulfillment by husband and children; whereas men worry about inadequacies in the fulfillment of the provider and father roles, insufficient time spent with the wife and the children, and lack of encouragement toward professional advancement and success from their wives.[39]

Differences in the ways that males and females are socially conditioned are largely responsible for the fact that men experience anxiety about their occupational performance and women experience anxiety about interpersonal competence. However, it is also possible that genetic factors are operative here. Some have suggested a biological basis for the male's greater need to master the world of object relationships and the female's greater need to master relationships with people.[40] In support of this, there is evidence that in infancy girls manifest a greater interest in looking at photographs of faces, while boys pay more attention to geometric forms.[41]

The question of whether men and women have different rates of psychosis has not been fully resolved. It is commonly believed that men are more susceptible to schizophrenia, while women have a higher prevalence of the manic-depressive psychoses. The Dohrenwends, however, contend that there is no clear sex differential among schizophrenics because half of the studies they investigated find schizophrenia to be more prevalent among men and the other half report it to occur more frequently among women.[42] This is also confirmed by a federal study of types of mental illness in *all* psychiatric facilities in the United States; approximately 22 percent of both male and female episodes are for schizophrenia.[43] The manic-depressive psychoses, however, generally affect women more often than men (eighteen of twenty-four studies reviewed by the Dohrenwends).[44] Kramer, using data from all United

[39]Josef E. Garai, "Sex differences in mental health," *Genetic Psychology Monographs,* 81 (1970), p. 136.

[40]Josef E. Garai and A. Scheinfeld, "Sex differences in mental and behavioral traits," *Genetic Psychology Monographs,* 77 (1968), pp. 169–299.

[41]M. Lewis, J. Kagan and J. Kalafat, "Patterns of fixation in the young infant," *Child Development,* 37 (1966), pp. 331–341; M. Lewis and others, "Infants' responses to facial stimuli during the first year of life," (paper presented at the annual meeting of the American Psychological Association, Chicago, Illinois, 1965).

[42]Bruce P. Dohrenwend and Barbara Snell Dohrenwend, "Sociocultural and social-psychological factors in the genesis of mental disorders," p. 369.

[43]National Institute of Mental Health, *Psychiatric Services and the Changing Institutional Scene, 1950–1985.* DHEW Publication No. (ADM) 77–433, Superintendent of Documents, U.S. Government Printing Office, Washington, D.C. 20402 (1977), p. 18.

[44]Bruce P. Dohrenwend and Barbara Snell Dohrenwend, "Sociocultural and social-psychological factors in the genesis of mental disorders", p. 369.

States psychiatric facilities in 1971, reports that psychotic depressive disorders comprise 9.8 percent of the male psychiatric population and 21.1 percent of the female psychiatric population.[45] However, it is likely that much of what is labeled "psychotic depression" includes both the manic-depressive psychoses and involutional melancholia, since the symptoms of the two disorders are quite similar. It was noted in chapter five that involutional melancholia is more prevalent among females because menopause, the common cause of the disorder among women, begins earlier in life than retirement, the typical cause of involutional melancholia among men. Therefore, although women are reported to be overrepresented among manic-depressives compared to men, this may be the result of clinicians diagnosing manic-depression when involutional melancholia is the proper diagnosis. Thus the higher female rates may result from researchers lumping the two disorders together into the category of psychotic depression.

Presently, the following conclusions can be drawn about the prevalence of types of psychosis by sex; schizophrenia is as common among men as it is among women; involutional melancholia is more prevalent among women; the manic-depressive psychoses *appear* to be more common among women; there are no reliable data on the distribution of the paranoid states by sex. Yet, while both sexes are equally susceptible to schizophrenia, there are vast differences in the clinical symptoms of male and female schizophrenics. Male schizophrenics adopt a feminine pattern of passivity, withdrawal, and submissiveness. Female schizophrenics, on the other hand, adopt masculine patterns of aggression and hyperactivity. It is as if schizophrenia forces the person into behavior appropriate to the opposite sex. A survey of thirty psychiatrists, men and women, lends strong support to this "sex role exchange" hypothesis among schizophrenics. The group of psychiatrists were in strong agreement that schizophrenic males are typically

> Better organized; more distant; better to deal with in a room; quieter, cleaner, more controlled; more constrained; more organized socially; better behaved; they exhibited more camaraderie; were more amenable to commands, requests and instructions; were less exhibitionistic; less hysterical; showed less acting out; there was less walking about, less screaming and crying; they were less hostile, more polite; clump in groups more; were less demanding, more cooperative, and better as a unit.[46]

The schizophrenic females were described by the same psychiatrists as

> More explosive; violent; displaying more homosexual and more general acting out; being more hysterical; more exhibitionistic; exhibiting more physical activity and showing more overt hostility; more noisy and pes-

[45]Morton Kramer, "Issues in the development of statistical and epidemiological data for mental health services research," *Psychological Medicine,* 6 (1976), pp. 185–215.

[46]Martin J. Weich, "Behavioral differences between groups of acutely psychotic (schizophrenic) males and females," *The Psychiatric Quarterly,* 42 (1968), p. 108.

ty; . . . more pent up; displaying more sexual material; more tearing of clothes; more disturbed; exhibiting more florid and interesting pathology; being more frenetic and volatile; more seductive; more agitated; more bizarre; more manipulative; more badgering; want to talk more; less conventional in approaching the doctor; grab your hand more; more clinging and dependent; there was more disrobing; they were less inhibited, "crazier," more psychotic, sillier, more expressive; had no group spirit; want more attention; were more outgoing, and more imploring; displayed wider extremes of behavior; look more dilapidated, unkempt, and neglect themselves more.[47]

The epidemiology of neurosis by sex follows a clear pattern; women are held to be more prone to neurotic reactions than are men. In fact, in twenty-eight of thirty-two studies reviewed by the Dohrenwends, rates of neurosis are higher for females regardless of time (pre–World War II or post–World War II) or place (rural and urban settings in North America and Europe).[48] The overrepresentation of females in the neurotic population is particularly marked in the thirty to fifty age group.[49] Because women are more susceptible to anxiety attacks, they are also more likely than men to develop psychophysiological disorders in which anxiety is displaced on to a body organ mediated by the autonomic nervous system.[50]

The rates of personality disorders are reportedly higher for men than women. The Dohrenwends found this to be true in twenty-two of twenty-six studies conducted throughout the twentieth century in both North America and Europe.[51] This is not true for all the mental illnesses classified as personality disorders in DSM–II since many of those conditions are simply prepsychotic or preneurotic states. As such, the prevalence of each prepsychotic or preneurotic condition follows the same sex-related pattern as its psychotic or neurotic counterpart. However, it is the *pure* personality disorders reviewed in chapter six that occur disproportionately among males. This is particularly true of the antisocial personality which has been the subject of most epidemiological research of personality disorders. In fact, many studies use the antisocial personality diagnosis interchangeably with the term "personality disorder."

Age Differences in Sex Patterns

It should also be noted that the prevalence of mental illness by sex is related to age. All of the findings presented above refer to males and

[47]Ibid., pp. 108–109.

[48]Bruce P. Dohrenwend and Barbara Snell Dohrenwend, "Sociocultural and social-psychological factors in the genesis of mental disorders," p. 369.

[49]R. C. Benfari and others, "Some dimensions of psychoneurotic behavior in an urban sample," *The Journal of Nervous and Mental Disease*, 155 (1972), pp. 77–90.

[50]F. Engelsmann and others, "Variations in responses to a symptom check-list by age, sex, income, residence and ethnicity," *Social Psychiatry*, 7 (1972), pp. 150–156.

[51]Bruce P. Dohrenwend and Barbara Snell Dohrenwend, "Sex differences and psychiatric disorders," p. 1453.

females beyond adolescence. Younger age groups, however, exhibit different patterns of mental illness by sex. Preadolescent males have higher rates of mental illness than do preadolescent females.[52] This is the result of a number of stress-producing problems that confront young boys. One problem is that the intellectual and physical development of boys is slower than that of girls yet they are expected to achieve as much as girls.[53] Another problem is that boys are more impulsive and aggressive than girls and also have a lower frustration threshold which often involves them in quarrels.[54] This in turn generates anxiety through conflicts with parents and teachers. Another stress-producing factor is the stringent set of sex role expectations placed on boys. Young boys are expected to act only in masculine ways while girls are usually allowed to pursue masculine activities. Perhaps this is clearest in the different social reactions tomboys and sissies receive; the female tomboy is "amusing," but the boy who is a sissy is shunned. At adolescence the situation of the sexes changes dramatically. During this period the girl experiences greater stress because suddenly she is expected to adopt the traditional feminine role and to drop any masculine traits she may have. Gove and Herb state that ". . . it is clear that girls who once sought and were rewarded for academic success find, in adolescence, that they should not surpass men and they come to fear success and to feel anxious over competitive behavior."[55] The move to adulthood is particularly trying for girls because they have been socialized to be dependent, yet in adolescence they are required to begin to act independently in preparation for adulthood. For these reasons, the rate of mental illness begins to increase among girls to the point where they outnumber boys in the ranks of the mentally disordered.

Marital Status

Marital status is associated with the likelihood of becoming mentally ill as well as the chances of recovering from it. Single persons have a greater prevalence of mental illness than married persons, and they also have a poor prognosis in comparison with married patients. Gove, reviewing fourteen studies of the rate of mental illness by marital status, reports that the rates of single persons are higher than those of married

---

[52]For a review of studies of mental illness among the young see: Walter R. Gove and Terry R. Herb, "Stress and mental illness among the young: a comparison of the sexes," *Social Forces,* 53 (1974), pp. 256–265.

[53]J. Kagan and M. Lewis, "Studies of attention in the human infant," *Merrill-Palmer Quarterly,* 11 (1965), pp. 95–127.

[54]Judith Bardwick, *The Psychology of Women* (New York: Harper and Row, 1971); M. Cohen, "Personal identity and sexual identity," *Psychiatry,* 29 (1966), pp. 1–14; Eleanor Macoby, *The Development of Sex Differences* (Stanford: Stanford University Press, 1966).

[55]Walter R. Gove and Terry R. Herb, "Stress and mental illness among the young," p. 258.

persons in the majority of the studies.[56] Both community surveys and analyses of patient records show a higher rate of mental disorder among single, widowed, separated, and divorced persons than among the married population. There is also a relationship between length of stay in a mental hospital and marital status; single persons have longer stays than those who are married.[57] Because of these associations, some consider marital status to be the best single demographic predictor of the chances of becoming mentally ill and recovering from it.

Theories of Differences Between Married and Single People

Marital status is probably a better predictor of mental illness for males than females due to the nature of the behaviors required of a man who marries. Typically, he must show initiative, independence, and aggressiveness in courtship. These qualities are inconsistent with the development of many types of disorders, particularly schizophrenia. The schizoid female, on the other hand, may be passive and aloof but to the untrained eye, her qualities fit in with the dependency expected of females during courtship. Consequently, more mentally disordered males than females are likely to be discovered before they marry. This theory of the relationship between marital status and mental illness holds that the association is the result of a *social selection process* which prevents the mentally ill from marrying because they are not perceived as good mates, particularly the males. From this perspective, mental illness precedes, and thereby influences marital status; that is, those who are mentally ill are not likely to marry. There is another view in which the temporal sequence is reversed; marital status preceeds mental illness. Proponents of this theory believe that marriage is a mental health haven which offers interpersonal security not available to single people. Studies indicate that married persons are better-adjusted and less depressed than single persons. Some interpret this as the result of more economic hardships and social isolation among single people.[58]

Differences Between Married Men and Women

It was stated earlier that female rates of mental illness are higher than male rates. This is quite apparent among married people. Married women have higher rates than married men but single women have lower rates than their male counterparts.[59] These data shed suspicion on

[56]Walter R. Gove, "The relationship between sex roles, marital status, and mental illness," *Social Forces*, 51 (1972), pp. 34–44.

[57]Ibid., p. 41.

[58]See, for example, Leonard I. Pearlin and Joyce S. Johnson, "Marital status, life-strains and depression," *American Sociological Review*, 42 (1977), pp. 704–715.

[59]Walter R. Gove, "The relationship between sex roles, marital status, and mental illness." Genevieve Knupler, Walter Clark and Robin Room, "The mental health of the unmarried," *The American Journal of Psychiatry*, 122 (1966), pp. 841–851.

the hypothesis that the high rates of psychiatric impairment among females result from a greater willingness of women to *admit* to problems. If this hypothesis were true, then the prevalence of mental illness should be equivalent among females in different marital categories, but it is not. Thus, the differences in rates of mental illness between the sexes are importantly affected by marital status.

Why is it that married women are more prone to mental illness than their husbands?[60] One reason stated earlier is that the mentally disordered female, particularly the schizoid type, may not be recognized as ill during courtship. It is not until she becomes more severely disordered that others recognize an actual illness. Often this is well after the wedding.

On the other hand, some researchers believe that married women are more likely to be mentally ill than their husbands, not because women are disordered before they marry, but because women find marriage more difficult than men. Gove lists a number of factors about the female role in marriage that are responsible for the unusually high rates of mental illness among married women.[61] One factor is that the married woman's role has fewer sources of gratification than does the married man's role. The woman generally has only her family to provide satisfaction whereas the man has his family and his work. A second factor is that a major instrumental role of married women, keeping house, is frustrating. It requires little skill and offers little prestige but must be constantly performed. A third factor is the lack of structure and visibility of the housewife role. This allows her to put things off and brood over her troubles in contrast to the jobholder who must meet structured demands which draw his attention from his troubles. Also, because the housewife role is only vaguely defined, the woman becomes responsible for "everything" that must be done in the house, while the husband has only a limited set of household duties. Thus, the wife may experience considerable anxiety concerning whether she has done "everything." Fourth, even the married woman with a job is less satisfied than the married male because she faces occupational discrimination in the form of low pay and underemployment. In addition, she puts in more hours than her husband because she must still perform household chores as well as job duties. The greater number of work hours per day places working wives under greater strain than their husbands. A final factor involved in psychopathology among married women is that their lives become meaningless when their children grow up and move out of

---

[60] Of 17 studies of the rates of mental illness among married men and women reviewed by Gove, all of the studies found that married women have higher rates of mental disorder than married men. See Walter R. Gove, "The relationship between sex roles, marital status, and mental illness," p. 37. It is also reported that the admission rates to mental hospitals are high for heads of female-headed families and of children who live in such families. See: Morton Kramer, "Issues in the development of statistical and epidemiological data for mental health services research."

[61] Ibid., pp. 34–35.

the home. At this time, the middle-aged housewife no longer is needed to nurture her children, one of the few sources of gratification available to her.

Among married women, the highest rate of mental disorder occurs among lower class females, especially those with little education.[62] This occurs for a number of reasons. First, the lower class woman is more likely than the middle class woman to fill only one aspect of the housewife role, that of mother.[63] Yet, while motherhood is more central to the lower class housewife, she is less likely to feel gratified by being a parent than is the middle class housewife because she is prone to view her children as creatures to be controlled rather than developed.[64] In addition, the lower class housewife is also frustrated by her husband who, compared to the middle class husband, helps less with household duties and care of the children and is more likely to desert his wife.[65] Presently, the greater prevalence of mental disorder among married women compared to married men seems to be largely due to the high concentration of mental illness among the lower class woman with less than a high school degree. Among women who are at least high school graduates, the differences between married and never married are inconsequential.[66] In addition, the differences between married men and women disappear after the male retires.[67] At retirement the male's social network shrinks, and his status becomes comparable to his wife's—limited and isolated.

Differences Between Single Men and Women

There are also differences in rates of mental illness between unmarried men and women but, contrary to popular opinion, unmarried men are more frequently disordered than unmarried women. The stereotypes of the carefree bachelor and the unhappy spinster are not reflected in the mental health statistics. Of fifteen studies of the rates of mental disorder among men and women who have never married, four studies found single women to have higher rates and eleven found single

[62]Richard L. Meile, David Richard Johnson and Louis St. Peter, "Marital role, education, and mental disorder among women: test of an interaction hypothesis," *Journal of Health and Social Behavior*, 17 (1976), pp. 295–301.

[63]Ibid., p. 295.

[64]T. S. Langner and S. T. Michael, *Life, Stress and Mental Health* (New York: Free Press, 1963); J. Veroff and S. Feld, *Marriage and Work in America: A Study of Motives and Roles* (New York: Van Nostrand Reinhold, 1970).

[65]R. S. Cavan, "Subcultural variations and mobility," in *Handbook of Marriage and the Family*, ed. H. T. Christensen (Chicago: Rand McNally, 1964), pp. 535–581.

[66]Richard L. Meile and others, "Marital role, education, and mental disorder among women," p. 299.

[67]S. Bellin and R. Handt, "Marital status and mental disorders among the aged," *American Sociological Review*, 23 (1958), pp. 155–162; B. Cooper, "Psychiatric disorder in hospitals and general practice," *Social Psychiatry*, 1 (1966), pp. 7–10.

men to have higher rates.[68] Why is it that single men are more impaired by their single status than single women? One reason involves the man's dominant role in courtship. If a man fails to get married, he is more likely than the single woman to feel that is his own fault since the single woman plays a less active role in courtship. If it is true that most women are eager to get married, then it is likely, as Srole suggests, that the man who is rejected probably suffers from the handicap of physical or personality deviations.[69] Thus it is the inadequate man who is left over after the pairing has taken place.

A second reason for the higher rate of mental illness among single males is that they are more introverted and socially isolated than are single women who have closer interpersonal ties. One team of researchers studying this issue reports that ". . . being unmarried creates 'expressive hardships' for a man at least as important as a single woman's economic hardships. Man's lesser ability to form and maintain personal relationships creates a need for a wife, as the expressive expert, to perform this function for him, just as the wife needs a husband, the economic expert, to function for her in the economic sphere."[70] Single women are happier than bachelors because they are better able to form attachments with others and avoid the anguish of social isolation.

A third reason for mental illness among single males involves early childhood experiences. Knupfer and others collected information on the childhoods of a group of single men and women; they found that a larger proportion of single men experienced stressful childhood situations.[71] They also found that single women had more favorable childhood environments than married men and women. Perhaps there is some truth to the old saying that "Happy marriages produce old maid daughters." The Knupfer group believes that their findings ". . . lend support to the idea that men who remain single are more apt to do so because they are handicapped to begin with, whereas single women do not give evidence of being handicapped in these ways."[72]

The Once-Married

The residence patterns in mental hospitals correspond to the sex differences between marrieds and singles discussed earlier; there are more married women than married men and more single men than single women. However, in addition to married persons and never married persons, there is another marital grouping to consider—the once-married. At the turn of the century Durkheim noted that the severing of the marital tie is particularly dangerous to mental health, as indicated by

[68]Walter R. Gove, "The relationship between sex roles, marital status and mental illness," p. 38.
[69]Leo Srole and others, *Mental Health in the Metropolis*, p. 186.
[70]Genevieve Knupfer and others, "The mental health of the unmarried," p. 848.
[71]Ibid., pp. 845–846.
[72]Ibid., p. 846.

a high suicide rate among widowed and divorced persons. Since that time, almost all of twenty-two studies comparing the mental illness rates of widowed and divorced males and females with the rates of married males and females found higher rates of mental illness among the divorced and widowed.[73] The rates of the widowed are slightly lower than the rates of the never-married, but the rates of the divorced are higher than most other marital status groups. Mental illness is particularly high among divorced men; they have higher rates than divorced women. The only other marital status group with more psychiatric impairment than the divorced are the separated—those en route to divorce.[74] Because impairment is greater among those closest to the disruption of a marriage (the separated as opposed to the divorced), we can conclude that there is something about the marital break-up itself that causes stress and high rates of mental illness, rather than that unstable people had been involved in the marriage. Otherwise the divorced and separated rates would be the same.

Religion

The Pathology of Religiosity

At the present time the relationship between mental illness and religious experience has not been fully delineated although there is a growing opinion that the interrelationships between the two should be studied. One basis for the connection between mental illness and religion is the religious imagery and delusions commonly found among psychotics in mental hospitals.[75] A good many behavioral scientists firmly believe that religiosity is either pathological per se, or it originates in an abnormal state of mind. Freud subscribed to such a view. He held that religion is an obsessional neurosis used by people as a means of repeating infantile experiences.[76] Other critics of religion contend that it is an escape from reality, a tactic originally used by primitive man to explain natural events that were mysteries at the time. In today's world, religion no longer serves such a purpose but instead is accepted by those who lack a rational perspective. Of course, it is quite possible that those behavioral scientists who think religious people are mentally disordered are reflecting their own biases against religion.[77]

[73]Walter R. Gove, "The relationship between sex roles, marital status, and mental illness," p. 41.
[74]Charles E. Holzer and others, "Sex, marital status and mental health: a reappraisal," (paper presented at the annual meeting of the American Sociological Association, San Francisco, 1975).
[75]Rodney Stark, "Psychopathology and religious commitment," *Review of Religious Research*, 12 (1971), pp. 165–176.
[76]Sigmund Freud, *The Future of an Illusion* (New York: Liveright, 1953).
[77]In 1934 Leuba reported that only 13 percent of distinguished sociologists and 12 percent of distinguished psychologists in the United States acknowledged the existence of

Perhaps religion per se is not as important as the individuals' response to it. In this sense, the way in which religion is taught by the family may be the key as to whether it is an infantile regression or simply a body of beliefs about the divine. Certain mental health experts hold that a body of beliefs is the true nature of religion. They dispute the views of their colleagues who believe religion is abnormal. How can this conflict be resolved? One useful approach is to distinguish between *traditional* religious commitment and *pathological* forms of commitment. The form of religious commitment examined by those in support of psychopathological theories is usually abnormal—people obsessed with holiness, extreme fears of the devil, or the belief that one has been given divine inspiration. This type of commitment existed among the members of the Peoples' Temple, a religious cult led by the Reverend Jim Jones who had the power to direct some 900 people to suicide-murder in the jungles of Guyana. In its conventional form, religious commitment may not be associated with mental illness at all. Indeed, one analysis of personality differences between religious and less religious persons found no significant differences.[78] Stark, in an investigation of religious affiliation (church membership) among mental patients and a random sample of normal people, found that mentally ill people were less religiously committed.[79] Stark concluded that mental illness and religious commitment are inversely related, but it is questionable whether church membership indicates true religious commitment. A number of studies have shown that church membership declines as social class declines, and, since lower-class people are overrepresented in mental hospitals, it is logical to expect that mental patients (in contrast to normal people) are reported more frequently to lack a religious affiliation.

Differences Between Religious Denominations

Although the nature of the relationship between religiosity and mental illness is still being argued, there has been some empirical research on the prevalence of mental illness among members of the nation's three major religious denominations—Protestantism, Catholicism and Judaism. One such study by Roberts and Myers examined the religious affiliation of mentally disturbed people in New Haven. Table 8.3 contains data on the distribution of the psychiatric and general population according to diagnosis and religious affiliation.

Protestants were slightly underrepresented in the psychiatric population compared to their number in the general population (31 percent to 33 percent). Catholics appeared in the psychiatric population in pro-

God. In addition, only 10 per cent of the sociologists and 2 per cent of the psychologists said they believed in life after death. See: James H. Leuba, "Religious beliefs of American scientists," *Harper's Magazine,* 169 (1934), pp. 291–300.

[78]Daniel G. Brown and Warner L. Lowe, "Religious beliefs and personality characteristics of college students," *Journal of Social Psychology,* 33 (1951), pp. 103–129.

[79]Rodney Stark, "Psychopathology and religious commitment," pp. 168–169.

Table 8.3. Distribution of Psychiatric and General Population According to Diagnosis and Religious Affiliation

	Catholic		Protestant		Jewish	
	Number	Percent	Number	Percent	Number	Percent
General population	6,736	57.5	3,869	33.0	1,108	9.5
Total psychiatric population	1,059	57.0	576	31.0	223	12.0
Psychoneurotic and character disorder	189	46.2	122	29.8	98	24.0
Alcohol and drug addiction	61	68.5	28	31.5	0	0.0
Schizophrenia	506	60.8	245	29.4	81	9.7
Affective disorders	86	55.1	53	34.0	17	10.9
Psychosis with mental deficiency	56	61.5	23	25.3	12	13.2
Disorders of senescence	100	55.9	67	37.4	12	6.8
Epilepsy	25	71.5	9	25.7	1	2.9
Other organic	36	53.8	29	43.4	2	2.8

Bertram H. Roberts and Jerome K. Myers, "Religion, national origin, immigration, and mental illness," *American Journal of Psychiatry*, 110 (1954), p. 760. Copyright 1954, The American Psychiatric Association. Reprinted by permission of publisher and authors.

portion to their numbers in the general population. What is noteworthy about the Catholic group is an inordinately high rate of alcoholism and epilepsy. Catholics comprised 68.5 percent and 71.5 percent of the alcoholic and epileptic populations respectively. The Jews were overrepresented in the psychiatric population (12 percent to 9.5 percent). Much of this was due to a high rate of neurosis (two and a half times above expectation). At the same time, it was remarkable that no Jews suffered from alcohol and drug addiction. Why is there such a high rate of neurosis among Jews? One factor is that Jewish parents provide extremely ambitious goals for their children. However, it is unclear whether a failure to achieve these goals produces neurosis or whether neurosis produces the failure. Another explanation of the high reported rates of neurosis among Jews involves their positive attitudes toward psychotherapy. Since psychiatric treatment does not conflict with their religious doctrine, Jews seek treatment more readily than do other groups. Catholics, for instance, are taught to deal with life problems through prayer and the counsel of priests. In the Midtown study, respondents were asked what they would do with a hypothetical psychiatric problem. About half of the Jewish respondents felt that psychotherapists were the most appropriate help source compared to only 23.8 percent of the Catholics and 31.4 percent of the Protestants.[80] Most of the Catholics and Protestants said they would not go to any type of professional, including a physician. The Midtown study also found that Jews have the highest treatment rate of the three major religious affiliations. In that study, Jews had an outpatient rate more than twice that of Protestants and approximately ten times that of Catholics.[81] Of course many psychotherapists are Jewish. This partly accounts for the high rate of treatment among Jews who can readily find psychiatric help from a "similar other." At the same time Jews are the least severely impaired of all three religious groupings. They simply seek help more readily than other groups even though they are less disordered. Why are Jews less prone to develop the more debilitating psychoses? The Midtown researchers believe it stems from the Jewish history which has immunized Jews against severe traumas. They state that

> ... mobilization of anxiety about the instability of the Jewish exilic environment may historically have been established as a conditioning pattern of the Jewish family structure. In one direction, such anxiety, subsequently magnified in the adult by extrafamily life conditions, may be reflected in our finding of an unusually large concentration of Midtown Jews in the subclinical mild category of symptom formation. On the other hand, this large component of historically realistic anxiety, as generated in the Jewish family, may function prophylactically to immunize its children against the

[80]Leo Srole and Thomas S. Langner, "Protestant, Catholic and Jew: comparative psychopathology," in *Changing Perspectives in Mental Illness*, eds. Stanley C. Plog and Robert B. Edgerton (New York: Holt, Rinehart and Winston, 1969), pp. 422–440.
[81]Ibid., p. 437.

potentially disabling sequelae of the more severe pressures and traumas of existence."[82]

The mental health status of the Jew is certainly a curiosity. On the one hand, a number of researchers have described the Jew as unimpaired relative to members of other religions. At the same time, Jews seek psychiatric help more often than others. *Why is it that the least impaired religious group receives the greatest amount of psychiatric consultation?* The answer probably lies in educational and occupational differences that separate Jews from Catholics and Protestants. Jewish people are concentrated in the upper echelons of the American stratification system and thus are more able to pay for treatment than are Protestants and Catholics, especially. They are typically professional people who are well-educated, and it is the educated mind which is most sensitive to the nuances of human psychology. It is also the educated mind which is oriented toward a sophisticated, scientific approach to problem-solving. Thus a Jew who feels distressed is simply cautious and educated enough to take the problem to the most scientific help source available—the psychotherapist. In the process, he becomes a registered patient even though his symptoms are mild or transient.

Ethnic Groups

Popular opinion has it that the United States is a melting pot in which people of differing national extraction are homogenized into Americans. In time that may be true, but presently there are a considerable number of ethnic groups that still maintain an identity separate from that of the host culture. The mental health status of some of these ethnic groups are reviewed here with the notable exception of blacks. Mental illness among blacks is best considered together with the literature on mental illness and social class which is presented in Chapter 10. The reason for this is that patterns of mental illness among blacks are chiefly the result of continued economic and racial discrimination. This is not to imply that blacks are more of a social class than an ethnic group but only that their economic hardships have caused mental health problems which typify low income groups.

Puerto Ricans

It is sometimes impossible to isolate the singular effects of ethnicity on mental illness because ethnicity is often intimately associated with religion as in the case of Puerto Ricans who are disproportionately Catholic. This makes it difficult to determine how much ethnicity contributes and how much religious membership contributes to the de-

[82]Ibid., p. 426.

velopment of mental illness. However, unlike Catholics in general, Puerto Ricans in the United States have a relatively high rate of mental illness. Dohrenwend found higher rates of reported symptoms among Puerto Ricans than among Jews, a group known to overreport symptoms.[83] Specifically, Puerto Ricans are particularly prone to develop somatic symptoms.[84] This is to be expected since many Puerto Ricans are not well-educated, a common characteristic among people who display somatic symptoms.[85]

Mexican-Americans

Mexican-Americans (Chicanos) have been described as relatively free of mental illness. In a study of the comparative rates of mental illness among Mexican-Americans and Anglo-Americans living in Texas, Jaco found Mexican-Americans to have 50 percent less psychosis than Anglo-Americans.[86] Another study of admissions to California state hospitals also uncovered a low rate of illness among Chicanos.[87] A number of hypotheses have been generated to explain these low rates. One theory is that the Mexican-American male actually is filled with feelings of insecurity and inferiority because of his subordinate social position in the United States. This stress is not very visible, however, because it may be masked by the Mexican machismo complex.[88] Another view suggests that some Mexican-Americans have primitive concepts of mental illness. Consequently, they are resistant to psychiatry and frequently use "witch doctors" rather than professional therapists, a practice most frequently found in the Southwest.[89] A third theory is that the strongly cohesive Mexican-American family is very tolerant of abnormal behavior and thus avoids or delays treatment. If this "postponement thesis" is true, then those Mexican-Americans who actually are hospitalized should be more disorganized and more severely psychotic than patients of other ethnic strains. There is evidence that this is the case.[90] But it is also possible that Chicanos feel alienated in Anglo hospitals and

[83]Bruce P. Dohrenwend, "Social status and psychiatric disorder: an issue of substance and an issue of method," *American Sociological Review,* 31 (1966), pp. 14–34.

[84]D. M. Kole, "A cross-cultural study of medical-psychiatric symptoms," *Journal of Health and Human Behavior,* 7 (1966), pp. 162–173.

[85]D. L. Crandell and Bruce P. Dohrenwend, "Some relations among psychiatric symptoms, organic illness, and social class," *American Journal of Psychiatry,* 23 (1967), pp. 1527–1538.

[86]E. G. Jaco, *The Social Epidemiology of Mental Disorders—A Psychiatric Survey of Texas* (New York: The Russell Sage Foundation, 1960), p. 474.

[87]Harry H. L. Kitano, "Japanese-American mental illness," in *Changing Perspectives in Mental Illness,* eds. Stanley C. Plog and Robert B. Edgerton (New York: Holt, Rinehart and Winston, 1969), pp. 256–284.

[88]Samuel Ramos, *Profile of Man and Culture in Mexico* (Austin, Texas: The University of Texas Press, 1962).

[89]William Madsen, "Mexican-Americans and Anglo-Americans: a comparative study of mental health in Texas," in *Changing Perspectives in Mental Illness,* eds. Stanley C. Plog and Robert B. Edgerton (New York: Holt, Rinehart and Winston, 1969), p. 238.

[90]Horacio Fabega Jr., Jon D. Swartz and Carole Ann Wallace, "Ethnic differences in

appear more ill as a result. A fourth theory holds that the reports of low rates of mental illness among Chicanos reflect the fact that there really is less mental illness among Mexican-Americans than among Anglo-Americans. It is argued that all members of the tightly knit Chicano family share the same values. This in turn, provides the Mexican-American with a clearer sense of identity and fewer role conflicts than the Anglos.[91] In addition, the Mexican-American view of the world allows the individual to avoid guilt and self-doubt by placing the blame for failure on witchcraft or fate, rather than on himself.[92]

One study investigated specific symptomatic differences between Chicano females and Anglo females in treatment.[93] Comparisons of diagnoses showed a relatively higher prevalence of personality disorders (preneurotic and prepsychotic) among the Anglo patients and a relatively higher rate of neurosis among the Chicano patients. A recurring symptom among the Mexican-American patients was depression. The researchers hypothesized that the depression resulted from the highly subordinate role of the Mexican-American female who is expected to be a good mother, uncomplaining and subservient to the males of the household. The women were frequently troubled by their husbands' "acting out" behavior which included sexual promiscuity, drunkenness, episodic desertion of the family, and physical assaults upon the wife and children. In contrast, the central symptom of the Anglo patients was guilt and defensive detachment from others, a presumed reflection of the Anglo societal ethic that holds individuals responsible for their own failures. Consistent with this, the Anglo patients were frequently troubled by economic matters, the symbols of personal achievement.

Japanese-Americans

Japanese-Americans have puzzled behavioral scientists over the years because they appear to be an exceptional group in that they are free of antisocial tendencies, as evidenced by an immeasurably small rate of delinquency.[94] The Japanese have not reacted to discriminatory treatment in the United States with high rates of crime and mental illness. For this reason, they are rarely considered to be a "problem minority." Kitano's investigation of hospitalization rates among the Japanese found that mental illness is not a major problem for the Japanese, compared to other groups.[95] Those Japanese that are hospitalized are typically single, old, lower-class males suffering from

---

psychopathology: specific differences with emphasis on a Mexican-American group," *Journal of Psychiatric Research*, 6 (1968), pp. 221–235.

[91]William Madsen, "Mexican-Americans and Anglo-Americans," p. 239.

[92]Ibid., p. 239.

[93]David H. Staker, Louis A. Zurcher and Wayne Fox, "Women in psychotherapy: a cross-cultural comparison," *International Journal of Social Psychiatry*, 15 (1969), pp. 5–22.

[94]Harry H. L. Kitano, "Changing achievement patterns of the Japanese in the United States," *The Journal of Social Psychology*, 58 (1962), pp. 257–264.

[95]Harry H. L. Kitano, "Japanese-American mental illness," p. 267.

schizophrenia. The hospitalization rates and symptomatic patterns are similar for the Japanese in Japan and in the United States.[96]

One important reason for the low rate of disorder among Japanese-Americans is the tightly knit family structure. Like the Chicano family, the Japanese family is a very cohesive group that exerts a high degree of social control over its members. This not only functions as a mental health haven by offering interpersonal security, but it also reduces the likelihood of outside "experts" being used to handle behavioral problems. Consequently, few Japanese become registered in the official mental illness statistics.[97] Another control on the expression of mental illness among the Japanese is their strong belief in directing reactions to stress and frustration inward without showing any external signs. This tendency among the Japanese to internalize problems and not bother others with them is known as the concept of "ga-man."

Certainly the strong sense of social solidarity within the Japanese family and in the Japanese community as a whole reduces the need for professional help with psychiatric problems. But other factors are at work as well. Kitano notes that the Japanese Americans are unsophisticated regarding the causes and treatment of mental illness.[98] Because of this, they have no clear conception of what mental illness is and consequently rarely use psychiatric facilities. In addition, there is the "Kibei" custom whereby American-born children are sent to be raised by relatives in Japan. Often these are children with behavioral problems who are never treated in this country and therefore not included in the mental illness statistics.[99]

Chinese-Americans

The Chinese in the United States exhibit mental illness patterns that in some ways parallel those of Japanese-Americans. Chinese-Americans have particularly low rates of antisocial behavior and alcoholism.[100] However, research indicates that the mental health status of Chinese-Americans has worsened throughout the last century. During that time, trends in mental hospital commitments among Chinese in California, for example, have changed significantly.[101] There has been a twofold increase for the general population compared to a sevenfold increase among the Chinese in that state. Like the Japanese, the Chinese commitment rates are especially high for aged males, particularly those who emigrated from China. Certainly, the Chinese have suffered much

---

[96]Ibid., p. 267.

[97]Although Japanese rarely seek professional help, they show a great deal of interest in mental health problems as evidenced by their high attendance at public lectures on the subject. Ibid., p. 260.

[98]Ibid., p. 278.

[99]Ibid., p. 271.

[100]Theodore Millon and Renée Millon, *Abnormal Behavior and Personality: A Biosocial Learning Approach* (Philadelphia: W.B. Saunders, 1974), p. 183.

[101]Bernard B. Berk and Lucie Cheng Hirata, "Mental illness among the Chinese: myth or reality?" *Journal of Social Issues*, 29 (1973), pp. 149–166.

physical and social violence in America. Until the 1950s the Chinese experience in America was one of blatant discrimination. Since that time discriminatory behavior has assumed subtler forms. In 1882, however, discrimination became official government policy when Congress passed the Exclusion Act which prevented further Chinese immigration. The psychiatric impact of this social policy was painfully clear; the rate of diagnosed paranoia (with persecutory content) increased from 3 percent to 9 percent.[102] This lends support to the sociological theory of paranoia which holds that behavior labeled as delusions of persecution is often a realistic reaction to actual social rejection. Such a formula seems to fit the Chinese experience quite well.

There has been an interesting change in the mental illness trends of Chinese-Americans from the 1850s to the 1950s. In the 1850s, 65 percent of Chinese mental patients committed to California hospitals were diagnosed as manic-depressives.[103] Less than 7 percent were so diagnosed in the 1950s; instead, the diagnosis of schizophrenia rapidly increased to the point where 85 percent of Chinese patients were labeled as schizophrenics.[104] If schizophrenia is a more disturbed state than manic-depression, and it certainly seems to be, then the shift from manic-depressive to schizophrenic conditions can be interpreted as a growing deterioration of the mental health of Chinese-Americans.

European Groups

For only a few of the many groups who emigrated from Europe are there well-documented mental illness characteristics. One group is the Irish. As noted earlier, their rate of alcoholism is exceedingly high. In fact, it is the specific contribution of the Irish that is responsible for the high rate of alcoholism among Catholics in general.[105] In many ways it is remarkable that the Irish can find an outlet for psychological conflict in this single form of escape. But, as noted earlier, the Irish version of the teachings of the Roman Catholic Church is exceptionally rigid, leaving few forms of behavior as socially acceptable. Malzberg reports that admission rates for the Irish to American hospitals are the highest of all European groups.[106] Polish immigrants also have above average rates, but one must be careful to separate the Slavic and Jewish streams.[107] The high rate for immigrants from Poland is due to the Slavic element, not the Jewish stream, which, as noted earlier, rarely requires hospitalization. The lowest rates are found among English, Italian, and Russian

[102]Ibid., p. 164.
[103]Ibid., p. 161.
[104]Ibid., p. 164.
[105]Bertram H. Roberts and Jerome K. Myers, "Religion, national origin, immigration and mental illness," p. 761.
[106]Benjamin Malzberg, "Are immigrants psychologically disturbed?" in *Changing Perspectives in Mental Illness,* eds. Stanley C. Plog and Robert B. Edgerton (New York: Holt, Rinehart and Winston, 1969), p. 408.
[107]Ibid., p. 408.

(disproportionately Jewish) immigrants while Germans have an average admission rate.[108]

Conclusions

Prevalence studies of mental illness have often produced inconsistent results because different researchers use different techniques of measuring prevalence. Methodology aside, a number of demographics appear to be related to rate and type of mental illness. Cross-cultural research indicates that there is less mental illness in primitive societies than in complex industrialized settings.

There is more mental illness reported among females than males. This is either because females are under greater stress or because they are more likely to admit to emotional problems than are men who are stigmatized for appearing weak and in need of help. Schizophrenia is reported to be equally common among men and women. Psychotic depression is held to be more common among females who are especially vulnerable to involutional melancholia. Neuroses are also said to be more common among women. Psychophysiologic and personality disorders, particularly the antisocial type, are found more frequently among males.

Married persons have lower reported rates of disorder than do nonmarried persons. Within marital categories, there are important differences by sex. Married women are known to be more disordered than married men either because women prone to mental illness are not as visible before marriage as are disordered men or because women find marriage more difficult than men do because of the particular strains of the housewife role. Single females are reported to be less disordered than single males. This is generally taken to indicate that women are better able to form attachments with others and thus avoid the anguish of social isolation.

Certain patterns emerge from the research on religious denomination and mental illness. One is a high rate of alcoholism noted among Catholics. Much of this is accounted for by the specific contribution of the Irish strain of Catholics. Jews are overrepresented in the psychiatric population. At the same time, they are rarely seriously impaired, suffering mainly from neurosis. The high prevalence of mild disorders among Jews is due in part to the fact that they seek and can afford treatment more readily than other groups.

The mental health status of different ethnic groups in America is far from homogeneous. High rates are reported among Puerto Ricans and Indians while the Japanese and Mexicans both with tightly knit family structures, have relatively low reported rates.

[108]Ibid., p. 408.

Patterns
of Mental Illness

Migration, Place of Residence, Age, and Family Variables

The Effect of Geographical Mobility

International Migration

"Social stress" is a common concept running through many etiological theories of mental disorder. One factor believed to produce stress is geographical mobility of which there are two types; one is international mobility or external mobility whereby a person moves from one country to another, and the other is internal mobility whereby a person moves to a different area of the same country. Since the two types of mobility may have different effects, they are considered separately here.

An overrepresentation of foreign-born people in the mental hospital population was noted as early as 1910. In that year, native-born constituted 69.8 percent of the population of New York State but only 52.6 percent of admissions to state hospitals. The foreign-born, on the other hand, constituted 30.2 percent of the general population and 47.4 percent of hospital admissions, exceeding their "quota" by 17 percent.[1] In 1939, Faris and Dunham reported a similar finding in Chicago—a pronounced overrepresentation of foreign-born in mental hospital admissions.[2] From 1949 to 1951, admissions for schizophrenia in New

---

[1]Benjamin Malzberg, "Are immigrants psychologically disturbed?" in *Changing Perspectives in Mental Illness* eds. Stanley C. Plog and Robert B. Edgerton (New York: Holt, Rinehart and Winston, 1969), pp. 397–398.

[2]Robert E. L. Faris and H. Warren Dunham, *Mental Disorders in Urban Areas* (Chicago: University of Chicago Press, 1939).

York State among the foreign-born exceeded that of the native-born by 28 percent.[3] The corresponding statistics for Canada from 1950 to 1952 agree closely with those of New York State.[4] And in New Haven in 1950 immigrants into the United States constituted 20.5 percent of the general population and 23 percent of the psychiatric population, a small overrepresentation of foreign-born compared to other studies but consistent with the observed pattern.[5] A review of all studies of prevalence of mental disorder among United States immigrants concluded that the rate of schizophrenia is markedly higher among the foreign-born than among the native-born.[6] The same review also noted that immigrant patients are often diagnosed as schizophrenic, paranoid type, a reflection of the suspiciousness that a person can develop living among unfamiliar people. This is also very evident among immigrants to Great Britain.[7]

A number of factors characterize the type of immigrant most vulnerable to mental illness. One factor is the duration of residence in the host country. Consistent with the concept of culture shock, those immigrants who have the shortest period of residence have the highest rate of hospital admissions.[8] Another factor is age as the older immigrants are particularly vulnerable to mental disorder.[9]

The central etiological question of the international migration studies is, "Do individuals who emigrate become mentally ill because of the stresses involved in adjusting to a new environment, or are individuals who are predisposed to mental illness more likely to emigrate?" The theories based on these two positions are known as the *stress model* and the *migration model*. The stress model holds that mental illness among the foreign-born results from the stresses of adapting to a new environment. Afro-Americans and Afro-Britains illustrate this model well. They are placed in a double-bind relationship with society because they are offered inducements to social mobility while at the same time they are discouraged from achieving such success. They are expected to strive but not to succeed. In fact, if a person emigrates to improve his social status, it is likely that he will first experience a decline in social status, a factor known to play an important role in the etiology of mental illness. Such is the case among Puerto Ricans who move to New York. Many of

[3]Benjamin Malzberg, "Mental disease among English-born and native-whites of English parentage in New York State, 1949-1951," *Mental Hygiene*, 48 (1964), p. 54.

[4]Benjamin Malzberg, "Are immigrants psychologically disturbed?" pp. 409–410.

[5]Bertram H. Roberts and Jerome K. Myers, "Religion, national origin, immigration, and mental illness," *American Journal of Psychiatry*, 110 (1954), pp. 761–762.

[6]U. Sanua, "The socio-cultural aspects of schizophrenia: a review of the literature", in *Schizophrenia: A Review of the Syndrome*, eds. L. Bellak and L. Loeb (New York: Grune and Stralton, 1969).

[7]Christopher Bagley, "The social aetiology of schizophrenia in immigrant groups," *International Journal of Social Psychiatry*, 17 (1971), pp. 292–304.

[8]Benjamin Malzberg, "Are immigrants psychologically disturbed?" p. 419.

[9]Ibid., p. 418.

them dream of a new life in New York where they think there are good economic opportunities. However, when they arrive they find themselves at the bottom of the socioeconomic structure.[10]

Psychoanalytic theory favors the stress model because moving is believed to reactivate the original anxiety of the child's first move away from the mother.

> Separation from the mother is not experienced as freedom, but as a feeling of being deserted by the protective figure. The anxiety reawakened by migration is much more traumatic than the original anxiety because the desertion by the mother country is made legal: all the formalities the immigrant has to go through to be able to live and work in a new country mark the severing of the 'umbilical cord,' the new process of 'weaning,' of leaving the mother's side. What is more, the new country appears as a 'wicked stepmother,' the 'bad mother' who has replaced the good one. The man who has left home with no hope of returning desires to be adopted by this new mother, but he also has doubts that generate a feeling of inner panic: Will she accept him? In addition to this, the immigrant can regress, as a result of the cultural shock, to the Oedipal stage: the policeman or the boss takes on the role of a restrictive father or even of a sadistic, castrating one. Any effort to integrate him into the value-system of the new country will be experienced as phallic or anal aggression. This is particularly disturbing for those who have not been able to reconstruct a community life that keeps the traditional values of the native land.[11]

Of course, the psychoanalytic explanation of mental illness among migrants assumes that the individual who regresses to an earlier stage of development because of the stress involved in the move is the person who is already fixated at an infantile stage. The move simply serves to reactivate the dynamics involved in the original fixation.

The migration model posits that mentally disturbed people are more prone to emigrate than those with stable personalities. Consequently, they leave their native country to escape from a society in which they are considered deviant. Actually there is little evidence to support the migration model over the stress model. One important factor in favor of the stress model is the discrimination the immigrant faces in attempting to obtain housing and jobs in the United States. In Great Britain, there are very stringent regulations against immigration, particularly of black people. All of these facts weigh in favor of the stress model over the migration model.

Some studies have concluded that the struggle between the stress and migration models is fruitless since mental illness may not be more common among the foreign-born than the native born. Only a few em-

[10]Mario Rendon, "Transcultural aspects of Puerto Rican mental illness in New York," *International Journal of Social Psychiatry,* 20 (1974), pp. 18–24.

[11]Roger Bastide, *The Sociology of Mental Disorder* (New York: David McKay, 1972), p. 146.

pirical studies support this proposition.[12] However, the fact that some studies report less mental illness among the foreign-born than among the native-born raises some interesting questions about intervening variables in the relationship between international migration and mental disorder. Not all international moves need be stressful as, for example, where the cultural practices of the original country are similar to those of the new environment. Thus, an individual who migrates from London to Boston is not as likely to be socially disoriented by the move as is the person who moves from the forests of New Guinea to the concrete of New York. As the cultural gap widens, the chances of mental illness increase.

Other intervening variables have been examined by Morrison who believes that the contradictory studies on migration and mental illness can not be integrated by grappling with the stress and migration models alone. Instead, Morrison insists that other factors must be examined to determine the ways in which migration affects different people.[13] One factor is the reason for leaving the old environment. A refugee who is forced to leave has no rationale for choosing a new location and thus is more vulnerable to mental illness than a voluntary migrant. Another factor is the attitude of the new country toward the migrant. Israel, for instance, has a very positive attitude toward immigrants which is reflected in lower rates of mental illness among the foreign-born than among the native-born. All of these factors indicate that the relationship between international migration and mental illness varies according to the nature of the move.

Internal Migration

The question of whether moving from one part of the country to another precipitates mental illness is highly relevant since about 20 percent of the population of the United States changes residence each year. However, research in this area has not produced consistent results. Some researchers have found that internal migration causes adjustment problems which in turn precipitate psychological disorder. Others have found that this holds true only under certain conditions. There are also reports that there is an inverse relationship between moving and mental illness.

One of the earliest reports suggesting a positive relationship between internal migration and mental illness was Malzberg's analysis of

[12]In Israel, for example, Halevi found that the native-born had a higher incidence of schizophrenia than immigrants. See: H. D. Halevi, "Frequency of mental illness among Jews in Israel," *International Journal of Social Psychiatry*, 9 (1963), pp. 268–287.

[13]S. David Morrison, "Intermediate variables in the association between migration and mental illness," *International Journal of Social Psychiatry*, 19 (1973), pp. 60–65.

interstate migrants in the United States.[14] He found higher rates of hospitalization among migrants into New York State than among non-migrant natives. Later investigations by other researchers supported Malzberg's findings in different states.[15] Freedman, using census data, defined migrants as persons who moved from one country to another between 1935 and 1940.[16] He found high admission rates among this type of migrant population for the manic-depressive psychoses but not for schizophrenia. A more recent investigation of patients using psychiatric facilities (state hospitals and psychiatric clinics) in Los Angeles County found a much higher proportion of migrants in the patient group than in the general population.[17]

Some of the studies reporting a preponderance of mental illness among internal migrants found such an association only for certain types of moves. For instance, most of the studies that differentiate between migration from one city to another and mobility within a city found that high rates of mental illness were more common among intracity migrants.[18] This is probably because intracity migrants are often rootless individuals who move to avoid bill collectors and landlords. The intercity migrant, on the other hand, is more likely to move in conjunction with upward occupational mobility. Additionally, those who migrate from one urban community to another have fewer adjustment problems than those who migrate from a rural to an urban area.[19]

The investigators who report high rates of mental disorder among internal migrants usually explain their results by drawing an analogy between the needs of a person new to the community and the needs of a newborn infant. Both need to belong and to be loved. A protracted absence from home decreases the fulfillment of these needs. Another line of reasoning is that the migrant must struggle to maintain his identity, a task which can weigh heavily on the already insecure person.

[14]Benjamin Malzberg, "Rates of mental disease among certain population groups in New York State," *Journal of the American Statistical Association,* 31 (1936), pp. 545–548.

[15]Locke, Kramer and Pasamanick analyzed rates of hospital admissions among migrant and native-born populations of Ohio and found lower rates among natives of Ohio. See: B. Z. Locke, M. Kramer and B. Pasamanick, "Immigration and insanity," *Public Health Reports,* 75 (1960), pp. 301–306.

[16]R. Freedman, *Recent Migration to Chicago* (Chicago: University of Chicago Press, 1950).

[17]Specifically, that study found that approximately one in four of the patients were migrants. Translated differently, there were at least two and a half times as many migrants in the patient population as in the general population of Los Angeles County. See: Arnold W. Wilson, Gordon Saver and Peter A. Lachenbruch, "Residential mobility and psychiatric help seeking," *American Journal of Psychiatry,* 121 (1965), pp. 1108–1109.

[18]Mildred B. Kantor, "Internal migration and mental illness," in *Changing Perspectives in Mental Illness,* eds. Stanley C. Plog and Robert B. Edgerton (New York: Holt, Rinehart and Winston, 1969), p. 379.

[19]A. M. Rose and L. Warshay, "The adjustment of migrants to cities," *Social Forces,* 36 (1957), pp. 72–76.

However, it is risky to assume that migration always engenders mental disorder because a number of studies have reached the opposite conclusion. A. O. Wright, using 1880 census data, noted that the hospitalization rate for "insanity" was higher in Massachusetts than in any other state.[20] The rate declined in rough proportion to the distance from that state traveling in any direction. He concluded that the more recently settled areas of the country are inhabited by ". . . a selected population, mostly young and middle aged people of sound minds and bodies. The insane are left behind. . .".[21] Other studies in this century report either an insignificant or an inverse relationship between migration and mental illness.[22] Kleiner and Parker, for instance, compared rates of admission to mental hospitals of interstate migrant and nonmigrant blacks in Pennsylvania.[23] They found lower rates among the southern black migrant population than among northern natives. They hypothesized that this was due to a greater discrepancy between level of aspiration and goal attainment among northern black natives than among southern migrants who have fewer ambitions. Another team of researchers investigated mobility patterns among a group of mental patients in Louisiana.[24] They found geographic mobility and mental illness to be inversely related since the mobility rate of the study population (4 percent annually) was much lower than the national mobility rate (20 percent annually). The researchers concluded that ". . . today the ability to be flexible, to move with the times, and to change one's life circumstances is indicative of good mental health. Moving to another environment can be an opportunity to test one's skills and mettle in competition with others for money and prestige. Thus mobility would afford a man the chance to develop and enhance his identity. The person with emotional problems is markedly restricted in competitive pursuits and consequently often settles for a job that helps him maintain his status quo."[25]

The large variation in research findings makes it clear that internal migration, like international migration, does not always precipitate mental illness. Instead it requires adjustments which, depending on the conditions of the move and the characteristics of the individual, may improve or worsen mental health. Such factors as the characteristics of the place of destination, the personalities of the migrants, and the circum-

[20]A. O. Wright, "The increase of insanity," *Conference on Charities and Corrections*, (1884), pp. 228–236.

[21]Ibid., p. 232.

[22]See: C. Tietze, P. Lemkau and M. Cooper, "Personality disorder and spatial mobility," *American Journal of Sociology*, 48 (1942), pp. 29–39; Rema Lapouse, Mary A. Monk and Milton Terris, "The drift hypothesis and socioeconomic differentials in schizophrenia," *American Journal of Public Health*, 46 (1956), pp. 979–986.

[23]Robert J. Kleiner and Seymour Parker, "Migration and mental illness: a new look," *American Sociological Review*, 24 (1959), pp. 687–690.

[24]Hilliard E. Chesteen, Veronica Bergeron and William P. Addison, "Geographical mobility and mental disorder," *Hospital and Community Psychiatry*, 21 (1970), pp. 43–44.

[25]Ibid., p. 44.

stances under which the move occurs (voluntary or involuntary) affect the amount of change experienced by the person, and it is change which is the crucial mental health hazard for those unprepared for it.

Place of Residence

Rural-Urban Differences

It is widely believed that the strains of urban living lead to high rates of mental disorder. A number of studies have tested this proposition by comparing rates between rural and urban dwellers. In eight out of ten of those studies the urban rate is higher than the rural rate, but the differences are not large; the median difference for total rates is only 1.1 percent.[26] However, the fact that the difference is greater than one would expect to occur just by chance indicates that living in the country or in a city does have a singular effect on mental health as measured by hospital admissions. Not all groups living in urban areas are susceptible to the reported mental health hazards of city living. A few groups have managed to preserve some aspects of rural life by creating small communities with traditional extended families within the larger city such as the Italian Americans of Philadelphia and Boston.

Some types of mental disorder are more prevalent in urban settings, while others are found more frequently in rural settings. The total rates for all the functional psychoses combined are higher in rural settings. This is due to the greater rural prevalence of the manic-depressive psychoses, not schizophrenia, which is more evenly distributed between the two areas.[27] The rates of neurosis and personality disorder are higher in urban settings in a majority of the studies.[28]

Why is there more mental illness in urban areas? A number of answers to this question have been offered. One explanation centers on the methodologies of the investigations that purport to measure rural-urban differences. Since all of the studies use hospital admissions as the measure of prevalence, it is to be expected that urban areas will have higher admission rates because treatment facilities are more readily available in and around cities.[29] Mental illness is also less stigmatizing among urban dwellers who, on the average, are more highly educated than their rural counterparts. Thus seeking professional help in the city involves fewer social costs than in the country. Additionally, cramped

[26]Bruce P. Dohrenwend and Barbara Snell Dohrenwend, "Social and cultural influences on psychopathology," *Annual Review of Psychology*, 25 (1974), pp. 434–435.

[27]Bruce P. Dohrenwend and Barbara Snell Dohrenwend, "Sociocultural and social-psychological factors in the genesis of mental disorders," *Journal of Health and Social Behavior*, 16 (1975), p. 370.

[28]Ibid., p. 370.

[29]W. W. Eaton, "Residence, social class, and schizophrenia," *Journal of Health and Social Behavior*, 15 (1974), pp. 289–299.

urban living conditions make disordered people more visible. Consequently, they are more likely to be brought to treatment centers than are rural dwellers living in isolated farmhouses where their families may try to care for them at home.

Another theory of rural-urban differences suggests that the quality of life varies between the two areas. The country is popularly viewed as a more benign environment in which human relationships are based on love, understanding, and an intimate concern with others, a *Gemeinschaft* type of community. Life in urban areas is said to be quite different; relationships between people are characterized by impersonality, tension, and competition, a *Gesellschaft* type of community. Not only is the quality of interpersonal relationships different between *Gemeinschaft* and *Gesellschaft* dwellers but there is an added feature of urban living that affects mental health—population density. A number of animal studies have shown that high population density creates stress which exhausts the vitality of animals.[30] Studies of humans also conclude that high density leads to social disorganization and emotional stress.[31] Research on men in the armed services correlated mental illness with population density. In one such study, persons from sparsely settled regions were found to have better mental health than those from more populated areas. In fact, mental tests of Selective Service inductees uncovered a rate of failure three times higher for those from the most populous states than for their counterparts from the least populated states.[32]

Aside from the "methodological" and "quality of life" theories, a third explanation has also been offered. According to this view, mental health differences between rural and urban dwellers are not attributable to the characteristics of one's home community but to a self-selection process whereby unstable people are more likely to settle in urban than rural areas.[33] Therefore, higher rates of mental illness among urban dwellers may be due in part to the unstable migrating from the country to the city.

Zones of the City

Earlier in the twentieth century, Burgess divided Chicago into five *concentric zones* which he contended were related to social problems of the city. The zones were (1) the central or business district, (2) the zone of

---

[30]Charles H. Southivick, "The biology and psychology of crowding," *Ohio Journal of Science* (1971).

[31]Griscom Morgan, "Mental and social health and population density," *Journal of Human Relations,* 20 (1972), pp. 196–204.

[32]United States Department of Health, Education and Welfare, *Digest of Educational Statistics* (National Center for Educational Statistics), (1970), p. 13.

[33]Leo Srole, "Urbanization and mental health: some reformulations," *American Scientist,* 60 (1972), pp. 576–583.

transition also called the zone of disorganization, (3) the zone of working class families, (4) the wealthy residential zone, and (5) the suburbs. He noted that the greatest concentration of social problems is in the second zone, the zone of transition. It is this area of the city which is typically occupied by rootless transients who lead lives of loneliness in the anonymity of their surroundings. In 1939, Faris and Dunham examined the spatial distribution of the functional psychoses in Chicago to determine the nature of the relationship between type of psychosis and zone of the city.[34] They discovered that mental illness, like other social problems, varies across the ecological zones of the city. Specifically, they found that the highest rates of schizophrenia were found in zone two, the zone of transition, and the rates of schizophrenia declined in all directions toward the periphery of the city. Although there was a slight tendency for the manic-depressive cases to be found in the wealthier sections of the city (zones four and five), most of these cases were scattered randomly throughout the city. This landmark study in psychiatric sociology led to the development of a new etiological theory of schizophrenia. Since the highest rates of hospitalized schizophrenia in Chicago were found in the inner city rooming house areas, Faris and Dunham offered their "social isolation hypothesis" to account for their findings. This theory, mentioned earlier in Chapter 5, holds that the anonymity of life in inner-city areas creates an extreme sense of isolation that, in turn, causes schizophrenia.

Some thirty years later, Levy and Rowitz retested the Faris and Dunham findings in Chicago and found essentially the same spatial distribution: a concentration of schizophrenia in the inner city and a random distribution of manic-depressive cases throughout the city.[35] Another study in Worcester, Massachusetts supported the Faris and Dunham findings as well.[36] However, that study found that the great number of schizophrenic cases in the lower socioeconomic areas of the city were predominantly single, separated, or divorced men living alone. There was little schizophrenia among inner city dwellers who lived with their families. Other studies were conducted in St. Louis, Milwaukee, Omaha, Kansas City, Rockford, Peoria, Cleveland, and Providence. All of these studies confirmed the pattern observed by the Chicago researchers. The only notable exception is Clausen and Kohn's study of schizophrenics in Hagerstown, Maryland.[37] They argue that their data show no relationship between zone of the city and hospitalization for

[34]R. E. L. Faris and H. W. Dunham, *Mental Disorders in Urban Areas* (New York: Hafner, 1960).

[35]Leo Levy and Louis Rowitz, *The Ecology of Mental Disorder* (New York: Behavioral Publications, 1973).

[36]Ibid., p. 5.

[37]J. A. Clausen and M. L. Kohn, "Relation of schizophrenia to the social structure of a small city," in *Epidemiology of Mental Disorders*, ed. B. Pasamanick (Washington, D.C.: American Association for the Advancement of Science, 1959).

schizophrenia. However, in light of the overwhelming evidence in support of the Faris and Dunham findings, the Hagerstown data must be considered an exception, possibly because Hagerstown is not large enough to have well-defined city zones.

The inner city concentration of mental illness as measured by hospital admissions has rarely been tested outside of the United States. A study of the Montreal metropolitan area, however, found a considerable amount of disorder among suburbanites.[38] In that study, prevalence was estimated through the use of psychiatric interviews of a random sample of Montreal residents. Because of a high rate of depressive symptoms among suburbanites, the researchers concluded that the high-income outer city group is nearly as disordered as the low-income inner city dwellers. The Montreal researchers hypothesized that, while suburban life may be materially rich, it is socially impoverished, particularly in the case of the isolated suburban housewife. Additionally, the higher class suburbanite is more likely to develop depressive symptoms than is the lower class inner city dweller because the outer city dweller does not usually have an external target on which to place blame for problems besetting him. He only has himself to blame should his chosen job, milieu, or lifestyle prove unsatisfying. Although the concentration of depression among suburbanites needs further clarification, it is not a suprising finding since the research on American cities hinted at such a relationship. The American city research did not uncover the strong association between outer city life and depression found in the Canadian city research because the former used hospital admissions as an index of prevalence while the latter used interviews with community residents. Since suburbanites appear to be most prone to depression, a disorder that does not necessarily require hospitalization, the suburban cases are not likely to be discovered in research using hospital data.

The concentration of schizophrenia among inner city dwellers has been the focus of much etiological controversy. Biogenic theorists believe that a predisposition to schizophrenia influences place of residence and socioeconomic status. On the other hand, environmental theorists contend that the stresses involved in inner city life directly contribute to the onset of schizophrenia. It is not necessary to choose between these two positions since both may be correct. In one case schizophrenia may preceed residence, and in another case residence may exert a causal influence on schizophrenia. It is also possible that residence and illness may exert an interdependent influence on one another as in the case of the person who is already disordered and chooses to live in a socially isolated section of the city.[39] Once he is there, he becomes increasingly disordered by the surroundings.

[38]F. Engelsmann and others, "Variations in responses to a symptom check-list by age, sex, income, residence and ethnicity," *Social Psychiatry*, 7 (1972), pp. 150–156.

[39]Weinberg suggests that the schizophrenics most likely to drift to inner city areas are the paranoids and hebephrenics who inhabit the "bohemian" sections of the city. See S.

Mental Illness and Age

In the earlier chapters on neurosis, psychosis, and personality disorder, reference was made to the average age of particular types of patients. But is there an overall relationship between mental illness and age? Is there a particular age group which is most vulnerable to mental disorder? A number of studies have analyzed this question, but the results have not been consistent. Reviewing twenty-four such studies, the Dohrenwends report that in five of the studies the maximum rate appeared in adolescence; in twelve, in the middle age years; and in seven, in the elderly.[40] Because the results are somewhat discrepant, it is difficult to identify any particular age group as the most susceptible one. However, since most studies show a minimum rate of illness in the youngest group, it is safe to assume that the chances of becoming disordered increase with age. Indeed a recent report on research in this area shows that "One of the most consistent patterns in rates of admission to mental hospitals is the general tendency toward higher rates with increasing age."[41]

Mental illness among the aged is a growing problem simply because the size of the elderly population is rapidly expanding. Since the turn of the century there has been an 80 percent increase in the proportion of persons sixty-five years of age and older. The social and psychological consequences of such longevity are not always favorable. Hospitalization rates for the over-fifty age group have increased alarmingly, in part because it is difficult to care for old people at home in an urbanized society. This sharp increase in admissions with age holds for all ethnic groups in the United States. [42] A similar pattern is also reported in Great Britain.[43] In Canada, the prevalence of mental illness increases rapidly

Kirson Weinberg, "Urban areas and hospitalized psychotics" in *The Sociology of Mental Disorders: Analyses and Readings in Psychiatric Sociology*, ed. S. Kirson Weinberg (Chicago: Aldine, 1967), p. 24.

[40]Bruce P. Dohrenwend and Barbara Snell Dohrenwend, *Social Status and Psychological Disorder: A Causal Inquiry* (New York: Wiley-Interscience, 1969), p. 13.

[41]Walter T. Martin, "Status integration, social stress, and mental illness: accounting for marital status variations in mental hospitalization rates," *Journal of Health and Social Behavior*, 17 (1976), p. 290. If impairment among age groups is measured by psychiatric screening of people in the community, the relationship is much weaker. In one such study, few age-related differences were noted in people's responses to instruments used to measure mental health. The researchers were at a loss to explain their findings. See Charles M. Gaitz and Judith Scott, "Age and the measurement of mental health," *Journal of Health and Social Behavior*, 13 (1972), pp. 55–67.

[42]Harry H. L. Kitano, "Japanese-American mental illness," in *Changing Perspectives in Mental Illness*, eds. Stanley C. Plog and Robert B. Edgerton (New York: Holt, Rinehart and Winston, 1969), pp. 265–266.

[43]Joseph L. Fleiss and others, "Cross-national study of diagnosis of the mental disorders: some demographic correlates of hospital diagnosis in New York and London," *International Journal of Social Psychiatry*, 19 (1973), pp. 180–186.

with age; a longer life span allows more years of exposure to the risk of mental illness. The Canadian male who survives to age ninety has a 24 percent chance of being admitted to a mental hospital. The Canadian female who lives to the same age has a 20 percent chance of being hospitalized.[44] The difference in rate of admissions between elderly men and women may be the result of the greater ability of the female to cope with single life.

Why is there a high risk of mental disorder among people of fifty-five years or older? Part of this risk stems from the nuances of the middle age years discussed in chapter five. Changes in physical appearance and strength, loss of childbearing ability, and retirement are certainly important factors in the origin of involutional melancholia. However, older persons are high mental illness risks also because they are socially dislocated. The attitudes of Americans towards aging persons create this social dislocation by funneling the elderly into isolated warehouses to live out their remaining years. Older people need social supports for feelings of psychological well-being more so than do younger people. Social interaction is important to an elderly person who thrives on the emotional support provided. One empirical study found that psychological well-being among elderly people is directly related to the number of significant others in their lives.[45] Unfortunately, this social support is often missing during the later years of life because Americans display a great deal of disinterest toward the aged. This disinterest is found in the scientific community as well, as evidenced by a significant lack of basic information on mental health and illness among the elderly. Further, there is a good deal of misdiagnosis of patients in later life because the medical community often confuses functional and organic forms of mental illness among the aged. Depression, for instance, probably occurs more frequently than most know because it is confused with senile deterioration and cerebral arteriosclerosis.

The suicide statistics yield some interesting information on age and mental health. Although some consider it risky to assume that a person who commits suicide is mentally ill, it is safe to assume that a suicidal person is at least temporarily disturbed. Since Durkheim's comprehensive investigation of suicide patterns in the earlier part of the century, a countless number of studies have found that the risk of suicide, like mental illness, increases with age. Since the 1960s, however, there has been a new surge of suicides among American youth, particularly among those in college. Depression among the young has been rising as evidenced by clinical studies, suicide data, and the widespread use of

[44]Gordon Johnson, Joseph Cooper and Jack Mandel, "Expectation of admission to a Canadian psychiatric institution," *Canadian Psychiatric Association Journal,* 14 (1969), pp. 295-298.

[45]Sharon Y. Moriwaki, "Self-disclosure, significant others and psychological well-being in old age," *Journal of Health and Social Behavior,* 14 (1973), pp. 226-232.

mood-elevating drugs.[46] Admission rates to mental hospitals have followed the same pattern. Since the early 1960s, the hospitalization rate among those from ages 15 to 24 has skyrocketed. However, it is not certain that this is purely the result of a heightened rate of disorder among the young or simply the consequence of earlier detection and treatment of mental illness.

Admission rates have also increased slightly in recent years among those in their thirties and forties. It is this group which is reported to be most disturbed by economic and occupational anxieties which may be the prime reason for their high rate of psychophysiological disorders.[47]

Family Size and Birth Order

Family Size

There is quite a bit of controversy in the scientific community regarding whether a large or small family is most conducive to mental health. Some argue that the material and emotional needs of the child are met better in a small family in which the child receives considerable parental attention. Others argue that the child in a large family has more opportunity to develop social skills through interaction with brothers and sisters. A minority opinion holds that there is no significant relationship between family size and mental health.[48]

There is an accumulation of evidence that a person's mental health is threatened when he is a member of a large sibship (five or more siblings). This was first argued in the early 1900s when Pearson noted an increased prevalence of "insanity" and criminality in unduly large families.[49] The hypothesized relationship between large family size and mental illness may not be the result only of the *amount* of attention children in large families receive from their parents. It may be that the *quality* of interaction between parents and children in large families is undesirable since at least one team of researchers reports that the men-

[46]George J. Warkeit, Charles E. Holzer III and John J. Schwab, "An analysis of social class and racial differences in depressive symptomatology: a community study," *Journal of Health and Social Behavior*, 14 (1973), pp. 291–299.

[47]Bernard Indik, Stanley E. Seashore and Johnathan Slesinger, "Demographic correlates of psychological strain," *Journal of Abnormal and Social Psychology*, 69 (1964), pp. 26–38.

[48]A. Chakrabortry, "Birth order and mental illness," *British Journal of Social Psychiatry*, 3 (1970), pp. 231–236; D. E. Domrin, "Family size and sibling age, sex and position as related to certain aspects of adjustment," *Journal of Social Psychology*, 29 (1949), pp. 93–102; C. Schooler, "Birth order and schizophrenia," *A. M. A. Archives of General Psychiatry*, 4 (1961), pp. 91–97.

[49]K. Pearson, *On the Handicap of Firstborns* (London: Eugenics Laboratory Section Service, 1914).

tal health of mothers and fathers declines as family size increases.[50] However, it is not clear whether the mental health status of the parents led them to have an excessively large family or whether the strains of raising a large number of children caused the parents to become disturbed.

The relationship between social class and sibship size is marked and highly significant; lower class families have larger sibships than families from higher social classes. Therefore any interpretation of the observed relationship between sibship size and mental illness must take account of the close relationship between social class and mental illness which is discussed in the following chapter. Studies indicate that neurosis usually occurs among people from sibships of five or less,[51] and it is neurosis rather than psychosis which is most common among those from higher social classes.

Much of the research on sibship size and mental illness has concentrated on the mental health status of the only child. Popular opinion has it that this child is most likely to be "spoiled" by his parents and thus develop a pathological sense of insecurity and dependency. Despite evidence that the child in a two-child family is more likely to be spoiled than is the only child,[52] the stereotype of the only child persists. The major difficulty in assessing the validity of this stereotype is a lack of objective data. The methodologies of some studies are suspect because they combine only children with first-borns into the same category so that it is impossible to determine which group accounts for any results. Furthermore, it is not psychologically valid to couple the two groups. Indeed, Riess and Safer found only children to have a significantly higher rate of neurosis, depression, and sexual disorder than a comparable group of first-borns.[53] Other studies define the only child in peculiar ways; one study considers a child "only" if he has been raised to the age of five as a single child member in an adult household without living siblings or the immediate prospect of a sibling.[54]

Despite the lack of objective data, controversy over the mental health status of the only child continues to rage. On the one hand, some professionals believe unequivocally that being an only child is a disease in itself. In support of this is a study comparing normal and psychiatrically disturbed soldiers which found that the only child was more frequently a member of the disturbed group.[55] Of course it is possible that the tem-

[50]E. H. Hare and G. K. Shaw, "A study in family health: health in relation to family size," *British Journal of Psychiatry,* 3 (1965), pp. 461–466.

[51]John Birtchnell, "Sibship size and mental illness," *British Journal of Psychiatry,* 117 (1970), pp. 303–308.

[52]D. M. Levy, *Maternal Over-protection* (New York: Columbia University Press, (1943).

[53]Bernard F. Reiss and Jeanne Safer, "Birth order and related variables in a large outpatient population," *The Journal of Psychology,* 85 (1973), pp. 61–68.

[54]Margaret G. Howe and Maribeth E. Madgett, "Mental health problems associated with the only child," *Canadian Psychiatric Association Journal,* 20 (1975), pp. 189–194.

[55]W. Vogel and C. G. Lauterback, "Sibling patterns and social adjustment among

perament of only children is not suited to army life. If this is true, the disturbance may be caused as much by army life as it is by being an only child.

Other studies of the only child report that they are more apt to be referred for psychiatric help[56] and to return for help more frequently than are children with siblings.[57] However these "findings" are also open to question since it is likely that only children require psychiatric help so frequently because their overprotective parents rush them to help sources at the slightest sign of unhappiness. Certainly there is a linkage between maternal overprotection and submissiveness on the part of only children. But it is far from clear whether this overprotection fosters children who truly need psychiatric care or whether the overprotective attitude leads only children into treatment channels where they become registered as "cases" more frequently.

It is also possible that being an only child affects mental health in a positive way, as much evidence in everyday life suggests. Schachter has documented the fact that eminent scientists, scholars, and other great achievers tend to be only children.[58] On a more widespread basis, Stuart gave mental hygiene tests to random samples of only children and children with siblings and concluded that only children are not prone to mental illness and that in fact they are more generous, gregarious, independent and responsible.[59] Ingham found no excess of only children among neurotic university students compared with a matched control group.[60] Glueck and Glueck, comparing 500 delinquent boys and an equal number of matched controls, discovered that fewer delinquents than controls were only children.[61] Obviously, research on the only child is highly polarized. Neither position has convincing evidence, creating the impression that the personal biases of the investigators color their findings since most researchers wholeheartedly support one or the other extreme.

Birth Order

Although there is much literature on the relationship between sibling position and personality type, a lot of it is speculative. However,

normal and psychiatrically disturbed soldiers," *Journal of Consulting and Clinical Psychology,* 27 (1963), pp. 236–242.

[56]Yung-ho Ko and Long chu Sun, "Ordinal position and the behavior of visiting the child guidance clinic," *Acta Psychologia Tiawanica,* 7 (1965), pp. 1016–1062.

[57]Margaret G. Howe and Maribeth E. Madgett, "Mental health problems associated with the only child," p. 190.

[58]S. Schacter, "Birth order, eminence and higher education," *American Sociological Review,* 28 (1963), pp. 757–768.

[59]J. C. Stuart, "Data on the alleged psychopathology of the only child," *Journal of Abnormal and Social Psychology,* 20 (1926), pp. 441–445.

[60]H. V. Ingham, "A statistical study of family relationships in psychoneurosis," *American Journal of Psychiatry,* 106 (1949), pp. 91–98.

[61]S. Glueck and E. Glueck, *Unraveling Juvenile Delinquency* (Cambridge, Mass.: Harvard University Press, 1950).

Barry and Barry have uncovered a "double-branched relationship" between birth order, sibship size, and schizophrenia.[62] They note that stress is greatest for late born members of large sibships who are subject to parental rejection or neglect. This in turn leads to the "shut-in" personality which can develop into full-blown schizophrenia. Other studies of schizophrenic patients also indicate an increasing trend toward later birth order with increasing sibship size.[63] Schooler examined religion as a variable that may affect the relationship between birth order and schizophrenia. He found a last-born effect to be more pronounced for Catholic and Jewish patients compared to Protestant patients.[64] Other evidence suggests that the paranoid and catatonic forms of schizophrenia are most common among last-born children.[65]

Studies of the birth order of patients suffering from the manic-depressive psychoses are few and contradictory. Grosz observed that, in sibships of three, those from the first two birth ranks are most vulnerable to a depressive breakdown.[66] Birtchnell's investigation, however, failed to replicate Grosz's findings, leaving the question of the relationship between birth order and depression unanswered.[67] But Grosz's hypothesis concerning three person sibships may have revealed an important linkage since there is evidence that the personalities of first-, second-, and third-born children manifest specific sets of characteristics.[68] Further, children in higher birth ranks may repeat these character types, fourth-borns resembling first-borns, fifths resembling seconds, and sixths resembling thirds. Indeed, Riess and Safer, investigating the effect of birth order in a large outpatient population, found significant differences in diagnostic type between first-, second-, and third-born children.[69] They also found that the first and fourth children tended to receive similar diagnoses, as did second and fifth, and third- and sixth-borns.

Considerable research by social psychologists has focused on personality differences between first-borns (including only children) and

[62]H. Barry, III and H. Barry, Jr. "Birth order, family size and schizophrenia," *Archives of General Psychiatry,* 17 (1967), pp. 435–440.

[63]K. L. Gronville-Grossman, "Birth order and schizophrenia," *British Journal of Psychiatry,* 112 (1966), pp. 1119–1126; L. Solomon and R. Nuttall, "Sibling order, premorbid adjustment and remission in schizophrenia," *Journal of Nervous and Mental Disease,* 144 (1966), pp. 37–46; M. Sundararaj and B. S. S. R. Rao, "Order of birth and schizophrenia," *British Journal of Psychiatry,* 112 (1966), pp. 1127–1129.

[64]C. Schooler, "Birth order and hospitalization for schizophrenia," *Journal of Abnormal and Social Psychology,* 69 (1964), pp. 574–579.

[65]Roger Bastide, *The Sociology of Mental Disorder,* p. 161.

[66]H. J. Grosz, "The depression-prone and the depression-resistant sibling: a study of 650 three-sibling families," *British Journal of Psychiatry,* 114 (1968), pp. 1555–1558.

[67]John Birtchnell, "Mental illness in sibships of two and three," *British Journal of Psychiatry,* 119 (1971), pp. 481–487.

[68]K. Konig, *Brothers and Sisters* (New York: Anthroposophic Press, 1963).

[69]Bernard F. Reiss and Jeanne Safer, "Birth order and related variables in a large outpatient population," p. 67.

later borns. Schachter first discovered a relationship between a person's birth order and his affiliative response in an anxiety-provoking situation.[70] First-borns become more anxious than later borns when exposed to an anxiety-arousing experience, such as being led to believe that they are about to participate in a physically painful experiment. It has also been demonstrated that first-borns show more symptoms of psychological distress when they are not in the company of others. Later borns, on the other hand, show more symptoms of distress when they are forced into social interaction. Therefore, conditions of social isolation are particularly threatening to first-borns who have stronger dependency needs than later borns who prefer socially isolated situations, presumably a manifestation of their self-reliance. The reader should note that these characterizations of first and later borns are not derived only from Schacter's experiment. A number of researchers, including the Dohrenwends, have found first-borns to be socially dependent and later borns to be more isolated.[71] This holds true not only in an experimental setting but in outside situations as well. The 1965 power failure in New York City provided an opportunity to test the experimentally-derived notions of the relationship between birth order, anxiety, and affiliation. First-borns stranded in the blackout were more anxious and more affiliative than were their later born counterparts.[72] This relationship was stronger for first-born women than for first-born men.

Considering all the studies on birth order and psychopathology, is there any evidence that a consistent relationship exists between the two? Some feel that the research is so contradictory that it is time to call a moratorium on the topic. It is true that many of the investigations are inconclusive, but this is not true of the studies which simultaneously consider sibship size *and* birth order. A number of such studies have found a concentration of youngest children from large sibships in patient populations. This is particularly true for schizophrenia. In addition, studies involving large samples of mental patients have uncovered an overrepresentation of eldest children from small families. This is particularly true for neurosis. Hare and Price, for instance, examined

[70]Stanley Schachter, *The Psychology of Affiliation* (Stanford, California: Stanford University Press, 1959).

[71]J. M. Darley and E. Aronson, "Self-evaluation vs. direct anxiety reduction as determinants of the fear-affiliation relationship," *Journal of Experimental Social Psychology*, suppl. 1 (1966), pp. 66–79; B. S. Dohrenwend and B. P. Dohrenwend, "Stress situations, birth order and psychological symptoms," *Journal of Abnormal Psychology*, 71 (1966), pp. 215–223; H. B. Gerard and J. M. Rabbie, "Fear and social comparison," *Journal of Abnormal and Social Psychology*, 62 (1961), pp. 586–592; I. Sarnoff and P. G. Zimbardo, "Anxiety, fear, and social isolation," *Journal of Abnormal and Social Psychology*, 62 (1961), pp. 356–363; L. S. Wrightsman Jr., "Effect of waiting with others on changes in level of felt anxiety," *Journal of Abnormal and Social Psychology*, 61 (1960), pp. 216–222; P. G. Zimbardo and R. Formica, 'Emotional comparison and self-esteem as determinants of affiliation," *Journal of Personality*, 31 (1963), pp. 141–162.

[72]R. A. Zucker, M. Monosevitz and R. I. Lonyon, "Birth order, anxiety, and affiliation during a crisis," *Journal of Personality and Social Psychology*, 8 (1968), pp. 354–359.

the family size and birth order of over 10,000 patients attending the Bethlem and Maudsley Hospitals in England from 1958 to 1966.[73] In sibships of two and three, there was an excess of first-born patients over last born. In sibships of five or more, there was an excess of last born patients over first-born. It appears that the first-born in a small family and the last born in a large family are particularly vulnerable to mental disorder. However, one should be cautious here since this is only a *tendency* over a large number of people and certainly not a universal.

Sexual Composition of the Sibship

Family size and birth order are not the only family structure variables related to mental illness. Other evidence suggests that the sexual composition of the sibship also affects personality. In one study of two-child families, it was found that those with an opposite-sexed sibling showed more neurotic symptoms than those with a same-sexed sibling.[74] Interpreting the finding, the researchers felt that "Since same-sexed siblings may show a greater communality of interests and provide each other support and sharing of responsibility, it seems less likely that they would seek elaborate defenses or withdraw into themselves. However, opposite-sexed siblings may perceive each other as rivals vying for the attention of the parents and more likely show neurotic responses and poor adjustment to stress."[75] An earlier study of sibling sex distribution and psychiatric status reached a similar conclusion. That study, conducted by Bauer and Ehrlich, found that females from opposite-sexed sibships (one girl and the rest boys) were more impaired than females from same-sexed sibships (all girls).[76] However, the exact opposite was found among males; the most impaired males were those from a same-sexed sibship. The logical conclusion from the study is that females benefit from a same-sexed sibling, and males benefit from an opposite-sexed sibling. Stated more simply, the inference is that a sister benefits mental health. Although this finding needs to be tested further, it is certainly an interesting proposition and one that is consistent with the literature on emotional and social differences between the sexes. Females, having more empathy and interpersonal skills than males, provide a compassionate ear for the problems of their brothers and sisters.

---

[73]E. H. Hare and J. S. Price, "Birth order and family size: bias caused by changes in birth rate," *British Journal of Psychiatry,* 115 (1969), pp. 647–657.

[74]Kathleen McCormick and Daniel J. Baer, "Birth order, sex of subject and sex of sibling as factors in extraversion and neuroticism in two-child families," *Psychological Reports,* 37 (1975), pp. 259–261. This study also found that birth order and sex affected sociability, with first born males and second born females having the highest scores on a standardized test of extraversion.

[75]Ibid., p. 261.

[76]Mary Lou Bauer and Howard J. Ehrlich, "Sibling sex distribution and psychiatric status," Psychological Reports, 18 (1966), pp. 365–366.

Season of Birth

Some epidemiological studies have examined the relationship between mental illness and the time of year a person was born. Although these studies are few in number and have been largely limited to psychotic patients, particularly schizophrenics, the conclusions have been so consistent that it would be foolhardy to dismiss them as astrological nonesense. Tramer was the first to report on season of birth in schizophrenia. Examining 2,100 cases of schizophrenia in Switzerland, he found an excessive number of patients born during December through March.[77] Subsequent studies have confirmed this "winter birth" finding and, in some instances, have extended it to the manic-depressive psychoses. Dalen, for instance, found a significant difference in month-of-birth distribution between schizophrenics and the general population of Sweden.[78] In that study schizophrenics demonstrated an excess of births from January to April and a deficiency from July to October. More recently a team of British researchers observed the distribution of mental patients' births compared with that of the general population of England and Wales.[79] They found an excess of winter births (first quarter of the year) among schizophrenics and manic-depressives. What accounts for this phenomenon? It may be related to social class. There is documentation that schizophrenics frequently come from the lower social class. Perhaps the lower class has a high winter birth rate, and this is what accounts for the observed pattern of births of schizophrenics. However, this explanation is questionable since the winter birth pattern is also found in nonstratified societies such as Sweden. Other causal hypotheses have been offered. Presently the most plausible hypothesis is that winter-born children are subject to nutritional deficiencies or infections which damage their biochemical systems.[80] Perhaps it is these people who become psychotic as a result of biochemical abnormalities. It is also possible that mental hospital patients have more opportunity for outdoor sexual contacts during the spring and summer. This would cause a birth rate increase in hospitals during the winter.

The Adopted Child

There is considerable evidence that the adopted child is especially vulnerable to mental disorder as measured by treatment rates.[81] Indeed,

[77]M. Tramer, "Uber die biologische Bedeutung des Geburtsmonates imbesondere für die Psychoses erkrankung," *Schweizer Archiv für* Neurologie und Psychiatrie, 24 (1929), pp. 17–24.

[78]P. Dalen, "Month of birth and schizophrenia," *Acta Psychiatrica Scandinavica,* Suppl. 203 (1968), pp. 48–54.

[79]Edward Hare, John Price and Eliot Slater, "Mental disorder and season of birth: a national sample compared with the general population," *British Journal of Psychiatry,* 124 (1974), pp. 81–86.

[80]Ibid., p. 85.

[81]See, for example: Nathan M. Simon and Audrey G. Senturia, "Adoption and

Schecter claims that adopted children are 100 times more likely to receive psychiatric care than would be expected on the basis of their numbers alone.[82] Although Schecter's study has been criticized by others for its methodological design,[83] his dismal view was supported by Toussieng who also reported high treatment rates for adoptees at a psychiatric treatment center.[84]

Among adoptees, there is a high frequency of personality disorders, particularly the antisocial type. A number of factors can account for this. Antisocial tendencies can result from neglectful parenting which produces a deficient superego in the absence of adequate role models. In the case of the adoptee, this may happen when the child is adopted by parents who raise him incorrectly because they adopted for the wrong reasons in the first place. Another reason for the high rate of psychiatric impairment among adoptees is the fact that many of these children are institutionalized (in an orphanage) for a period of time before they are adopted. During that time, they lack the intensive one-to-one relationship between infant and caretaker that is required for normal personality formation. Instead they are shifted from one institution to another and are deprived of the opportunity for normal parenting. For this reason, the risk of impairment increases as the time span between birth and adoption lengthens. In the case of adoption closely following birth, the child is likely to be mentally healthy provided he is adopted by stable parents. On the other hand, adoption can be particularly risky if the infant has already established a relationship with an individual who has been specifically identified as the nurturing figure. Such is the case when a child loses his parents through death after he had known them for years. The transition to another nurturing figure is an unsettling experience which can engender a psychiatric disturbance. If, however, there is a similarity between the original nurturing figure and the replacement, the experience may not be problematic at all. For this reason, adoption by a relative carries less risk for mental illness than adoption by a stranger.[85]

Socioeconomic factors also play a role in the high rate of disturbance among adoptees. Generally adoptive families are from relatively high socioeconomic groups, and it is these groups which can afford

---

psychiatric illness," *American Journal of Psychiatry,* 122 (1966), pp. 858–868; H. David Kirk, Kurt Jonassohn and Ann D. Fish, "Are adopted children especially vulnerable to stress?" *Archives of General Psychiatry,* 14 (1966), pp. 291–298.

[82]M. D. Schecter, "Observations on adopted children," *Archives of General Psychiatry,* 3 (1960), pp. 21–32.

[83]Schecter only observed a small group of children seen in private practice by one psychiatrist.

[84]P. W. Toussieng, "Thoughts regarding the etiology of psychological difficulties in adopted children," *Child Welfare,* 41 (1962), pp. 59–65.

[85]Nathan M. Simon and Audrey G. Senturia, "Adoption and psychiatric illness," p. 863.

private psychiatric and counseling services. Therefore an adoptee may be more likely to become a patient partly because his relatively wealthy parents bring him to treatment centers with little hesitation.

Another factor involved in the mental health of the adopted child has been emphasized by adoptees themselves. Reflecting on their upbringing, some adoptees feel that their emotional diffficulties stem from the void created by their lack of personal history.[86] They use such words as "conspiracy" and "underground" to describe the emotional dishonesty they were subjected to as children. This sense of emotional dishonesty is usually created by the adoptive parents who either repeatedly tell the child not to ask about his natural parents or lie to the child about them.

Conclusions

Those who migrate from one country to another are overrepresented in the mental hospital population. This is either because of the stress of moving to an unfamiliar environment or because mentally ill people are more likely to migrate. The research on internal migration is contradictory. This type of move can have a positive or negative effect on mental health depending on the nature of the move and the personality of the individual. Aside from physical mobility, geographical place of residence is related to mental illness in other ways. Rural dwellers are reported to have lower rates than urban dwellers. Although this is commonly interpreted as indicating a better quality of life in rural areas, it is also possible that the greater availability of treatment centers in urban areas results in more urban than rural dwellers becoming registered cases. Within urban settings there is a concentration of schizophrenia in the center city area while the manic-depressive psychoses are distributed more randomly with a noticeable concentration among suburbanites.

The overall relationship between prevalence of mental illness and age is direct; there are higher rates among increasingly older age groups. This is the result of the negative experiences that accompany aging, such as loss of loved ones through death, diminished physical vitality, and societal attitudes which ostracize the aged. Recently there has been a rise in psychiatric disorder among adolescents although this may be the result of earlier detection and treatment.

The question of the mental health status of the only child has not been resolved. It is true that only children have higher treatment rates than do children with siblings, but these rates may result from overprotective parents who rush their child to treatment centers more spontaneously than do the parents of larger families.

Birth order must be considered together with family size. Combining the two, a few patterns stand out: a concentration of schizophrenia

---

[86]Nancy Greenberg, "A most militant adoptee comes out of the closet," *The Evening Bulletin*, April 7, 1976, p. 6.

among those born late in a large sibship and a concentration of neurosis among those born early in a small sibship.

There is also some evidence that season of birth is related to mental illness since researchers have found an excess of winter births among schizophrenics. This may be due to either lower class birth patterns, nutritional deficiencies that threaten winter-borns, or patterns of sexual behavior among mental hospital patients.

Adopted children have an unusually high rate of mental illness, particularly the antisocial personality disorder. This probably stems from a number of forms of improper parenting. In some cases the child was adopted for the wrong reasons and functions as an outlet for the adoptive parents' hostilities and unconscious drives. Other children become disordered because they were adopted after having formed a relationship with a nurturing figure from whom they are suddenly separated. It is also possible that mental disorder among adoptees stems from a lack of personal history and identity.

10

Patterns of Mental Illness

Social Class, Race, and Social Mobility

The Meaning of Social Class

The important effect which membership in a specific social class has on the lives of Americans has been demonstrated in numerous studies. The chances for a long life, for example, are positively related to social class; the higher one's social class, the longer his life expectancy. General unhappiness with life is greatest in the lower social classes.[1] Actually, there is an endless list of studies that have uncovered important relationships between social class and such phenomena as fertility rates, sexual behavior, political ideology, religious beliefs, and work satisfaction, to name just a few. As a result of these findings, it is now commonplace for social scientists to consider social class in many behavioral investigations. Social class has particular relevance for epidemiological analyses of mental health since many differences exist between social classes in the structure of interpersonal relationships, especially parent-child interaction patterns. It is these family interaction patterns that are partly responsible for different expressions of mental illness in various social classes. This chapter examines the ways that members of different classes view the world and raise their children. These distinctions will then be used to explain why people of various social classes and races develop different types of mental illness.

Before proceeding, it is necessary to understand what social class is.

[1]Norman M. Bradburn and David Caplovitz, *Reports on Happiness* (Chicago: Aldine, 1965).

In many ways, the classes that comprise highly industrialized, democratically oriented societies, such as the United States, are made up of individuals who are similar to other members of their class yet significantly different from people of other classes. While there is little disagreement among social scientists regarding the use of the concept of social class, there is some controversy concerning the techniques used to measure social class as well as the number of discreet classes which exist. The most accepted method of assessing social class is an objective ranking of the occupational, educational, and financial standing of the head(s) of a family. Most scales measuring class center around these interrelated characteristics, particularly occupation, because education and income can usually be inferred from it. Customarily, the stratification system of the United States is described in terms of five major classes as below:[2]

The Upper Class

This group is comprised of wealthy families whose money is passed down from one generation to the next. Upper class families occupy positions of high social prestige and frequently have members who are community leaders. At the very least, they are college graduates. Despite their reverence for the past, these people have the social security to be individualists and indulge their idiosyncrasies. The Kennedy, Du Pont, and Ford families serve as modern examples.

The Upper Middle Class

These families are headed almost entirely by adults who are college educated. They are well-to-do but their income is *acquired* from executive and professional work. These are self-made men and women who lack the qualifications of ancestry and inherited wealth for membership in the upper class. Common occupations include medicine, law, corporate management, and university teaching.

The Lower Middle Class

This group includes small proprietors, white-collar workers, and many skilled manual employees. The lower middle class has expanded to almost half of the nation's population. This is the class of the "common men" who are predominantly high school graduates but who may have completed part of college. Their incomes are modest but large enough to support a comfortable life style. Their strivings for upward mobility

---

[2]A five-class breakdown is the most manageable approach to differentiating between social classes. Other scales are more specific but often their specificity sacrifices practical usage. For a review of this issue see: *Class, Status and Power*, eds. R. Bendix and S. M. Lipset (New York: Free Press, 1953).

are especially projected on their children who are attending college in increasing numbers.

The Working Class

This stratum consists of manual workers who have finished the elementary grades and, in many cases, high school as well. The boundary line between working class and middle class is blurred since many blue-collar workers[3] earn more than lower-middle-class people in clerical and sales jobs. The force of ethnic tradition is more of a differentiating factor in the working class because they are closer to their European or Asian roots than those from the lower middle class.

The Lower Class

Lower class adults are either semiskilled or unskilled workers or among the ranks of the unemployed. They differ from members of the working class in terms of the instability of their employment as well as the kind of work they do. Most have not completed elementary school and are familiar with the hardships of poverty and ghetto living.

Social Class, Child Rearing and Personality

A person's view of the social world is affected by his position in the social class hierarchy. In general, there is a feeling of autonomy among members of the middle and upper classes while those in the working and lower classes express a sense of being controlled by others.[4] This is to be expected in light of the fact that the privileged classes enjoy more power and freedom, a luxury rarely experienced among the relatively power-less working and lower classes. This phenomenon was well described by Melvin Kohn in his analysis of social class and values.

> The essence of higher class position is the expectation that one's decisions and actions can be consequential: the essence of lower class position is the belief that one is at the mercy of forces and people beyond one's control, often, beyond one's understanding. Self-direction—acting on the basis of one's own judgment, attending to internal dynamics as well as to external consequences, being open-minded, being trustful of others, holding personally responsible moral standards—this is possible only if the actual conditions of life allow some freedom of action, some reason to feel in control

[3]"Blue-collar worker" is a synonym for the working class person.

[4]Most research in this area is limited to studies of the middle and working classes only and has systematically ignored the extreme ends of the social hierarchy. This is particularly true for the literature on differences in child-rearing by class. Here it is assumed that what exists among the working and middle classes is even more common among the lower and upper classes respectively.

of fate. Conformity—following the dictates of authority, focusing on external consequences to the exclusion of internal processes, being intolerant of non-conformity and dissent, being distrustful of others, having moral standards that strongly emphasize obedience to the letter of the law—this is the inevitable result of conditions of life that allow little freedom of action, little reason to feel in control of fate.[5]

A major psychological difference between social classes is a feeling of *autonomy* among the middle and upper classes and a preoccupation with *conformity* among the working and lower classes. How are these differences fostered? An important agent for their development is the specific expectations placed on children of different social classes by their parents. There is mounting evidence that much of the variance in the personalities of children can be explained by the social class position of the child's family. The resultant personalities are a direct function of the specific child-rearing practices with which they were tempered. The Lynds, in their classic study of Middletown, found that working class mothers placed more emphasis on teaching their children obedience than did mothers of higher social class position.[6] Consequently, these mothers transmit to their children an orientation that is inflexible and incapable of dealing with change. In the higher social classes parents place an emphasis on *developmental* ambitions which involve raising children to be individualistic and self-directing, rather than conforming. Other social class differences in parental values express the *internally oriented,* autonomous concerns of higher social classes and the *externally oriented,* conformity needs of lower social classes. Middle-class parents, for example, see consideration for others and honesty as highly desirable traits for their children while working-class parents see obedience and physical neatness as highly desirable.

Research on disciplinary practices demonstrates that punishment techniques are structured quite differently between classes, consistent with parental expectations. The *internally oriented* parent tends to use psychological punishment, and the *externally oriented* parent typically employs physical forms of punishment. Bronfenbrenner summarizes the results of relevant studies as indicating that "... working-class parents are consistently more likely to employ physical punishment, while middle-class families rely more on reasoning, isolation, appeals to guilt, and other methods involving the threat of loss of love."[7]

The physical disciplinary techniques of lower social classes have typically been viewed as a dangerous approach to raising children. But

[5] Melvin L. Kohn, *Class and Conformity: A Study in Values* (Homewood, Illinois: Dorsey, 1969), p. 189.

[6] Robert S. Lynd and Helen M. Lynd, *Middletown: A Study in Contemporary American Culture* (New York: Harcourt, Brace, 1929).

[7] Urie Bronfenbrenner, "Socialization and social class through time and space," in *Readings in Social Psychology,* ed. Eleanor E. Macoby (New York: Holt, Rinehart and Winston, 1958), p. 424.

few have considered that the psychological techniques employed by the middle class may also be damaging to the child's developing personality. Green suggests that the middle-class environment is sometimes even less conducive to healthy personality formation since the parent manipulates the child's fragile self-concept by threatening the withdrawal of love.[8] This approach to raising children may create a "slavish dependence" on the parents in that the personality of the child is partially absorbed by them. Dependence on the parents may direct the child into neurotic behavior patterns by fostering the threat of withdrawal of parental love because his personality has been absorbed by these two persons, because he has been conditioned to have a slavish-emotional dependence upon them. Not the need for parental love, but the constant threat of its withdrawal after the child has been conditioned to the need, lies at the root of the most characteristic modern neurosis."[9]

It is possible that class differences in child-rearing practices may produce different *rates* of mental illness as well as predispose members of different classes toward specific *types* of disorder. Differences uncovered in the rate and type of mental disorder must thus be considered in light of the *internal-external* social class variations in world view, parental expectations, and punishment techniques.

Occupation and Mental Illness

The first attempts to examine the rate of mental illness by class did so indirectly by studying prevalence as a function of occupation, one component of social class. It was originally believed, on the basis of rather weak evidence, that professional people were most affected by psychiatric disorder and that the lowest rate of mental disorder was to be found among less prestigious occupational groups, such as agricultural workers. Today there is still a great deal of speculation on the relationship between work roles and psychiatric impairment, but it is known that attitudes toward psychiatric treatment vary by occupational status. The proportion of self- and family referrals increases as one ascends the occupational status continuum.[10] This is generally taken to indicate more positive attitudes toward psychiatry among those in more prestigious occupations and not necessarily a greater *true prevalence* of mental illness.

Much of the speculative literature suggests a high degree of psychiatric impairment among lower-middle-class white-collar workers employed in large companies. These people are believed to suffer stress

---

[8]Arnold W. Green, "The middle class child and neurosis," *American Sociological Review,* 11 (February, 1946), pp. 31–41.

[9]Ibid., p. 39.

[10]Robert J. Kleiner and Seymour Parker, "Potential sources of error in epidemiological studies of mental illness," *International Journal of Psychiatry,* 17 (1971), p. 123.

because their work roles are repetitive and meaningless. This may be true, but it is a relative statement since empirical data indicate even more psychiatric impairment among those in lower class jobs.[11] This may mean that the absence of regular work role participation is a more significant pathogenic force than factors indigenous to work organizations. This is not to say that the clerical worker is satisfied with the highly routinized aspects of his job. On the contrary, many clerical workers are consciously depressed about the state of their lives. In fact they report greater general unhappiness and more worries about their marriages and self-images than other white-collar workers.[12] This is particularly true of those employees who are least involved with their job, a group most likely to develop neurotic anxiety.[13] Consistently, "worries about work" are associated with greater impairment at all occupational levels.[14]

Studies to date indicate an inverse relationship between occupational prestige and rate of mental illness. This relationship holds within occupational categories as well. Blauner, studying the degree of alienation among industrial workers, found that the most alienated workers were those whose jobs were connected to the repetitive assembly line as opposed to those workers whose jobs allowed some sense of freedom and creativity.[15] Automobile workers, for instance, suffer a greater sense of meaninglessness in life than do workers in a craft industry such as printing. Even within the auto industry, there is a relationship between mental health and job type. Kornhauser found that mental illness is most common among auto workers in the low prestige jobs which were highly repetitive, dirty, offered little opportunity for advancement, and required almost total isolation from other workers.[16] These workers are most susceptible to the *automation syndrome,* a pattern of depression and psychophysiological symptoms associated with workers' attempts to deal with the constrictions brought about by automation.

The major problem with the literature on occupation and mental illness is that while it is known that psychiatric impairment increases as one moves down the occupational prestige continuum, a more pressing question is left unanswered; namely, does occupation cause mental illness or do people with certain personalities choose particular types of jobs? It seems likely that occupation and mental health can affect each other. Some people seek out a job which suits their particular personality make-up. The belief that the mentally disturbed are the very ones at-

[11]Paul M. Roman and Harrison M. Trice, "Psychiatric impairment among 'Middle Americans': surveys of work organizations," *Social Psychiatry,* 7 (1972), pp. 157–166.

[12]G. Gurin, J. Veroff, and S. Feld, *Americans View Their Mental Health* (New York: Basic Books, 1960).

[13]R. Kahn and others, *Organizational Stress* (New York: Wiley, 1964).

[14]T. Langner and S. Michael, *Life, Stress and Mental Health* (New York: The Free Press, 1963).

[15]Robert Blauner, *Alienation and Freedom: The Factory Worker and His Industry* (Chicago: University of Chicago Press, 1964).

[16]A. Kornhauser, *Mental Health of the Industrial Worker* (New York: Wiley, 1965).

tracted to mental health occupations may not be just a myth since these jobs may prove attractive to those who are curious about their own make-up. Dentistry may provide another example of personality pre-ceeding occupational choice. Common sense dictates that an occupation like dentistry which demands attention to fine detail and order would appeal most to those with obsessive-compulsive needs. Consistently, dentists have the highest suicide rate of all occupational groups. This may not be simply because the job is stressful but because obsessive-compulsives are prime candidates for suicide since they are too inflexible to cope with the changes associated with aging.

There are a variety of examples of how an occupation can affect personality. The high rate of lesbian behavior among strippers is at least partly due to the conditions provided by the occupation such as isolation from male, affective social relationships.[17] In addition, these women experience unsatisfactory relationships with those males that do cross their path because the men view the women only as sex objects, as evi-denced by their masturbatory behavior in the audience. Another exam-ple of occupation affecting personality is the proliferation of the use of drugs by musicians (rock and jazz)[18] and physicians.[19] In both instances, occupationally-imposed pressure is relieved through deviant, socially unacceptable behavior.

Education and Mental Illness

Education interacts with mental illness in an inverse way just as occupation does; those with higher levels of educational attainment have a lower reported rate of psychiatric impairment.[20] This is probably a true relationship and not simply due to reporting biases since it has been demonstrated that more educated persons are more likely to seek psychiatric help for personal problems.[21] There are some exceptions to this norm—those whose educational and occupational statuses are dis-similar (a phenomenon known as *status inconsistency*).

[17]Charles H. McCaghy and James K. Skipper, Jr., "Lesbian behavior as an adapta-tion to the art of stripping," *Social Problems*, 17 (Fall, 1969), pp. 262–270.

[18]Charles Winick, "The use of drugs by jazz musicians," *Social Problems*, 7 (Winter, 1960), pp. 240–253.

[19]Richard M. Hessler, "Junkies in white: drug addiction among physicians," in *The Social World of Occupations*, eds. Bernard J. Gallagher III and Charles S. Palazzolo (Dubuque: Kendall Hunt Publishing Company, 1977), pp. 298–305. Estimates are that the narcotics addiction rate is a hundred times greater for physicians than the addiction rate for the public at large. The drug used most by physician junkies is meperidine (demerol).

[20]This has been confirmed by a number of studies. See, for example: Richard L. Meile, David Richard Johnson and Louis St. Peter, "Marital role, education, and mental disorder among women: test of an interaction hypothesis," *Journal of Health and Social Behavior*, 17 (1976), pp. 295–301.

[21]Richard A. Kulka, Joseph Veroff and Elizabeth Douvan, "Social class and the use of professional help for personal problems: 1957–1976" (paper presented at the annual meeting of the American Sociological Association, San Francisco, California, 1978).

What is noteworthy about the relationship between level of education and prevalence of psychiatric symptoms is that it is not peculiar to Western cultures. One research team uncovered an inverse relationship between educational level and the prevalence of mental illness for both sexes in Lebanon.[22] The same study also confirmed what researchers had previously discovered about the relationship between educational level and type of mental disorder in the Western world; people with high educational levels are most likely to develop a neurosis if they become disordered while those of low educational attainment are predisposed toward psychosis. Additionally, that minority of the "low education" group who become ill in a nonpsychotic way typically develop disorders with external symptoms such as conversion reactions and antisocial behavior.

The Prevalence of Mental Illness by Social Class

The combined effect of occupation and education on mental illness is measured in a number of studies that examine patterns of mental disorder between members of different social classes. In 1950, August B. Hollingshead and Frederick C. Redlich undertook a landmark study in psychiatric sociology by analyzing the relationship between social class and mental illness in the urban community of New Haven, Connecticut. That classic study is used as the nexus for discussion here because it can serve as a common reference to most easily evaluate other relevant studies and also because its findings have been replicated in the last few decades. The social class breakdown of a 5 percent random sample of New Haven households was compared to the class breakdown of the psychiatric population which consisted of people currently receiving psychiatric care on both an inpatient and outpatient basis.[23] The New Haven population was divided into five social classes equivalent to those outlined at the beginning of the chapter. A major hypothesis of the study was that the *expectancy* of a psychiatric disorder is significantly related to an individual's position in the class structure of his society. Simply stated, a person's chances of being mentally disordered, regardless of the type or severity of the illness, are related to his social class. This hypothesis was strongly supported by the New Haven data. The New Haven researchers compared the social class distribution of the general popula-

---

[22]H. A. Katchadourian and C. W. Churchill, "Education and mental illness in urban Lebanon," *Social Psychiatry*, 8 (1973), pp. 152–161.

[23]This study was concerned with diagnosed or treated prevalence rather than *true prevalence*. *True prevalence* figures, while theoretically more desirable, may not be as useful in studies of social class since methodological problems encountered in estimating those figures can bias the findings. This is due to the fact that researchers' evaluations are a vital part of their studies of mental illness and their own social class affects their evaluation of who is mentally ill. See Derek L. Phillips and Kevin J. Clancy, "Response biases in field studies of mental illness," *American Sociological Review*, 35 (1970), pp. 503–514.

tion of New Haven with the social class distribution of the psychiatric part of the community. If there were no relationship between social class and the prevalence of mental illness, then each social class would comprise the same percentage of the psychiatric population and the overall population. The data in Table 10.1 demonstrate that this is not the case. In New Haven the upper class contains 3.1 percent of the community's population but only 1.0 percent of all known psychiatric cases. Upper middle, lower middle, and working-class individuals are also underrepresented in the patient population but not to the same degree as are upper-class people. On the other hand, the percentage of lower-class people in the patient population is more than twice that which would be expected on the basis of their representation in the general population.

The researchers further tested their finding that social class is related to the likelihood of a person becoming a mental patient by controlling for the specific effects of sex, age, race, and marital status. In doing so they discovered some interesting ways in which these four demographic factors interacted with social class. They found that there is a particular abundance of female patients in the lower middle class and a concentration of male patients in the lower class. Age is especially related to being a mental patient in the lower middle class where adolescents and young adults are overrepresented in the psychiatric population. This may be due in part to excessive upward mobility ambitions which are likely to be the particular burden of young people striving to surpass their parents' class position by training for and/or entering more prestigious lines of work. Blacks exhibit the same pattern as whites by social class although, as a group, they are found more frequently in the lower social classes. Therefore, if the chances of becoming a mental patient were assessed on the basis of race alone, one would have to conclude that a black is more predisposed. But the real truth is that race itself is

Table 10.1. *Distribution of Normal and Psychiatric Population by Social Class*

Social Class	Normal Population		Psychiatric Population	
	Number	*Percent*	*Number*	*Percent*
Upper	358	3.1	19	1.0
Upper Middle	926	8.1	131	6.7
Lower Middle	2500	22.0	260	13.2
Working	5256	46.0	758	38.6
Lower	2037	17.8	723	36.8
Unknown	345	3.0	72	3.7
Total	11,422	100.0	1,963	100.0

Reprinted from August B. Hollingshead and Frederick C. Redlich, "Social stratification and psychiatric disorders," *American Sociological Review*, 18 (1953), p. 167. By permission of authors and publisher.

unrelated to the likelihood of being in treatment. It is membership in the lower social class that is responsible for excessive mental illness among blacks since it is the lower class to which many blacks belong, not because of an innate tendency for blacks to be lower class, but as a result of prejudicial treatment in the United States.

Married members of the four higher classes are less likely to be mentally ill than separated, widowed, divorced, and unmarried members of these same classes. In the lower class, however, married patients are as common as unmarried patients, suggesting that marriage does not function as a mental health haven in the miserable, deprived conditions of lower-class life.

The New Haven study concluded that a definite association exists between social class and being a psychiatric patient; the lower the class, the greater the proportion of people in the patient population. The greatest difference is between the four higher classes and the lower class; the lower class has a much higher ratio of patients to normal population than other classes.

Other researchers also report an inverse relationship between social class and rate of mental illness. An early study conducted by the Selective Service reported on 60,000 male registrants examined at the Boston Area Induction Station in 1942.[24] The psychiatric rejection rates were noticeably greater among lower-class registrants. The Midtown Manhattan study tested the class-impairment relationship among members of a population not in treatment and also found that lower social class carries a larger risk of impaired mental health.[25] The Midtown researchers estimated that 47.3 percent of the lowest social stratum was mentally impaired contrasted to only 12.5 percent of the highest stratum. In 1974 the Dohrenwends analyzed the findings of all studies of the *true prevalence* of psychopathology by social class.[26] They found that the most consistent result reported was an inverse relationship between overall rates of mental disorder and social class. In fact, of thirty-three communities examined by different researchers, twenty-eight yielded the highest rate of mental illness in the lowest class. This relationship holds for both rural and urban areas but may not be valid outside of the United States since one study of the prevalence of mental illness by class in Lebanon found the highest concentration of cases in the lower and upper classes while the middle class showed the lowest rate.[27]

---

[24]R. W. Hyde and L. V. Kingsley, "Studies in medical sociology: the relation of mental disorder to the community socioeconomic level," *New England Journal of Medicine,* 231 (1944), pp. 543–548.

[25]Leo Srole and others, *Mental Health in the Metropolis: The Midtown Manhattan Study* (New York: McGraw-Hill, 1962).

[26]Bruce P. Dohrenwend and Barbara Snell Dohrenwend, "Social and cultural influences on psychopathology," *Annual Review of Psychology,* 25 (1974), pp. 417–452.

[27]H. A. Katchadourian and C. W. Churchill, "Components in prevalence of mental illness and social class in urban Lebanon," *Social Psychiatry,* 8 (1973), pp. 145–151.

The Societal Reaction Hypothesis

The concentration of mental illness in the lower class has been explained in a number of ways. Some have concluded that the reported relationship of the prevalence of mental illness by social class is partly due to a middle-class bias that pervades psychiatric diagnosis. The middle-class prototype and the prototype of mental health are equivalent in many respects. This is a reflection of the large proportion of middle-class people who enter the mental health field and in turn project their own class-based values into their evaluations of who is mentally ill. Attitudes toward problem-solving, the control of emotions and planning ahead vary significantly by social class.[28] These are all traits found more commonly in the higher classes. So also is self-expression, a skill highly valued by psychiatrists. Wilkinson uncovered a strong tendency for middle-class people to rate a lower-class patient as more seriously impaired than an equally disordered member of their own class.[29] He interpreted this as support for the *societal reaction hypothesis* and concluded that part of what is seen as a psychiatric disorder among lower-class people is actually their social class characteristics.

The inherent biases of psychiatric diagnosis against lower-class people are particularly apparent in the projective tests used to assess mental health.[30] These instruments rely on test-taking experience, motivation to perform, familiarity with the vocabulary of the tester, and reading ability, in all of which the lower-class person is less skilled than his higher-class counterparts. It is these social class differences in abilities and norms that can be confused with pathological symptoms. In addition, higher-class individuals may be more aware than lower-class persons of what are considered the most socially desirable responses to questions used to assess mental health.

Some work has been done by the National Association for Mental Health to educate the public and increase their credence in mental health counseling. But such efforts have had an impact only on the pamphlet-receiving and reading group, which is comprised almost completely of middle- and upper-class people. The result of all this is a network of mental health communications disseminated and received by the higher social classes. This problem, which functions to maintain lower-class ignorance regarding mental health and illness, must be considered at least partly responsible for the reported inverse relationship between social class and prevalence of mental illness.

[28]Orville R. Gursslin, Raymond G. Hunt, and Jack L. Roach, "Social class and the mental health movement," *Social Problems,* 7 (1960), pp. 210–218.

[29]Gregg S. Wilkinson, "Patient-audience social status and the social construction of psychiatric disorders: toward a differential frame of reference hypothesis," *Journal of Health and Social Behavior,* 16 (1975), pp. 28–38.

[30]Projective tests typically involve telling a story about a picture that is presented to the subject. One widely-used projective test, the Rorschach Technique, involves free-associating about an inkblot design, an ambiguous stimulus that allows the subject to reveal his unconscious motivations.

The Social Stress Hypothesis

Another theory of the preponderance of mental illness in the lower class holds that the miserable conditions of lower-class life generate stress which in turn fosters psychiatric impairment. Social stress in the lower class takes many forms including childhood deprivation, broken homes, degrading treatment by others, social isolation, and resource deprivation which prevents educational and occupational attainment. Of utmost importance is the fact that unemployment is highest in the lower class. Unemployment is reported to have an undesirable effect on feelings of self-esteem and estrangement from family and friends.[31] A number of studies of mental illness and social class have been interpreted as supporting the *social stress hypothesis* which is also called the *social causation hypothesis*.[32] The social stress explanation is plausible in light of the finding that the most disadvantaged members of the lower class have the greatest degree of impairment; blacks and Puerto Ricans, for example, common objects of discrimination in the United States, are more frequently and severely impaired than their lower-class Irish peers.[33]

Several other possibilities have been suggested regarding the impact of stress on the mental health of the lower class. One is that it is not the stress of lower-social-class life per se that is the principle issue but living in areas where other ethnic groups predominate. In Boston, for instance, Italian Americans living in non-Italian neighborhoods have higher rates of disorder than those living in predominantly Italian neighborhoods.[34]

Melvin Kohn has developed an interesting proposition regarding the predominance of schizophrenia in the lower class. He contends that schizophrenia is caused by the stresses of lower-class life on genetically susceptible people.[35] The stresses that lower-class people experience are not alterable by individual actions because many of the stresses arise from economic circumstances over which there is little control. This is true for the lower-class person who is typically socialized to have a conformist orientation system so rigid that it can not possibly deal with stress or change. The genetic component of Kohn's theory of schizophrenia in the lower class is consistent with existing biogenic evidence. It also ex-

[31]Ramsay Liem and Joan Liem, "Social class and mental illness reconsidered: the role of economic stress and social support," *Journal of Health and Social Behavior*, 19 (1978), pp. 139–156.

[32]For a review of studies in this area see: Blair Wheaton, "The sociogenisis of psychological disorder: reexamining the causal issues with longitudinal data," *American Sociological Review*, 43 (1978), pp. 383–403.

[33]Bruce P. Dohrenwend and Barbara Snell Dohrenwend, *Social Status and Psychological Disorder: A Causal Inquiry* (New York: Wiley-Interscience, 1969), pp. 71–72.

[34]D. T. Schwartz and N. L. Mintz, "Ecology and psychosis among Italians in 27 Boston communities," *Social Problems*, 10 (1963), pp. 371–374.

[35]Melvin L. Kohn, "Social class and schizophrenia: a critical review and a reformulation," *Schizophrenia Bulletin*, 7 (1973), pp. 60–79.

plains why no study has found important differences in patterns of parent-child relationships between schizophrenics and normal persons of lower-social-class background. Genetic predisposition coupled with the rigid orientation system programmed into lower-class children can cause schizophrenic breakdown when stress is imposed. Mechanic, however, takes issue with Kohn's theory because it fails to consider that the lower-class person may be equally capable or even superior to higher-class persons in dealing with stress.[36] Mechanic finds it more challenging to discover why so many lower class persons do so well in facing adversity, rather than why some fail. He believes that the stresses of lower-class life give people greater opportunity to develop coping mechanisms rather than rendering them psychologically inoperative.

The Social Selection Hypothesis

There is another explanation of the preponderance of mental illness in the lower class that is the opposite of the social stress hypothesis. This theory, known as the *social selection hypothesis,* or *drift hypothesis,* holds that social class is not a cause but a consequence of psychopathology. According to this view, the mentally disordered person is likely to be a member of the lower class because his illness did not allow him to function at a higher-class level. As a consequence, he became downwardly mobile and *drifted* into the lower class. This theory is consistent with a biogenic orientation to etiology whereas the social stress hypothesis is consistent with an environmental orientation. The social selection view is gaining respect from sociological researchers who previously denied its validity. Dunham, for instance, has recently argued against his and Faris' earlier interpretations of the high concentration of schizophrenia in socially and economically disadvantaged communities.[37] Previously, he offered a social stress interpretation that emphasized the isolated conditions of inner city living. Since that time, a number of studies have impressively argued that social selection processes play a part in etiology, particularly for schizophrenia and the antisocial personality disorder.[38] All of these studies employ a similar logic; if the parents of mentally ill people are in higher social classes than their offspring, then the mental disorder preceded social class, and the

---

[36]David Mechanic, "Social class and schizophrenia: some requirements for a plausible theory of social influence," *Social Forces,* 50 (1972), pp. 305–309.

[37]H. Warren Dunham, *Community and Schiozphrenia: An Epidemiological Analysis* (Detroit, Michigan: Wayne State University Press, 1965).

[38]See, for example: J. Birtchnell, "Social class, parental social class, and social mobility in psychiatric patients and general population controls," *Psychological Medicine,* 1 (1971), pp. 209–221; E. M. Goldberg and S. L. Morrison, "Schizophrenia and social class," *British Journal of Psychiatry,* 109 (1963), pp. 758–802; Lee N. Robins, *Deviant Children Grown Up: A Sociological and Psychiatric Study of Sociopathic Personality* (Baltimore: Williams and Wilkins, 1966); R. J. Turner and M. O. Wagenfeld, "Occupational mobility and schizophrenia: an assessment of the social causation and social selection hypotheses," *American Sociological Review,* 32 (1967), pp. 104–113.

social selection hypothesis is supported. One team of researchers examined the social class of fathers of mental patients (schizophrenics and neurotics) in Great Britain.[39] They found that the social class distribution of patients' fathers did not differ from that of the general population. The patients, however, were often downwardly mobile, particularly the schizophrenics.

More recently, a study by Harkey and others presented a different twist on the relationship between mental illness and downward drift into the lower class.[40] They used a wide index of psychological health which essentially measured a person's general ability to function in society and administered it to over 16,000 individuals in Southern Appalachia. Their results partly supported the social selection hypothesis, as they found that the primary effect of psychological disorder is to retard upward mobility rather than contribute to downward mobility. This may result in two schools of thought within social selection theory: those that believe mental illness causes downward mobility and those that believe that mental illness limits upward mobility.

One sophisticated test of the social selection-social stress controversy contrasted psychological distress levels of Anglos, blacks, and Mexican Americans at the same social class level.[41] If the social stress model were correct, distress would be greater among blacks, Chicanos, and other minority group persons than among Anglos of similar social class because minority groups confront added stress in the form of racial bigotry and discrimination. If the social selection model were correct, there would be less impairment among disadvantaged minorities than among Anglos of the same class. The reason for this is that opportunities for upward mobility are more restricted, and downward pressures are much greater among disadvantaged groups compared to Anglos who are not forced into lower classes by racial constraints. Therefore, the lower-class Anglo was more likely to be impaired since some psychological dysfunction caused his social class position. The data from the study strongly support the social selection hypothesis since the disadvantaged ethnics had appreciably fewer symptoms of mental illness than Anglos of similar social class. It seems that, for every study supporting the social stress model, there is another verifying the social selection model. This is not surprising because the two models are not mutually exclusive; class can determine illness in one case and illness can determine class in another.

[39]E. H. Hare, J. S. Price and E. Slater, "Parental social class in psychiatric patients," *British Journal of Psychiatry,* 121 (1972), pp. 515–524.

[40]John Harkey, David L. Miles and William A. Rushing, "The relation between social class and functional status: a new look at the drift hypothesis," *Journal of Health and Social Behavior,* 17 (1976), pp. 194–204.

[41]George Antunes and others, "Ethnicity, socioeconomic status, and the etiology of psychological distress," *Sociology and Social Research: An International Journal,* 58 (1974), pp. 361–368.

Social Class and Type of Mental Disorder

The New Haven Findings

The literature is rich with studies reporting a relationship between types of mental illness and social class. Unfortunately, the classification system used by the New Haven researchers was rather simplistic since they divided all psychiatric cases into only two possible types: the neuroses and the functional psychoses. There are other types of illness ignored by such a breakdown, such as the personality disorders. In addition, the New Haven classification system did not treat the different types of psychoses and neuroses separately. Although the New Haven methodology was limited in this respect, the study did find a sharp contrast in the distribution of these two gross categories of disorders by social class as the data in Table 10.2 indicate.

There is a definite concentration of the neuroses at the higher-class levels and the psychoses at the lower levels of the class structure. The New Haven team suggested that the small number of neurotic cases in the lower classes was caused by the high cost of private psychiatric treatment for neurosis which is beyond the economic means of the lower class person. This explanation is not that compelling since case analyses by other researchers revealed that the *social distance*[42] between therapist and patient is as important as any economic considerations in determining who goes to private practitioners and who does not.[43] The *social distance* between a middle-class therapist and a lower-class patient is not conducive to mutual understanding and a desire for interaction.

Other studies have confirmed the major findings of the New Haven findings. One investigation reported a higher rate of hospitalized psychoses in a lower- and working-class area of Boston than in an upper- and middle-class section.[44] A prevalence study of psychiatric disorder in Baltimore found that psychotic disorders decreased as income increased.[45] The preponderance of psychoses, particularly schizophrenia, among the lower classes has also been found in similar research outside

---

[42]*Social distance*, a term coined by Georg Simmel, refers to a feeling of separation between individuals or groups. The greater the social distance between two groups of different status or culture, the less sympathy, understanding, intimacy, and desire for interaction there is between them.

[43]Jerome K. Myers and Leslie Schaffer, "Social stratification and psychiatric practice: a study of an out-patient clinic," *American Sociological Review*, 19 (1954), pp. 307–310.

[44]B. Kaplan and others, "A comparison of the incidence of hospitalized and nonhospitalized cases of psychosis in two communities," *American Sociological Review*, 21 (1956), pp. 472–479.

[45]B. Pasamanick and others, "A survey of mental disease in an urban population: prevalence by race and income," in *Epidemiology of Mental Disorder*, ed. B. Pasamanick (Washington, D.C.: American Association for the Advancement of Science, 1959), pp. 183–201.

Table 10.2. *Distribution of Neuroses and Psychoses by Social Class*

Social Class	Neuroses		Psychoses	
	Number	*Percent*	*Number*	*Percent*
Upper	10	52.6	9	47.4
Upper Middle	88	67.2	43	32.8
Lower Middle	115	44.2	145	55.8
Working	175	23.1	583	76.9
Lower	61	8.4	662	91.6
Total	449		1,442	

Reprinted from August B. Hollingshead and Frederick C. Redlich, "Social stratification and psychiatric disorders," *American Sociological Review*, 18 (1973), p. 168. By permission of authors and publisher.

of the United States including studies conducted in England[46] and Lebanon.[47] Research findings on the relationship between social class and type of mental disorder are not entirely consistent, however. Clausen and Kohn, for example, found no relationship between the prevalence of schizophrenia and social class in a small Maryland town.[48] In a study of the black population of Philadelphia, Parker found an increase in the rate of schizophrenia as social class decreased, but neuroses showed no social class differences.[49] Prevalence studies in Australia,[50] Norway,[51] and Formosa[52] also failed to confirm the New Haven finding of more psychosis and less neurosis among lower class people. Apparently these differences exist because the New Haven findings are appropriate only for the type of population from which the sample was drawn, that is, white, urban America. The Parker study examined a black population, and the other studies dealt with populations outside of the United States.

[46]J. N. Morris, "Health and social class," *Lancet*, 1 (1959), pp. 303–305.

[47]H. A. Katchadourian and C. W. Churchill, "Components in prevalence of mental illness and social class in urban Lebanon."

[48]J. A. Clausen and M. L. Kohn, "Social relations and schizophrenia: a research report and a perspective," in *The Etiology of Schizophrenia*, ed. Don D. Jackson (New York: Basic Books, 1960), pp. 295–320.

[49]S. Parker and others, "Social status and psychopathology" (paper presented at the annual meeting of the Society of Physical Anthropology, Philadelphia, Pennsylvania, 1962).

[50]J. F. J. Cade, "The aetiology of schizophrenia," *Medical Journal of Australia*, 2 (1956), pp. 135–139.

[51]Ornub Odegaard, "The incidence of psychosis in various occupations," *International Journal of Social Psychiatry*, 2 (1956), pp. 85–104.

[52]Tsung-yi Lin, "A study of the incidence of mental disorder in Chinese and other cultures," *Psychiatry*, 16 (1953), pp. 313–336.

Types of Psychosis

In addition to the New Haven investigation, other researchers have examined the relationship between social class and functional disorders. These investigations have been more specific than the New Haven study in that they have researched particular types of neuroses and psychoses rather than only the two gross categories utilized by the New Haven researchers. One early study by Fuson analyzed the social class distribution of two major types of functional psychosis: schizophrenia and the manic-depressive illnesses.[53] From an examination of the records of 1,496 mental patients, Fuson found that there is relatively more schizophrenia in lower-class groups and relatively more manic-depressive illness in higher class groups. It is important to note here that schizophrenia involves a greater break with reality than the manic-depressive psychoses which are more internal.

The social class gradient in schizophrenia has been examined in more than 50 studies to date. Almost without exception these studies have found a preponderance of schizophrenia at the lowest social class levels of urban society. Some of this evidence even comes from research conducted in a number of countries outside of the United States including England, Denmark, Finland, Canada, Norway, Sweden and Taiwan. Kohn's etiological argument is relevant here; he explains the preponderance of schizophrenia in the lower class as the result of the interaction of genetics and a psychological inability of lower-class people to deal with stress because of an inflexible, conformist conception of reality grounded in their socialization experiences.[54] Presently, Kohn's stress hypothesis is faced with some opposition since Levy and Rowitz found that first admissions for schizophrenia tend to come from more affluent communities while readmissions tend to emanate from poorer communities.[55] This indicates that the schizophrenic condition occurs in all classes and causes a *drift* down the social class ladder over time.

Neuroses and Personality Disorders

Given the large number of studies showing that there are certain ways in which members of different classes become psychotic, is there a particular way in which the various classes develop neuroses or personality disorders? Some researchers have found suggestive differences among the social classes in this regard.[56] The most common neurotic

[53]William M. Fuson, "Research note: occupations of functional psychotics," *American Journal of Sociology,* 48 (1943), pp. 612–613.

[54]Melvin L. Kohn, "The interaction of social class and other factors in the etiology of schizophrenia," *American Journal of Psychiatry,* 133 (1976), pp. 177–180.

[55]Leo Levy and Louis Rowitz, *The Ecology of Mental Disorder* (New York: Behavioral Publications, 1973), p. 148.

[56]S. M. Miller and Elliot G. Mishler, "Social class, mental illness, and American

reaction in the higher classes is the obsessive-compulsive neurosis, a relatively internal type of disorder compared to the phobic neurosis which occurs more frequently among those lower in the social hierarchy. Additionally, it is not by chance that the antisocial personality disorder is found among lower-class people since this also involves external symptoms in the form of social disobedience.

The Logic of Social Causation

The relationships between social class and type of mental illness lend support to the major hypothesis of this chapter; *there is an increasing predisposition toward external forms of mental disorder among those lower in the social class hierarchy.* Perhaps this is best exemplified by the high rate of psychosis in the lower class. In earlier discussions of psychoanalytic theory it was noted that the essential difference between a neurosis and a psychosis is the role of the ego in acting against two different agencies of the personality as a means of resolving intrapsychic conflict. Freud held that "... one of the features which differentiates a neurosis from a psychosis ... (is) that in a neurosis the ego, in its dependence on reality, suppresses a piece of the id (of instinctual life), whereas in a psychosis, this same ego, in the service of the id, withdraws from a piece of reality. Thus, for a neurosis the decisive factor would be the predominance of the influence of reality, whereas for a psychosis it would be the predominance of the id."[57] It seems logical that a response against social reality and in support of one's instinctual drives (a psychosis) is more likely to be found among those whose real world is unfulfilling. This is the reality of lower-class life. On the other hand, a response against instinctual drives and in support of social reality (a neurosis) is more consistent with the relatively desirable conditions of life in the higher classes.

The explanation of social class differences in type of mental illness preferred by this author is the *social stress* proposition that people from lower class settings develop *antireality* types of illnesses because their world is miserable and they were socialized as children toward external reactions. People from higher classes lead more rewarding lives, have less reason to retreat from that reality, and are not prone to act out their feelings because of an upbringing that emphasized internal control. For these reasons, *antiinstinctual* types of illnesses are their most common way of exhibiting mental disorder. This theory is useful beyond explaining the general neurosis/psychosis breakdown by social class since it is also possible to differentiate *within* these two categories in terms of the

---

psychiatry: an expository review," *Milbank Memorial Fund Quarterly*, 37 (1959), pp. 174–199.

[57]Sigmund Freud, "The loss of reality in neurosis and psychosis" in *Sourcebook in Abnormal Psychology*, eds. Leslie Y. Rabkin and John E. Carr (Boston: Houghton Mifflin, 1967), p. 192.

degrees to which specific disorders reflect a discontent with the real world. For example, both schizophrenia and the manic-depressive psychoses are considered to be a withdrawal from reality, but schizophrenic fantasies are much less associated with the real world than are the unexplained mood swings of manic-depressives, many of whom function within reality on a temporary basis. Within the neurotic and personality disorder categories the instinct/reality distinction also holds. The lower classes are most susceptible to antisocial reactions which are a clear-cut rejection of the social structure. The obsessive-compulsive tendencies of the higher classes, on the other hand, are experienced in more internal ways. This is not to say that the end result of psychological conflict is a simple function of social class. It would be true only if all higher-class people developed only specific types of neuroses while all lower-class people developed only severe psychotic reactions. This is not the case. There is, however, a significant relationship in this direction which should compel any responsible psychiatric researcher to consider social class as an important factor in the etiology of mental disorder.

Racial Differences

Blacks in the Nineteenth Century

Mental illness among blacks is presented here because their patterns of mental disorder roughly conform to what is known about mental illness patterns among economically deprived people. In the 1800s, there were a number of reports that blacks were relatively free of mental illness because of the special care they received as slaves.[58] These beliefs were strengthened by the 1840 census which reported higher rates among northern blacks than southern blacks. Interpreting these data, Edward Jarvis, a Massachusetts physician, endeared himself to the southern slave states by declaring that "... slavery must have a wonderful influence upon the moral faculties and intellectual powers of the individual, for in refusing many of the hopes and responsibilities which the free, self-thinking and self-acting enjoy and sustain, of course it saves him from some of the liabilities and dangers of active self-direction. The false position of the Negro in the North had a disturbing effect on his 'character.'"[59] Although the census report was falsified and Jarvis later issued a complete repudiation of his statements, the harm was already

[58]J. Babcock, "The colored insane," *Alienist and Neurologist,* 16 (1895), pp. 423–447; M. O. Malley, "Psychoses in the colored race," *American Journal of Insanity,* 71 (1914), pp. 309–337; T. Powell, "The increase in insanity and tuberculosis in the southern Negro since 1860 and its alliance and some of the supposed causes," *Journal of the American Medical Association,* 27 (1896), pp. 1185–1188; A. Witmer, "Insanity in the colored race in the United States," *Alienist and Neurologist,* 12 (1891), pp. 19–30.

[59]Edward Jarvis, quoted in Seymour Leventman, "Race and mental illness in mass society," *Social Problems,* 16 (1968), p. 73.

done and proslavery interests were strengthened. The 1860 census also reported some suspicious findings; only 766 "colored insane" were reported out of a total black population of 4,441,830. The number increased to 6,776 in 1890, a rate change from 17.5 per 100,000 in 1860 to 88.6 per 100,000 in 1890. The racist mentality of the era linked this increase with the abolition of slavery which altered the "peaceful" conditions blacks had enjoyed as slaves and introduced them to the stresses of competitive life. It is disheartening to realize that ethnocentrism was so common among researchers at that time. Many of them either did not recognize mental illness among blacks, or they attributed it to the "natural inferiority" of the race. Only since the civil rights movement of the 1950s has the idea been challenged that blacks are happiest in their "place."

The Mental Health Status of Blacks Today

In 1969, the Dohrenwends reported that of eight studies of black-white differences in rate of mental illness, four reported higher rates for blacks and four reported higher rates for whites.[60] However, the methodologies of many of those studies were poor since they were conducted at a time when statistical analyses were underdeveloped. The Midtown Manhattan study did not suffer such weaknesses; it uncovered higher rates among blacks. It is curious that the Dohrenwends are more critical toward the Midtown study than the less sophisticated designs of earlier studies. They suggest that the results of the Midtown study were affected by using white interviewers and by asking questions that better educated people would know how to answer on the basis of social desirability.[61]

More recent studies of the relationship between race and mental illness have consistently found that blacks have more mental illness than whites, but the differences are minimal when social class is held constant.[62] In other words, much of the greater prevalence of mental disorder among blacks is due to the fact that they are overrepresented in the lower social class which is known to be hazardous to mental health. In 1970 blacks had higher rates of mental illness than whites in every age, sex, and marital status group.[63] But these data are based on records of admissions to public institutions, the type of help-source the poor are

[60]Bruce P. Dohrenwend and Barbara Snell Dohrenwend, *Social Status and Psychological Disorder*, p. 16.

[61]Ibid., p. 76.

[62]George J. Warheit, Charles E. Holzer III and Sandra A. Arey, "Race and mental illness: an epidemiologic update," *Journal of Health and Social Behavior*, 16 (1975), pp. 243–256.

[63]R. Redick and C. Johnson, "Statistical note 100: marital status, living arrangements and family characteristics of admissions to state and county mental hospitals and outpatient psychiatric clinics, United States, 1970," Department of HEW, Public Health Service, NIMH, Office of Program Planning and Evaluation, Biometry Branch, Survey and Reports Section.

likely to utilize. Affluent whites, on the other hand, can better afford private care. As a consequence of these socioeconomic differences between blacks and whites, blacks are more likely to appear as cases in studies using public records. To control for this, one study used the Monroe County case register which not only includes all patients seen by public and private hospitals and clinics but also patients treated by psychiatrists in private practice.[64] Using these data, the prevalence rates were still higher for blacks than whites (11.55 per 1,000 population for blacks, 8.39 per 1,000 population for whites). Another study applied a "general psychopathology scale" to a nonhospitalized population and found that blacks were significantly more impaired than whites.[65] Additionally, one study of 2,000 randomly chosen adults living in the South found a significantly higher percentage of blacks (38 percent) than whites (28 percent) were impaired.[66]

The higher rates among blacks can be accounted for in two ways. First, since blacks are overrepresented in the lower social class, it is expected that they will manifest more impairment than whites as a group. Second, even within the same social class, stress situations are more frequent and severe among disadvantaged blacks than among their relatively advantaged white counterparts.

Types of Mental Illness

There are a number of differences in type of mental illness by race that closely follow known differences between social class groups. Functional psychosis, especially schizophrenia, appears more frequently among blacks than whites.[67] The manic-depressive psychoses, on the other hand, appear less frequently among blacks than they do in the lower social class in general.[68] But, when the rates for the manic-depressive psychoses are compared between blacks and whites of the same social class, these differences disappear.[69] Consistent with the labeling theory perspective that paranoia is often diagnosed among people who suffer

[64]E. A. Gardner and Associates, "A cumulative register of psychiatric services in a community" (paper presented at the annual meeting of the American Public Health Association, 1962).

[65]George J. Warheit and others, "Race and mental illness."

[66]John J. Schwab, Nancy H. McGinnis and George J. Warheit, "Social psychiatric impairment: racial comparisons," *American Journal of Psychiatry,* 130 (1973), pp. 183–187.

[67]William A. Scott, "Social psychological correlates of mental illness and mental health," *Psychological Bulletin,* 55 (1958), pp. 72–87.

[68]B. Malzberg, "Mental disease among Negroes: an analysis of first admissions in New York State," *Mental Hygiene,* 43 (1959), pp. 422–459; A. Pronge and M. M. Vitols, "Cultural aspects of the low incidence of depression in southern Negroes," *International Journal of Social Psychiatry,* 62 (1961), pp. 104–111; B. H. Roberts and J. K. Myers, "Religion, national origin, immigration, and mental illness," *American Journal of Psychiatry,* 110 (1954), pp. 759–764.

[69]George J. Warheit, Charles E. Holzer III, and John J. Schwab, "An analysis of social class and racial differences in depressive symptomatology: a community study," *Journal of Health and Social Behavior,* 14 (1973), pp. 291–299.

actual social exclusion, it has been found that paranoid tendencies are more common among blacks than whites.[70] Blacks are also more susceptible to antisocial reactions, which are known to be more common among people in the lower classes.[71]

Organic disorders appear more frequently among blacks. For example, organic brain syndromes due to the consequences of chronic alcoholism are reported to be nine times as high for blacks than whites.[72] Blacks also have higher rates of mental retardation,[73] a disorder known to be associated with premature birth and complications of pregnancy which are more likely to be encountered in lower class groups.

Consistent with their prevalence in higher classes, whites are more susceptible to neurotic breakdowns[74] with the exception of the phobic reactions which appear more frequently among blacks, as they do in general among people in the lower classes.[75] Whites also have higher rates of psychophysiologic disorders that may be a consequence of the greater propensity of higher-class persons to report symptoms which fall into this diagnostic category.[76]

The social class element underlying the mental health status of blacks is most apparent when they are compared with Jews, a group which is overrepresented in the higher classes. The black and Jewish populations manifest psychic strain in radically different ways. Jews have high rates of neurosis but low rates of alcoholism and antisocial reactions.[77] The Jew turns his stress inward because of the internally oriented socialization practices common among higher-class families and because of taboos in Jewish culture against the outward expression of hostility. This taboo apparently transcends social class constraints since there are also low rates of antisocial behavior among the few Jews in the lower class.[78]

Black-Jewish differences even occur when members of the two groups suffer the same illness. Blacks are most susceptible to the paranoid form of schizophrenia, a reflection of the outward expression of aggression and actual assault found in black culture.[79] The Jewish

[70]Bruce P. Dohrenwend and Barbara Snell Dohrenwend, *Social Status and Psychological Disorder,* p. 71.

[71]Ibid., p. 71.

[72]Benjamin Pasamanick, "A survey of mental disease in an urban population VII: an approach to total prevalence by race," *American Journal of Psychiatry,* 119 (1962), p. 304.

[73]Ibid., p. 304.

[74]Ibid., p. 303.

[75]George J. Warheit and others, "Race and mental illness," pp. 247–249.

[76]Benjamin Pasamanick, "A survey of mental disease in an urban population," pp. 303–304.

[77]R. M. Hyde and R. M. Chisholm, "Studies in medical sociology, III: the relation of mental disorders to race and nationality," *New England Journal of Medicine,* 231 (1944), pp. 612–618.

[78]Matthew Figelman, "A comparison of affective and paranoid disorders in Negroes and Jews," *International Journal of Social Psychiatry,* 14 (1968), p. 277.

[79]Michael Breen, "Culture and schizophrenia: a study of Negro and Jewish schizophrenics," *International Journal of Social Psychiatry,* 14 (1968), pp. 282–289.

schizophrenic, on the other hand, is usually diagnosed as simple, hebephrenic, or catatonic, diagnoses which Breen terms "dependency schizophrenia" because these types of schizophrenic patients are usually in need of greater care and direction by the hospital staff than the more independent, paranoid schizophrenic.[80] The preponderance of "dependency schizophrenia" among Jewish patients is assumed to be a reflection of the excessive mothering many Jews receive as children.

Northern-Southern Differences

There are also differences within the black population itself. Blacks living in the northern part of the United States have higher reported rates of mental illness than black residents of the southern part of the country.[81] This has been interpreted in a number of ways. One explanation is that unstable blacks migrate to the North where they swell the mental illness statistics. Another theory holds that most northern blacks are urban dwellers and most southern blacks are rural dwellers. Therefore, North-South differences are a result of differences in the quality of living conditions between urban and rural areas. A third explanation of the greater prevalence of mental illness among blacks living in the North involves attitudinal differences between northern and southern blacks. Northern blacks, raised in an environment that presents the goals and aspirations of an affluent society, do not have the means for achieving these ideals. Southern blacks, raised in a more oppressive environment, have learned to strive for less ambitious goals and are therefore less likely to experience frustration than northern blacks who are strained by the large discrepancy between their ambitions and their actual accomplishments.

The Effect of the Civil Rights Movement

Ironically, there has been a tremendous reported increase in the black mental hospital admission rate since the advent of the civil rights movement. The change in the social status of black Americans has apparently not been without its costs. This social change has transformed blacks from a deprived but homogeneous group to one which is riven with divisions based on new-found identities and ambitions. For many blacks, the result has been an unsettling sense of marginality because they find themselves somewhere between black society and white society. This is particularly apparent in the case of blacks who were educated for prestigious occupations and used their recently acquired wealth to move to the white suburbs.[82] Here they find themselves burdened with racist

[80]Ibid., p. 285.

[81]Fred R. Crawford, "Variations between Negroes and Whites in concepts of mental illness, its treatment and prevalence," in *Changing Perspectives in Mental Illness*, eds. Stanley C. Plog and Robert B. Edgerton (New York: Holt, Rinehart and Winston, 1969), p. 243.

[82]This group was aptly termed the "black bourgeoisie" by E. Franklin Frazer. See E. Franklin Frazer, *Black Bourgeoisie* (London: Collier-Macmillan Ltd., 1957).

stigmas and labeled as "block busters." It is no small wonder that mental illness has grown among blacks, given the frustrations and insecurities middle-class blacks face from breaking with their own cultural traditions while simultaneously suffering isolation as a result of their rejection by the "white world."

The psychiatric effect of the marginal position of the black American is perhaps best exemplified by the high rate of impairment among young blacks (under thirty). This group was exposed during their formative years to the social change that has taken place since the 1950s. They witnessed the turbulent 1960s and participated in the struggle for desegregation. Yet their opportunities for sharing in the lifestyles and material benefits of the wider society are limited compared to their aspirations. This frustration is probably responsible for a substantially higher rate of impairment among young blacks than among young whites.[83]

If, through integration, blacks eventually become fully accepted members of American society, their mental illness patterns will change as they become more evenly distributed throughout the stratification system. Then they will be more subject to the psychological environment of traditional middle-class life which in turn will increase neurosis and decrease psychosis, antisocial behavior, and the organically based syndromes to which lower-class people are subject.

Social Mobility

Does movement up or down the social class ladder cause stress which in turn leads to mental illness? A number of studies have tested this proposition, but the results have been inconclusive and contradictory. One reason for this is that mobility studies often use different measures of social class. Since mobility is typically measured in terms of the difference between the subject's attainments and that of his parents, those studies that use education as the sole criterion of social class are especially problematic since educational opportunities have changed so much over time that intergenerational differences in educational levels are common and thus no real index of mobility.

Durkheim first reported an association between economic change and abnormal behavior in his classic study of suicide. He reported that the suicide rate increases during periods of economic depression and prosperity. He concluded that any type of economic change produces a state of normlessness which leads to feelings of frustration. During an economic crisis, the downwardly mobile individual is forced to restrain his desires, a requirement that some persons are not able to tolerate. Durkheim postulated a similar process operating in the upwardly mobile person who finds himself with unexpected wealth resulting from an

[83]John J. Schwab, "Social psychiatric impairment: racial comparisons," p. 186.

economic boom. Although some persons react with happiness, others fail to perceive the practical limitations of the situation, and they begin to strive for unrealistic goals. They are frustrated by "the futility of an endless pursuit." Since Durkheim's study of suicide, others have reported a direct relationship between any type of social mobility (upward or downward) and a number of psychological and interpersonal disturbances.[84] At the same time, some studies have shown no important relationship between social mobility (regardless of direction) and mental illness.[85]

The Pathology of Upward Mobility

The psychoanalytic researcher, Karen Horney, believed that deep-seated personality factors are involved in the drive for upward mobility.[86] She held that persons who sought power, prestige, and wealth were neurotics who were deprived of affection during childhood. Typically this took the form of a "series of humiliating experiences," such as parental preference for other children, unjust reproaches, rejection by parents, jealousy of a parent or sibling, and minority group membership. These experiences wounded the child's self-esteem and created a sense of unconscious hostility toward others whom the person desires to humiliate. According to Horney, the drive for upward mobility occurs in such persons who vindictively strive to rise above others. Horney's hypothesis that mobility is frequently inspired by emotional drives generated by unsatisfactory early family relations was tested by Ellis who compared the backgrounds of upwardly mobile and nonmobile women.[87] She found that the mobile women had a significantly larger number of humiliating experiences during childhood, more often rated their childhood as "less than average," and were considerably more lonely as adults than nonmobile women. A later study found that psychological disturbances are only common among upwardly mobile

[84]P. M. Blau, "Social mobility and interpersonal relations," *American Sociological Review,* 21 (1956), pp. 290-295.; J. Greenbaum and L. I. Pearlin, "Vertical mobility and prejudice: a social psychological analysis" in *Class, Status and Power: A Reader in Social Stratification,* eds. R. Bendix and S. M. Lipset (Glencoe, Illinois: The Free Press, 1953), pp. 480-491.

[85]John Clausen and Melvin Kohn, "Relation of schizophrenia to the social structure of a small city" in *Epidemiology of Mental Disorder,* ed. Benjamin Pasamanick (Washington, D.C.: American Association for the Advancement of Science, 1959), pp. 69-86; D. L. Gerard and L. Houston, "Family setting and the social ecology of schiozphrenia," *Psychiatric Quarterly,* 27 (1953), pp. 90-101; August B. Hollingshead and Frederick C. Redlich, *Social Class and Mental Illness* (New York: Wiley, 1958); R. M. Lapouse, M. A. Monk and M. Terris "The drift hypothesis in socio-economic differentials in schizophrenia," *American Journal of Public Health,* 48 (1956), pp. 978-986.

[86]Karen Horney, *The Neurotic Personality of Our Time* (New York: Norton, 1937), pp. 80-82, 178-179.

[87]Evelyn Ellis, "Social psychological correlates of upward social mobility among unmarried career women," *American Sociological Review,* 17 (1952), pp. 558-563.

individuals at relatively high social-class levels.[88] Apparently status climbing can have pathogenic effects for those who are unprepared for it. However, it would be unreasonable to hold that upward mobility is always linked with mental illness since there are many people who are upwardly mobile and display no signs of psychopathology. For them, sound mental health is either a preparatory asset that helps them improve their position or the rewards of upward mobility improve their mental health.

The Pathology of Downward Mobility

The most consistent finding in the mobility literature is a positive association between downward mobility and mental illness. This has been verified by a number of studies using patient records[89] as well as the Midtown Manhattan study of people in the community. The Midtown study found that impaired people were frequently downwardly mobile in relation to their parents' status level. Most of the studies reporting downward mobility to be a commonplace among disturbed people have been limited to hospitalized schizophrenics who undoubtedly are prone to drift into the lower class because of the severity of their condition. However, some researchers believe that the downwardly mobile experience itself generates sufficient stress to cause psychiatric impairment of varying degrees. Other researchers specify that impairment rates for the downwardly mobile are only high at the lowest status level and for the upwardly mobile at the high end of the status scale.[90] All of these mixed reports make it apparent that Durkheim's assumption of an invariant association between *any* type of mobility and abnormal behavior is untenable. Downward mobility appears to be a greater mental health hazard than upward mobility, although this is only generally true. Much depends on the way the person perceives the experience. For some people status climbing may have costly effects in the form of shifting reference groups and concomitant interpersonal experiences that would have been avoided had they remained stationary. For others downward mobility may stabilize mental health by permitting an escape from taxing stresses at higher-class levels.

Status Inconsistency

Closely related to social mobility is the phenomenon known as *status inconsistency*. A status inconsistent individual is one whose occu-

[88]R. J. Turner, "Social mobility and schizophrenia," *Journal of Health and Social Behavior,* 9 (1968), pp. 194–203.

[89]See, for example, H. Warren Dunham, *Community and Schizophrenia*; E. M. Goldberg and S. L. Morrison, "Schizophrenia and social class"; M. Lystad, "Social mobility among schizophrenic patients," *American Sociological Review,* 21 (1957), pp. 288–292; R. J. Turner, "Social mobility and schizophrenia," *Journal of Health and Social Behavior,* 9 (1968), pp. 194–203.

[90]Robert J. Kleiner and Seymour Parker, "Social mobility, anomie, and mental dis-

pational, educational, and income attainment are incongruous. In a sense, this resembles social mobility, as in the case of the individual with high educational attainment who is employed in a lower-class job, a downwardly mobile experience since the individual failed to function at the level of his training. Studies of status inconsistency and mental illness allow researchers to more thoroughly understand the relationship between mobility and illness by examining the particular effects of each component of class.

A study of rates of first admission to mental hospitals found rates to vary inversely with status integration; individuals with inconsistent statuses were more likely to require hospitalization.[91] However, not all types of status inconsistency cause stress leading to mental disorder. Schizophrenics, for instance, tend to have backgrounds with a particular type of status imbalance—their occupational level is lower than their years of education merit. This finding is substantiated by a number of studies.[92] In fact, the greater the magnitude of this type of inconsistency, the higher the proportion of schizophrenia.[93] The literature consistently notes that those with high education-low occupation inconsistencies are disproportionately diagnosed as schizophrenics. This discrepancy between the individual's education and his occupational attainment is consistent with the *social selection* explanation of the great number of schizophrenics who are members of the lower class. Their aspirations are linked to middle-class goals because of the achievement-oriented influence of their formal education yet their psychological condition prevented them from functioning at occupational levels consistent with their training. The consequence is a drift into the lower class. However, it is also plausible that status inconsistency is a cause of schizophrenia as well as a consequence but in both instances lower-social-class membership does not precede schizophrenia as *social stress* theory would predict.

It is important to note that only one type of status inconsistency—high education-low occupation—is associated with schizophrenia. The

---

order," in *Changing Perspectives in Mental Illness,* eds. Stanley C. Plog and Robert B. Edgerton (New York: Holt, Rinehart and Winston, 1969), pp. 462–463.

[91] Walter T. Martin, "Status integration, social stress, and mental illness: accounting for marital status variations in mental hospitalization rates," *Journal of Health and Social Behavior,* 17 (1976), pp. 280–294.

[92] See, for example, H. W. Dunham, P. Phillips and B. Scinivason, "A research note on diagnosed mental illness and social class," *American Sociological Review,* 31 (1966), pp. 223–227; E. M. Goldberg and S. L. Morrison, "Schizophrenia and social class"; A. B. Hollingshead, R. Ellis and E. Kirby, "Social mobility and mental illness," *American Sociological Review,* 19 (1954), pp. 577–584; Seymour Parker, R. J. Kleiner and H. G. Taylor, "Level of aspiration and mental disorder: a research proposal," *Annals of the New York Academy of Sciences,* 84 (1960), pp. 878–886; J. Tuckman and R. J. Kleiner, "Discrepancy between aspiration and achievement as a predictor of schizophrenia," *Behavioral Science,* 7 (1962), pp. 443–447.

[93] D. Stanley Eitzen and Jeffrey H. Bair, "Type of status inconsistency and schizophrenia," *The Sociological Quarterly,* 13 (1972), pp. 61–73.

opposite type of inconsistency—low education-high occupation—is associated with a very different form of behavior. The first type of inconsistent individual is prone to schizophrenia because he becomes frustrated when investments (educational level) exceed rewards (occupational level). The second type of inconsistent individual is more prone to neurosis because of the guilt he may experience when rewards (occupational level) exceed investments (educational level).[94]

Differences in Psychiatric Treatment by Social Class

The New Haven Findings

The New Haven study examined treatment differences by social class. All treatments were grouped into three categories: psychotherapy, organic therapy, and custodial care. Psychotherapy includes all techniques which rest on verbal interaction between the patient and someone else in a helping role. This ranges from the highly individualistic and lengthy psychoanalytical approach to the cheaper, group method technique typically employed in state hospitals. Organic therapy includes all techniques which involve alteration of bodily state. The two major types of organic therapy are chemotherapy (the use of drugs, such as tranquilizers, to maintain temporary psychic equilibrum) and shock treatment (insulin shock therapy and ECT). Custodial care is a polite term for no treatment at all. The custodial approach is based on the assumption that the patient can not be rehabilitated, but he must be separated from the rest of society for security reasons. The New Haven study found a roughly equal distribution of these three therapeutic approaches over the entire patient population, but the percentage of persons who received organic therapy or custodial therapy was greatest in the lower class. Psychotherapy was used more frequently in the higher classes, and, within the psychotherapy category, there were important differences in the type administered by class. Psychoanalytic techniques were predominant among upper- and upper-middle-class patients. The few patients in the lower class who received psychotherapy were typically administered a group method approach. The breakdown of type of treatment received by patients of various social classes is presented in Table 10.3.

The New Haven findings have caused considerable controversy since some regard the report as a blatant indictment of prejudicial systems of psychiatric care which favor the higher-class patients with expensive, individually oriented therapy and relegate lower-class patients to inexpensive, less effective therapeutic programs. This charge has been strengthened by other studies showing that lower-class patients are socially disadvantaged in treatment settings. One study of depressed

[94]Ibid., p. 66.

Table 10.3. *Distribution of the Principal Types of Therapy by Social Class*

Social Class	Psychotherapy		Organic Therapy		No Treatment	
	Number	*Per-cent*	*Number*	*Per-cent*	*Number*	*Per-cent*
Upper	14	73.7	2	10.5	3	15.8
Upper Middle	107	81.7	15	11.4	9	6.9
Lower Middle	136	52.7	74	28.7	48	18.6
Working	237	31.1	288	37.1	242	31.8
Lower	115	16.1	234	32.7	367	51.2

Reprinted from August B. Hollingshead and Frederick C. Redlich, "Social stratification and psychiatric disorders," *American Sociological Review*, 18 (1953), p. 169. By permission of authors and publisher.

patients found that only 17 percent of the depressed lower-class patients were referred for psychotherapy in contrast to 33 percent in the middle class and 100 percent in the upper class.[95] Another study of prospective patients at a psychiatric outpatient clinic found that lower-class people are more frequently misdiagnosed and less likely to receive psychotherapy than higher class persons.[96] Many are claiming that equality of care is far from the norm, especially in the case of lower-class people who are also members of minority groups. Before examining the bases of this argument, it is important to note that usually the psychotic illnesses found in the lower classes are not effectively treated through psychotherapeutic techniques. This is particularly true in the case of psychoanalysis which requires transference for successful treatment. Transference is the process by which a patient sees in the psychoanalyst the return—the reincarnation—of some important figure from childhood and consequently transfers on to the analyst feelings and reactions that originally applied to the past figure. Not only does this seem impossible to accomplish with a psychotic, but it is particularly difficult to achieve between a lower class patient and an analyst from a higher class. The social distance problems are enormous since few patients can relate to an analyst as a significant figure from the past when the analyst makes the patient feel uncomfortable and cautious. In addition, psychoanalysis relies on the patient assuming an active role in the therapeutic process by verbalizing his thoughts and feelings. This is not likely to occur with lower-class patients who generally are not self-expressive. Psychotherapeutic techniques are most useful with higher class, nonpsychotic patients who are better able to engage in a "talking-out" approach.

[95]John J. Schwab and others, "Current concepts of depression: the sociocultural," *International Journal of Social Psychiatry*, 14 (1968), p. 230.
[96]Marvin Karno, "The enigma of ethnicity in a psychiatric clinic," *Archives of General Psychiatry*, 14 (1966), pp. 516–520.

Unfortunately, psychiatry seems to be hamstrung in its effort to cure the most severely disturbed patients, and some feel that the "behavior control" approach of organic and custodial treatments is the best available treatment.

Lower-Class Patients in Treatment

In defense of the underrepresentation of lower-class patients in psychotherapy, some have suggested that lower-class patients do not understand the psychotherapeutic process and are uninterested in it.[97] On the other hand, some fault therapists who are believed to negatively stereotype lower-class patients and relegate them to organic or custodial forms of therapy on the simple basis of social-class characteristics.[98] It has been reported that therapists consider lower-class persons as poor candidates for psychotherapy, not because they are lower class per se, but because they typically lack "insight-verbal ability."[99] It is true that lower-class patients often lack verbal skills but it is important to realize that this is frequently the result of family and peers discouraging the person from talking about feelings. Thus, the absence of talking-out skills among lower class persons is a *trained incapacity*. For this reason, perhaps it is the lower-class patients who really should be favored with psychotherapy since they can learn new skills from it.

The lack of verbal ability among lower-class persons is not the only reason why they are so frequently considered as poor candidates for psychotherapy. There are other forces at work as well. One of these is *status homophily*, a term that refers to the degree of social similarity between two individuals. From this perspective, therapists are believed to select patients who have social class characteristics similar to their own. This was demonstrated by Kandel who found that psychotherapists have an elitist bias toward higher-class patients.[100] They prefer to treat patients socially similar to themselves, and they screen their patients in terms of an orientation that underlies many forms of social interaction—that "birds of a feather flock together." Participation in psychotherapy is inversely related to the extent of class discrepancy between psychotherapists and potential patients. However, this may not be true of psychotherapists from the lower social classes since at least one

[97]Herta Mayer and Gerald Schamess, "Long term treatment for the disadvantaged," *Social Casework*, 50 (1969), pp. 138–145; John E. Mayer and Noel Timms, "Clash in perspective between worker and client," *Social Casework*, 50 (1969), pp. 32–40.

[98]James T. McMahon, "The working class psychiatric patient: a clinical view," in *Mental Health of the Poor*, eds. Frank Riessman, Jerome Cohen and Arthur Pearl (New York: Free Press, 1964), pp. 283–302.

[99]David W. Rowden and others, "Judgments about candidates for psychotherapy: the influence of social class and insight-verbal ability," *Journal of Health and Social Behavior*, 11 (1970), pp. 51–58.

[100]Denise Bystryn Kandel, "Status homophily, social context, and participation in psychotherapy," *American Journal of Sociology*, 71 (1966), pp. 640–650.

study found that even this group of therapists tends to underselect lower-class patients.[101]

All of these findings on status homophily come from studies of psychotherapists in organizationally based practices, such as state mental hospitals. Marx and Spray tested the "homophilic hypothesis" among psychiatrists and clinical psychologists in private practice.[102] They found that college graduates are clearly preferred as patients by all psycho-therapists although those from higher social class origins have a much greater concentration of college graduates as patients than their colleagues from lower-class backgrounds. Marx and Spray also evaluated another component of status homophily—religiocultural values. They found that therapists also prefer patients from their own religious origins even when the therapist is an apostate. This partly accounts for the large number of Jews receiving psychotherapy; although only three percent of the United States population is Jewish, about a third of psychiatrists are Jewish.[103] Catholic patients, on the other hand, typically seek treatment from clinical psychologists who tend to come from Christian backgrounds.

The literature convincingly demonstrates that what happens therapeutically to people who become psychiatric patients is largely determined by their social c. ss. However, this may not be true in all types of treatment settings, such as community mental health centers which are publicly funded to serve the needs of all persons in a geographical area. Mental health centers offer a variety of treatments, not all of which have social-class-related requirements. This, coupled with the fact that such centers are supposedly based on a democratic dispensation of therapy, reportedly weaken the relationship between social class and acceptance for some type of psychotherapy in this setting.[104] However, much of what is written about community mental health centers is a function of the specific centers a researcher chooses to investigate since there are also reports that lower-class patients are typically assigned to the least competent therapists.[105]

The community mental health center may be dealing more effectively with another class-related problem in psychotherapy—the high attrition rates of lower-class patients.[106] The patient characteristics com-

---

[101]David W. Rowden and others, "Judgments about candidates for psychotherapy," p. 56.

[102]John H. Marx and S. Lee Spray, "Psychotherapeutic 'birds of a feather': social class status and religio-cultural value homophily in the mental health field," *Journal of Health and Social Behavior,* 13 (1972), pp. 413–428.

[103]Ibid., p. 421.

[104]Maxine Springer Stein, "Social class and psychiatric treatment of adults in the mental health center," *Journal of Health and Social Behavior,* 18 (1977), pp. 317–325.

[105]Roberta Satow and Judith Lorber, "Cultural congruity and the use of paraprofessionals in community mental health work" (paper presented at the annual meeting of the Society for the Study of Social Problems, San Francisco, California, 1978).

[106]See, for example, Leonard Scheiderman, "Social class, diagnosis and treatment,"

monly associated with attrition are poor verbal ability, lack of introspection or emotional responsiveness, and a lack of concern about interpersonal relations, all of which are associated with low social class. Some community mental health centers have reduced attrition among lower-class patients by using techniques designed to increase their comfort and reduce their fears.[107] The techniques include an informal atmosphere in the clinic and the selection of motivated therapists and employees drawn from the community.

There is evidence that therapy differences by social class can be controlled by economic variables as well. The Midtown Manhattan Study, for instance, did not show the poor to be receiving less psychotherapy. As a matter of fact, that study reported no relationship at all between class and treatment. This surprising departure from the New Haven findings was explained by different types of treatment programs available in the two communities. In Manhattan, the availability of both high- and low-cost treatment facilities resulted in people of all classes being able to afford better care. This was not the case in New Haven where the better types of treatment were more expensive.

Those that defend the selective tendencies of psychotherapists are not entirely wrong in stressing that "good patients" are required for successful treatment and that the likelihood of finding this type of patient declines with social class. On the other hand, those critical of these selective admission standards seem justified in taking issue with the intellectually sophisticated definition of a "good patient" which often rests on evaluations of social worth. These judgments include a multitude of issues related to the definition of a "good patient" including the ability to verbalize problems, hold common values and pay bills.[108] The resolution of the dilemma requires a reexamination of psychotherapeutic techniques with respect to broadening approaches. This should be done with the goal of imparting psychiatric care by therapists who are not class-biased and who employ techniques with special reference to lower-class values, life style, educational level, and verbalizing ability.

Conclusions

Epidemiological analyses of mental illness by social class have revealed important relationships between social classes and prevalence,

American Journal of Orthopsychiatry, 35 (1965), pp. 99–105; Joe Yamamoto, "Social class in psychiatric therapy," _Current Psychiatric Therapy,_ 5 (1965), pp. 87–90.

[107]Myrna M. Weissman, Effie Geanakoplos and Brigitte Prusoff, "Social class and attrition in depressed patients," _Social Casework,_ 54 (1973), pp. 162–170.

[108]The diagnosis and treatment of mental illness are not unique in incorporating social judgments of patients. This seems to be a more general phenomenon that is prevalent in many facets of the medical world. See Julis A. Roth, "Some contingencies of the moral evaluation and control of clientele: the case of the hospital emergency service," _American Journal of Sociology,_ 77 (1972), pp. 839–856.

type, and treatment of mental disorder. In general, rates of treated psychiatric cases are highest in the lower class while the working, middle and upper classes are underrepresented in the psychiatric population. This finding is open to criticism because the rates are based on known psychiatric cases. This type of study may underreport mental disorders among higher social class individuals who have a greater ability to avoid publicity. In addition, the types of illnesses that typically affect members of these classes are not as likely to result in institutionalization since they are less severe and visible.

It is well documented that the higher social classes experience mental disorders that are *internally oriented* while the lower classes experience more *externally oriented* disorders. This finding itself is sufficient cause to question whether the conclusions on rate of disorder by class are simply a reflection of the need to hospitalize disordered members of the lower class because their disturbances involve more overt, less controllable symptoms while members of the higher classes display more covert, controlled symptoms.

There are three major explanations for the higher reported rates of illness among lower-class people. The *societal reaction hypothesis* holds that what is seen as a psychiatric disorder among lower class people is actually their social class characteristics which higher class diagnosticians consider to be abnormal. The *social stress hypothesis* holds that lower-class people are more prone to become disordered because their life styles are miserable and stressful. The *social selection hypothesis* holds that the high rate of impairment in the lower class is the result of disordered people from higher classes drifting down the social class ladder. There is evidence that all three of these propositions are true to some extent.

Blacks have higher reported rates of mental illness than whites. Even within the lower class, stress is more severe among blacks who are disadvantaged compared to their white counterparts. Blacks are also more likely to develop more severe disorders, including schizophrenia, mental retardation, and organic brain syndromes. Much of the high reported rate of mental illness among blacks is a result of limited opportunities for socioeconomic advancement.

The literature on the relationship between mental disorder and social mobility is inconsistent. There are reports of no association between the two, of a positive relation between mental disorder and upward mobility, as well as a positive relation between pathology and downward mobility. The latter relationship is documented most frequently. It is also supported by studies showing the high education-low occupation status inconsistent individual is particularly vulnerable to serious mental illness.

Type of psychiatric treatment varies significantly between patients of different social classes. Patients of the upper and middle classes are more likely to receive psychotherapeutic care while their working- and lower-class counterparts are generally treated organically or custodially. Much of this relationship can be explained by the fact that the types of illnesses that are prevalent among the various classes require different treatments. However, more refined investigations which hold type of illness constant have also found that patients of different classes do not receive the same kind of therapy. This is because most psychotherapists come from the higher social classes and prefer to treat patients who are similar to them (*status homophily*). For this reason, few lower-class patients receive psychotherapy. In response to this problem, community mental health centers are working to make psychotherapy a feasible alternative for the lower class person.

The research reported in this chapter should be evaluated in light of social class differences in values and child-rearing practices. Children whose parents are favorably situated in the social class hierarchy are oriented toward inner needs. Working- and lower-class children, on the other hand, are oriented toward external behavior. It is suggested that these differences in world view and socialization patterns are partly responsible for the relationship between mental illness and social class.

The Social Role
of the
Mental Patient

11

Becoming
a Mental Patient

The Prepatient Process

Psychiatric disorders are quite varied as was evident from the elaborate symptoms of various illnesses presented in earlier chapters. Even within specific categories of illness, the reported experience of mentally ill individuals is diverse. Beyond these differences, however, are common social experiences which lead to the recognition of psychiatric conditions. These processes constitute the focus of this chapter which is concerned with the behavioral, interpersonal, and legal events which the prospective patient confronts as he seeks help. Together they comprise the *prepatient process.* More specifically, the temporal sequence of events preceeding treatment consists of four stages. The first is the personal onset which includes the subjective experience of pathological feelings that frequently occur after a stressful life event. The second stage involves the reaction of relatives and friends as they attempt to cope with an individual's changed behavior. The third stage of the prepatient process is the community response. This includes all experiences associated with seeking help from the larger community, mental health experts included. The final stage consists of the psychiatric and legal aspects of formal evaluation.

The Personal Onset

Autobiographical Reports

There are a few approaches available to those interested in understanding the onset of mental illness. Autobiographical accounts, for example, primarily describe the subjective experience of being mentally ill. Most of these accounts portray radical alterations in the character of the consciousness and perception of the subject. Consider, for example, the following reports by schizophrenics decribing the changes they underwent:

> Case 1: Something has happened to me—I do not know what. All that was my former self has crumbled and fallen together and a creature has emerged of whom I know nothing. She is a stranger to me—and has an egotism that makes the egotism that I had look like skimmed milk; and she thinks thoughts that are—heresies.[1]

> Case 2: I can't concentrate on television any longer because I can't watch the screen and listen to what is being said at the same time. I can't seem to take in two things like this at the same time, especially when one of them means watching and the other means listening.[2]

> Case 3: When I have been rushing about I have to stop and be still for a minute. It's like watching a miniature railway. There is split second timing. One train misses the other by a split second. If I could walk slowly I would get on all right. My brain is going too quickly. If I move quickly I don't take things in. My brain is working all right but I am not responding to what is coming into it. My mind is always taking in little things at the side.[3]

> Case 4: Half the time I am talking about one thing and thinking about half a dozen other things at the same time. It must look queer to people when I laugh about something that has got nothing to do with what I am talking about, but they don't know what's going on inside and how much of it is running round in my head. You see, I might be talking about something quite serious to you and other things come into my head at the same time that are funny and this makes me laugh.[4]

Life Events

The influence of social events on the beginning of an illness is more relevant to sociological analysis than an autobiographical perspective.

[1]Bert Kaplan, *The Inner World of Mental Illness* (New York: Harper and Row, 1964), p. 6.

[2]Reprinted from Andrew McGhie and James Chapman, "Disorders of attention and perception in early schizophrenia," *British Journal of Medical Psychology*, 34 (1961), p. 105. By permission of publisher.

[3]Ibid., p. 106.

[4]Ibid., p. 109.

The celebrated Swiss American psychiatrist, Adolph Meyer, pioneered in developing a systematic framework in this regard in the early decades of this century. He constructed a "life chart" which showed the relationship between major events of a patient's life and psychiatric disorder. Subsequent work by others has more succinctly elaborated the mechanisms by which social events can influence the inner state. Holmes and Rahe have constructed a scale to gauge the specific influence of various social events in the production of stress. Not all of the events in their scale are intrinsically unpleasant, but all reportedly involve some impingement on the steady state of the individual's life. The rank ordering of these events according to the amount of stress each produces as measured by the subjective feelings of test subjects is presented in Table 11.1. A high score (mean value) indicates that a particular life event produced a greater amount of stress (as measured by readjustment) than an event with a lower score.

The Holmes and Rahe study generated the hypothesis that those individuals who had a very high life crisis score during a given period of time would be more likely to become ill than those who had a low score during the same period. For example, a person would be more likely to become disturbed over sex difficulties (mean value of 39) than from a change in his sleeping habits (mean value of 16). Other investigations have confirmed the basic hypothesis. Rahe and his associates tested the scale on a Navy population and found that subjects in the highest decile for a life crisis score developed illnesses twice as often as did those in the lowest decile.[5]

The Holmes and Rahe scale has been further developed by a group of researchers who expanded the list of 43 life events to 102.[6] This is called the Psychiatric Epidemiology Research Interview (PERI) Life Events Scale. However, others have criticized life events scales for failing to consider the quality of life events, particularly the desirability-undesirability of the change. Additionally, these same critics report research findings which strongly indicate that only undesirable changes are significantly associated with psychological impairment while desirable events are hardly related at all.[7] While the debate continues, other questions remain unanswered, such as the issue of individual differences in reactions to major life changes. Do some people have an "emotional

---

[5]R. H. Rahe and others, "Life crisis and health change" in *Psychotropic Drug Responses: Advances in Prediction,* eds. P. R. A. May and J. R. Wittenborn (New York: Charles C. Thomas, 1969).

[6]Barbara Snell Dohrenwend and others "Exemplification of a method for scaling life events: the PERI life events scale," *Journal of Health and Social Behavior,* 19 (1978), pp. 205-229.

[7]Joanne C. Gusten and others, "An evaluation of the etiologic role of stressful life-change events in psychological disorders," *Journal of Health and Social Behavior,* 18 (1977), pp. 228-244; Daniel P. Mueller, Daniel W. Edwards and Richard M. Yarvis, "Stressful life events and psychiatric symptomatology: change or undesirability?" *Journal of Health and Social Behavior,* 18 (1977), pp. 307-317.

Table 11.1. *Social Readjustment Rating Scale*

Rank	Life Event	Mean Value
1	Death of Spouse	100
2	Divorce	73
3	Marital Separation	65
4	Jail Term	63
5	Death of close family member	63
6	Personal injury or illness	53
7	Marriage	50
8	Fired at work	47
9	Marital reconciliation	45
10	Retirement	45
11	Change in health of family member	44
12	Pregnancy	40
13	Sex difficulties	39
14	Gain of new family member	39
15	Business readjustment	39
16	Change in financial state	38
17	Death of close friend	37
18	Change to different line of work	36
19	Change of number of arguments with spouse	35
20	Mortgage over $10,000	31
21	Foreclosure of mortgage or loan	30
22	Change in responsibilities at work	29
23	Son or daughter leaving home	29
24	Trouble with in-laws	29
25	Outstanding personal achievement	28
26	Wife begins or stops work	26
27	Begin or end school	26
28	Change in living conditions	25
29	Revision of personal habits	24
30	Trouble with boss	23
31	Change in work hours or conditions	20
32	Change in residence	20
33	Change in schools	20
34	Change in recreation	19
35	Change in church	19
36	Change in social activities	18
37	Mortgage or loan less than $10,000	17
38	Change in sleeping habits	16
39	Change in number of family get-togethers	15
40	Change in eating habits	15
41	Vacation	13
42	Christmas	12
43	Minor violations of the law	11

Reprinted from T. Holmes and R. H. Rahe, "The social readjustment scale," *Journal of Psychosomatic Research*, 11 (1967), pp. 213–218. By permission of Pergamon Press, Ltd.

insulation" to these changes as has been reported?[8] If so, who are susceptible to these changes—the genetically vulnerable, the biochemically imbalanced, or those who were improperly socialized? Perhaps the influence of life changes is different for each of these groups. Another unresolved issue is the nature of the causal linkage between life changes and psychiatric symptoms. It is generally assumed that life changes can cause symptoms, but it is also possible that certain types of symptoms can lead to self-induced stressful events.

The Crisis Within the Family

The Tendency to Ignore

The next set of events on the path to treatment occurs within the prepatient's interpersonal world. There are a number of published findings that explore the reactions of the family in attempting to cope with the behavior of one of its members who later becomes a mental patient.[9] All of these studies have consistently documented ". . . the monumental capacity of family members, before hospitalization, to overlook, minimize and explain away evidence of profound disturbance in an intimate".[10] In short, *the person's illness is typically ignored at first and then tolerated.* The high tolerance for abnormal behavior in certain types of families seems to be caused, at least in part, by "shameful" attitudes toward mental illness. These attitudes are more frequently found among less educated families who tend to hide their mental illness problems more than those who hold less superstitious views. This phenomenon of hiding mental illness among the lower classes partially explains the tendency of these same people to develop the more disturbed illnesses since persons from these families are left untreated longer, and their sicknesses fester as a consequence.

Geographical area of residence also affects the tendency of families to ignore behavioral disturbances because it is much easier for a family to look after a mentally disturbed member in an isolated farmhouse than it is in the cramped living conditions of an urban area.[11] Mental illness is

[8]L. E. Hinkle, Jr., "The effect of exposure to culture change, social change, and changes in interpersonal relationships on health," in *Stressful Life Events: Their Nature and Effects,* eds. Barbara Snell Dohrenwend and Bruce P. Dohrenwend (New York: Wiley, 1974), pp. 9–44.

[9]See, for example: Harold Sampson and others, "Family processes and becoming a mental patient," *American Journal of Sociology,* 68 (1962), pp. 88–96; Marion Yarrow and others, "The psychological meaning of mental illness in the family," *Journal of Social Issues,* 11 (1955), pp. 12–44; Charlotte G. Schwartz, "Perspectives on deviance—wive's definitions of their husband's mental illness," *Psychiatry,* 20 (1957), pp. 275–291.

[10]Harold Sampson and others, "Family processes and becoming a mental patient," p. 88.

[11]E. G. Jaco, "Attitude toward and incidence of mental disorder," *Southwestern Social Science Quarterly,* 38 (1957), pp. 27–38.

simply more visible in urban than in rural areas because of the greater population density. This affects the likelihood of a mental illness being treated because certain cases, particularly the visible ones, are more difficult to ignore.

Types of Family Response

The social psychological styles employed by different families to accommodate the bizarre behavior of the prepatient have been analyzed and to some extent, categorized. Toward this end, Sampson and his associates examined families in which the wife was eventually hospitalized for schizophrenia.[12] They detected two types of family response. In the first case, the marital relationship was characterized by the mutual withdrawal of husband and wife and the construction of "separate worlds of compensatory involvement." Typically this took the form of the husband becoming increasingly involved in his work or in other interests outside of the marriage. In fact, one case is reported where the husband would tinker in the basement every evening while his wife engaged in conversations and arguments with imaginary others upstairs! The husband became even less concerned with his wife's behavior and accepted it as a matter of course. This situation continued for two years.

The second type of family response differs from the first in that family life was organized around the presence of a maternal figure (the wife's mother) who took over the wife's domestic and child-rearing functions. The wife's mother established a relationship with her daughter based on helplessness. The husband, on the other hand, ". . . withdrew to the periphery of the family system, leaving the wife and mother bound in a symbiotic interdependency."[13]

There are a multitude of feelings generated within the family toward the prepatient which cannot adequately be summarized by observing behavioral patterns. Although it is difficult to completely penetrate a family's attitudes toward the prepatient's illness, it has been ascertained that there is a spectrum of feeling among families ranging from sympathetic understanding to overt hostility.[14] There are those who vent anger and those who express chagrin, puzzlement, fear, and guilt. The most commonly expressed feelings are confusion and ambivalence. In fact, a considerable number of families manifest these uncertainties by viewing the illness as physical or by denying that the person is ill at all. In general, most families seek an adjustment by reducing their expectations of the prepatient and by reassigning the responsibilities formally assumed by the prepatient to other family members. This is particularly likely to occur when another family member is able to act as a functional equiva-

---

[12]Harold Sampson and others, "Family processes and becoming a mental patient."
[13]Ibid., p. 93.
[14]U. S. Lewis and A. M. Zeichner, "Impact of admission to a mental hospital on the patient's family," *Mental Hygiene*, 46 (1960), pp. 66–74.

lent, such as the son who assumes economic responsibilities previously held by his now-disordered father.

Factors Affecting Help-Seeking

Typically these intrafamilial patterns of accommodation and denial fail to preserve harmony permanently. Usually situations worsen as the prepatient's illness progresses, and the ability of the family to tolerate his changing behavior decreases. At this point, the outside community is called on for assistance. Often members of the community are the first to recognize the problem as a mental illness. One study reports that this is true for over 85 percent of the cases they investigated.[15] In that study, the community member most likely to spot the disorder was a physician, although this varied by social class; policemen, ministers, judges, and other community authorities accounted for bringing a large proportion of lower-class people to psychiatric help sources.

There are a number of factors that affect if and when people realize that a relative is mentally disturbed. Zola has outlined five "triggers" that relate to the decision to seek professional help.[16] The first is an *interpersonal crisis* which calls attention to the symptoms, such as hostile behavior on the part of the prepatient toward his family. The second involves *social interference* which brings the disorder into conflict with a socially valued activity. The third is *sanctioning* in which others actually tell the person to seek help. The fourth involves the prepatient seeing the symptoms of his illness as a *threat to himself and/or those around him* and the fifth is the *actual recognition* by the patient of the mental nature of his illness. Zola reports that these "triggers" vary in importance by ethnic group; sanctioning is prevalent among the Irish; interpersonal crisis and social interference among Italians; and recognition of the nature of the illness among Anglo Saxons.

Mechanic has also dealt with the question of how people recognize the existence of a mental disorder and which factors affect the likelihood of a prospective mental patient seeking help outside of the family.[17] He developed a list of factors related to help-seeking, all of which are associated with a high probability of soliciting assistance. Some of these are

1. *The visibility and recognizability of deviant signs and symptoms.* Visible symptoms are more likely to engender help outside of the family.
2. *The extent to which the prepatient perceives the symptoms as serious.* This is his estimate of the present and future probabilities of something physically or socially dangerous occurring.
3. *The extent to which symptoms disrupt family, work, and other social activities.*

[15]Ibid.
[16]I. Zola, "Illness behavior of the working class" in *Blue Collar World: Studies of the American Worker,* eds. A. Shostak and W. Gomberg (Englewood Cliffs: Prentice Hall, 1964) pp. 351–361.
[17]David Mechanic, *Medical Sociology: A Selective View* (New York: Free Press, 1968).

The more disruptive they are, the more likely it is that others will become aware of the problem and either offer assistance or suggest a professional help source. This is related to the visibility of symptoms as well.

4. *The frequency of the appearance of deviant signs or symptoms, or their persistence.* Many families can tolerate bizarre behavior that is infrequent or transient. But ability to tolerate decreases as the family more frequently encounters psychiatric symptoms in a member.

5. *The tolerance threshold of those who are exposed to and evaluate the deviant signs and symptoms.* This threshold naturally varies from one personality to another. There are important differences, however, as a function of the person's familial relationship. Spouses, for example, tolerate less from their mates than do parents from their children.

6. *The information available to, the knowledge of, and the cultural assumptions and understandings of the evaluator.* Social class is important here since lower class people are less informed regarding the nuances of mental illness than their higher class counterparts. As mentioned earlier, this results in more lower class cases going untreated.

7. *The degree to which autistic psychological processes are present.* These are perceptual processes that distort reality and alarm others by their visible departure from the commonly accepted view of the world.

8. *The availability of treatment resources, their physical proximity, and the psychological and monetary costs of taking action.* This includes not only physical distance from the treatment center and costs of time, money and effort, but also such costs as stigmatization and feelings of humiliation resulting from being considered sick and in need of help. These costs are less in higher social classes, not only because such people are better able to pay fees, but also because there is less stigmatization since these classes have more open-minded attitudes toward mental illness.

One team of researchers has noted a sequential pattern of familial responses to mental illness.[18] The phases, which usually overlap and often vary in intensity, are (1) beginning uneasiness, (2) the need for reassurance that the problem is not serious, (3) denial and minimizing the symptoms, (4) anger and placing the blame, (5) guilt, shame, and grief when the family recognizes that a member is mentally ill, (6) confusion in the changed family and in those families who come to terms with the presence of mental illness, (7) acceptance of reality.

The sex of the patient is also a factor related to help-seeking. Since women are more likely than men to discuss their problems with others and to willingly enter psychiatric treatment as a solution to their problems, their families are more likely to seek help for them.[19]

---

[18]Margaret E. Raymond, Andrew E. Slaby and Julian Lieb, "Familial responses to mental illness," *Social Casework*, 56 (1975), pp. 492–498.

[19]James R. Greenley and David Mechanic, "Social selection in seeking help for psychological problems," *Journal of Health and Social Behavior*, 17 (1976), pp. 249–262; Allan Horwitz, "The pathways into psychiatric treatment: some differences between men and women," *Journal of Health and Social Behavior*, 18 (1977), pp. 169–178.

The Community Response

The Recognition Process

Although relatives tend to "normalize" bizarre psychiatric symptoms, there is a limit to this rationalization process. The limit is a function of the family's willingness to tolerate disruptive behavior.[20] There are vast differences in toleration capacities, but few relatives can cope with a person who is suicidal, homicidal, hallucinatory, or disoriented. When such situations develop, in most states the police have considerable leeway in arresting on an "emergency basis." This may occur when there is (1) an indication of violence by the individual, (2) incongruous behavior in physical appearance, such as odd posturing or nudity, (3) evidence of attempted or potential suicide, (4) disruptive behavior, such as creating a nuisance in public places and (5) situations in which the police have been summoned by a complainant in the family or a physician, employer and so on.[21] These conditions are linked by a behavioral characteristic common to those who are most likely to be treated—visible symptoms which engender public recognition. These are situations in which individuals usually become labeled as mentally ill since they have attracted the judgment of others. It is important to note that prepatients displaying visible symptoms are not necessarily more disordered than those with more hidden psychopathologies. If this were so, the transvestite, for example, would be considered more disordered than the paranoid schizophrenic. On the simple basis of symptoms, the transvestite is more visible since overt behavior such as cross-dressing is common in the disorder. But the paranoid schizophrenic does not always exhibit such external signs. Those who do display visible symptoms, however, are more likely to experience enduring problems because of the greater stigmatization associated with the public display of psychopathology. Below are some cases representative of this "publicly disordered" group.

J. P. C., a thirty-eight-year-old single man, had been arrested on a charge of drunkenness, growing out of an incident in which he was behaving in a very strange way near a neighbor's apartment building. When questioned

[20]There are a number of reports that public recognition of psychiatric symptoms has increased dramatically in the last two to three decades. If this is true, it would be expected that disordered people would enter treatment sooner, but this does not seem to be the case since most families wait until the behavior becomes extreme. One recent study found that public recognition of mental illness has not changed as much as most believe. What has changed is the methodology of the studies designed to test attitudinal change. Thus, any reported change over time may simply be an artifact of changed research methods. For an elaboration of this issue see: Carl D'Arcy and Joan Brockman, "Changing public recognition of psychiatric symptoms? Blackfoot revisited," *Journal of Health and Social Behavior,* 17 (1976), pp. 302–310.

[21]Egon Bittner, "Police discretion in apprehending the mentally ill," *Social Problems* 14 (1967), pp. 278–292.

by the police he said that he was looking for his sister who he believed was in the tree and said that she had dropped her child in a culvert and that he had retrieved the baby. He explained that his sister, while changing the baby's diaper, was snatched up into the tree.[22]

R. U., a twenty-one-year-old married man, was referred to the courts after an incident in which he was arrested in a downtown department store dressed in women's clothing and sitting in the fitting room of the dress department. Upon examination by the police physician, it was discovered that he was completely dressed in women's clothing including padded bra, women's hose etc.[23]

In the cases above, the recognition process proceeds rapidly. This is particularly true of mentally ill people who are both severely and chronically disordered since they are frequently unable to provide good reasons to account for their actions. Most cases of mental illness, however, are not both severe and chronic. With such cases, the recognition process becomes more complex, and the degree of agreement among observers concerning the existence of an illness diminishes accordingly.[24]

The procedures by which people in need of psychiatric treatment are identified are frequently unclear, largely because their first help source is usually a nonprofessional. Even if the help source is a physician, the criteria he applies to deviant behavior "... are at times indefinite and the physician who practices in large treatment centers often *must assume the illness of the patient* who appears before him and then proceed to prescribe treatment."[25] The consequences are that the initial decisions about mental illness take place prior to the patient's examination by mental health experts. Although this is an important phase of the recognition process, it is essentially managed by nonprofessionals who lack the time and psychiatric insight to render a valid diagnosis. This is especially true of nonpsychiatric physicians (general practitioners, family specialists, internists, obstetricians, and gynecologists) who rarely even bother to send a disturbed patient to other persons or agencies for psychiatric care.[26] The police and judicial systems do not have a better

---

[22]Reprinted from Clarence J. Rowe, *An Outline of Psychiatry* (Dubuque: Wm. C. Brown Company, Publishers, 1975), p. 147. By permission of publisher.

[23]Ibid., p. 127.

[24]It is reported that there is a greater consensus as to what constitutes mental illness in communities which are culturally homogeneous as measured by (1) political consensus, (2) common economic interests, and (3) racial-ethnic homogeneity. In this type of setting, there is a greater consensus about mental illness because social similarity causes a prompt rejection of deviants. See: Arnold S. Linsky, "Community homogeneity and exclusion of the mentally ill: rejection versus consensus about deviance," *Journal of Health and Social Behavior*, 11 (1970), pp. 304–311.

[25]David Mechanic, "Some factors in identifying and defining mental illness," *Mental Hygiene*, 46 (1962), pp. 66–74.

[26]Virginia Aldige Hiday, "Mental health problems in primary care: a new study" (paper presented at the annual meeting of the Society for the Study of Social Problems, San Francisco, California, 1978).

Figure 11.1. *Degree of social rejection of individuals seeking mental health counsel by degree of professionalism of help source.*

Professionalism of Help Source

No Help	Clergyman	General Physician	Psychiatrist	Mental Hospital

Social Rejection of Patients

record as they commonly fail to refer those with psychological problems, particularly young, lower-class males.[27]

Community Rejection

Those who are diagnosed as mentally ill resist the label because it involves a negative change in their self-image. This is not an ungrounded fear in light of evidence that there is a social penalty exacted from the mentally ill, especially when they are considered to be violently dangerous, a condition which is diagnosed much too frequently.

The price that these people pay for "being different" is often rejection by others in the community. Derek Phillips investigated the factors involved in the social rejection of those seeking mental health counsel.[28] He found that the degree of rejection by others in the community is a function of the type of help source utilized. Individuals are increasingly rejected as they seek no help, utilize a clergyman, a physician, a psychiatrist, or a mental hospital in that order. In other words, prepatients are increasingly ostracized as they go to more professional help sources. This ironic phenomenon is portrayed in Figure 11.1.

This explains why there is such a large number of disturbed people trying to live with their problems rather than paying the costs in ostracism and self-image that are a consequence of seeking help. It can also account for the findings of other studies that have discovered a high percentage of people *reporting* that they were helped more by clergymen or physicians than by psychiatrists or mental hospitals.[29] These people may *say* nonprofessionals are more helpful, but they are probably reacting to differences in social cost by type of help source. That is, clergymen do not actually *help* more than psychiatrists, they just engender less social rejection of the prepatient by others.

---

[27]Milton Mazer, "Two ways of expressing psychological disorder: the experience of a demarcated population," *American Journal of Psychiatry*, 128 (1972), pp. 933–938.

[28]Derek L. Phillips, "Rejection: a possible consequence of seeking help for mental disorders," *American Sociological Review*, 29 (1963), pp. 963–972.

[29]Maxwell Jones, *Social Psychiatry* (Springfield, Illinois: Thomas, 1962), p. 31.

The Social Psychology of Legal Commitment

Early Mental Health Laws

When the prepatient reaches the point at which commitment to a mental hospital is a real possibility, he will then be exposed to the professional evaluation of psychiatrists and legal experts. There is a historical conflict between psychiatry and law that is dark, painful, and too lengthy to recount here in detail. Simply stated, the psychiatrist is involved with the commitment of patients to mental hospitals on the basis of his specialized knowledge of mental illness while legal experts are involved on the basis of the principle of protecting citizens' rights. This conflict is exemplified in the case of the prospective patient who requires hospitalization from the psychiatrist's point of view but who is seen as a criminal in need of a prison stay from a legal point of view. The psychiatrist may possess the expertise to support his convictions, but the law possesses all the power to institutionalize or incarcerate the individual. Judges and lawyers often view psychiatrists as interfering with the operation of the law, and psychiatrists view lawyers as skeptics who question the wisdom of psychiatric treatment. While these stereotypes may hamper cooperative efforts between the two professions, they do exist and are the inevitable result of involving both medical judgments and legal issues in the decision to commit a person to a mental hospital.

At this point, a brief examination of the legal steps of commitment is relevant in order to understand the last phase of the prepatient process. During the nineteenth century, this country began to grapple with the question of the legal rights of the mentally ill. The era was chaotic, particularly in regard to the best means of ascertaining whether a person was disordered and deserving of institutionalization. The problem of properly committing patients to institutions ("the propriety of confinement") is intimately woven into the history of psychiatry since it is a question which must be resolved before any treatment requiring hospitalization can be undertaken. Laws were passed, tested, evaluated, and often repealed when they failed to deal with the problem adequately. In the 1890s, in Illinois, for example, a law was in effect that decided on commitment by jury trial with the patient present. It was also a law that permitted barbaric treatment of the mentally ill. The result was a return to the old and ugly procedures of dealing with mentally ill people that had supposedly ended ages before. The inhumane aspects of this law were graphically expressed by a respected physician of the time:

> I have seen a man suffering, unfortunately for him from acute mania, shackled hand and foot and then placed in a great canvas sack which was tied around his neck, and in that condition, carried thirty miles to the county seat and subsequently, in the same day, brought fifty miles to the asylum without an opportunity to attend to the calls of nature. I have found that man one mass of bruises from the top of his head to the soles of

his feet, and I have seen him succumb in six days, and I attribute it to this treatment. When you have seen such things under this law it needs no argument to show that it is not the law for this time and this community.[30]

Laws change slowly, particularly the laws governing the commitment of the mentally ill. As late as 1933, there were still fourteen states in which potential mental patients were jailed while they waited for commitment proceedings! This supports the contention that those reported as disturbed are presumed to be just that before they are formally evaluated.

Commitment in Recent Times

Although the idea of voluntary commitment was first given legal recognition by Massachusetts in 1881, this procedure did not become a frequent practice until well into the twentieth century. Today each state has its own laws governing commitment. Consequently, there is great diversity among the states regarding legal procedures, many of which still subject the patient to indignities and humiliations. In 1949, the National Advisory Mental Health Council developed a *Model Act* governing hospitalization of the mentally ill in an attempt to develop uniformity among the states. Modern thinking reflected in the provisions of this proposal is gradually being incorporated into state laws as they are modified. As of this writing, considerable interstate variation still exists. Many states do not require that the person be present at the commitment hearing. Other states only require the sworn statement of a legal guardian or close relative to enact commitment. Almost all states have laws that permit a person to voluntarily apply for admission to a mental hospital, but the number who do so is negligible in many states.

Because of the great diversity of state laws at the present time, a person can be committed by a court order based upon the findings of an "insanity" commission, the conclusions of one or more medical examiners, or a jury trial. These approaches have been designed to protect the legal rights of the prospective patient by attempting to insure that normal people are not railroaded into mental hospitals. Arthur P. Noyes, the author of one of the leading psychiatric textbooks in the United States, contends that railroading is theoretically possible but probably quite rare. There are numerous cases in the sociological literature, however, which describe situations in which a person was forced into a mental hospital on the basis of unconventional behavior. Frequently this behavior is nothing more than a value conflict between the person and others who wield power over him as is often the case between rebellious youths and revengeful parents. One researcher describes a case of a twenty-two-year-old veteran who returned from the service and pursued a "hippie-like life style" which did not include regular employment and

---

[30]J. K. Hall and others, *One Hundred Years of American Psychiatry* (New York: Columbia University Press, 1944), p. 538.

family life.[31] His parents consulted their family physician who was instrumental in having the man arrested as a person "dangerous to himself and others and in need of immediate hospitalization," a key legal concept of the Wisconsin Mental Health Act. This is not an isolated case. In fact, newspapers regularly report instances of unjust commitment, including people who wasted their lives in mental institutions for no good reason. It is impossible to measure accurately the extent of railroading in this country but it would be naive to insist, as Noyes does, that it is negligible.

The Presumption of Illness

Each year approximately 400,000 people are committed to mental hospitals. This figure includes voluntary commitments, although in some states, such as Florida, they comprise less than 5 percent of the total.[32] Serious questions have been raised about the judgments that lead to these commitments, particularly in regard to whether commitment procedures are psychiatrically valid and meet legal requirements. To deal with these questions, some investigators have turned their attention from the behavior of the mentally ill to the behavior of psychiatrists who have been accused of hospitalizing people for nonpsychiatric reasons. Thomas Scheff, on the basis of psychiatric evaluations of patients who have been committed as well as observations of the commitment procedures themselves, has data demonstrating that psychiatrists indiscriminately diagnose people as mentally ill.[33] Kutner, describing commitment procedures in Chicago, also reports a strong presumption of illness by the staff of the Cook County Mental Health Clinic. He states:

> Certificates are signed as a matter of course by staff physicians after little or no examination... The so-called examinations are made on an assembly-line basis, often being completed in two or three minutes, and never taking more than ten minutes. Although psychiatrists agree that it is practically impossible to determine a person's sanity on the basis of such a short and hurried interview, the doctors recommend confinement in 77% of the cases. It appears in practice that the alleged-mentally-ill is presumed to be insane and bears the burden of proving his sanity in the few minutes allotted to him.[34]

Since the commitment laws are so loosely defined, there is no precise way of determining whether a case is sufficiently severe to require hos-

---

[31]David Mechanic, "Therapeutic intervention: issues in the care of the mentally ill," *American Journal of Orthopsychiatry,* 37 (1967), pp. 703–718.

[32]D. W. Oberhausen, "Contingencies in involuntary hospitalization: have the laws governing commitment changed and does it really matter?" (unpublished Master's thesis, Florida State University, 1973).

[33]Thomas J. Scheff, *Being Mentally Ill* (Chicago: Aldine, 1966).

[34]Luis Kutner, "The illusion of due process in commitment proceedings," *Northwestern University Law Review,* 57 (1962), pp. 383–394.

pitalization. In a Wisconsin study, for example, only 25 percent of the persons involuntarily committed were reported to be in need of hospitalization by an outside pool of judges.[35] Furthermore, Scheff has found that the commitment procedures are incomplete and the hearings are perfunctory. He reports that medical examiners spend an average of only ten minutes deciding upon each case and nearly always recommend hospitalization![36] Others have supported Scheff's findings, discovering that psychiatrists who do not have "sufficient time" sign commitment certificates after little or no examination. In Ohio, the commitment hearing is reported to average 8.12 minutes in length while the shortest observed took 45 seconds, and 80.3 percent of eighty-one cases seen by the researchers were committed.[37] The chances of being involuntarily committed are reportedly greater if the person is old, being evaluated by a committee which includes a psychiatrist, and was brought to the hospital by a petition from the community rather than from the family.[38] Hence persons who come to a hospital for evaluation are very likely to be absorbed into the patient population regardless of their capacity to live in outside society.

It is startling to discover that the decision to commit is so routinely made since psychiatric diagnosis is such a crucial step in the social process of mental illness. Scheff explains this phenomenon as a reaction by psychiatrists to the ambiguities of mental illness. They assume illness and recommend commitment as a safe alternative. This was clearly demonstrated by David Rosenhan who, with a team of colleagues, feigned schizophrenia before commitment evaluators at twelve mental hospitals around the country.[39] Not only were all diagnosed as schizophrenic and committed, but their guise was never detected even though they acted completely "normal" immediately after admission! This study deals a crushing blow to those who believe that current psychiatric procedures of evaluation are viable. The findings of the Rosenhan study also suggest that labeling theorists are correct in their assertion that the label of mental illness is difficult to eradicate once it has been applied to someone.

Within sociological circles, some have taken issue with the "presumption of illness" findings by holding that hospitalization can be a *positive* experience because it shifts a person's label from "obnoxious" and "intolerable" to "being ill" and "in need of help." While this argument merits consideration, it does not answer the question at hand; namely, are com-

[35]Thomas J. Scheff, "Legitimate, transitional and illegitimate mental patients in a midwestern state," *American Journal of Psychiatry,* 120 (1963), pp. 267–269.

[36]Thomas J. Scheff, "The societal reaction to deviance," *Social Problems,* 11 (1964) pp. 401–413.

[37]Dennis L. Wegner and C. Richard Fletcher, "The effect of legal counsel on admissions to a state mental hospital: a confrontation of professions," *Journal of Health and Social Behavior,* 10 (1969), pp. 66–72.

[38]C. Allen Haney and Robert Michielutte, "Selective factors operating in the adjudication of incompetency," *Journal of Health and Social Behavior,* 9 (1968), pp. 233–242.

[39]David L. Rosenhan, "On being sane in insane places," *Science,* 179 (1971), pp. 250–258.

mitment procedures conducted thoroughly and ethically? If they are not, and most evidence indicates that they are not, it must be concluded that some who are committed are not mentally ill.

Others who have analyzed the "presumption of illness" phenomenon in greater detail conclude that, while the probability of being committed is suspiciously large for the *general* population, it does vary substantially along certain socioeconomic lines. For example, those with greater individual resources and higher standing in the community are less likely to be committed.[40] This is supported by the fact that those from the lower classes are most likely to be involuntarily committed,[41] particularly lower-class blacks.[42] It is consistent with the *status resource hypothesis* which states that persons with more socioeconomic resources are better able to control their fates and thereby resist legal coercion that would lead to hospitalization.

In addition, there is a greater tendency to commit someone if he has no relatives or others currently available for psychological support.[43] People who are referred for psychiatric evaluation by physicians are more likely to be committed than nonphysician referrals. Males are more likely to be committed than females. Those with no previous record of hospitalization are also committed more frequently than those who have previously been hospitalized.[44] To summarize, the prime candidate for commitment is the lower class, single, black, male, who has no relatives, no previous hospitalization record, and is referred by a physician. These selection biases are particularly noticeable in state hospitals. The psychiatric day hospital has different prejudices. In this setting, there is selectivity as a function of the person's symptoms. This type of hospital is more likely to admit the prepatient with less conceptual and perceptual disorder and greater interpersonal competence than is observed among inpatient admissions.[45]

The tendency to presume illness and recommend commitment, while it is not universal, is certainly quite widespread. How can this phenomenon best be explained? The explanations are different for judges and lawyers than they are for psychiatrists. Many judges consider it pointless to conduct extensive examinations on each prospective patient since

---

[40]William A. Rushing, "Individual resources, societal reaction, and hospital commitment," *American Journal of Sociology,* 77 (1971), pp. 511–525.

[41]William A. Rushing, "Status resources, societal reactions, and type of mental hospital admission," *American Sociological Review,* 43 (1978), pp. 521–533.

[42]Beverly Ann Baldwin, H. Hugh Floyd, Jr. and Dennis R. McSeveney, "Status inconsistency and psychiatric diagnosis: a structural approach to labeling theory," *Journal of Health and Social Behavior,* 16 (1975), pp. 257–267.

[43]See for example: E.G. Mishler and N. E. Waxler, "Decision processes in psychiatric hospitalization: patients referred, accepted, and admitted to a psychiatric hospital," *American Sociological Review,* 28 (1963), pp. 576–587; Allen D. Wade, "Social agency participation in hospitalization for mental illness," *Social Service Review,* 26 (1967), pp. 27–43.

[44]E. G. Mishler and N. E. Waxler, "Decision processes in psychiatric evaluation".

[45]G. E. Hogarty and others, "A critical evaluation of admissions to a psychiatric day hospital," *American Journal of Psychiatry,* 124 (1968), pp. 934–944.

they are quite busy with other cases and because most persons considered for commitment are unusual in either appearance or behavior. Mechanic contends that this fact, coupled with a tendency to see an accused person as a different type of individual, predisposes judges to rubber stamp commitment papers.[46] Furthermore, there is a pervasive belief that mentally ill persons are dangerous and should therefore be hospitalized for the safety of others. This attitude is commonly found among judges who view their function as legal guardians of society's welfare.

The "presumption of illness" phenomenon among psychiatrists, however, is more complex. Scheff interviewed diagnosticians who indicated that they perform hasty examinations in part because their pay is determined by the number of examinations they conduct. Aside from financial reasons, a set of ideological assumptions also accounts for the presemption of illness by psychiatric examiners. These assumptions are:

1. Unlike surgery, there are no risks involved in involuntary psychiatric treatment. It either helps or is neutral, but it can't hurt.
2. Exposing a prospective mental patient to questioning, cross-examination, and other screening procedures exposes him to the unnecessary stigma of trial-like procedures and may do further damage to his mental condition.
3. There is an element of danger to self or others in most mental illnesses. It is better to risk unnecessary hospitalization than the harm the patient might do himself or others.[47]

In response to each of these assumptions, Scheff has respectively constructed counterpoints. He holds that:

1. There is very good evidence that involuntary hospitalization and social isolation may affect the patient's life, his job, his family affairs, etc. There is some evidence that too hasty exposure to psychiatric treatment may convince the patient that he is "sick," prolonging what may have been an otherwise transitory episode.
2. This assumption is correct, as far as it goes. But it is misleading because it fails to consider what occurs when the patient who does not wish to be hospitalized is forcibly treated. Such patients often become extremely indignant and angry, particularly in the case, as often happens, when they are deceived into coming to the hospital on some pretext.
3. The element of danger is usually exaggerated. In the psychiatric survey of new patients in state mental hospitals, danger to self or others was mentioned in about a fourth of the cases. Furthermore, in those cases where danger is mentioned, it is not always clear that the risks involved are greater than those encountered in ordinary social life.[48]

---

[46]David Mechanic, *Medical Sociology: A Selective View* (New York: Free Press, 1968).

[47]Thomas J. Scheff, "The societal reaction to deviance," *Social Problems,* 11 (1964), p. 412.

[48]Ibid., p. 412.

The arguments continue over the dangers of commitment versus the dangers of keeping a prospective patient in the community, but one thing seems painfully clear; many of the patients involved in commitment proceedings *are* sick and in need of help, but the superficial and prejudicial inquiries conducted by medical examiners and judges result in the institutionalization of others who do not belong in a hospital. It seems likely that these "errors", so damaging to the lives of those affected, will continue until the laws on commitment are rewritten. But changes in the law depend on changes in the values and ideology of our culture. It is difficult to effect these changes because such deeply ingrained beliefs are not easily altered.

New Mental Health Laws

In recent years, concern for patients' rights has increased as witnessed by the patients' rights movement and the resultant laws some states have passed to protect those rights. The patients' rights movement is legally embodied in the law of *informed consent.* The core of this legal doctrine is the concept that the psychiatrist must inform the patient of the risks and benefits of the proposed treatment and then accept the patient's decision about the appropriate treatment.

An example of new laws regarding mental patients is Pennsylvania where the Mental Health Procedures Act (MHPA) was passed in 1976. It established new procedures and standards for voluntary and involuntary commitments and is considered to be the most modern of all state statutes. The policy of the MHPA is to prefer voluntary commitment over involuntary commitment. Before a person is accepted for voluntary treatment, a full explanation must be made of the type of treatment procedures in which the person will be involved. Under the new law, involuntary commitments are limited to persons who pose a clear danger to themselves or others. A patient committed on an involuntary basis must be either (1) discharged within 72 hours, (2) admitted as a voluntary patient, or (3) certified for extended involuntary emergency treatment by a judge or mental health review officer after a hearing. Under the MHPA, a court-ordered involuntary commitment can not extend for any longer than ninety days. Court hearings in these cases are open to the public unless the person whose case is being heard requests privacy. In addition, the person has the right to confront and cross-examine all witnesses and to present evidence in his or her behalf. The MHPA also specifies that every patient must have an individualized treatment plan which is reviewed every thirty days by a treatment team.

Unfortunately, Pennsylvania's law has created some new problems in its attempt to insure that prospective patients are accorded full civil liberties. One major problem is that it has resulted in a growing number of severely disturbed people in the community since it states that a person must commit some violent or dangerous act before being involuntarily committed. Clearly there are a number of very disturbed people who are in need of treatment yet are not violent or dangerous in some way. Additionally, since the new law provides for short commitment periods, other disturbed people are being prematurely released. Of course, this may appear to be beneficial because it keeps people out of mental hospitals where their problems may be exchanged for another set of ills.[49] But there are not adequate community facilities to care for these people. Therefore they are being forced to fend for themselves without any supervision in the community. The pendulum has apparently swung too far in the direction of upholding civil liberties. Now sick people are not getting treated because they are too sick to know they need it. The new law actually makes it necessary for people to harm themselves or others to get help!

The Pennsylvania law may reflect a nationwide trend against treating mental patients against their will. If it does, the country is in deep trouble because this kind of extreme change can only mean added grief to patients, their families, and the community in the absence of adequate outpatient facilities. Under the previous law, families could spot warning signs and get professional help before the patient regressed to violence. Now treatment is withheld from many people who desperately need it.

The major problem with mental health laws such as that found in Pennsylvania is that they are frequently formulated without the advice of mental health experts. Lawyers and state senators play a large role in such policies and, because they are untrained in regard to mental illness, the result is a naive, unrealistic set of legal guidelines that may win political favors but certainly worsen the plight of the mentally ill. Presently, there is a movement to reform this law so that it reflects good psychiatry. Hopefully, this will be accomplished before other states also overreact in reconstructing mental health laws. In the meanwhile, the Pennsylvania state hospital system is being invaded by a swarm of lawyers instructing the staff in the "new ways" and checking to see that patients were committed according to the principles of the present law. The reaction of the staff has not been favorable. In fact, there is at least one report that the staff behavior does not even approximate what the law prescribes.[50] In short, they are ignoring it.

Conclusions

Social forces are important in the recognition and treatment of mental illness. Investigations of the effect of these forces suggest damaging consequences for prospective patients. These people, often driven to seek help by stress-producing changes in their lives, first encounter the

[49]See Chapter 12 of this book for an elaboration of the negative aspects of life in a mental hospital.

[50]Charles W. Lidz, "Legal rights vs. how staff process patients," (paper presented at the annual meeting of the Society for the Study of Social Problems, San Francisco, California, 1978).

reactions of family and friends who typically deny the possibility of a mental aberration. In the case of an actual illness, this acts to complicate the disorder by extending its duration and delaying treatment.

When the outside community is called on for help, nonprofessionals generally respond first, and these people often assume that a disorder exists even though the person may simply be seeking advice on transitory life difficulties. Here the label of mental illness is first applied to the individual who is then penalized with social rejection. These social costs exacerbate the trauma of the experience by creating feelings of inferiority and social isolation.

The formal process of commitment often proceeds at the expense of the prospective patient through decision-making actions that manifest haste, value judgments, and an inability to ascertain validly who is actually disturbed. Consequently, many people enter the mental hospital population who do not belong there. In an effort to guard the civil liberties of prospective patients, some states, notably Pennsylvania, have passed new laws that only allow for involuntary commitment if the person poses a danger to himself or others. Since this is generally taken to mean violence, many nonviolent people who are seriously disturbed are left in the community without treatment.

The social psychology involved in becoming a mental patient reflects some of society's inappropriate attitudes regarding mental illness. These attitudes are based on embarrassment, ignorance, shame, and an exaggerated fear of the behavior of mentally disordered people, beliefs which reflect an underlying view of mental illness that is a problem itself. This is the view that mentally ill people are entirely responsible for their own unhappiness. The truth is that social forces are also responsible for mental illness. Some individuals are simply not fortunate enough to avoid these damaging influences while others have weak psychological make-ups that do not permit a healthy response to stressful changes in their lives.

12

The Patient
in Treatment

The Mental Hospital

Types of Hospitals

Today there are two major types of psychiatric hospitals: the traditional "institution-centered," or custodial hospital, and the emerging "patient-centered," or therapeutic hospital.[1] The custodial hospital is primarily concerned with segregating the mental patient from the rest of society. In this setting, the patient is considered to be qualitatively different from other human beings. He is expected to conform to the authoritarian routines of the hospital and passively accept impersonal treatments including ECT and drugs. There is a strict ordering of power in the custodial hospital; only the psychiatrist has a therapeutic role while other personnel are merely ancillary and serve only to control patients. The patient conforms out of fear of physical sanction.

The patient-centered hospital is concerned with rehabilitating patients rather than simply controlling them. In this setting, the needs of the patients are the focus around which the organization of the hospital is structured. The patients' problems are treated individually, not impersonally. All hospital personnel, including the patient himself, are ex-

---

[1]Lawrence Appleby and others, "Institution-centered and patient-centered mental hospitals: a comparative analysis of polar types" in *The Sociology of Mental Disorders,* ed. S. Kirson Weinberg (Chicago: Aldine, 1967), pp. 212–218.

pected to play active roles in the process of rehabilitation to normal social roles.

Not all hospitals can be classified as either institution-centered or patient-centered. Most large state mental hospitals are obliged to pursue the goals of custody-control and treatment simultaneously. The demand of custody-control for the patient's conformity and the subordination of his needs to institutional routines sharply contrast with therapeutic treatment based on resolving patients' individual problems. Why are both of these conflicting goals pursued simultaneously? Schwartz and Schwartz believe that this dual function performed by the state mental hospital is the result of the ambivalence felt toward mental patients by society.[2] Because mental patients are viewed as dangerous deviants, the mental hospital is expected to isolate and restrain them. But, since they are also seen as sick people in need of help, the mental hospital is expected to rehabilitate them as well. Because of this dual mandate, the psychiatric staff is often split into two factions: psychiatric attendants represent custody and control while the professional staff represents treatment.

In the United States today there are approximately 495 mental hospitals, 313 of which are run by state governments. Until 1955, most state mental hospitals were primarily custodial. Before this time, hospitals had earned the reputation of being snake pits. Treatment was brutal and inhuman. Physical restraints were commonly used. Under these conditions patients often deteriorated and became more disoriented and remote than they had been when they were admitted. The introduction of tranquilizers in the 1950s paved the way for reformers to control the negative effects of hospitalization by reducing the length of stay. Long-term hospitalization was widely abandoned, and mental hospitals became short-term treatment facilities.

Not all hospitals have followed the trend toward short-term stays, however. Newer hospitals (post-1955) express a short-term orientation toward their patients while the older hospitals (pre-1955) are more likely to require longer stays.[3] Small private hospitals, usually regarded as being at the opposite pole from the state mental hospitals in terms of the quality and intensity of treatment, have higher rates of patient turnover. Much of this difference is due to the fact that state mental hospitals have a large number of patients and a small number of staff members to care for these patients. Another part of the variation in length of patient stay is due to differences in the types of patients admitted to private and state hospitals; a greater proportion of private hospital patients are diagnosed as neurotic, while state hospital patients are more likely to be psychotic. In addition to hospital type, quality and orientation of staff, and patient

[2]Morris S. Schwartz and Charlotte Green Schwartz, *Social Approaches to Mental Patient Care* (New York: Columbia University Press, 1964), p. 198.

[3]William R. Rosengren, "Organizational age, structure, and orientations toward clients," *Social Forces*, 47 (1968), pp. 1–11.

diagnosis, there is another reason why an individual may spend a considerable part of his life in a mental institution; he may simply be destitute and not be able to function in outside society.[4]

The Psychiatric Staff

There is a formal hierarchy within the staff of the mental hospital. The psychiatrist occupies the position at the apex of the power structure; he makes the final decision on all requests and recommendations. Next in power are the occupational therapists and social workers, followed by the nurses. At the bottom of the hierarchy are the psychiatric attendants. While this is the *formal* hierarchy of power in the state hospital, it does not necessarily represent the everyday reality of hospital life. Because the psychiatrist, occupational therapist, and social workers rarely appear on the ward, the head nurse occupies a crucial power position. She serves to link the ward with the rest of the hospital world, and she acts as a funneling agent by emphasizing negative aspects of those patients she disfavors and positive aspects of those patients she likes.[5] She is the immediate authority figure for the patients and attendants. Student nurses also play important roles in the daily lives of patients because they are responsible for individual patient care. The permanent personnel are occupied with administrative functions and have impersonal contact with patients, while student nurses provide companionship, escort patients to off-ward activities, and help them in their personal hygiene.

The psychiatric attendants are the low people on the staff totem pole. They are responsible for housekeeping functions, keeping records, and maintaining order on the ward. However, the attendants themselves deemphasize these aspects of their work and stress their contacts with patients. In fact, attendants have been noted by some to have more contact and more *raw* knowledge of the patients than anyone in the hospital.[6] To the patient it appears that he is under the control of these nonmedical custodians because they seem to control such essentials as access to professional staff, ground privileges, and even eligibility for discharge. In fact, some studies of hospital life have concluded that the *real* control of a state mental hospital is exercised by the psychiatric attendant since other staff members are so occupied with bureaucratic details that they spend very little time with the patients.[7] Stone reports that, because of time constraints, the psychiatrist is likely to turn to the

---

[4]Aaron Rosenblatt, "Providing custodial care for mental patients: an affirmative view," *Psychiatric Quarterly*, 48 (1974), pp. 14–25.

[5]Gregg S. Wilkinson, "Interaction patterns and staff response to psychiatric innovations," *Journal of Health and Social Behavior*, 14 (1973), pp. 323–329.

[6]Robert Perrucci, *Circle of Madness: On Being Insane and Institutionalized in America* (Englewood Cliffs, N.J.: Prentice-Hall, 1974), p. 47.

[7]See, for example, I. Belknap, *Problems of a State Mental Hospital* (New York: McGraw-Hill, 1956).

nonprofessional staff for an "educated guess" on a patient's condition.[8] This practice is quite alarming in light of the fact that psychiatric attendants are usually recruited from the ranks of the uneducated.

The nursing staff enjoys a higher status than do the attendants because nurses are better educated. However, the unfortunate fact is that nurses typically have little knowledge about mental illness and its treatment since they rarely have formal training in psychiatry beyond a short affiliation as a student nurse.[9] Consequently, psychiatric nurses do not have the sense of professional identity that their medical hospital counterparts enjoy. Because psychiatric nurses feel undertrained, mental patients can pose a threat to them. This may cause the nurse to take on an authoritarian disciplinary role and endorse the use of control techniques such as shock treatment and heavy medication.

Of course, the problem of the quality of treatment administered to patients in large mental hospitals is, in part, the result of unfavorable staff-patient ratios. Few patients ever have as much as a five minute conversation a week with the nurses. Psychiatrists, or "ward physicians" as they are called, have even less patient contact. A large part of the psychiatrist's time on the ward is spent writing medical orders and handling administrative duties. Because of the understaffing problem, actual contact between patients and the ward physician may be limited to a bimonthly "ward round" in which all the patients as a group meet in the dayroom where they are given the "opportunity" to present their problems.[10]

Understaffing and undertraining are two important reasons for the impersonal atmosphere that typically pervades the state hospital ward. As Stone puts it, "The system tends to reward standard performance by staff, impartiality toward patients, and the preservation of kindly but formal relationships. The system also arouses guilt in those staff members who find themselves responding in spontaneous ways to patients who have singled them out for attention."[11] There are, nevertheless, many personal adaptations which staff have applied to make the relationship with patients less impersonal. One technician, for example, suggests to patients who beg for a demonstration of affection that they "blow kisses" to each other. However, it would be inaccurate to describe the psychiatric nurse as universally impersonal and authoritarian since the nurse's behavior toward a patient is, at least in part, a function of the patient's behavior toward her. If a patient derogates the nurse, the

[8]Olive M. Stone, "The three worlds of the back ward," *Mental Hygiene*, 45 (1961), pp. 18–27.

[9]One possible exception is the nursing program that is part of a full-time college curriculum. Here the student is usually exposed to sociological, psychological, and psychiatric concepts in the classroom.

[10]To avoid what state hospital psychiatrists see as a never-ending line of patient requests, the physician's office is usually located off the ward and often in a separate building.

[11]Olive M. Stone, "The three worlds of the back ward," p. 22.

nurse's response may be total withdrawal.[12] On the other hand, the patient who approaches the nurse in a warm, interested manner is typically favored over the cold, indifferent patient.[13]

A number of psychological and demographic variables affect nurses' attitudes toward patients as well as the degree of social distance they maintain from them. The most negative attitudes toward patients are usually exhibited by the older, least educated staff members and those with the longest employment in the ward.[14] These persons display the greatest amount of authoritarianism, and they restrict themselves socially from the patients. Conversely, more humanitarian attitudes toward patients are found among nurses who are younger, better educated, and who have had experience in a number of different wards. Apparently nursing personnel become embittered toward mental patients over time. This may be due to a sense of futility and helplessness which develops through treating hospitalized psychotics. One longitudinal study clearly demonstrates that student nurses' attitudes toward the usefulness of psychiatric treatment become less favorable over time.[15]

Relations among staff members also affect the quality of care patients receive. When coordination among staff members is high, there is a therapeutic atmosphere on the ward.[16] If staff relations are weakened, staff members do not obtain support from one another, and they lose their sense of competence in dealing with the patients who, in turn, become agitated or depressed. In fact, conditions of weak relations among the staff are reported to be directly linked with patient suicides.[17]

Many methods for overcoming staff problems have been explored, but one relatively untapped help source is the college student volunteer. A number of benefits accrue to both patients and staff from the use of student volunteers. The enthusiasm of the students is contagious and often helps to renew or even initiate enthusiasm among patients and staff.[18] Perhaps the greatest strength the college student brings to the

[12]Marge Stringer, "Therapeutic nursing intervention following derogation of the nurse by the patient," *Perspectives in Psychiatric Care*, 3 (1965), pp. 36–46.

[13]William G. Bye and Martha E. Bernal, "The effects of two patient behaviors upon psychiatric nurses' ratings of the patient," *Nursing Research*, 17 (1968), pp. 251–255.

[14]J. M. Bordeleau and others, "Authoritarian-humanitarian index in a large mental hospital," *Disorders of the Nervous System*, 31 (1970), pp. 166–174; John F. Leckwart, "Social distance: an important variable in psychiatric settings," *Psychiatry*, 31 (1968), pp. 352–361.

[15]L. C. Toomey and others, "Attitudes of nursing students toward psychiatric treatment and hospitals," *Mental Hygiene*, 45 (1961), pp. 589–602. Attitudes toward psychiatric treatment have also been linked with shift work. Day shift staff members report more improvement in patient functioning over time as opposed to those working other hours. It is believed that this is because most therapy is scheduled during the day. See Edmund G. Doherty and Joseph Harry, "Structural dissensus in the therapeutic community," *Journal of Health and Social Behavior*, 17 (1976), pp. 272–279.

[16]Alfred H. Stanton and Morris S. Schwartz, *The Mental Hospital* (New York: Basic Books, 1954).

[17]Rose Laub Coser, "Suicide and the relational system: a case study in a mental hospital," *Journal of Health and Social Behavior*, 17 (1976), pp. 318–327.

[18]Barry S. Brown and Toaru Ishiyoma, "Some reflections on the role of the student in the mental hospital," *Community Mental Health Journal*, 4 (1968), pp. 509–518.

treatment setting is his ability to get close to the patient because he is not viewed as a formal member of the hospital hierarchy. The student himself also benefits from being immersed in the hospital environment because he develops a greater sense of self-awareness and gains more knowledge about the mentally ill than books could ever offer.

Types of Wards

Another factor that affects the quality of interaction between patients and staff is the organization of the mental hospital ward. Large wards that are organized according to a rigid status hierarchy in which authority and decision making ultimately rest with a few staff members are likely to produce staff conflict and unusual problems among patients.[19] For this reason, many large state hospitals are decentralized into small, semiautonomous units, or buildings. The smaller treatment units establish closer ties between patients and staff, and they also allow for easier evaluation and modification of therapy programs. Decentralized staffs have also been found to have more personalized therapy programs than do the hierarchically controlled staffs.[20] Whether a hospital has a centralized or decentralized staff is largely a function of the staff's psychiatric ideology. A medically oriented staff typically employs organic forms of therapy and is usually organized according to a strict status hierarchy.[21] On the other hand, the staff oriented toward psychotherapy is usually decentralized to allow for flexibility and individualism.

Perhaps the most important distinction between different types of patient wards is in terms of the length of the patients' hospital stay. Chronic (long-stay) patient wards are typically separated from the acute (short-stay) patient wards. Some feel that it is more useful to define "chronicity" in terms of patient behavior rather than in terms of a specific amount of time spent in the hospital. The chronic patient is one who has become so dependent on the hospital that he can no longer function in the outside world.[22] However, the likelihood of this "dependency syndrome" is directly related to length of hospitalization.

It appears that being placed in a chronic ward is a self-fulfilling prophesy since residence in a chronic ward calls forth the types of behavior that insure a patient will become more and more dependent on the hospital, and hence will never leave. The atmosphere of chronic wards is depressing at best. Patients go through the same set of activities in a zombie-like state, day after day. They rise, they eat, they take their

[19]John M. Meyer, "Collective disturbances and staff organization on psychiatric wards: a formalization," *Sociometry,* 31 (1968), pp. 180–199.

[20]Thomas P. Holland, "Organizational structure and institutional care," *Journal of Health and Social Behavior,* 14 (1973), pp. 241–251.

[21]Simon Dinitz, Mark Lefton and Benjamin Pasamanick, "Status perceptions in a mental hospital," *Social Forces,* 38 (1959), pp. 124–128.

[22]Robert Sommer and G. Witney, "The chain of chronicity," *American Journal of Psychiatry,* 118, pp. 111–117.

medication, and they idle their lives away within the sterile confines of the dayroom. They are stereotypically viewed by the staff as hopelessly ill and not quite human. Over time, relatives and friends stop visiting them and eventually letters end as well.[23] It is no small wonder that patients on chronic wards feel alienated from outside society[24] and are especially threatened by the idea of returning to the community.[25] Can these problems be alleviated? One solution is to integrate the acute and chronic patients. This would help to eliminate the stagnant atmosphere of the chronic ward and combat the tendencies of the staff to treat all patients according to group sterotypes. A mixed ward more closely resembles the outside world and can also promote the patient's eventual return to it. Simply by witnessing other patients leaving the hospital, the chronic patient can be made aware that it is possible to return to outside society.

Patient Society

Is there a patient society, a system in which patients interact on the basis of prescribed statuses and roles? Erving Goffman, in his famous sociological examination of the social conditions of mental hospitals, portrayed the patient as such a dehumanized and embittered person that it seems unlikely that, if there is a patient society, it is modeled after outside society.[26] Empirical investigations of patient attitudes toward the hospital and staff support Goffman's descriptions. Over half of the patients in one study reported that the hospital unduly restricted their freedom[27] and 99 percent of the chronic patients in another study viewed the psychiatric staff as oppressors and expressed anger toward them.[28]

Because of the oppressive conditions found in many mental hospitals, there is little incentive for patient interaction. However, some friendships and cliques do form among patients, and these have been

[23]One study reports that only 10 percent of chronic patients have visits from relatives and friends once a month compared to 42 percent of recently admitted patients. As regards receipt of letters from friends and relatives, 46 percent of recently admitted patients received such letters once a month or more often while the corresponding figure for chronic patients is only 12.5 percent. See K. Bhaskaran and N. Dhawan, "A comparison of the effects of hospitalization on long-stay and recently admitted female schizophrenic patients," *International Journal of Social Psychiatry*, 20 (1974), pp. 72–77.

[24]Robert Sommer and Robert Hall, "Alienation and mental illness," *American Sociological Review*, 23 (1958), pp. 418–420.

[25]Bernard J. Bergen and Claudewell S. Thomas, "An attempt to examine the perception of self and hospital among chronically ill mental patients," *International Journal of Social Psychiatry*, 15 (1969), pp. 307–313.

[26]Erving Goffman, *Asylums: Essays on the Social Situation of Mental Patients and Other Inmates* (New York: Anchor Books, 1961).

[27]Lawrence S. Linn, "The mental hospital from the patient perspective," *Psychiatry*, 31 (1968), pp. 213–223.

[28]Madeline Karmel, "The internalization of social roles in institutionalized chronic mental patients," *Journal of Health and Social Behavior*, 11 (1970), pp. 231–235.

the focus of some research. On the open psychiatric ward, friendship choices are made on the basis of social similarity, much as they are in the outside world.[29] But on a locked psychiatric ward social similarity does not influence friendship choice at all,[30] perhaps because the most severely impaired patients are placed in the locked wards and these patients are generally uninterested in friendships. Unlike outside society, patients in a locked ward are apparently unconcerned about reciprocity of feeling since they frequently desire as friends patients who are uninterested in the friendship.[31] In other words, liking does not beget liking but rather begets interaction.

The likelihood of a patient having fellow patients as friends is significantly related to type of illness. Manic-depressives and schizophrenics (without paranoid symptoms) have the greatest number of friends.[32] This is particularly true of manic-depressives who are most frequently chosen as friends by other patients.[33] Hostile patients are generally ignored by other patients. Hostility is most common among paranoids, a group of patients who rarely make friendships. When they do, they tend to select other paranoids.[34]

One unsettling aspect of friendships among mental patients is that popular patients have lower rates of contact with staff than do unpopular patients.[35] Assuming staff contact is positively related to recovery (and it may not be), the patient appears forced to choose between social affiliations and recovery. This is a serious problem because patients need some rapport with each other to survive what is otherwise a very meaningless and undirected existence. Patient interaction helps to combat the boredom which is a major problem of ward living. Patient friendship networks also provide a means to assert independence and self-identity. Interaction among patients also serves as a reference point by means of which the patient can judge his own recovery.

The Sick Role

The "sick role" concept was popularized by Talcott Parsons. It is widely used in medical sociology to refer to the attitudes and behavior

[29]E. J. Murray and M. Cohen, "Mental illness, milieu therapy, and social organization in ward groups," *Journal of Abnormal and Social Psychology*, 58 (1959), pp. 48–54.
[30]Ibid.
[31]Julia S. Brown and Powhatan J. Woolridge, "Interpersonal attraction among psychiatric patients: patterns of interaction and choice," *Journal of Health and Social Behavior*, 14 (1973), pp. 299–310.
[32]G. W. Gilliland and R. A. Sommer, "A sociometric study of admission wards in a mental hospital," *Psychiatry*, 24 (1961), pp. 367–372.
[33]Julia S. Brown, "Sociometric choices of patients in a therapeutic community," *Human Relations*, 18 (1965), pp. 241–251.
[34]E. J. Murray and M. Cohen, "Mental illness, milieu therapy, and social organization in ward groups"; W. G. Shipman, "Similarity of personality in the sociometric preferences of mental patients," *Journal of Clinical Psychology*, 13 (1957), pp. 292–294.
[35]Robert Perrucci, "Social distance strategies and interorganizational stratification: a study of the status system on a psychiatric ward," *American Sociological Review*, 28 (1963), pp. 952–962.

expected of a person when he becomes a patient. Initiation into the sick role is begun early in childhood with the first physical illnesses. It is taught by the parents and reinforced by the physician, all of whom expect the child to follow their orders submissively. This sick role is appropriate for a medical patient who passively follows others' instructions, lest he injure himself by independent activity.

The sick role of the psychiatric patient differs from the medical sick role. Not only does the psychiatric sick role last much longer than the medical sick role, but the expected behavior of the "good" psychiatric patient is quite divergent from that of the medical patient. To be a mental patient requires participation in one's own rehabilitation. The mental patient must actively deal with people in the environment to create a new concept of reality for himself and gradually to test his ability to fulfill autonomy, responsibility, and independence demands made on him. A common problem is that many mental patients perceive their role as a passive, dependent one because they transfer the role they learned during physical illnesses.[36] This inconsistency between the expectations of the medical sick role and the psychiatric sick role can cause problems in treatment. Typically, the mental patient complains that the staff should be doing more for him or that the psychiatrist should be telling him what to do.

Psychiatric patients with a medical sick role orientation appear well-adjusted to hospital life, but the adjustment is only apparent and actually dysfunctional since they are likely to become dependent on the institution and fail to anticipate discharge.[37] There is ample evidence that this problem is most common among the lower-class patients who have been socialized toward conformity and passivity. Consequently, they are not as able to shift from a submissive, medical role to an independent, psychiatric role as their higher-class counterparts.[38] This is one of the reasons that lower-class patients tend to be hospitalized longer than do higher class patients. But, given the fact that lower-class patients are usually treated organically, their submissive behavior may not really be so inappropriate.

Treatment Techniques

Unlike general hospitals, mental hospitals do not usually function as active treatment centers. This is particularly true of state mental hospitals which do not have a sufficient number of skilled personnel to administer intensive and individualized treatment. As a result, few patients receive psychotherapy which is oriented toward insight into their problems and eventual care. Instead, treatment techniques which control

---

[36]Raymond Sobel and Ardis Ingalls, "Resistance to treatment: explorations of the patient's sick role," *American Journal of Psychotherapy*, 18 (1964), pp. 562–573.

[37]Rose Laub Coser, "A home away from home," *Social Problems*, 4 (1956), pp. 3–17.

[38]Frank A. Petroni, "Correlates of the psychiatric sick role," *Journal of Health and Social Behavior*, 13 (1972), pp. 47–54.

psychotic symptoms are employed, although they make little contribution to permanent rehabilitation. Earlier, shock treatments and psychosurgery were the favored control approaches. Recently, chemotherapy has replaced shock as the predominant control treatment mode. ECT has always been controversial because permanent loss of memory can result from it. Additionally, serious questions have been raised as to whether ECT directly relieves psychotic symptoms or whether it simply exerts a strong placebo effect through the self-fulfilling powers of suggestion. The possible self-fulfilling function of ECT was suggested in a British press release reporting that for two years patients in a mental hospital had been given electric shock treatments on an inoperative machine. Although none of the staff discovered that the machine was not working, patients were reported to benefit as much from being put to sleep (with anaesthetics) in preparation for the shock treatment as did other patients who were actually treated on functioning machines!

Mental hospitals are frequently described as prisons for people who have not broken the law. In light of the types of treatment patients usually receive, this position seems justified. However, as the number of patients in mental hospitals has dropped over the past few decades, a greater effort has been made to give patients some psychotherapy. There is no doubt that being in psychotherapy significantly improves the patients' chances for recovery. This is particularly true of patients who receive individual psychotherapy over extended periods of time.[39] However, the patient-staff ratio in mental hospitals has not reached the point where individual psychotherapy is a realistic option. Accordingly, group psychotherapy is used as a substitute for individual treatment. Group therapy is based on the idea that emotional disorders originate in pathological relationships with other people and can therefore best be worked through in a group setting which reproduces the original situation which led to the disorder.

Many consider group therapy to be a poor substitute for individual therapy because the patient gets less attention, may be embarrassed in discussing some problems before a group, and is denied the confidentiality that only an individual therapeutic experience can provide. However, there are some positive aspects to group therapy. First of all, it is usually the only way that treatment needs can be met within an institutional setting. It also helps patients overcome feelings of isolation and provides them with skills in interacting with others. Additionally, members of the group can point out each others' maladaptive behavior more readily than an individual therapist can. If an individual therapist bluntly confronts the patient with an unpleasant fact about himself, the patient may

---

[39]S. D. Imber and others, "A ten-year follow-up study of treated psychiatric outpatients," in *An Evaluation of the Results of the Psychotherapies,* ed. Stanley Lesse (Springfield, Illinois: Thomas, 1968), pp. 70–81; Ronald Maris and Huell E. Connor, Jr., "Do crisis services work?: a follow-up of a psychiatric outpatient sample," *Journal of Health and Social Behavior,* 14 (1973), pp. 311–322.

feel hurt or angry and become less cooperative but if a fellow patient in a group makes the same criticism, the therapist is then free to discuss it.

Related to group therapy is the community meeting in which all patients on a ward meet as a group with the staff. This exposes the staff to the social networks which operate on the ward. It can also help provide the patients with an opportunity to obtain information about hospital life as well as possible insight into their own problems. The meetings allow patients to actively participate in discussions about various aspects of the hospital. In the process, undesirable passive-dependent attitudes can be modified. The community meeting also fosters a team approach to treatment since different staff members can combine and integrate their treatment efforts after they interact together with the patients. In turn, patients are less likely to be subjected to differing sets of expectations by different members of the staff.

The primary goal of the community meeting is to increase patients' participation in their own care and treatment. In some hospitals, patients also participate in the administration of the hospital through patient government. This is a democratic organization comprised of an executive council of patient-members who transmit patients' opinions about the administration as it affects their activities. Generally, the issues decided on by patient government are simple things, such as decorating the ward, but occasionally the patients are invited to express opinions on more important questions, such as admission and discharge policies. Both the community meeting and patient government help to take the despondent edge off mental hospital life by treating patients as people with social rights that are to be respected.

Over the past several years, token economy programs based on the principles of operant conditioning, or behavior modification, have been increasingly used. The aim is to elicit desired patient behavior by providing tangible rewards for acts viewed by the staff as adaptive. The rewards are tokens that can be exchanged for items selected by patients at a small in-hospital variety store. Token economy programs are reported to be beneficial in modifying a number of patient behaviors including troublesome meal and bedtime behavior as well as a number of personal care behaviors, such as combing hair, making a bed, and bathing.[40] Many mental patients can not perform these acts because of their impairment or as a result of an extended stay in a mental hospital which deteriorates personal habits. At least one study reports that token economy principles can also modify the delusional speech of schizophrenics.[41] Although token programs are reported to be positively related to hospital

---

[40]For a review of research on the efficacy of token economy programs see: Jesse B. Milby, "A review of token economy treatment programs for psychiatric inpatients," *Hospital and Community Psychiatry*, 26 (1975), pp. 651–658.

[41]J. P. Wincze, H. Leitenberg and W. S. Agras, "The effects of token reinforcement and feedback on the delusional verbal behavior of chronic paranoid schizophrenics," *Journal of Applied Behavior Analysis*, 5 (1972), pp. 247–262.

discharge,[42] most studies of token program efficacy examine only reported improvement in the patients' hospital behavior rather than actual symptoms of the illness.[43] Undoubtedly, token programs are useful in controlling the behavior of chronic hospitalized schizophrenics, an otherwise unmanageable group, but it is false to assume that they also effect cure of psychotic symptoms.

Other forms of therapy also provide opportunities for the development and expression of the patient's individuality which is usually undermined by the restrictive mental hospital world. By being encouraged to act spontaneously, patients can gain insight into themselves.

> Traditional avenues for fostering the expression of the patients' individuality are the ancillary therapies found in some form in most mental hospitals—occupational therapy, music therapy, recreational therapy, bibliotherapy, and so forth. With the explicit aim of individualizing care and treatment, the patient may be given a plastic medium and told he may make with it anything he wishes. Neither usefulness nor excellence enter in, the objective being to help him find ways of expressing himself through the medium. His productions may be used both diagnostically and therapeutically; for example, the finger-paintings, drawings, or clay figures may be used as clues to his illness and his progress.[44]

The reader should not get the impression that the typical mental hospital provides a multitude of therapeutic activities. Many provide nothing but an excessively routinized, inactive, dehumanizing existence. Even when an effort is made to reach the patients individually, the results are largely a function of the staff person's skills. Since a large portion of the staff is undertrained, the benefits in terms of patient improvement are minimal. What else can account for the damaging ways in which some activities are conducted? For example, the author and a group of students on a hospital tour witnessed "music therapy" that required the patients to individually sing about how "crazy" they were!

It would be dishonest to investigate therapy within mental hospitals without mentioning the increasing number of reports concerning the dangerous and punishing practices that sometimes occur. ECT is more frequently used than public relations officials of mental hospitals lead outsiders to believe. Injecting a shock into an already shocked mind can

[42]R. F. Heap, "Behavior-milieu therapy with chronic neuropsychiatric patients," *Journal of Abnormal Psychology,* 76 (1970), pp. 349–354.

[43]R. F. Gripp and P. A. Magaro, "A token economy program evaluation with untreated control ward comparisons," *Behavior Research and Therapy,* 9 (1971), pp. 137–149; L. Krasner, "Assessment of token economy programmes in psychiatric hospitals," in *The Role of Learning in Psychotherapy,* ed. R. Porter, J. London and A. Churchill (London: Ciba Foundation, 1968), pp. 155–173; G. D. Shean and Z. Zeidberg, "Token reinforcement therapy: a comparison of matched groups," *Journal of Behavior Therapy and Experimental Psychiatry,* 2 (1971), pp. 95–105.

[44]Morris S. Schwartz and Charlotte Green Schwartz, *Social Approaches to Mental Patient Care,* pp. 122–123.

result in brain injury and amnesia, yet it is used to punish uncontrollable patients and to force them to submit to rules and routines.[45] There are also "seclusion rooms" where disagreeable patients are locked in solitary confinement to exhaust their energy. A panel of former mental patients and psychiatrists have reported that dangerous major tranquilizers, such as Thorazine, are used indiscriminately to control and discipline patients in hospitals.[46] These drugs induce a zombie-like state and can cause permanent damage to the central nervous system.

Antisocial patients run the greatest risk of injury in mental hospitals. Although psychosurgery is supposed to be used only under careful guidelines and with the approval of the hospital board, a Senate report claims that it is being widely used on patients who exhibit antisocial behavior.[47] One "behavior-control experiment" implanted radio transmitter-receivers in the brains of known offenders to control their behavior through a computer. Another program used the drug Apomorphine, which can cause uncontrolled vomiting for up to an hour, on patients who used abusive language. In addition, another hospital tried to suppress assaults and suicide attempts with the drug Anectine which causes prolonged seizure of the respiratory system and muscular paralysis.

Collective Disturbances

Sometimes all the patients on a given ward become disturbed at once. These outbreaks are called collective disturbances, and they are not just chance occurrences. Sometimes they are precipitated by drinking, a real source of stress in ward management. At other times, they are caused by a patient suicide which in turn can set off a wave of suicidal acts by other patients.[48] At least two studies have concluded that suicide waves occur during periods of social disorganization within the hospital.[49] This anomic condition is frequently caused by weakened relations among staff members. As a result, the staff members lose confidence in their abilities to deal with patients who in turn develop feelings of hopelessness. Staff resignations and conflicts are common causes of a breakdown in staff morale. In addition, Kahne's study of psychiatrists whose patients committed suicide found that psychiatrists who keep a great deal of social distance between themselves and their patients have high rates of patient suicide.[50] This problem is most common among psychiatrists of foreign birth or training. There is also a high rate of

[45]Olive M. Stone, "The three worlds of the back ward," p. 21.
[46]"Patients describe overdose," *The Evening Bulletin* (August 19, 1975), p. 33.
[47]"Behavior control study out," *The Philadelphia Inquirer* (December 1, 1974), p. 19-A.
[48]Rose Laub Coser, "Suicide and the relational system."
[49]Ibid.; Merton J. Kahne, "Suicide among patients in mental hospitals: a study of the psychiatrists who conducted their psychotherapy," *Psychiatry*, 31 (1968), pp. 32–43.
[50]Merton J. Kahne, "Suicide among patients in mental hospitals."

suicide among patients of psychiatric residents, not simply because of their lack of experience, but also because the hospital often assigns high-risk cases to beginners who are considered by their supervisors to be talented.

Reported cases of collective disturbances occur mainly in private hospitals which have a high ratio of staff members (especially psychiatrists) to patients and which emphasize psychotherapeutic methods of treatment.[51] There are fewer disturbances in state hospitals because of a heavier use of drugs which tranquilize patients. Private hospitals are more likely than state hospitals to have psychiatric residents in training. This leads to a constant turnover which threatens the control system. It has also been suggested that the larger number of residents and students results in more reporting of collective disturbances in private hospitals. This may be because the greater interest of staff novices makes them respond more eagerly to a display of agitated behavior. Or perhaps the presence of concerned staff motivates patients to reveal bizarre symptoms because they believe that the staff will react with concern and tolerance. If the last hypothesis is true, more disturbances should occur on weekdays when more staff is present. Melbin tested this proposition and discovered that there is a timetable of collective disturbances; consistent with the prediction, patients behave "crazily" much more often during weekdays than they do during evenings or weekends.[52] Also, certain conditions in the patient group seem to incite collective disturbances. These include the admission of new disruptive patients, a concentration of schizophrenic patients, and the lack of patient cliques.[53]

The Relatives of Hospital Patients

No description of the life of the mental hospital patient would be complete without some consideration of the patient's relatives since they can play an important role in increasing the patient's agony. Over time they abandon the patient by terminating visits and even mail.[54] Yet, perhaps this is not as detrimental to the patient as it may seem because the painstaking results of weeks of work can easily be undone in half an hour by a relative's visit, as exemplified by the case below:

> A paranoid schizophrenic, with additional catatonic ailments, was treated quite successfully, with electric shock and psychotherapy, at a state hospital. His social recovery was indicated by the fact that after nine weeks of

[51]John W. Meyer, "Collective disturbances and staff organization on psychiatric wards."

[52]Murray Melbin, "Behavior rhythms in mental hospitals," *American Journal of Sociology*, 74 (1969), pp. 650–665.

[53]John W. Meyer, "Collective disturbances and staff organization," p. 186.

[54]Paul G. Swingle, "Relatives' concepts of mental patients," *Mental Hygiene*, 49 (1965), pp. 461–465.

treatment, he had progressed from a closed ward to an open, working ward and was making good at a hospital job. About this time, however, he received a visit from his wife, upon whom he was extremely dependent. During the course of the visit he questioned her, obviously in a paranoid manifestation, about her possible relations with other men. The wife's response was to belabor him with an umbrella. The following day found the patient . . . showing marked disturbance and complete loss of contact.[55]

As suggested by the genetic and social theories of familial transmission of mental disorder, the relatives of mental patients may have as much psychopathology as the patients themselves. This allows some insight into the family dynamics involved in the patient's problems. In some instances, it is appropriate that the relative be treated as well. Frequently it is important that the relative at least stay away from the patient, rather than risk additional stress or relapse. This is particularly advisable in light of reports that relatives have more pessimistic views toward mental patients than do nonrelatives.[56] They view the hospitalized patient as unpredictable, hopeless, and unable to understand a letter or participate in conversation, and these negative attitudes are not reduced by more frequent visits.

It is no small wonder that staff members often feel hostile toward patients' relatives. They perceive the family as responsible for having produced a mentally ill member, and they commonly joke about the wrong family members being in the hospital.[57] The hostility between staff and relatives is mutual since the families view the staff as being difficult to deal with and deliberately denying their rights, requests, and needs.[58] The relatives often complain that the staff does not give them any information on the patient's treatment and progress, while the staff is frustrated by the family's reluctance to accept the authority of the hospital. All of this creates additional chaos which further minimizes the patients' chances for recovery.

Relatives of patients who are placed in day hospitals and returned home at night are often more uncooperative than are relatives of full-time patients. They are particularly difficult to deal with at admission time because they are disappointed to learn that the patient will be home at night.[59] However, if they are provided with an emergency phone number and given medication themselves, they appear better able to cope.[60]

[55]Karl R. Beutner and Russell Branch, "The psychiatrist and the patient's relatives," *Psychiatric Quarterly,* 33 (1959), p. 4.

[56]Paul G. Swingle, "Relatives' concepts of mental patients," p. 463.

[57]Norman W. Bell and Robert A. Zucker, "Family-hospital relationships in a state hospital," *Mental Hygiene,* 51 (1967), p. 201.

[58]Ibid.

[59]John F. Odenheimer, "Day hospital as an alternative to the psychiatric ward: attitudes and responses of relatives," *Archives of General Psychiatry,* 13 (1965), pp. 46–53.

[60]Ibid., p. 50.

The Future of the Mental Hospital

Psychiatric inpatients enjoy some definite benefits. One is the benefit derived from living apart from the family. This removes the person from the demands and stresses of everyday living and allows him to suspend obligations as a spouse, parent, or worker. Hospitalization also allows treatment to be repeated, monitored frequently, and evaluated for its results. This may sound inconsistent in light of the previously stated negatives of mental hospital life, but many of those negatives are due to the attitudinal problems of a small and undertrained staff. If the staff were larger, better trained, and able to communicate openly with the patients, much better care would be available than is presently the case.

From a practical point of view, the remarkable drop in hospital populations will probably lead to a major change in hospital functions or to total shutdowns. The hospital population decline was ushered in by advances in psychopharmacology in the mid 1950s. A moderate decline occurred until 1969, but, since then, the total population has decreased by about 30 percent to 255,000. Today some hospital buildings stand empty or have already been razed. If the size of the hospital staff can be maintained, the population drop will provide the opportunity to treat patients on the individualistic basis that good psychiatry requires.

Since the etiology of the psychoses is often organic, it is not likely that mental hospitals will be totally abolished in the future. Medical treatment is absolutely necessary for controlling the symptoms of many psychotic patients, and it would not be feasible to administer such treatment on an outpatient basis where the patient is not constantly monitored. Additionally, legal offenders, the confused, the acutely disturbed, those with actual brain diseases, and the potentially dangerous can be housed only in hospital wards inside locked doors. Anything short of institutional care for such patients poses a real threat to both the patients and the community.

Institutionalization

The Meaning of Institutionalization

The fact that hospitalized mental patients are not treated individually but as a homogeneous group of people is a routine feature of life in what Goffman calls the "total institution."[61] The features of this atmosphere include: (1) barriers between the "inmate" and the outside world; (2) requirements that the "inmate" must show deference to the staff; (3) admission procedures which strip the "inmate" of personal possessions and a full name; (4) verbal and/or gestural profanations such as calling

[61]Erving Goffman, *Asylums.*

312

an "inmate" obscene names, cursing him and publicly pointing out his negative traits. The highly regulated style of life in the mental hospital can cause long-stay patients to develop a syndrome which is not part of their original mental disorder. The syndrome is usually referred to as *institutionalization* although some prefer other labels such as *chronic institutional reaction,*[62] the *social breakdown syndrome,*[63] and *dysculturation.*[64] Institutionalization frequently develops in patients who have been hospitalized for two or more years. The syndrome consists of a varying combination of apathy, lack of concern for one's future, deterioration in personal habits, oversubmissiveness and an overdependency on the hospital and staff. The accepted explanation of this syndrome is that it results from the authoritarian, impersonal routines in the mental hospital which force the person to succumb to institutional demands and to minimize his individual needs for a prolonged period of time. However, it is not clear whether patients become institutionalized because the hospital inducts them into a sick role by convincing them they are mentally ill or whether institutionalization is simply a passive acceptance of institutional life caused by an inability to cope in the outside world.[65]

The Effects of Institutionalization

There can be little doubt that hospital expectations and requirements contribute to the institutionalization process. This is most pronounced in a custodial institution where the patient's most pressing need is often, not how to cope with his disorder, but how to emotionally survive the hospital experience. For this reason, some sociological discussions of mental hospitals imply that the patient is victimized by institutionalization.[66] Although it may take years to damage the patient's personality permanently, the process of institutionalization begins with admission experiences that diminish ego strength and can cause a partial regression to a childhood stage during which the outer world was perceived as an extension of the self.

Admission to the mental hospital is all too often a humiliating experience, reinforcing the patient's low self-esteem. In an atmosphere of impersonality and indifference, he waits for attention. He is stripped of clothes, spectacles, money, watches, wedding rings. He is put in a shower. He is given a

---

[62]D. H. Miller, "Psycho-social factors in the aetiology of disturbed behavior," *British Journal of Medical Psychology*, 34 (1961), pp. 43–52.

[63]J. Zusman, "The social breakdown syndrome," *International Journal of Psychiatry*, 3 (1967), p. 216.

[64]K. Bhaskaran and N. Dhawan, "A comparison of the effects of hospitalization on long-stay and recently admitted female schizophrenic patients."

[65]J. Marshall Townsend, "Self-concept and the institutionalization of mental patients: an overview and critique," *Journal of Health and Social Behavior*, 17 (1976), pp. 263–271.

[66]J. K. Wing, "Institutionalism in mental hospitals," *British Journal of Social and Clinical Psychology*, 1 (1952), pp. 38–51.

perfunctory examination and is probably not told where he is and why and what will be done to and for him and why.[67]

Hospitalization can cause a loss in self-esteem and a loss of social identity. This is the result of a process of *self-mortification* which subjects the patient to a number of humiliating experiences.[68] Every detail of the patient's life comes under the scrutiny and control of the staff, including when to sleep, what to eat, what to wear, and how to behave. The hospital is a world of "unfreedom," particularly in the conventional state hospital where the patient is given no significant responsibility and little opportunity to make important decisions. Here the patient is desocialized; that is, he is not helped to move toward the outside world since self-direction, as well as his personhood, is virtually eliminated. He is treated as if he were an inanimate object having no psychosocial existence.

The factors that cause institutionalization have not been contrived by liberal social scientists; they have also been reported by researchers who have had themselves admitted as patients to observe firsthand the conditions of mental hospitals.[69] However, it only requires a tour through a state hospital to see the visible correlates of institutionalization. The lives of ward-bound patients are repetitive and boring. They are confined to the dayroom which rarely contains anything more than uncomfortable chairs, a few ashtrays, and the ever-present television, the only contact with the outside world. In this setting, time becomes boundless, and some patients shrink into a vegetative state. In fact, some actually curl up in a corner and wither away.

Goffman argues that many long-term patients adjust to being hospitalized through what he calls *conversion*.[70] This is the process by which the patient accepts the hospital's definition of him as sick and belonging in an institution. To accomplish this, Goffman argues that the hospital discredits the patient's self-concept so that he comes to view himself as simply another sick patient, rather than as an individual. Goffman believes that conversion is most likely to occur in a patient-centered hospital which employs psychotherapy and group therapy, both of which are powerful tools in changing the patient's self-concept.[71] Goffman states that, "The more it (the hospital) attempts to be therapeutic and not merely custodial—the more he (the patient) may be confronted by high-ranking staff arguing that . . . if he wants to be a person he will have to change his way of dealing with people and his conceptions of himself."[72]

[67]Morris S. Schwartz and Charlotte Green Schwartz, *Social Approaches to Mental Patient Care*, p. 124.

[68]Madeline Karmel, "Total institution and self-mortification," *Journal of Health and Social Behavior*, 10 (1969), pp. 134–141.

[69]A. R. Goldman, R. H. Bohr and T. A. Steinberg, "On posing as mental patients: reminiscences and recommendations," *Professional Psychology*, 2 (1970), pp. 427–434.

[70]Irving Goffman, *Asylums*, pp. 61–62.

[71]Ibid., pp. 366–377.

[72]Ibid., p. 150.

Some research lends support to Goffman's propositions concerning institutionalization and conversion. One study found that chronic patients exhibit more dependency on and identification with the hospital than do acute patients.[73] As a result, these patients, particularly the females, become very anxious about returning to the community. On the other hand, a number of studies fail to demonstrate that mental patients think of themselves as mentally ill.[74] However, most of these studies examined the self-concepts of acutely ill patients, not the chronic patients that Goffman has studied. Short-term patients tend not to change their self-concepts because they view their "apart state" as temporary and are therefore not likely to loose their social identities. But even short-term patients easily accept institutional life and believe that hospital routines are intended to benefit them.[75] In one study, for instance, 66 percent of the short-term patients agreed with the statement, "Locked doors help you get well."[76]

A behavioral explanation can also be employed to analyze institutionalization and conversion. Some researchers utilizing this approach define institutionalization in terms of behavioral symptoms which include a specific posture and gait.[77] Interestingly, these behaviors can be modified by restructuring the physical environment of the hospital through rearranging the furniture or moving to a new building.[78] Such changes have beneficial effects because they disrupt the monotony of hospital life. The changes also place the otherwise withdrawn patients into an unfamiliar situation, thus forcing them to interact more with others.

Providing a Therapeutic Milieu

Because social conditions often contribute to mental disorder, the mentally ill can be effectively rehabilitated only in an environment which projects a remedial social character. Although it is probably impossible to totally avoid institutionalization, some steps can be taken to mitigate its

---

[73]Bernard J. Bergen and Claudewell S. Thomas, "An attempt to examine the perception of self and hospital among chronically ill mental patients."

[74]B. M. Craginsky, D. Braginsky and K. Ring, *Methods of Madness: The Mental Hospital as a Last Resort* (New York: Holt, Rinehart and Winston, 1969); Joint Commission on Mental Illness and Health, *Action for Mental Health* (New York: Basic Books, 1961); D. J. Levinson and E. B. Gallagher, *Patienthood in the Mental Hospital* (Boston: Houghton Mifflin, 1964); J. M. Townsend, "Cultural conceptions, mental disorders and social roles: a comparison of Germany and America," *American Sociological Review*, 40 (1975), pp. 739–752.

[75]J. Marshall Townsend, "Self-concept and the institutionalization of mental patients."

[76]Madeline Karmel, "Total institution and self-mortification."

[77]Russell Barton, *Institutional Neurosis* (Bristol: John Wright and Sons, 1959).

[78]David L. DeVries, "Effects of environmental change and of participation on the behavior of mental patients," *Journal of Consulting and Clinical Psychology*, 32 (1968), pp. 532–536

effects. Maxwell Jones recognized that the mental hospital is a community which has a great therapeutic potential if it is properly structured.[79] His concept of the *therapeutic community* hinges on a number of assumptions about the curing of mental patients without their developing a dependency on the hospital. One assumption is that patients do have certain conflict-free areas of their personalities that can facilitate recovery if programs can be geared to make use of them. A second assumption is the importance of pervasive staff involvement, including nurses and aides, as well as psychiatrists and social workers, with patients. A third assumption is the constructive role that patients can play in designing their own treatments and influencing the organization of the hospital through patient government.

A fundamental component of the social organization of a therapeutic community is the daily community meeting with the entire patient and staff population of a ward or building. Jones contends that the community meeting activates patient tensions which can then be worked through in smaller group meetings. In addition to patient-staff meetings, the therapeutic community also emphasizes treatment programs including individual therapy, psychodrama, and occupational-recreational therapy.

Perhaps what most accurately characterizes the therapeutic community is its attitudinal climate. The atmosphere created by personalized treatment, which encourages patient autonomy and social interaction without tolerating deviant behavior, reduces the risk of institutionalization. Patients are encouraged to express their anger and aggression openly. They share decisions with the staff regarding such matters as the discharge of patients, transfers to other wards, and actions to be taken with disagreeable patients. Of course, none of this is possible without a large staff which is properly trained, highly motivated, and of high morale. Such a favorable treatment situation is not easy to accomplish at the present time due to the limited funding for mental health care. If therapeutic communities ever do become widespread, however, mental hospitals will no longer be places in which a horrible fate awaits patients. Furthermore, the barriers between the hospital and the community will be broken down when visitors can see patients who are treated like the human beings they are.

The Community Mental Health Clinic

Basic Services

The mental hospital is often unable to effect proper care for the mentally disordered. As has been discussed earlier, a number of factors account for this inability, including the size and training of staff and the

[79]Maxwell Jones, *The Therapeutic Community* (New Haven: Yale University Press, 1953).

risk of institutionalization. Another problem is the tendency of psychiatrists, judges, and others involved in the commitment process to assume the person is ill. This floods hospitals with many people who do not belong there although mental health laws are changing to correct this. Hospitalization itself may also unduly stigmatize mental patients because others in the community tend to view the hospitalized as qualitatively different from the rest of the population. The stigma attached to institutionalized patients remains long after discharge and in some cases is irreversible. All of these factors indicate that mental hospitals constitute as much of a problem as does mental illness itself. In fact, a number of studies, including the Midtown Manhattan study, have demonstrated that mentally disordered people function more effectively in the community than do those who have been hospitalized and released. Perhaps this is because the hospitalized person must unlearn hospital routines and become resocialized into the outside community while the never-hospitalized person has learned to adapt his illness to the routines of mainstream society.

In the United States during the 1960s, the traditional mental hospital came increasingly under attack. In 1961 the Joint Commission on Mental Illness and Health placed the burden of treatment of the mentally ill upon the community, rather than psychiatrists and other mental health workers in hospitals.[80] This ushered in *community psychiatry*, a movement based on the idea that community resources should be used for the treatment and prevention of mental disorder.[81] The focus of mental health care began to shift from long-term care of chronic aspects of mental illness to short-term treatment of acute aspects. Short-term hospitalization and crisis-oriented outpatient care were added to the long-term approaches. Tranquilizers played a significant role in this change by easing the problem of otherwise uncontrollable behavior.

Suicide prevention centers were the original models of the principles of community action for mental health,[82] but today a number of different programs exist. These include day hospitalization, immediate crisis intervention at home by "flying teams," brief stays in a foster home, and, most recently, the multipurpose community mental health clinic. A primary function of these clinics is to nurture adaptive behavior in individuals by promoting positive mental health attitudes in the community as a whole. A second function of the community mental health clinic is to shorten the length of illness through early evaluation and treatment, rather than ignoring symptoms until the illness becomes chronic. A third function is to assist chronic patients in their return from the mental hospital to the community. All of these functions are oriented toward

[80]Joint Commission on Mental Illness and Health, *Action for Mental Health*.

[81]The community psychiatry movement is commonly referred to as the "third revolution" in psychiatry, following Pinel's reform treatments and Freud's discoveries.

[82]Richard K. McGee, "Community mental health concepts as demonstrated by suicide prevention programs in Florida," *Community Mental Health Journal*, 4 (1968), pp. 144-152.

avoiding or shortening hospitalization since the longer a patient stays in the hospital, the less chance he has of getting out and staying out.[83] The community mental health clinics are designed to offer disturbed people immediate attention. An impetus for this approach came during World War II when it was found that quick intervention for the treatment of shell shock at the front lines was more successful than taking soldiers back to the states for long periods of hospitalization.

The typical community mental health clinic serves a population unit varying from 75,000 to 200,000 people, the size required to qualify for federal funding. This unit is a geographic area called a "catchment area," and it may be a city, a county, or a neighborhood. Most clinics are located near the center of a large urban community. They provide a number of services to persons of varying economic levels by setting fees on a sliding scale basis so that a person pays what he can afford.

Community mental health clinics were formally established with the passage of the Community Mental Health Centers Construction Act in 1963 and its staffing implementation in 1965. Federal funds have been awarded to assist in the development of over 400 community mental health centers to date. Each of these centers is somewhat unique because each serves a specific community with its own political structure, social system, and medical organization. The most common type of clinic is the multiple agency center operated by from two to twelve agencies, each of which provides a basic service. The agencies include general hospitals, social work agencies, family therapy groups, and mental health programs which are affiliated with a university. Some clinics are part of a general hospital or a state mental hospital. All clinics are required to provide five basic services—inpatient, outpatient, partial hospitalization, emergency and consultation, and education. Some have special services for children, alcoholics, drug addicts, the suicidal, juvenile delinquents, geriatric patients, and the mentally retarded.

Consultation and education is often aimed at school systems. The clinic's staff can train guidance counselors, administrators, and teachers to provide mental health services to situations within their scope or ability. Psychiatric emergency services are helpful for less severely disordered persons who need immediate aid at times of crisis. During the 1970s, there has been an astounding growth rate in these services which include drug abuse clinics, suicide prevention centers, alcoholism programs, and "hot lines."

Partial hospitalization is a treatment modality between in-patient and outpatient care. It includes day hospitals, night hospitals, and weekend hospitals. The day hospital, which provides care for those who are too disordered to be treated as outpatients, is the most common part time facility. Patients in day hospitals participate in a full program of hospital activities during the day and return home in the evening. The

[83]G. L. Paul, "The chronic mental patient: current status—future directions," *Psychological Bulletin*, 71 (1969), pp. 81–94.

night hospital has the opposite treatment schedule of the day hospital; the patients work during the day and are treated in the evening. The night hospital is especially helpful for patients who do not function well during leisure time, such as alcoholics. The weekend hospital offers more intensive treatment than an outpatient clinic and is especially helpful to those who live far from treatment centers. Any of these forms of partial hospitalization may be sufficient for patients who need to be removed from temporary environmental stresses, as in the case of a housewife who is suicidal when her family is away during the day but is calm when they are home in the evening.

Partial hospitalization provides custodial care without the restrictive measures of full time hospitalization. Patients are free to come and go as they choose. They are not locked into a small area but are at liberty to move about the community. They are not forced to accomodate themselves to the needs of the staff. This approach can be useful with mildly disordered patients who would otherwise endure miserable days. Unfortunately, the concept of partial hospitalization as an alternative to total hospitalization is relatively unknown among the general public.[84]

Effectiveness

Approximately 10 percent of all the psychiatric facilities in the United States are federally funded community mental health clinics. Since these centers have been expected to reduce admissions to mental hospitals, one measure of their effectiveness is the changes that occur in admissions to such hospitals. Since the 1960s there has been a vast shift in the locale of care from predominantly in-patient settings to predominantly outpatient settings. In California, for instance, the mental hospital population declined from 34,955 to 6,476 between 1963 and 1974.[85] The same trend has been observed in Canada where there was a dramatic decrease of 43 percent in the mental hospital population between 1960 and 1970.

Of the total number of patient admissions to mental health facilities in this country during 1973, 31 percent were in-patient episodes, 65 percent were outpatient episodes, and 3 percent were day care episodes.[86] Much of this decline in inpatient care is the result of the increasingly important role played by community mental health clinics, as evidenced by the fact that care episodes in these clinics constituted almost one quarter (23 percent) of all episodes in 1973, while they comprised only 4 percent of all episodes in 1967.[87] As one would expect, a substan-

---

[84]John F. Odenheimer, "Day hospital as an alternative to the psychiatric ward."

[85]Jack Anderson, "Mental patients turned out into the cold," *The Evening Bulletin* (February 19, 1978).

[86]There were 5,475,000 patient care episodes in 1973. See: Carl A. Taube and Richard W. Redick, "Provisional data on patient care episodes in mental health facilities, 1973," *Mental Health Statistical Note No. 127*, (1976), pp. 1–7.

[87]Ibid., p. 1.

tial portion of the patients remaining in mental hospitals are mentally retarded. However, it is surprising that the percentage of hospitalized schizophrenics has declined as a result of increased treatment of schizophrenics in community clinics.[88] This may prove to be a dangerous practice unless a very conservative screening process is employed to separate those schizophrenics who can function in the community on a part time basis from those who definitely require custodial care.

The drop in the mental hospital population has actually closed some state mental hospitals. An extreme reaction occurred in California whose state legislature decided to close *all* psychiatric hospitals. Although this decision was later reversed, some hospitals were closed, and the state legislature refused to build any new ones. Needless to say, this kind of action has had an unsettling effect on hospital staff members who feel that it jeopardizes promotional opportunities and leads to layoffs.

The community response to local mental health care centers oriented to outpatient care has not been favorable. Some studies report that the public resists community-based programs,[89] even when intensive educational campaigns designed to develop progressive attitudes towards mental illness are used.[90] Many people simply fear a mass invasion of mental patients into their neighborhoods. Consequently, they often fight the establishment of community-based programs, particularly board-and-care homes for patients discharged from hospitals. Zoning ordinances, city ordinances, neighborhood pressures, fire regulations, and bureaucratic maneuvering have all been employed to fight off community mental health programs.

One of the questionable aspects of treating the mentally disordered in the community is the risk incurred with psychotic patients. The community clinics have been accused of handling the manageable neurotics and avoiding the psychotic patients.[91] This is not the case, but in some ways it would be better if it were since community clinics are not properly equipped to handle many psychotics. These patients require constant supervision which can not easily be provided within a community treatment setting. Yet some dangerously believe that every psychotic patient can eventually be returned to the community.[92] Hopefully, this

[88]Robert H. Barnes and Russell L. Adams, "The impact of a mental health center on admissions to a state hospital system," *Hospital and Community Psychiatry*, 25 (1974), pp. 402–407.

[89]D. DeSole, P. Singer and E. Swietnicki, "A project that failed" in *Mental Health and Urban Social Policy*, eds. L. Duhl and R. Leopold (San Francisco: Jossey-Bass, 1968), pp. 163–183; F. Hladky, "A psychiatric program in a rural mental health plan" in *Mental Health and Urban Social Policy*, pp. 141–160.

[90]J. Cumming and E. Cumming, *Closed Ranks: An Experiment in Mental Health Education* (New York: Commonwealth Fund, 1957).

[91]Mike Gorman, "Community mental health: the search for identity," *Community Mental Health Journal*, 6 (1970), pp. 353–354.

[92]Hugh G. Lafave, Alex Stewart and Frederic Grunberg, "Community care of the mentally ill: implementation of the Saskatchewan plan," *Community Mental Health Journal*, 4 (1968), p. 39.

ideology will not dominate the community clinics because it poses a great risk to both the community and to those psychotic patients who are not prepared to handle life in mainstream society. It is really nothing more than an undesirable shift of patients from the back wards to the back alleys.[93]

A major problem of the typical community clinic is staffing. In many instances the clinics have even fewer professionals than do the state hospitals. One survey reveals that 42 percent of full time positions at community mental health centers are occupied by nonprofessional mental health personnel, most of whom are drawn from the catchment are served by the center.[94] This occurs, not by design, but as a result of the fact that the community clinics are unappealing to many mental health personnel, particularly psychiatrists. Since psychiatrists are presently trained as medical specialists, they often lack the training in the social sciences which good community psychiatry requires. In addition, the team approach utilized by community clinics requires the psychiatrist to shift from individual-centered or family-centered therapy to group-centered or community-centered practice. All of this demands an attitude of mind for which the psychiatrist has not been prepared. He must accept the notion that he is only one of a team of "caretakers" which includes physicians, psychologists, social workers, and nurses as well as judges, lawyers, probation officers, employers, family, friends, and neighbors or anyone who can lend a helping hand at an opportune time.[95] Psychiatrists also have difficulty performing consultation and education functions since these functions are rarely included in their training. Of course, no explanation of the underrepresentation of psychiatrists in community clinics would be complete without mention of the vital role of income factors. Income is an important determinant of professional contentment among psychiatrists and, since community psychiatry is a poor source of remuneration, most psychiatrists choose to work in a more lucrative setting, such as private practice.[96]

Besides the staffing issue, community mental health clinics face other problems as well. One is the uncertain nature of funding from the federal government. Consequently, citizens and their local governments have had to raise more than 50 percent of the funds for these centers.[97]

[93]For a more detailed analysis of the problem of caring for psychotics in the community as well as other weaknesses of community mental health clinics see: Jonathan L. Borus, "Issues critical to the survival of community mental health," *American Journal of Psychiatry*, 135 (1978), pp. 1029–1035.

[94]Alan I. Levenson and Shirley R. Reff, "Community mental health center staffing patterns," *Community Mental Health Journal*, 6 (1970), pp. 118–125.

[95]Victor F. Lief and Richard Brotman, "The psychiatrist and community mental health practice," *Community Mental Health Journal*, 4 (1968), pp. 134–143.

[96]A community psychiatrist earns between one-half and two-thirds of what a private psychiatrist earns for a comparable number of hours. See: Edward H. Lehman and Ethna Lehman, "Psychiatrists and community mental health: normative versus utilitarian incentives," *Journal of Health and Social Behavior*, 17 (1976), pp. 364–375.

[97]Mike Gorman, "Community mental health," p. 354.

Another nagging issue is how to deal effectively with patients who have returned to the community after a long stay in a mental hospital. Roominghouse programs are intended to provide these people with a comfortable place to live, but this is often not accomplished. One problem is the resistance encountered by these programs in the form of hostility from nearby residents who resent ex-mental patients in their neighborhood. Another problem is the quality of life in the boarding homes. They can be as detrimental to the patient as state hospitals are unless additional programs for reintegrating the ex-patient into the community are available. Without such programs, ex-patients will continue to waste away their lives in social isolation. Indeed, some contend that boardinghouses are small hospital wards in the community and represent more of a retreat from the world than the mental hospital.[98] This is an accurate description of many of these boarding homes which are little more than storage sheds, converted tenements, or old hotels.

The real measure of the effectiveness of the community mental health clinics is whether they have significantly reduced the prevalence of mental illness. Unfortunately, it is not presently possible to answer that question objectively although there is no shortage of researchers who have tried. Consequently, a number of conflicting reports have appeared regarding the supposed merits and disadvantages of the community approach to treatment. On the positive side is the commonly cited fact that, since the creation of community clinics, hundreds of thousands of people have received care who would never have been reached before, people whose emotional problems were not severe enough to warrant traditional treatment. Certain of the community clinic programs appear to be quite effective with these problems, particularly the problems that emergency services are equipped to handle.[99]

On the other hand, the critics of the community clinics charge that they are not more effective than the state hospitals. In fact they may even be less effective because they are not equipped to handle psychotics.[100] This is reportedly also the case in Great Britain where the community psychiatry movement was started before it was begun in the United States. Questions have also been raised regarding the efficacy of short-term and day hospitalization, both of which require immediate prescriptions of high drug dosages for psychotics and allow little time for a careful observation of the patient's symptoms. Short-term hospitalization has certainly increased the number of discharges to the point where they outnumber new admissions. There is, however, an undesirable side effect of this reform: readmissions have also increased dramatically since the initiation of short-term hospitalization. This is usually interpreted as

[98]H. R. Lamb and V. Goertzel, "Discharged mental patients—are they really in the community?" *Archives of General Psychiatry*, 24 (1971), pp. 29-34.

[99]Ronald Maris and Huell E. Connor, Jr., "Do crisis services work?"

[100]Ronald O. Rieder, "Hospitals, patients, and politics," *Schizophrenia Bulletin*, 11 (1974), p. 11.

the consequence of the ineffectiveness of the short-term-stay approach for seriously ill patients. The label, "revolving door phenomenon," aptly describes the combined effect of shortened periods of hospitalization with a high probability of readmission.

The community mental health movement certainly has its merits, as evidenced by the large number of people using community clinics who otherwise would go untreated. The underlying philosophy of the movement is also sound because it is based on the recognition that the effects of long-term hospitalization can be as debilitating as the mental disorder itself. However, the danger of the movement lies in the enthusiastic way in which some people have extended the community clinic concept beyond its appropriate sphere. As a consequence, many seriously disturbed psychotics are being treated as outpatients in clinics staffed by overambitious and undertrained people.

Conclusions

A number of problems exist within today's system of mental hospitals, particularly the large state hospitals. One problem is the frequency of contact between patients and the generally untrained, nonprofessional staff and the dearth of patient contact with the professional staff that is often too small and primarily concerned with administrative functions. A second problem is the oppressive atmosphere of the typical hospital ward which, in turn, minimizes interpersonal contacts among patients and between patients and others. A third problem is the inconsistency between the medical sick role and the psychiatric sick role. Most patients unconsciously assume that the submissive behavior of the medical sick role is appropriate for the psychiatric sick role. This interferes with recovery from mental illness since effective therapy requires the patient to participate actively in his own cure. A fourth problem with today's mental hospitals is the lack of any effective therapy for treating large numbers of patients. There is virtually no psychotherapy in large hospitals; there is only group therapy which is a poor substitute for individual therapy. The custodially oriented hospitals are especially likely to use ECT and seclusion rooms, both of which are as much punishment as therapy. Other problems encountered within the mental hospital include collective disturbances among patients and the threats posed by patients' relatives who are frequently disordered themselves. Presently there is no way of alleviating the problems of traditional hospitals although attempts have been made to reduce them, such as the use of decentralized wards, community meetings, and patient government.

A major problem that patients encounter in mental hospitals is that over time they develop an institutionalization syndrome which is distinct from mental illness per se. The syndrome includes a sense of apathy, lack of concern for the future, extreme submissiveness, and overdependency on the hospital. This syndrome was a major impetus for the development of community mental health clinics where patients can receive treatment without being institutionalized full time. These clinics provide a variety of services ranging from emergency and consultation services to part time hospitalization. The community approach to treatment is based on the recognition that hospitalization can do more harm than good. While the problems of hospitalization are enormous, there is no evidence that the community clinics are doing a better job than the traditional hospitals, particularly in light of their staffing problems and their inability to care for many psychotics.

In summary, the present system of psychiatric care in the United States is far from ideal. On the one hand, the hospitalization approach subjects the patient to the risks of institutionalization and stigmatization by society. On the other hand, the community approach may be quite helpful for those who are not severely impaired, but it appears totally inappropriate for many psychotics. Hopefully, a mental health care system will evolve which channels milder cases to community centers staffed with more professionals and severe cases to an inpatient therapeutic milieu.

13

Life as an Ex-Mental Patient

At this point it should be clear to the reader that the methods used to treat people with mental disorders are far from scientific and are frequently nontherapeutic. The process by which prepatients are led to help-sources is typically complicated by the inappropriate reactions of others, such as family members who ignore the problem, physicians and clergy with no professional insight, and psychiatric evaluators who generally presume the person is disordered, rather than run any risks. This ill-defined and subjective process can both delay the treatment of the seriously disturbed as well as result in the institutionalization of those who do not need it. Both of these types of patients are likely to deteriorate further during their stays in mental hospitals because there are no clear guidelines to curing mental illness. Instead, a wide variety of organic prescriptions are used which may alleviate symptoms but often produce new and undesirable side effects at the same time.[1]

Having examined the prepatient and inpatient experiences, it is now appropriate to evaluate the life of the ex-mental patient. Logic

[1]The reader would be informed by glancing at a current issue of *The American Journal of Psychiatry*. A large portion of each issue contains ads for drugs to help psychotic and neurotic patients. On the back of each ad sheet is a list of "adverse reactions." It is amazing how many undesirable effects a single drug can produce. Some side effects of antipsychotic medications include drowsiness, motor restlessness, muscle group contraction, blurring of vision, nausea, dry mouth, urinary retention, constipation, cardiovascular changes, skin rash as well as dyskinesia. Dyskinesia is characterized by rhythmical involuntary movements of the tongue, face, mouth or jaw and includes protrusion of tongue, puffing of cheeks, puckering of mouth and chewing movements. There is no known effective treatment for dyskinesia.

would suggest that this group of people would have fewer stresses than those headed for mental hospitals or those being treated within them. However, logic is a rather weak tool in understanding how the mentally ill are treated in society. Perhaps this is most obvious in the case of ex-patients. Those who are discharged from hospitals would be expected to have shown notable signs of recovery, be protected from a setback by suitably tailored aftercare programs, and be accepted back into society as competent persons. Unfortunately, these expectations are rarely realized because the experiences of ex-mental patients are guided more by social accident than by objective standards. Consequently, ex-patients, like prepatients, undergo subjective and often negative experiences with discharge criteria, aftercare programs, and the problems of stigma and community readjustment. Each of these sets of experiences is treated separately in this chapter.

Criteria for Discharge

The mental hospital does not have objective standards for evaluating patients for discharge. Even the behavior of the patient is not a useful standard because he may appear quite "well" in the hospital setting but "fall apart" in the outside world. The medical model logically postulates that a patient should be released on the basis of the seriousness of his illness. This is not always possible, however, because mental health professionals have not proven to be good predictors of a patient's behavior in the community.[2] Of course, they argue that they can estimate a patient's readiness for life in the outside world and they insist that the timing of discharge depends on the type and severity of the illness. Yet actual observations indicate that discharge decisions frequently do not relate to the patient's psychopathology.[3] This is also true of patients discharged from day hospital aftercare programs.[4] The increasing release of still disordered people from mental hospitals is indicative of the trend towards community treatment. Unfortunately, the community mental health programs are not equipped to deal with these patients, a dangerous contradiction which benefits neither the patients nor the community. For this reason, arrest rates of discharged patients have

[2]G. Dix, "'Civil' commitment of the mentally ill and the need for data on the prediction of dangerousness," *American Behavioral Scientist,* 19 (1976), pp. 318–334; D. G. Langsley, J. T. Barter and J. M. Yarvis, "Deinstitutionalization—the Sacramento Story" (paper presented at the annual meeting of the American Orthopsychiatric Association, Atlanta, Georgia, 1976).

[3]Joan Sall, William W. Vosburgh and Abby Silverman, "Psychiatric patients and extended visit: a survey of research findings," *Journal of Health and Human Behavior,* 7 (1966), pp. 20–28.

[4]Shirley H. Heinemann, Lee W. Yudin and Felice Perlmutter, "A follow-up study of clients discharged from a day hospital aftercare program," *Hospital and Community Psychiatry,* 26 (1975), pp. 752–754.

noticeably increased since the beginning of the community treatment movement.[5]

The reader should not get the impression that the mental hospitals are giving chronic patients priority for release. Actually, as one might expect, younger patients with less than two years of hospitalization are more likely to be released than their chronic counterparts.[6] However, there is a growing movement to release chronic patients exhibiting severe symptoms. The hospitals that are most likely to favor release of chronic patients to the community are often motivated by practical concerns such as overcrowding or what some call "statistical pressure," rather than interest in the patients' welfare.

It is alarming to discover that criteria for release are not based solely on the patient's present mental health condition but more on his life circumstances. For example, whatever his pathology, a patient has a better chance of release if he has a place to live and a job waiting for him.[7] Consistent with this, one researcher found that among women patients, married women are more likely to be discharged than single women,[8] because the married woman is more likely to have a home to which she can return. The sex of the patient is not *directly* related to the probability of discharge although it is *indirectly* related as a function of life circumstances; a major prerequisite for male patients' release is employment, a condition not imposed upon women who are more likely to be released if they have an acceptable level of self-care, housekeeping, and social contacts.[9]

Another factor supports the societal reaction contention that the treatment of mental patients is largely determined by the judgments of nonprofessionals. This is the very important role played by family wishes regarding release. The attitudes of the family toward the patient's release are more likely to affect length of hospitalization than is the degree of the patient's impairment.[10] The formal request for discharge nearly always comes from the patient's family. Furthermore, the attitudes of the family are the single most important determinant of when the patient is released; if the family is in favor of release, the patient's chances of exit from the hospital are improved and, conversely, release is delayed if the

---

[5]Henry J. Steadman, Joseph J. Corozza, and Mary Evans Mclick, "Explaining the increased arrest rate among mental patients: the changing clientele of state hospitals." *American Journal of Psychiatry,* 135 (1978), pp. 816–820.

[6]John Cumming and Elizabeth Markson, "The impact of mass transfer on patient release," *Archives of General Psychiatry,* 32 (1975), pp. 804–809.

[7]R. S. Rock, M. A. Jacobson and R. M. Janopaul, *Hospitalization and Discharge of the Mentally Ill* (Chicago: University of Chicago Press, 1968).

[8]Edmund G. Doherty, "Are differential discharge criteria used for men and women psychiatric inpatients?" *Journal of Health and Social Behavior,* 19 (1978), pp. 107–116.

[9]A. Keskiner and J. J. Zalcman, "Advantages of being female in psychiatric rehabilitation," *Archives of General Psychiatry,* 28 (1973), pp. 689–692.

[10]James R. Greenley, "The psychiatric patient's family and length of hospitalization," *Journal of Health and Social Behavior,* 13 (1972), pp. 25–37.

family does not favor it.[11] What determines the attitudes of the family toward release? Typically the family wishes are based on factors totally unrelated to their relative's psychiatric condition, such as the need for help with childcare, loneliness, guilt, social freedom without the patient living at home, or even the timing of a vacation.

Perhaps a more important question is why are hospital psychiatrists so heavily influenced by the family's preferences? Greenley investigated this question and has found several possible reasons.

> First, the psychiatrist is much more likely to successfully place the patient in the home if the family supports his return. The family who wants the patient released is likely to be supportive and to help the patient re-integrate into the community; the reluctant family may undermine the plans of the psychiatrist, exacerbate the patient's symptoms, and drive the patient back to the hospital. Rational planning of treatment decisions, such as discharge, may demand seriously taking into account the desires of the family. Second and possibly more important, the psychiatrist may follow the wishes of the family to avoid a range of possible family actions. At one extreme, the family may use the judicial system in seeking a release or further retention. The psychiatrist may wish to avoid a hearing or other courtroom processes because they have a damaging impact on the patient or consume a considerable amount of his time and effort. The therapist may prefer to discharge the patient "Against Medical Advice" or to hold a patient while seeking a non-family placement in the community. Families may also place psychiatrists in awkward positions by taking their questions and demands to unit chiefs, department heads, or superintendents of the institutions involved. Institutional leaders both expect and easily tolerate a few such complaints. Yet if such complaints multiply beyond a scattered few, these leaders may come to question not the assertive families but the accused psychiatrists. This may give a family considerable leverage of which even it is unaware. Most commonly, a family's persistent questions and demands constitute a significant nuisance to the psychiatrist himself. In the state hospital studied, the work load was so heavy that a moderately interested and aggressive family could cause a substantial and disruptive drain on the psychiatrist's available time and energy. Under the pressure of too many patients, the psychiatrist appears to welcome the family which wishes to remove the patient from the hospital and the responsibility for him from the psychiatrist. On the other hand, if the family resists the patient's return, the over-worked psychiatrist often redirects his limited energies toward patients whose return to the community seems more likely, thus continuing the hospitalization of the unwanted patient. Finally, the psychiatrist may seek to please the family because he feels it to be as much his client as is the patient himself. The family is often the complainant, the patient only its symptom.[12]

[11]Daniel Levinson and Eugene Gallagher, *Patienthood in the Mental Hospital—An Analysis of Role, Personality, and Social Structure* (Boston: Houghton Mifflin, 1964).

[12]From James R. Greenley, "The psychiatric patient's family and length of hospitalization," *Journal of Health and Social Behavior*, 13 (1972), pp. 34–35. By permission of publisher.

Undoubtedly, the attitude of the hospital's "disposition staff" toward release is heavily influenced by the family's desires. This is not to say that the patients do not influence their own release at all. In fact, before the disposition staff examination, which is supposed to determine discharge, patients are known to counsel each other on the "right" answers that are usually based on stories of past successes and failures.[13] Patients who initiate their own release have a higher probability of discharge, particularly if their relatives are supportive than do those who wait for initiation by the psychiatrist. Thus the most realistic view of discharge is as a process of social negotiation rather than as a process of psychiatric evaluation. Negotiation includes the expressed wishes of the family and the attempts made by the patient to be discharged. When both are oriented toward release, the resultant coalition is the most powerful predictor of reentry into the community, even though the mental health of the patient may not warrant discharge.[14]

The Problems of Aftercare

Many ex-patients are unfit to resume living in outside society because institutionalization, resulting from a lengthy hospital stay, has atrophied their social and occupational skills. In addition, many patients still exhibit the symptoms of their illness. Both of these problems require aftercare programs to aid the ex-patient in reentering the community. Unfortunately, there is a deficiency of programs designed to provide discharged patients with the skills needed to function in ordinary life.[15] Consequently, many ex-patients, conditioned by long-term chronic care to be socially and economically dependent, fail to become functioning members of society, and are either readmitted to the hospital or pursue a meaningless existence in a boarding home. Gove and Lubach state that "... the patient cannot reenter the community and start again exactly where he left off. During his extended separation from the community his family may have adjusted to living without him, his friends may have grown accustomed to his absence, and his job may have been filled by someone else. Furthermore, hospital procedures are designed to insure control and order and do not usually allow, much less encourage, the patient to assume responsibility for his own welfare and to behave in ways appropriate for the community.[16]

[13]James R. Greenley, "The negotiating of release from a mental hospital: substantive and methodological considerations" (paper presented at the annual meeting of the Midwest Sociological Association, Milwaukee, Wisconsin, 1973).
    [14]Ozzie G. Simmons, James A. Davis, and Katherine Spencer, "Interpersonal strains in release from a mental hospital," *Journal of Health and Human Behavior*, 7 (1967), pp. 20–28.
    [15]National Institute of Mental Health, "Deinstitutionalization: an analytical review and sociological perspective," DHEW Publication No. (ADM) 76–351, Superintendent of Documents, U.S. Government Printing Office, Washington, D.C. 20402 (1976), p. 11.
    [16]Walter Gove and John E. Lubach, "An intensive treatment program for psychia-

Some of these problems can be minimized by an in-hospital treatment program that prepares chronic patients for returning to the community. One such program allows patients to pass through a series of different living arrangements, each of which increasingly resembles a responsible life style in mainstream society.[17] Patients should not be completely and suddenly released from the hospital. Rather, they should be prepared for reentry by a series of passes to go home for brief visits. Another useful practice is to carry over some of the secure aspects of life in the hospital to the outside world. For instance, patients are often afraid to try to live outside because they do not know what will be expected of them, while in the hospital expectations are quite clear.[18] If the expectations of discharged patients in outside society are defined for them, and if they are within the patients' capabilities, there is a greater chance that patients will feel useful, adequate, and successful.

Of course, the best approach to the problem of institutionalization is a program which involves a minimum period of hospitalization. For this reason, some advocate brief but frequent hospitalization as the means of sustaining the patient in the community. This approach is called "intermittent patienthood." It makes sense in terms of controlling the undesirable side effects of hospitalization, and there is some empirical evidence that a "short stay" approach minimizes the socially disruptive impact of mental illness upon the patient and family.[19] At the same time, the "short stay" approach is not realistic for seriously disturbed psychotics who require an extended leave from mainstream society because they are unable to care for themselves at all. These people must be hospitalized for an extended period of time, and it is these cases in which the problem of institutionalization is most apparent. Another problem with the "short stay" approach is that more released patients still require some treatment for the symptoms of their illness. Thus, there is a trade-off between the symptoms of the mental disorder itself and the deterioration of social skills that accompanies long-term hospitalization.

Regardless of the length of hospital stay, it is highly probable that the ex-patient has some kind of problem which interferes with his attempts to rejoin society. Thus, posthospital follow-up in the community can be useful in reducing hospital recidivism and increasing occupational success and satisfaction.[20] Of equal importance is the role that

---

tric inpatients: a description and evaluation," *Journal of Health and Social Behavior*, 10 (1969), p. 225.

[17]This program is currently used at Norristown State Hospital in Pennsylvania. For a complete description see: Paul Becker and Christopher Bayer, "Preparing chronic patients for community placement: a four-stage treatment program," *Hospital and Community Psychiatry*, 26 (1975), pp. 448–450.

[18]Wanda Partridge, "The positive side of institutionalization," *Mental Hospitals*, (1961) pp. 38–40.

[19]Walter Gove and John E. Lubach, "An intensive treatment program for psychiatric inpatients," pp. 225–236.

[20]For empirical verification see: S. A. Purvis and R. W. Miskimins, "Effects of community follow-up on post-hospital adjustment of psychiatric patients," *Community Mental Health Journal*, 6 (1970), pp. 374–382.

aftercare programs can play in the patients' interpersonal world, an area of life that is often unsatisfactory to mental patients, particularly because their interpersonal relationships may have caused their problems in the first place. To return the released patient to the same stressful situation that led to hospitalization is not good psychiatry. Posthospital help in interpersonal relations is necessary if the patient is to retain any progress he has made in the hospital.

Each aftercare program should be tailored to the particular needs of the ex-patient. However, there are some useful principles that can be used within any aftercare situation. One of these is what the Schwartzes call the process of "grading stress."[21] This is a strategy of providing opportunities for the graduated assumption of responsibilities. This simply means no more than the common sense idea that one must learn to crawl before he can walk. In relation to ex-patients, this principle can guide the gradual reintegration of the person into the community by giving him increased doses of responsibility. Each new dose should go beyond his current level of performance. Higher expectations of oneself are necessary for improvement because they create the possibility of changing one's behavior, an essential condition for mental health progress.[22]

Undoubtedly, aftercare programs are important in the treatment of mentally disordered people. This is evident from the high recidivism rates among ex-patients who do not receive some form of structured follow-up. However, it is often difficult to get ex-patients into posthospital programs simply because they are not motivated to follow through on the referral from the mental hospital.[23] This is not necessarily a dangerous behavior, however, since ex-patients who expect changes in their social and occupational lives constitute a large part of those who do not continue treatment.[24] Often these people stop treatment because they were able to enter a life situation that itself was conducive to their rehabilitation. On the other hand, dependency appears to be the underlying motivation for participation in aftercare programs, as evidenced by a high rate of participation by first-borns and single persons.[25] This is not to say that all dependent personalities seek aftercare and all independent types avoid it. It can be said only that there is a significant relationship in that direction. Many ex-patients do not receive aftercare simply because there is often no concerted effort by hospital personnel or by the family to encourage them to do so. What kind of efforts are required? Certainly

[21]Morris S. Schwartz and Charlotte Green Schwartz, *Social Approaches to Mental Patient Care* (New York: Columbia University Press, 1964), chapter 15.

[22]Ibid., p. 249.

[23]One study estimates that only one-third of patients referred to aftercare programs actually enter the program. See: George H. Wolkon, "Effecting a continuum of care: an exploration of the crisis of psychiatric hospital release," *Community Mental Health Journal*, 4 (1968), pp. 63–73.

[24]George H. Wolkon, "Characteristics of clients and continuity of care into the community," *Community Mental Health Journal*, 6 (1970), pp. 215–221.

[25]Ibid., pp. 218–219.

aftercare programs should be integrated with in-patient care so that the patient will view a posthospital program as a natural next step. For example, an intake worker from the local community mental health clinic should see the patient in the hospital before his release. This kind of personal contact helps to effect a successful referral.[26]

Counteracting institutionalization and motivating patients to seek posthospital help are the two major problems of aftercare programs today. However, there are other problems as well. One problem is that, because aftercare programs are in the initial stage of development, only a few offer innovative programs that enhance the quality of life for chronically ill people.[27] A second problem has been the failure to establish a liason between hospitals and community-based facilities. As a result, some ex-patients have to fight through massive red tape in order to be treated in the community.[28] A third problem with effecting posthospital treatment is that many patients do not have a family and home to return to, so they resort to living in substandard housing. This group of isolated ex-patients then forms a new ghetto subpopulation. In other words, these patients are not actually being returned to the community but to a fringe element. Discussing readjustment of the ex-patient to the "community" makes little sense in this situation, especially because members of the "normal" community are often quite hostile toward ex-patients. They will use city ordinances, zoning codes, police arrests, and various informal approaches to exclude them from mainstream life. Consequently ex-patients may be neglected in the community more than in state hospitals.[29] A fourth problem with effective aftercare is the risk of exchanging one set of ills for another since providing the ex-patient with continued protection may foster overdependency and psychiatric hypochondriasis. In addition, the stigma of having been a mental hospital patient may be strengthened by this extended treatment so that the person continues to consider himself sick.

The Stigma of Mental Illness

Much of the literature on the life of the ex-mental patient is couched in terms of the stigma attached to mental illness. The word *stigma* was used by the Greeks to refer to bodily signs that demonstrated something negative about the person's worth. Today stigma refers to the disgrace itself rather than any bodily evidence of it. The person who is or was mentally ill is stigmatized because he is deeply discredited for his failure to live up to societal expectations and frequently rebuffed whenever he attempts social intercourse.

[26]George H. Wolkon, "Effecting a continuum of care."
[27]Ellen L. Bassuk and Samuel Gerson, "Deinstitutionalization and mental health services," *Scientific American*, 238 (1978), pp. 46–53.
[28]National Institute of Mental Health, "Deinstitutionalization," p. 16.
[29]Ibid., p. 13.

Research into public attitudes toward the mentally ill has become polarized into two schools of thought: those who contend that society stigmatizes the mentally ill and those who believe society accepts the mentally ill and is compassionate toward them. The former perspective is linked with the traditional view of mental illness which characterizes the mentally ill as unpredictable, bizarre, and violent. The latter perspective represents the psychiatric ideology which views the mentally ill simply as sick persons who can be treated and cured, just like people with physical ailments. The traditional view is usually learned during early childhood and reinforced by the mass media whereas the psychiatric ideology is usually developed through higher education.[30]

Some empirical studies report that the public is somewhat tolerant of mental illness and does not automatically stigmatize mental patients.[31] However, these findings usually apply only to people of a higher educational background or to those who were socialized in a more liberal cultural milieu, such as the 1960s. It takes no great insight to realize that the modal attitude of the American public towards the mentally ill is far from positive and accepting. Many people do not consider the mentally ill to be legitimately sick. They see them as a separate class of beings who are dangerous and incapable of cure.[32] These attitudes are largely responsible for the rejection of ex-patients. Even patients themselves fear the "mental patient!"[33] This situation is depressing, particularly because neither patients nor ex-patients typically live up to their popular portrayal as uncontrolled monsters. In fact, ex-patients are less likely to act violently or commit crimes than are those who have never been judged mentally ill.[34]

How have these inappropriate and damaging views toward the mentally ill been created? Much of the blame must be placed on the mass media which reinforce the traditional view of mental illness by giving the public the impression that former patients harass their fellow citizens. The media is not interested in reporting on ex-patients who are good citizens because they do not make interesting news. Instead, the media concentrate on the sensational acts of those ex-patients who may have broken the law. For this reason, the psychiatric background of former mental patients is always reported in news stories while the nonpsychiatric history of most people who commit crimes is conveniently ignored.

---

[30]Richard James Bord, "Rejection of the mentally ill: continuities and further developments," *Social Problems,* 18 (1970), p. 497.

[31]Elaine Cumming and John Cumming, *Closed Ranks* (Cambridge, Massachusetts: Harvard University Press, 1957); Donald W. Olmsted and Katherine Durham, "Stability of mental health attitudes: a semantic differential study," *Journal of Health and Social Behavior,* 17 (1976), pp. 35–44.

[32]J. C. Nunnally, *Popular Conceptions of Mental Health* (New York: Holt, Rinehart and Winston, 1961).

[33]J. M. Giovannoni and L. P. Ullmann, "Conceptions of mental health held by psychiatric patients," *Journal of Clinical Psychology,* 19 (1963), pp. 398–400.

[34]J. M. Giovannoni and L. Gurel, "Socially disruptive behavior of ex-mental patients," *Archives of General Psychiatry,* 17 (1967), pp. 146–153.

Much research indicates that the mass media has an enormous influence on societal opinion. Attitudes created toward the mentally ill are particularly slow to change because they have been hardened through years of biased reporting. Consequently, ex-patients are relegated to extremely difficult lives in the community. They report that the fact of their illness was used as a threat or "club over their heads" which blocked communication with friends and family, resulted in feelings of low self-esteem, and seriously diminished their chances for meaningful employment.[35] Perhaps the difference between the mythical aspects of mental illness and the reality of mental illness is best summarized by the report of a patient's relative making her first visit to a mental hospital:

> I felt all the patients would be stark-staring mad and expected padded cells and screaming and shouting. When at last the time came for my first visit, I could hardly walk up the drive, my knees were shaking so. I wasn't afraid to visit my husband. I knew he wasn't mad but I did expect the others to be. I just couldn't believe my eyes when I saw it all. It wasn't only the place, . . . it was the amazing fact that the other patients all looked . . . normal . . .[36]

Changes in Public Opinion

Although the average lay person in the United States is uninformed about mental illness, there is less ignorance today than in past decades. Since World War II, the psychiatric movement has made a variety of attempts to reeducate the public about the nature of mental illness. At the beginning of the movement, fear, stigmatization, and rejection strongly characterized public feeling about the mentally ill.[37] Later studies have uncovered an increased awareness about the real nature of mental illness as well as a more sympathetic understanding of it.[38] In 1974, a large scale study of public attitudes toward mental illness concluded that

> . . . people are almost unanimous in believing that the mentally ill are truly sick and thus require medical treatment "just as any other sick person"

[35]Dorothy Miller and William H. Dawson, "Effects of stigma on re-employment of ex-mental patients," *Mental Hygiene*, 49 (1965), pp. 281–287.
[36]M. Yvonne Dudgeon, "The social needs of the discharged mental hospital patient," *International Journal of Social Psychiatry*, 10 (1964), pp, 52–53.
[37]L. Allen, "Study of community attitudes towary mental hygiene," *Mental Hygiene*, 27 (1943), pp. 248–254.
[38]See, for example, the following studies which are chronologically ordered: G. V. Ramsey and M. Siepp, "Attitudes and opinions concerning mental illness," *Psychiatric Quarterly*, 22 (1948), pp. 428–444; G. Gurin, V. Veroff and S. Feld, *Americans View Their Mental Health: A Nationwide Interview Survey* (New York: Basic Books, 1960); J. K. Meyer, "Attitudes toward mental illness in a Maryland community," *Public Health Reports*, 79 (1964), pp. 769–772; W. J. Edgerton and W. K. Bentz, "Attitudes and opinions of rural people about mental illness and program services," *American Journal of Public Health*, 59 (1969), pp. 470–477.

does. . . They do not believe that most mentally ill are especially prone to criminal behavior. Quite consistently they do not believe that mental patients should be "locked up" or that mental hospitals should be fenced off and guarded. The public believes to the point of consensus that the mentally ill can be cured with proper treatment, and almost all are willing to accept people who have been severely mentally ill as neighbors, fellow club members, and workmates.[39]

It is not difficult to accept the proposition that there has been a growing acceptance of mental illness among Americans. However, the findings quoted above are not entirely consistent with the everyday experiences of ex-patients who are by no means welcomed back into the community with open arms. A more recent study by Olmsted and Durham concluded that the liberalization of attitudes toward mental illness has reached a plateau as they found no substantial differences in outlook from the 1960s to the 1970s.[40]

Without waging an unnecessary debate over the actual progress the psychiatric movement has made in educating the public, it is important to point out some problems with survey research. First, attitudinal surveys tend to generalize about the entire population rather than to point out differences between social groups. For example, certain groups exhibit more enlightened opinions about mental illness and acceptance of the mentally ill. This tends to be true of younger, educated people; college students, for instance, are much less authoritarian about mental illness than is the public at large.[41] Secondly, an increased awareness of the psychiatric view does not imply a decrease in the rejection of patients returned to the community. People's responses to public opinion polls do not necessarily reflect their everyday behavior accurately. Opinion polls may measure beliefs to some degree, but they rarely capture emotions. Consequently, a growing number of Americans may say they do not stigmatize the mentally ill even though they actually behave negatively toward them. Hence the shift in reported attitudes has not been paralleled by more humanitarian treatment of ex-patients. In fact, the problems of ex-patients are currently so great that the APA recently felt compelled to issue a position statement on discrimination against ex-patients. Part of it reads:

Knowledge of previous psychiatric treatment and/or the possession of a psychiatric label is blatantly used in a variety of settings to influence immigration, licensure, employment, insurance, the granting of permits, and credit. Such knowledge is not infrequently used prejudiciously to exclude

[39]Guido M. Crocetti, Herzl R. Spiro and Iradj Siassi, *Contemporary Attitudes Toward Mental Illness* (London: University of Pittsburgh Press, 1974), pp. 121–122.

[40]Donald W. Olmsted and Katherine Durham, "Stability of mental health attitudes."

[41]H. P. Halpert, "Public acceptance of the mentally ill," *Public Health Reports,* 84 (1969), pp. 59–64; Lervin R. Lieberman, "Attitudes toward the mentally ill, knowledge of mental illness, and personal adjustment," *Psychological Reports,* 26 (1970), pp. 47–52.

individuals, as if society's institutions were attempting to protect them-selves against what is felt to be a threat. Such exclusionary practices are arbitrary and prejudgmental, irrelevant to the purpose at hand, and sub-versive of fundamental needs for privacy, confidentiality, and the civil rights of individuals.[42]

Stigma and Type of Illness

No account of the stigma of mental illness would be complete with-out pointing out that the degree of stigma is associated with the charac-teristics of the person's past illness. One important characteristic is the severity of the disorder; the neurotic, for instance, is not stigmatized to the same degree as is the psychotic.[43] A number of studies indicate that this difference occurs not because people evaluate a disorder according to the psychodynamics involved, but because more serious illnesses typi-cally involve more bizarre, disruptive, and unpredictable behavior which is perceived as *overtly* more threatening by others.[44]

The relationship between external symptoms and degree of stigma was first uncovered in a 1950 national survey conducted by Star. That study involved interviews with 3,500 persons.[45] One of the key parts of the interview included six case descriptions of mentally ill people: a paranoid schizophrenic; a simple schizophrenic; an anxiety neurotic; an obsessive-compulsive neurotic; an alcoholic; and a child with a behavior disorder. Star found that only the paranoid schizophrenic was recog-nized as ill by a majority of the sample. This was the only case described which included threatening, assaultive behavior. Some of the other cases involved equally serious pathology, but the symptoms were not as visible as the paranoid schizophrenic case, so they were not perceived as ill.

Another factor which influences the degree of stigma is the type of treatment the patient received. Although stigma declines when the pa-tient is released from the hospital,[46] noticeably more stigma is suffered

[42]American Psychiatric Association, "Position statement on discrimination against persons with previous psychiatric treatment," *American Journal of Psychiatry*, 135 (1978), p. 643.

[43]Walter J. Johannsen, "Attitudes toward mental patients: a review of empirical research," *Mental Hygiene*, 53 (1969), pp. 218–228; David Schroder and Danuta Ehrlich, "Rejection by mental health professionals: a possible consequence of not seeking appro-priate help for emotional disorders," *Journal of Health and Social Behavior*, 9 (1968), pp. 222–232.

[44]Bruce P. Dohrenwend and Edwin Chin-Shong, "Social status and attitudes toward psychological disorder: the problem of tolerance of deviance," *American Sociological Review*, 32 (1967), pp. 417–433; Howard E. Freeman and Ozzie G. Simmons, "Feelings of stigma among relatives of former mental patients," *Social Problems*, 8 (1961), pp. 312–321; Donald W. Olmsted and Katherine Durham, "Stability of mental health attitudes"; Derek L. Phil-lips, "Rejection of the mentally ill: the influence of behavior and sex," *American Sociological Review*, 34 (1964), pp. 679–687.

[45]S. A. Star, "What the public thinks about mental health and mental illness" (paper presented at the annual meeting of the National Association for Mental Health, Inc., 1952).

[46]Robert M. Swanson and Stephen P. Spitzer, "Stigma and the psychiatric patient career," *Journal of Health and Social Behavior*, 11 (1971), pp. 45–51.

by those who have been patients in a state mental hospital than by those who have been in private hospitals.[47] This is especially true for those who were involuntarily committed.[48] The relationship between stigma and involuntary commitment may be due to the tendency for more visible cases to be forced into treatment, a phenomenon which was discussed in Chapter 11.

Social Status and Stigma

A considerable number of studies report that attitudes toward the mentally ill are largely determined by social class. However, it is apparently not social class per se which affects attitudes but the educational component of social class. Studies have measured the specific effect of education on attitudes toward the mentally ill. The results of these investigations have consistently shown a positive relationship between education and the psychiatric ideology; as the amount of formal education a person receives increases, so does the likelihood that he will hold the psychiatric view of mental illness because educational experiences provide the individual with more accurate information about mental illness.[49]

There is some debate in regard to whether a person who is knowledgeable about mental illness is also more tolerant of the mentally ill than is an individual with less information about the topic. A sophisticated ideology may not necessarily imply a reduced tendency to stigmatize and tolerate psychopathology because knowledge is intellectually-based whereas stigmatization is an emotional phenomenon. Research on this question has not yielded consistent results. Some researchers report that stigma decreases with higher levels of education; that is, better-educated people tend to have less derogatory attitudes toward the mentally ill and to be willing to tolerate more contact with them than do poorly educated people.[50] On the other hand, there is a growing body of evidence that knowledge of mental illness and stigmatization of the mentally ill do not vary together. Miller, for instance, reports that ex-patients living with grade-school-educated people report feeling less stigmatization than do those returned to more highly educated environments.[51] Others report a greater tolerance of mental illness

[47]Vytautas J. Bieliauskas and Harvey E. Wolfe, "The attitude of industrial employers toward hiring of former state mental hospital patients," *Journal of Clinical Psychology*, 16 (1960), pp. 256–259.

[48]Dorothy Miller, "Is the stigma of mental illness a middle-class phenomenon?" *Mental Hygiene*, 51 (1967), pp. 182–184.

[49]Richard James Bord, "Rejection of the mentally ill," p. 497; Bruce P. Dohrenwend and Edwin Chin-Shong, "Social status and attitudes toward psychological disorder," p. 426; Howard E. Freeman, "Attitudes toward mental illness among relatives of former mental patients," *American Sociological Review*, 26 (1961), pp. 59–66.

[50]E. Cumming and J. Cumming, *Closed Ranks*; Robert M. Swanson and Stephen P. Spitzer, "Stigma and the psychiatric patient career."

[51]Dorothy Miller, "Is the stigma of mental illness a middle class phenomenon?"

in less-educated groups as well.[52] If future studies also uncover less stigmatization among people of limited education, the reason for that relationship may prove to be controversial. Presently, two explanations have been offered. One suggests that since lower-educated people have little knowledge about mental illness, they have a narrow definition of it so that they consider only extremely disordered behavior to be abnormal. The other explanation is that mental illness is more common among less-educated (lower-class) people and consequently they are more tolerant of abnormal behavior because they are regularly exposed to it.

Other demographics are associated with stigma and knowledge of mental illness. All of them, however, are related to educational attainment and can thus be explained from that perspective. Older generations in the United States have less educational attainment than do younger age groups. Consequently, older people harbor more traditional, custodial views of mental illness.[53] They are also more prone to stigmatize the mentally ill than are younger people.[54] This is part of a process of aging which involves a movement toward authoritarianism, a personality type which is rigidly conventional.[55] These negative attitudes among older people are not ameliorated by exposure to the mentally ill since they are also found more prominently among older employees than younger employees in mental hospitals.[56]

Other demographics that are reported to correlate with attitudes toward mental illness can also be explained as a function of educational differences. Race, religion, and intelligence are known to be related to educational attainment. Consequently, they are related to attitudes toward mental illness as well; blacks exhibit more negative responses toward the mentally ill than do whites;[57] Catholics have the most negative attitudes about mental illness than do members of the other major denominations;[58] people with lower intelligence have less positive attitudes toward the mentally ill than do those of higher intelligence.[59]

[52]Bruce P. Dohrenwend and Edwin Chin-Shong, "Social status and attitudes toward psychological disorder."

[53]Josephine A. Bates, "Attitudes toward mental illness," *Mental Hygiene,* 52 (1968), pp. 250–253; A. W. Clark and Noel M. Binks, "Relation of age and education to attitudes toward mental illness," *Psychological Reports,* 19 (1966), pp. 649–650.

[54]Edwin Chin-Shong, "Rejection of the mentally ill: a comparison with the findings of ethnic prejudice" (Ph.D. dissertation, Columbia University, 1968); Robert M. Swanson and Stephen P. Spitzer, "Stigma and the psychiatric patient career," p. 48.

[55]David F. Bush, Bernard J. Gallagher III and Wendy Weiner, "Intergenerational patterns of authoritarianism" (paper presented at the annual convention of The Society for the Study of Social Problems, San Francisco, California, 1978).

[56]J. M. Bordeleau and others, "Authoritarian-humanitarian index in a large mental hospital," *Diseases of the Nervous System,* 31 (1970), pp. 166–174.

[57]Guido M. Crocetti, Herzl R. Spiro and Iradj Siassi, *Contemporary Attitudes Toward Mental Illness,* p. 24.

[58]Walter J. Johannsen, "Attitudes toward mental patients," p. 222.

[59]Ibid.

Prevalence of Stigma

The reader should not get the impression from the above discussion that stigma is limited to certain social groups. It tends to be found in varying degrees in different social settings, but it is by no means limited to specific sectors of society. On the contrary, it is a widespread social problem that can cause considerable hardship to both the ex-patient and his family.

There are many reports of the isolation of ex-patients from society. This isolation tends to affect the relatives of ex-patients as well; one study reports that over 70 percent of relatives experience stigma due to the presence of an ex-patient in the home.[60] What is particularly sad is that ex-patients frequently hold the same negative views of themselves that society does, due to the effects of labeling.[61] Even more depressing are the ignorant views toward the mentally ill that nonpsychiatrically trained physicians maintain. One study found that physicians view neurotics as foolish and twisted and psychotics as dirty and dangerous.[62] These physicians' attitudes are dangerous not only because many physicians are mistakenly treating mentally disordered people but also because their views can influence those of many other people due to the unrealistic way that many Americans perceive physicians as a tabernacle of knowledge.

Unfortunately, for the ex-patient, stigmatization is not a temporary phenomenon. Years after former patients have been living in the community, their families still struggle with the burden of stigma.[63] Some ex-patients do manage to avoid the threat of stigma, but this is not because they return to a sympathetic community. On the contrary, those who do not feel that being an ex-patient is difficult are those who somehow have managed to keep their status a secret.[64] Others avoid stigma by moving to a new residence where they and their families are not known. Moving is most common among middle class families who tend to be more concerned with the visible deviance of the ex-patient than families of other social classes.[65]

[60]Howard Freeman and Ozzie G. Simmons, *The Mental Patient Comes Home* (New York: Wiley, 1963), p. 162. In an earlier study, the same researchers, using a less appropriate methodology, reported stigma among only a minority of relatives. See: Howard E. Freeman and Ozzie G. Simmons, "Feelings of stigma among relatives of mental patients."

[61]Walter J. Johannsen, "Attitudes toward mental patients," pp. 222-223; Robert M. Swanson and Stephen P. Spitzer, "Stigma and the psychiatric patient career," p. 44.

[62]Walter J. Johannsen, "Attitudes toward mental patients," p. 220.

[63]Mollie Grob and Golda Edinburg, "How families view psychiatric hospitalization for their adolescents: a follow-up study," *International Journal of Social Psychiatry*, 18 (1973), pp. 14-21.

[64]Dorothy Miller and William H. Dawson, "Effects of stigma on re-employment of ex-mental patients," *Mental Hygiene*, 49 (1965), p. 285.

[65]Howard E. Freeman, Ozzie G. Simmons and Bernard J. Bergen, "Residential mobility inclinations among families of mental patients," *Social Forces*, 38 (1960), pp. 320-324.

Readjustment into the Community

Perhaps no other aspect of mental illness is as clearly determined by sociological factors as is the success or failure of the patient's attempt to rejoin society. A number of social variables are responsible for the readjustment of ex-patients into the community. Among these are employment and financial problems, the attitudes of relatives toward the patient, as well as the problems of stigma and effective aftercare programs discussed previously. To be sure, psychiatric hospitalization alone does not insure positive posthospital community adjustment to the extent that factors in the ex-patient's social world do.

Most of the studies of the determinants of adequate functioning in the community have used rehospitalization as the criterion for successful functioning. Presently, however, there is some controversy over the use of rehospitalization as a measure of readjustment. On one side, are those who argue that rehospitalization data do not ". . . take into account the uniqueness of the situation confronted by the former patient."[66] This argument seems particularly cogent today since patients are being hospitalized for shorter lengths of time and may require periods of respite to compensate for the brief treatment. If this is true, then rehospitalization may not necessarily be an index of community readjustment as much as an indication that the patient was released prematurely.

On the other side are those researchers who feel that rehospitalization is a valid indicator of unfavorable community adjustment. They argue that ". . . rehospitalization represents one of the most serious and clearcut manifestations of the breakdown in social arrangements which are necessary for people to live together in toleration, if not harmony.[67] Most of these researchers agree that rehospitalization does not yield a *total* picture of ex-patients' functioning since there are undoubtedly some who remain in the community but can not perform the social roles expected of them. Studies using rehospitalization as an evaluation index overlook these types of individuals, but they do identify extreme groups of ex-patients since the avoidance of rehospitalization is a minimum standard for evaluating the person's ability to cope with the real world.

Methodological issues aside, the fact is that studies of patients returning to the community usually use rehospitalization as a measure of functioning for the very practical reason that such data are readily available. However, another factor supports such a practice—the high readmission rate which reportedly accounts for as many as 40 percent of all admissions to prolonged-care hospitals in the United States today. The factors that separate readmitted psychiatric patients from those who

[66]Stephen P. Spitzer and Norman K. Denzin, eds., *The Mental Patient: Studies in the Sociology of Deviance* (New York: McGraw-Hill, 1968), p. 470.

[67]Alan F. Fontana and Barbara Noel Dowds, "Assessing treatment outcome II: the prediction of rehospitalization," *The Journal of Nervous and Mental Disease,* 161 (1975), p. 231.

are not readmitted provide important clues to the social control of mental illness. Are particular social roles conducive to eventual cure? Are these a function of family type, relatives' attitudes, and/or the ex-patient's occupational experiences? The findings of studies on these and related questions are presented below.

The Role of the Family

The interpersonal life of the ex-patient is one of the most important determinants of rehospitalization. Those with little involvement with others are particularly vulnerable to readmission, as evidenced by the unusually high rate of rehospitalization among discharged patients who live alone.[68] Interaction with significant others affects the community tenure and adjustment of ex-patients by encouraging them to perform normal roles.[69] However, it is not the mere presence of significant persons in the ex-patient's life that aids readjustment as much as it is their behavioral expectation of the discharged patient to perform an active, normal social role. Evidence for this proposition comes, not only from comparisons of ex-patients living alone with those living with others, but also from studies of the effects of different types of family arrangements.

Being married is known to be a stabilizing influence on community adjustment for both patients released from state hospitals who were psychotically disordered[70] and for less severe cases discharged from community mental health clinics.[71] Married patients are less likely to return than single patients. However, this is not simply because single patients are more likely to live alone; the phenomenon stems from deeper sources. Patients returned to parental (nuclear) families have much lower performance levels than patients returned to conjugal (marital) families.[72] Simply stated, the probability of rehospitalization is noticeably

[68]Simon Dinitz and others, "Psychiatric and social attributes as predictors of case outcome in mental hospitalization," in *The Mental Patient*, eds. Stephen P. Spitzer and Norman K. Denzin, pp. 437–445.

[69]Howard E. Freeman and Ozzie G. Simmons, "Mental patients in the community: family settings and performance levels," *American Sociological Review*, 23 (1958), pp. 147–154; Howard E. Freeman and Ozzie G. Simmons, "Wives, mothers, and the post-hospital performance of mental patients," *Social Forces*, 37 (1958), pp. 153–159; Howard E. Freeman and Ozzie G. Simmons, *The Mental Patient Comes Home*.

[70]George Serban and Christina B. Gidynski, "Significance of social demographic data for rehospitalization of schizophrenic patients," *Journal of Health and Social Behavior*, 15 (1974), pp. 117–126; R. Jay Turner and John W. Gartrell, "Social factors in psychiatric outcome: toward the resolution of interpretive controversies, "American Sociological Review, 43 (1978), pp. 368–382.

[71]Robert H. Richart and Lawrence M. Millner, "Factors influencing admission to a community mental health center," *Community Mental Health Journal*, 4 (1968), pp. 27–35.

[72]Ozzie G. Simmons and Howard E. Freeman, "Familial expectations and post-hospital performance of mental patients," in *The Sociology of Mental Disorders: Analyses and Readings in Psychiatric Sociology*, ed. S. Kirson Weinberg (Chicago: Aldine 1968), pp. 248–254.

higher among patients returned to their parents than among those returned to a spouse. Husbands and wives are less tolerant of deviant behavior than are mothers and fathers. Furthermore, spouses have higher expectations of the way in which the ex-patient should function in the community. The patient returned to the parental family occupies the "child" role of son or daughter which has low expectations of performance. In fact, one respected team of researchers warns against the practice of releasing the patient to the parental family since that type of family setting can worsen the patient's condition because parents are prone to allow deviant behavior which engenders regression.[73]

There is also a significant relationship between family size and performance in the community. Male patients returned to large families are very likely to be rehospitalized.[74] This is not because the ex-patient is ignored in this type of family setting but because fewer expectations are placed on him due to the presence of other family members who are available as functional equivalents. Such is the case where a man has many sons or daughters who can assume financial responsibility for the household. This reduces the expectations placed on the ex-patient as breadwinner and simultaneously undercuts his opportunities for independent action, so necessary for reintegration into society. Role performance also affects the chances of rehospitalization among married women, as evidenced by the fact that mothers are less likely to be readmitted than nonmothers.[75]

Of course, all of the research which reports a positive effect of the marital role on community adjustment of ex-patients is based on cases in which the conjugal family is intact upon release. Unfortunately, this is not always the case. An alarmingly high number of marriages deteriorate to the point of separation or divorce before release.[76] This is particularly true when the patient is schizophrenic. A number of factors are responsible: long periods of separation result in loss of interest; financial burdens become too great for the nonhospitalized spouse; and discouragement stemming from the patient's lack of progress can lead to the spouse's denial of the patient's existence.[77]

Other family variables are related to community adjustment. One of these is place of residence; rural families provide a better milieu for rehabilitation than do urban families.[78] Although the researchers report-

[73]Howard E. Freeman and Ozzie G. Simmons, "Mental patients in the community," p. 154.

[74]Howard E. Freeman and Ozzie G. Simmons, "Familial expectations and post-hospital performance of mental patients," pp. 251–252.

[75]Robert H. Richart and Lawrence M. Millner, "Factors influencing admission to a community mental health center," p. 31.

[76]One study reports a marital attrition rate of 51 percent. See: Roy Johnston and Karel Planansky, "Schizophrenia in men: the impact on their wives," *The Psychiatric Quarterly*, 42 (1968), pp. 146–155.

[77]Saul H. Fisher, "The recovered patient returns to the community," *Mental Hygiene*, 42 (1958), pp. 463–473.

[78]Mary H. Michaux and others, "Relatives' perceptions of rural and urban day center patients." *Psychiatry*, 36 (1973), pp. 203–212.

ing the "urban-rural" finding explain it as a function of more realistic demands placed on ex-patients by rural families, it is also possible that the communal quality of rural life in general is simply more conducive to patient rehabilitation. Other family variables that affect recovery relate to the relatives' knowledge of mental illness and their propensity to stigmatize the ex-patient, as evidenced by reports that recovery is greatest among those returned to family members who are young and well-educated.[79]

Symptoms and Rehospitalization

Contrary to popular belief, the type and severity of the patient's symptoms at discharge are not useful predictors of rehospitalization. Studies of this question have concluded that the extent to which the patient's symptoms are ameliorated in the hospital is not related to future readmission.[80] The fact that psychiatric variables bear little relationship to case outcome is another indication of the extreme importance of the social milieu to which the patient is returned.

There is, however, one social psychological variable that is related to rehospitalization—a lengthy hospital stay. Long hospital stays produce institutionalization which prevents reintegration into normal social roles. Those who spend less time in the hospital have a greater ability to function interpersonally regardless of the degree of their pathology. A number of investigations confirm this.[81] However, this should not be interpreted as evidence for the utility of brief hospitalizations because most of the studies compared patients hospitalized for a year or two with those who remained for five years or more. If comparisons were made between patients hospitalized for a year with those hospitalized for three months or less (a growing tendency today), this author would expect poorer performance and more rehospitalizations among members of the short-stay group simply because the hospitalization period has not been long enough to monitor and treat symptoms adequately. This point

[79]Simon Dinitz and others, "Instrumental role expectations and post-hospital performance of female mental patients," *Social Forces,* 40 (1962), pp. 248–254; Robert M. Swanson and Stephen P. Spitzer, "Stigma and the psychiatric patient career."

[80]Jack L. Franklin, Lee D. Kettredge and Jean H. Thrasher, "A survey of factors related to mental hospital readmissions," *Hospital and Community Psychiatry,* 26 (1975), pp. 749–751; L. Guel and T. W. Lorei, "Hospital and community ratings of psychopathology as predictors of employment and readmission," *Journal of Consulting and Clinical Psychology,* 39 (1972), pp. 286–291; R. Williams and R. Walker, "Schizophrenics at time of discharge," *Archives of General Psychiatry,* 4 (1961), pp. 87–90.

[81]Alan F. Fontana and Barbara Noel Dowds, "Assessing treatment outcome"; Theodore W. Lorei, "Prediction of length of stay out of the hospital for released psychiatric patients," *Journal of Consulting Psychology,* 28 (1964), pp. 358–363; Stanford H. Simon, Wayne Heggestad and Joseph Hopkins, "Some factors relating to success and failure of male chronic schizophrenics on their first foster home placement," *Community Mental Health Journal,* 4 (1968), pp. 314–318; Morton O. Wagenfeld, R. Jay Turner and Gary Labreche, "Social relations and community tenure in schizophrenia," *Archives of General Psychiatry,* 17 (1967), pp. 428–434.

remains to be demonstrated empirically. The widely supported finding that type and severity of disorder during hospitalization are not useful predictors of readmission is valid only for the functional disorders discussed in this book. For the organic disorders, such as mental retardation, organic psychosis, and drug addiction, there is a poor prognosis which worsens as the severity of the illness increases.[82] This difference reflects the etiology of functional disorders which is often interpersonal, so that case outcome is more dependent on the social structure of the posthospital community whereas organic disorders leave little hope for rehabilitation through socially oriented approaches. Additionally, the likelihood of rehospitalization is influenced by the state of the patient's physical health which is unrelated to his psychopathology. The patient in poor health is less able to care for himself or carry out expected roles in the community setting. In one study almost 70 percent of released patients with physical ailments were rehospitalized compared to 35 percent of those without such complications.[83]

The Role of Employment

Occupational activity is a very useful therapy for successfully reintegrating ex-patients into the community since a job leads to increased independence and elevated self-esteem, both of which promote mental health. Steady employment in a fulfilling job is a meaningful form of social participation which simultaneously reduces the stigma of the patient label by demonstrating competence and an ability to interact with others in a normal fashion. Having a job is importantly related to successful functioning in the community as evidenced by significantly higher readmission rates among discharged patients who are unemployed.[84]

Unfortunately, many discharged patients *are* unemployed. This is particularly true for blacks who face discrimination because of their patient status and their race.[85] If ex-patients do find work, it is typically in a job involving less skill, prestige, and pay than the one they had before they were hospitalized,[86] not because they are unfit for employment, but because employers are leary of the frightening stigma attached to mental patients. Patient status directly prevents the discharged

[82]Simon Dinitz and others, "Instrumental role expectations and post-hospital performance"; Richard L. Wessler and Donna Iven, "Social characteristics of patients readmitted to a community mental health center," *Community Mental Health Journal*, 6 (1970), pp. 69–74.

[83]John Cumming and Elizabeth Markson, "The impact of mass transfer on patient release."

[84]This is true for both men and women. See: Robert H. Richart and Lawrence M. Millner, "Factors influencing admission to a community mental health center," pp. 30–32.

[85]Richard Wessler and Donna Iven, "Social characteristics of patients readmitted to a community mental health center."

[86]Dorothy Miller and William H. Dawson, "Effects of stigma on re-employment of ex-mental patients."

from seeking, obtaining, or holding a job. Indeed, more patients are occupationally active during their hospital stay (with in-hospital jobs) than during their stay in the community following release[87]—another example of the hostile way in which patients are treated by society. The reader should not fall victim to the widespread myth that ex-patients are employment risks. The fact is that even the most disturbed group of released patients are employable in certain jobs, provided that they have the incentive to work.[88]

Employers' attitudes are as negative as those expressed by the general public. They believe that mental illness connotes character weakness, and they have practical fears regarding the ex-patient's ability to handle an employment situation.[89] This is particularly a problem when the ex-patient describes his hospitalization to a prospective employer in terms of "mental illness" or "nervous breakdown" rather than in terms of "difficulty with interpersonal problems."[90] Some studies report that employers express a willingness to hire former mental patients.[91] However, these employers are usually connected with large, manufacturing businesses which have many unskilled, repetitive jobs.[92] Receptive attitudes toward former patients are rarely found among employers in service companies.

Some have suggested that it is not unemployment per se that most significantly contributes to readmission but the humiliation suffered by having to depend on welfare. For example, one study reports that 70 percent of a group of ex-patients on welfare are rehospitalized within a year of discharge.[93] Obviously, there is a real need for special employment centers staffed by mental health specialists to act as liasons between ex-patients and prospective employers. This need should be met by the community mental health clinics, but, as noted earlier, these organizations have consistently failed to deal with the plight of ex-patients, including their employment needs. This is particularly depressing because the psychological, social, and economic rewards of employment can be invaluable to ex-patients seeking an accepted position in the community.

[87]Robert Walker and James McCourt, "Employment experience among 200 schizophrenic patients in hospital and after discharge," *American Journal of Psychiatry,* 122 (1965), pp. 316–319.
[88]Simon Olshansky, "Some assumptions challenged," *Community Mental Health Journal,* 4 (1968), pp. 153–156.
[89]Walter J. Johannsen, "Attitudes toward mental patients," p. 221.
[90]P. Rothaus, and others, "Describing psychiatric rehospitalization: a dilemma," *American Psychologist,* 18 (1963), pp. 85–89.
[91]Vytautas J. Bieliauskas and Harvey E. Wolfe, "The attitude of industrial employers toward hiring of former state mental hospital patients," pp. 256–259; D. Landry and W. P. Griffith, "Employer receptivity toward hiring psychiatric patients," *Mental Hygiene,* 3 (1958), pp. 383–390.
[92]Lawrence C. Hartlage, "Factors influencing receptivity to ex-mental patients," *American Psychologist,* 21 (1966), pp. 249–251.
[93]Karl Easton, "Boerum Hill: a private long-term residential program for former mental patients," *Hospital and Community Psychiatry,* 25 (1974), pp. 513–517.

Social Class and Readjustment

It is appropriate that the final topic of this book concerns social class since it is probably the most significant sociological influence on mental illness. In an earlier chapter it was noted that social class influences rate, type, and treatment of mental disorder. It also affects the ability of a returned patient to function in society. A follow-up of the patients in the landmark New Haven study revealed that lower social class patients have the highest rate of rehospitalization.[94] Not only are they readmitted more frequently than are patients of other classes, but their instrumental performance in the community (steadiness of employment and extent of participation in social activities) is also more limited.[95] There are several reasons for this relationship. One factor is family attitudes; since posthospital adjustment is related to the reactions of relatives, higher-class ex-patients function better in the community because their relatives place greater expectations on them than do the relatives of ex-patients from the lower class. Another factor is stigma which is more profound among lower-class people because they have little education. This in turn forces the returned lower-class patient into social isolation rather than subject himself to possible ridicule or avoidance by friends and neighbors.[96] Thus, low familial expectations, a high degree of stigma, as well as the generally depressing quality of lower-class life, are together responsible for the frequent rehospitalization of lower-class patients.

The community mental health movement should be directing some effort toward the plight of lower-class discharged patients through public education programs, employment counseling, and a variety of methods to enrich ex-patients' social lives. Unfortunately, this has not occurred. In fact, the community movement may have worsened the situation by pushing for the mass release of hospitalized patients into the community. This is particularly inappropriate for lower-class patients because their community environment is not conducive to rehabilitation. Consequently, they waste their lives away in the loneliness and anonymity of a boardinghouse or rundown hotel until they are either rehospitalized or die prematurely from social and physical neglect.

Conclusions

The problems faced by ex-patients in the community are enormous and are largely responsible for the present high rate of readmission to

---

[94]Jerome K. Myers and Lee L. Bean, *A Decade Later: A Follow-up of Social Class and Mental Illness* (New York: Wiley, 1968) chapters 6–9.

[95]Howard E. Freeman and Ozzie G. Simmons, "Social class and post-hospital performance levels," *American Sociological Review*, 24 (1959), pp. 345–351.

[96]Jerome K. Myers and Lee L. Bean, *A Decade Later*, pp. 192–193.

mental hospitals. Often discharged on the basis of outside pressure rather than cure of their symptoms, they face a hostile community which offers only deficient aftercare programs. Employment opportunities are limited because ex-patients are believed to be dangerous, unpredictable creatures who disrupt work environments. Consequently, rather than being given a chance to rejoin society through occupational activity and the mental health benefits that flow from it, they are relegated to the ranks of the unemployed, the underemployed, or welfare recipients.

The most fundamental problem involved with discharged patients rejoining society is the stigma attached to the mental patient role. The public harbors such negative and hostile attitudes toward the mentally ill that ex-patients are doomed to permanent social ostracism before they leave the hospital, even if their symptoms are gone. The attitudinal climate in the United States appeared to have become more sophisticated and open-minded during the 1960s, but the change was pronounced only in certain groups such as the young and the educated.

Some people do leave mental hospitals and rejoin society as functioning members. Usually these are persons who are fortunate enough to be returned to a social environment that is conducive to reintegration. The most favorable environment is a higher-class, conjugal family with young members. However, most patients are not that fortunate. Many of them are poor people, without families, who are returned to a ghetto community and waste their lives away while on welfare. Clearly this situation is a social problem which will grow as more states pass legislation resulting in the mass release of patients. These people can assume a normal social role only with the help of agencies devised to educate the public (and reduce stigma), provide individualized aftercare counseling, and structure occupational programs, to name a few. Some of these tasks have been given to the community mental health clinics which have failed miserably to provide anything of real value to ex-mental patients. At the risk of sounding extremely pessimistic, the only real hope for remedying this crisis situation lies in a compassionate federal administration which is progressive enough to invest sufficient sums of money into community clinics. Without a considerable economic investment, these clinics will never attract the professional personnel required to deal with the problems ex-patients face in their attempt to rejoin society.

Selected
Bibliography

ABRAHAMSEN, DAVID
    1967. *The Psychology of Crime.* New York: Columbia University Press.

BASTIDE, ROGER
    1972. *The Sociology of Mental Disorder.* New York: David McKay.

BORUS, JONATHAN F.
    1978. "Issues critical to the survival of community mental health," *American Journal of Psychiatry,* 135: 1029–1035.

CHESLER, P.
    1972. *Women and Madness.* New York: Avon.

CLINARD, MARSHALL B.
    1974. *Sociology of Deviant Behavior,* New York: Holt, Rinehart and Winston Inc.

CROCETTI, GUIDO M., HERZL R. SPIRO and IRADY SIASSI
    1974. *Contemporary Attitudes Toward Mental Illness.* Pittsburgh: University of Pittsburgh Press.

D'ARCY, CARL and JOAN BROCKMAN
    1976. "Changing public recognition of psychiatric symptoms? Blackfoot revisited," *Journal of Health and Social Behavior,* 17: 302–310.

DOHERTY, EDMUND G.
    1978. "Are differential discharge criteria used for men and women psychiatric inpatients?" *Journal of Health and Social Behavior,* 19: 107–116.

DOHRENWEND, BRUCE P. and BARBARA SNELL DOHRENWEND
    1969. *Social Status and Psychological Disorder: A Causal Inquiry.* New York: Wiley-Interscience.

1974.   "Social and cultural influences on psychopathology," *Annual Review of Psychology,* 25: 417–452.

DOHRENWEND, BRUCE P.
1975.   "Sociocultural and social-psychological factors in the genesis of mental disorders," *Journal of Health and Social Behavior,* 16: 365–392.

EITZEN, S. D. and J. H. BLAU
1972.   "Type of status inconsistency and schizophrenia," *Sociological Quarterly,* 13: 61–73.

GALLAGHER, BERNARD J., III
1977.   "The attitudes of psychiatrists toward etiological theories of schizophrenia," *Journal of Clinical Psychology,* 33: 99–104.

GERSTEN, JOANNE C. and others
1977.   "An evaluation of the etiologic role of stressful life-change events in psychological disorders," *Journal of Health and Social Behavior,* 18: 228–244.

GOFFMAN, ERVING
1961.   *Asylums: Essays on the Social Situation of Mental Patients and Other Inmates.* New York: Anchor Books.

GOVE, WALTER R. and TERRY R. HERB
1974.   "Stress and mental illness among the young: a comparison of the sexes," *Social Forces,* 53: 256–265.

GREENLEY, JAMES R.
1972.   "The psychiatric patient's family and length of hospitalization," *Journal of Health and Social Behavior,* 13: 25–37.

HARKEY, JOHN, DAVID L. MILES and WILLIAM A. RUSHING
1976.   "The relation between social class and functional status: a new look at the drift hypothesis," *Journal of Health and Social Behavior,* 17: 194–204.

HORWITZ, ALAN
1977.   "The pathways into psychiatric treatment: some differences between men and women," *Journal of Health and Social Behavior,* 18: 169–178.

HSU, FRANCIS, L. K., ed.
1972.   *Psychological Anthropology.* Cambridge: Schenkman.

KARLEN, ARNO
1971.   *Sexuality and Homosexuality: A New View.* New York: W. W. Norton.

KOHN, MELVIN
1973.   "Social class and schizophrenia: a critical review and reformulation," *Schizophrenia Bulletin,* 7: 69–79.

1976.   "The interaction of social class and other factors in the etiology of schizophrenia," *American Journal of Psychiatry,* 133: 177–180.

LEMERT, E. M.
1962.   "Paranoia and the dynamics of exclusion," *Sociometry,* 25, 2–20.

LESTER, DAVID
1975.   *Unusual Sexual Behavior: The Standard Deviations,* Springfield, Illinois: Charles C. Thomas, Chaps. 6–14.

LEVY, LEO and LOUIS ROWITZ
 1973. *The Ecology of Mental Disorder.* New York: Behavioral Publications.
LYNN, R.
 1971. *Personality and National Character.* Oxford: Pergamon Press.
MECHANIC, DAVID
 1969. *Mental Health and Social Policy.* Englewood Cliffs, N.J.: Prentice-Hall, Chap. 5.
MYERS, JEROME K. and LEE L. BEAN
 1968. *A Decade Later: A Follow-up of Social Class and Mental Illness.* New York: Wiley.
OLIVEN, JOHN F.
 1974. *Clinical Sexuality: A Manual for the Physician and the Professions.* Philadelphia: J. B. Lippincott.
OLMSTED, DONALD W. and KATHERINE DURHAM
 1976. "Stability of mental health attitudes: a semantic differential study," *Journal of Health and Social Behavior,* 17: 35-44.
PEARLIN, LEONARD I. and JOYCE S. JOHNSON
 1977. "Marital status, life-strains and depression," *American Sociological Review,* 42: 704-715.
PERRUCCI, ROBERT
 1974. *Circle of Madness: On Being Insane and Institutionalized in America.* Englewood Cliffs, New Jersey: Prentice-Hall.
PLOG, STANLEY C. and ROBERT B. EDGERTON, eds.
 1969. *Changing Perspectives in Mental Illness.* New York: Holt, Rinehart and Winston.
RANDELL, JOHN
 1976. *Sexual Variations,* Westport, Connecticut: Technomic Publishing Company, Inc.
RAYMOND, MARGARET E., ANDREW E. SLABY and JULIAN LIEB
 1975. "Familial responses to mental illness," *Social Casework,* 56: 492-498.
SPITZER, STEPHAN P. and NORMAN K. DENZIN, eds.
 1968. *The Mental Patient: Studies in the Sociology of Deviance.* New York: McGraw-Hill.
SZASZ, THOMAS S.
 1961. *The Myth of Mental Illness.* New York: Hoeber.
TUDOR, JEANNETTE F. and WALTER R. GOVE
 1977. "The effect of sex role differences on the social control of mental illness," *Journal of Health and Social Behavior,* 18: 98-112.
WALDMAN, ROY D.
 1968. "Neurosis and the social structure." *American Journal of Orthopsychiatry,* 38: 89-93.
WARHEIT, GEORGE J., CHARLES E. HOLZER III, and SANDRA A. AREY
 1975. "Race and mental illness: an epidemiologic update," *Journal of Health and Social Behavior,* 16: 243-256.
WEINBERG, S. KIRSON, ed.
 1967. *The Sociology of Mental Disorders: Analyses and Readings in Psychiatric Sociology.* Chicago: Aldine.

WHEATON, BLAIR
    1978.   "The sociogenesis of psychological disorder: reexamining the
            causal issues with longitudinal data," *American Sociological Review*,
            43: 383–403.

Index